Private Pilot
Test Guide
Including Recreational

**Questions, Answers & Explanations
in Numerical Order** for the Recreational and Private Airplane, Helicopter, Gyroplane, Glider, Free Balloon and Airship Certificates…
Plus the official *Computerized Testing Supplement*

Aviation Supplies & Academics, Inc.
Newcastle, Washington

Private Pilot Test Guide

Aviation Supplies & Academics, Inc.
7005 132nd Place SE
Newcastle, Washington 98059-3153
(206) 235-1500

© 1995 ASA, Inc.

FAA Questions herein are from United States government sources and contain current information as of July 13, 1995.

None of the material in this publication supersedes any documents, procedures or regulations issued by the Federal Aviation Administration.

Important: This Test Guide should be sold with and used in conjunction with *Computerized Testing Supplement for Recreational Pilot and Private Pilot* (FAA-CT-8080-2A).
 ASA reprints the FAA test figures and legends contained within this government document, and it is also sold separately and available from aviation retailers nationwide. Order #ASA-CT-8080-2A.

ISBN 1-56027-240-6
ASA-P010G

Printed in the United States of America

97 96 95   5 4 3 2 1

Contents

Instructions
Preface v
Free Test Update Coupon vii
Description of the Tests ix
   Cheating or Other Unauthorized Conduct x
   Taking a Knowledge Test by Computer x
      Computer Testing Designees x
   Testing and Scoring xi
      Retesting Procedures xi
Eligibility Requirements for the
   Private Pilot Certificate xii
Certificate and Logbook Endorsement xiii
Test-Taking Tips xiv
Suggested Materials for the
   Private Pilot Certificate xv
ASA Test Guide Layout xvi

Private Pilot Questions 1-64

Answers, References & Explanations ... 1-78

Cross-References
A: Answer, Subject Matter Knowledge
    Code & Category 1-10
B: Subject Matter Knowledge Code
    & Question Number 1-10

Preface

Welcome to ASA's Test Guide Series. ASA's test books have been helping pilots prepare for the FAA Knowledge Tests since 1984 with great success. We are confident that with proper use of this book, you will score very well on any of the private pilot certificate tests.

All of the questions in the FAA Private and Recreational Pilot Test Question Bank are included here. We suggest you begin by reading the book cover-to-cover. Then go back to the beginning and place emphasis on those questions most likely to be included in your test (identified by the aircraft category above each question).

It is important to answer every question assigned on your FAA Knowledge Test. If in their ongoing review, the FAA authors decide a question has no correct answer, is no longer applicable, or is otherwise defective, your answer will be marked correct no matter which one you chose. However, you will not be given the automatic credit unless you have marked an answer. Unlike some other exams you may have taken, there is no penalty for "guessing" in this instance.

The FAA does not supply the correct answers to questions reproduced in this book, is not responsible for answers contained herein, and will not reveal what they consider the correct answers to be. Our answers are based on research from the reference sources provided with each question. If your study leads you to question an answer choice, we recommend you seek the assistance of a local ground or flight instructor. If you still believe the answer needs review, please forward your questions, recommendations, or concerns to:

Aviation Supplies & Academics, Inc.
7005 132nd Place SE
Newcastle, WA 98059-3153

Phone (206) 235-1500
Fax (206) 235-0128
CompuServe 102105,223

Technical Editor:
Jackie Spanitz, ASA

Editor:
Jennie Trerise, ASA

Instructions

Free Test Update Coupon

Complete this coupon and mail to ASA to receive updates to the FAA computerized tests.
The update will include information from FedWorld on the changes made to each computerized test, and will be mailed to you as changes take place.

This will be your mailing label, so please print clearly.

Please send me ASA's Free Test Update:

Name _____

Address _____

City _____ State _____ Zip _____

Mail this coupon to:

Aviation Supplies & Academics, Inc.
7005 132nd Place SE
Newcastle, WA 98059-3153

Which ASA Test Book do you currently use?
❏ Private   ❏ Commercial   ❏ Instrument   ❏ CFI   ❏ FE   ❏ ATP

Does this book meet all your needs? Yes ❏   No ❏
If no, please explain:
_____
_____

General comments or suggestions:
_____
_____
_____

P010G / 10-12-95

Description of the Tests

All test questions are the objective, multiple-choice type, with three choices of answers. Each question can be answered by the selection of a single response. Each test question is independent of other questions, that is, a correct response to one does not depend upon or influence the correct response to another.

The maximum time allowed for taking each test is based on previous experience and educational statistics. This amount of time is considered adequate for applicants with proper preparation and instruction.

The following tests each contain 50 questions and 2 hours is allowed to take each test:

Recreational Pilot — Airplane
Recreational Pilot — Rotorcraft/Helicopter
Recreational Pilot — Rotorcraft/Gyroplane

The following tests each contain 30 questions and 1.5 hours is allowed to take each test:

Private Pilot — Airplane/Recreational Pilot–Transition
Private Pilot — Helicopter/Recreational Pilot–Transition
Private Pilot — Gyroplane/Recreational Pilot–Transition

The following tests each contain 60 questions and 2.5 hours is allowed to take each test:

Private Pilot — Airplane
Private Pilot — Rotorcraft/Helicopter
Private Pilot — Rotorcraft/Gyroplane
Private Pilot — Glider
Private Pilot — Free Balloon – Hot Air
Private Pilot — Free Balloon – Gas
Private Pilot — Lighter-Than-Air – Airship

A score of 70 percent must be attained to successfully pass each test.

Instructions

Cheating or Other Unauthorized Conduct

Computer testing centers follow rigid testing procedures established by the FAA. This includes test security. When entering the test area, you are permitted to take with you only scratch paper furnished by the test administrator, and an authorized aviation computer, plotter, etc., approved for use in accordance with FAA Order 8080.6, "Conduct of Airman Knowledge Testing via the Computer Medium, and AC 60-11, Aids Authorized for Use by Airman Written Test Applicants." The FAA has directed testing centers to stop a test any time a test administrator suspects a cheating incident has occurred. An FAA investigation will then follow. If the investigation determines that cheating or other unauthorized conduct has occurred, any airman certificate that you hold may be revoked, and you may not be allowed to take a test for 1 year.

Taking a Knowledge Test By Computer

Testing center personnel cannot begin the test until you provide them with the proper authorization. You should always check with your instructor or local Flight Standards District Office if you are not sure what kind of authorization you need to bring to the testing facility.

The next step is the actual registration process. Most computer testing centers require that all applicants contact a central 1-800 phone number. At this time you should select a testing site of your choice, schedule a test date, and make financial arrangements for test payment. You may register for tests several weeks in advance of the proposed testing date. You may also cancel your appointment up to 2 business days before test time, without financial penalty. After that time, you may be subject to a cancellation fee as determined by the testing center.

You are now ready to take the test. Remember, you always have an opportunity to take a sample test before the actual test begins. For the actual test you will be under a time limit, but if you know your material, there should be sufficient time to complete and review your test.

Computer Testing Designees

The following is a list of the computer testing designees authorized to give FAA knowledge tests. The services on this list should be helpful in choosing where to register for a test or for requesting additional information.

Aviation Business Services
1-800-947-4228
Outside U.S. (415) 259-8550

Drake Prometric
1-800-359-3278
Outside U.S. (612) 896-7702

Sylvan Learning Systems, Inc.
1-800-967-1100
Outside U.S. (410) 880-0880, Extension 8890

Testing and Scoring

Within moments of completing the test, you will receive an airman test report, which contains your score. It will list the subject matter knowledge areas in which you answered questions incorrectly. The total number of subject matter knowledge codes shown on the test report is not necessarily a reflection of the total number of incorrectly-answered questions. You can study these knowledge areas to improve your understanding of the subject matter. See the *Subject Matter Knowledge Code/Question Number Cross-Reference* in the back of this book, for a complete list of which questions apply to each subject matter knowledge code.

Your instructor is required to review each of the knowledge areas listed on your airman test report with you, and complete an endorsement that remedial study was conducted in these deficient areas. The examiner may also quiz you on these areas of deficiency during the practical test.

The airman test report, which must show the computer testing company's embossed seal, is an important document. DO NOT LOSE THE AIRMAN TEST REPORT as you will need to present it to the examiner prior to taking the practical test. Loss of this report means that you will have to request a duplicate copy from the FAA in Oklahoma City, which is costly and time-consuming.

Retesting Procedures

If the score on the airman test report is 70 percent or above, it is valid for 24 calendar months. The ground instructor instrument and instrument foreign pilot tests do not have an expiration date. You may elect to retake any test, in anticipation of a better score, after 30 days from the date your last test was taken. Prior to retesting, you must give your current airman test report to the computer testing administrator. Remember, the score of the latest test you take will become the official test score. The FAA will not consider allowing anyone with a passing score to retake a test before the 30-day remedial study period.

A person who fails a knowledge test may apply for retesting before 30 days of the last test providing that person presents the failed test report and an endorsement from an authorized instructor certifying that additional instruction has been given, and the instructor finds the person competent to pass the test. A person may retake a failed test after 30 days without an endorsement from an authorized instructor.

Eligibility Requirements for the Private Pilot Certificate

To be eligible for a private pilot certificate with an airplane, helicopter, or glider rating a person must:

1. Be at least 17 years old (16 for a glider or free balloon rating).
2. Be able to read, speak, and understand English or have a limitation placed on the certificate.
3. Have at least a third-class medical certificate issued within the preceeding 24 months. This medical certificate is usually, but not always, also the student pilot certificate. Glider and free balloon applicants need only certify that they have no known medical deficiency that would prevent them from piloting a glider or free balloon safely.
4. Score at least 70 percent on a written examination on the appropriate subjects.
5. Pass an oral exam and flight check on the subjects and maneuvers outlined in the Private Pilot Practical Test Standards (#ASA-8081-14S, 8081-14M, 8081-HB, or 8081-3).
6. For an airplane or helicopter rating, have a total of 40 hours of instruction and solo flight time which must include the following:
   a. 20 hours of flight instruction (15 hours must be in a helicopter for a helicopter rating) including at least—
      i. 3 hours cross-country,
      ii. 3 hours at night including 10 takeoffs and landings, and
      iii. 3 hours in an airplane or helicopter within the last 60 days in preparation for the flight test.
   b. 20 hours of solo flight time including at least—
      i. 10 hours in airplanes (15 hours in helicopters),
      ii. 10 hours cross-country, each flight with a landing more than 50 NM from the point of departure and one flight of at least 300 NM with 3 landings, one of which must be at least 100 NM from the departure point. In helicopters, 3 hours of cross-country with landings at three points at least 25 miles from each other, and
      iii. 3 takeoffs and landings to a full stop at an airport with an operating control tower, each landing separated by an enroute phase of flight in a helicopter.
7. For a glider rating, have at least one of the following:
   a. 70 solo glider flights including 20 in which 360-degree turns were made,
   b. 7 hours solo flight time including 35 ground launched or 20 aerotow flights, or
   c. 40 hours of flight time in gliders and single-engine airplanes including 10 solo glider flights in which 360-degree turns were made

Certificate and Logbook Endorsement

When you go to take your FAA Knowledge Test, you will be required to show proper identification and have certification of your preparation for the examination, signed by an appropriately Certified Flight or Ground Instructor. Ground Schools will have issued the endorsements as you complete the course. If you choose a home-study for your Knowledge Test, you can either get an endorsement from your instructor or submit your home-study materials to an FAA Office for review and approval prior to taking the test.

Private and Recreational Endorsement

I certify that Mr./Ms. _____
has received the ground instruction or completed home study required by FAR §61.35, §61.97, and §61.105.

Signed _____ Date _____

CFI Number _____ Expires _____

Test-Taking Tips

The following test-taking hints have proven helpful in creating a smooth process for taking the test:

1. Take a sign-off from an instructor, photo I.D., the testing fee, calculator, flight computer (ASA's E6-B or CX-1a Pathfinder), plotter, magnifying glass, and a sharp pointer like a safety pin to the testing center.

2. Your first action upon sitting down should be to write on the scratch paper the weight and balance and any other formulas and information you can remember from your study. Remember, some of the formulas may be on your E6-B.

3. Answer each question in accordance with the latest regulations and procedures.

4. Read each question carefully before looking at the possible answers. You should clearly understand the problem before attempting to solve it.

5. After formulating an answer, determine which answer choice corresponds the closest with your answer. The answer chosen should completely resolve the problem.

6. From the answer choices given, it may appear that there is more than one possible answer. However, there is only one answer that is correct and complete. The other answers are either incomplete or are derived from popular misconceptions.

7. If a certain question is difficult for you, it is best to mark it for RECALL and proceed to the other questions. After you answer the less difficult questions, return to those which you marked for recall and answer them. The recall marking procedure will be explained to you prior to starting the test. Although the computer should alert you to unanswered questions, make sure every question has an answer recorded. This procedure will enable you to use the available time to the maximum advantage.

8. Perform each math calculation twice to confirm your answer. If adding or subtracting a column of numbers, reverse your direction the second time to reduce errors.

9. When solving a calculation problem, select the answer nearest to your solution. The problem has been checked with various types of calculators; therefore, if you have solved it correctly, your answer will be closer to the correct answer than any of the other choices.

10. Remember that information is provided in the FAA Legends and FAA Figures.

11. Be cautious about changing an answer, as your first impression is right more often than not. If in doubt, answer "C", but only if that is not the totally incorrect answer.

12. Remember to answer every question, even the ones with no completely correct answer, to ensure the FAA gives you credit for a bad question.

13. Take your time and be thorough but relaxed. Take a minute off every half-hour or so to relax the brain and the body. Get a drink of water halfway through the test.

Suggested Materials for the Private Pilot Certificate

Instructions

The following are some of the publications and products recommended for the Private and Recreational Pilot certificates. All are reprinted by ASA and available from authorized ASA dealers and distributors.

ASA-ANA	*Aerodynamics for Naval Aviators*
ASA-AC00-6A	*Aviation Weather*
ASA-AC00-45D	*Aviation Weather Services*
ASA-AC61-13B	*Basic Helicopter Handbook*
ASA-PPT	*The Complete Private Pilot (textbook), by Bob Gardner*
ASA-PPT-W	*The Complete Private Pilot Workbook*
ASA-PPT-S	*The Complete Private Pilot Syllabus*
ASA-PPT-MM1	*The Complete Private Pilot Maneuvers Manual*
ASA-PPT-DL-E	*The Complete Private Pilot Deluxe Electronic Computer Kit (141)*
ASA-PPT-DL-M	*The Complete Private Pilot Deluxe Metal Manual Computer Kit (141)*
ASA-PPT-DL-P	*The Complete Private Pilot Deluxe Paper Manual Computer Kit (141)*
ASA-PPT-STD	*The Complete Private Pilot Standard Kit (141)*
ASA-PPT-BAS	*The Complete Private Pilot BasicKit (61)*
ASA-FR-AM	*Federal Aviation Regulations and Aeronautical Information Manual (combined)*
ASA-AC61-21A	*Flight Training Handbook*
ASA-AC67-2	*Medical Handbook for Pilots*
ASA-AC61-23B	*Pilot's Handbook of Aeronautical Knowledge*
ASA-AC91-23A	*Pilot's Weight and Balance Handbook*
ASA-8081-14S	*Private Pilot Practical Test Standards — Airplane (Single-Engine Land)*
ASA-8081-14M	*Private Pilot Practical Test Standards — Airplane (Multi-Engine Land)*
ASA-PM-1	*Flight Training (textbook), by Trevor Thom*
ASA-PM-2	*Private & Commercial (textbook), by Trevor Thom*
ASA-PM-S-P	*Private Pilot Syllabus*
ASA-CP-RLX	*Ultimate Rotating Plotter*
ASA-OEG-P	*Private Oral Exam Guide, by Michael Hayes*
ASA-SP-30	*Pilot Logbook*
ASAS-CX-1A	*Electronic Flight Computer*
ASA-E6B	*E6-B Flight Computer*

ASA Test Guide Layout

The FAA Private Pilot test questions are taken directly from FedWorld (the government's Internet site) and are reprinted in numerical order in the first section of this Test Guide. In the next section, the answers, codes, references and explanations to these FAA questions are listed in numerical order. *See* the EXAMPLES below.

Some FAA Questions refer to Figures or Legends immediately following the question number, i.e., "3201. (Refer to Figure 14.)." These are FAA Figures and Legends which can be found in the separate booklet: *Computerized Testing Supplement* (CT-8080-XX). This supplement is bundled with the Test Guide and is the exact material you will have access to when you take your computerized test. We provide it separately, so you will become accustomed to referring to the FAA Figures and Legends as you would during the test.

Figures referenced by the Explanation and pertinent to the understanding of that particular question are labeled by their corresponding Question number. For example: the caption "Questions 3245 and 3248" means the figure accompanies the Explanations for both Question 3245 and 3248.

Answers to each question are found within brackets [X] above each Explanation, and in the Cross-Reference at the back of this book.

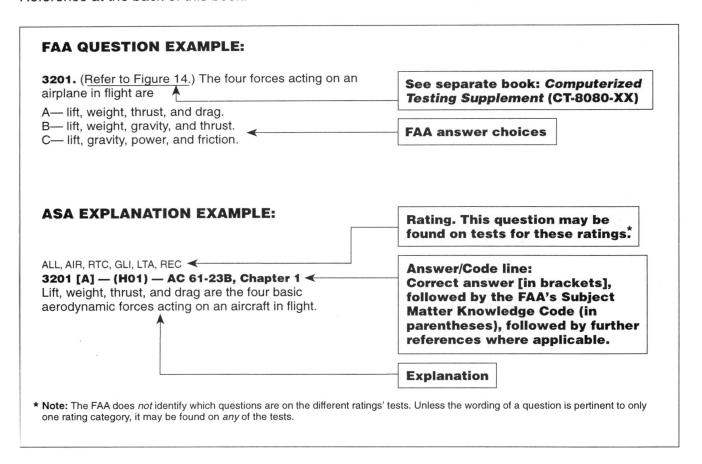

xvi ASA **Private Pilot Test Guide**

Private Pilot
Knowledge Test Questions

Note: Figures referred to in these FAA questions can be found in the separate booklet, *Computerized Testing Supplement for Recreational Pilot and Private Pilot* (#ASA-CT-8080-2A).

3001. With respect to the certification of airmen, which is a category of aircraft?

A—Gyroplane, helicopter, airship, free balloon.
B—Airplane, rotorcraft, glider, lighter-than-air.
C—Single-engine land and sea, multiengine land and sea.

3002. With respect to the certification of airmen, which is a class of aircraft?

A—Airplane, rotorcraft, glider, lighter-than-air.
B—Single-engine land and sea, multiengine land and sea.
C—Lighter-than-air, airship, hot air balloon, gas balloon.

3003. With respect to the certification of aircraft, which is a category of aircraft?

A—Normal, utility, acrobatic.
B—Airplane, rotorcraft, glider.
C—Landplane, seaplane.

3004. With respect to the certification of aircraft, which is a class of aircraft?

A—Airplane, helicopter, glider, hot air balloon.
B—Normal, utility, acrobatic, limited.
C—Transport, restricted, provisional.

3005. The definition of nighttime is

A—sunset to sunrise.
B—1 hour after sunset to 1 hour before sunrise.
C—the time between the end of evening civil twilight and the beginning of morning civil twilight.

3006. Which V-speed represents maneuvering speed?

A—V_A.
B—V_{LO}.
C—V_{NE}.

3007. Which V-speed represents maximum flap extended speed?

A—V_{FE}.
B—V_{LOF}.
C—V_{FC}.

3008. Which V-speed represents maximum landing gear extended speed?

A—V_{LE}.
B—V_{LO}.
C—V_{FE}.

3009. V_{NO} is defined as the

A—normal operating range.
B—never-exceed speed.
C—maximum structural cruising speed.

3010. V_{SO} is defined as the

A—stalling speed or minimum steady flight speed in the landing configuration.
B—stalling speed or minimum steady flight speed in a specified configuration.
C—stalling speed or minimum takeoff safety speed.

3011. Which would provide the greatest gain in altitude in the shortest distance during climb after takeoff?

A—V_Y.
B—V_A.
C—V_X.

3012. After takeoff, which airspeed would the pilot use to gain the most altitude in a given period of time?

A—V_Y.
B—V_X.
C—V_A.

3013. Preventive maintenance has been performed on an aircraft. What paperwork is required?

A—A full, detailed description of the work done must be entered in the airframe logbook.
B—The date the work was completed, and the name of the person who did the work must be entered in the airframe and engine logbook.
C—The signature, certificate number, and kind of certificate held by the person approving the work and a description of the work must be entered in the aircraft maintenance records.

3014. Which operation would be described as preventive maintenance?

A—Servicing landing gear wheel bearings.
B—Alteration of main seat support brackets.
C—Engine adjustments to allow automotive gas to be used.

3015. Which operation would be described as preventive maintenance?

A—Repair of landing gear brace struts.
B—Replenishing hydraulic fluid.
C—Repair of portions of skin sheets by making additional seams.

3016. What document(s) must be in your personal possession while operating as pilot in command of an aircraft?

A—Certificates showing accomplishment of a checkout in the aircraft and a current biennial flight review.
B—A pilot certificate with an endorsement showing accomplishment of an annual flight review and a pilot logbook showing recency of experience.
C—An appropriate pilot certificate and an appropriate current medical certificate.

3017. When must a current pilot certificate be in the pilot's personal possession?

A—When acting as a crew chief during launch and recovery.
B—Only when passengers are carried.
C—Anytime when acting as pilot in command or as a required crewmember.

3018. Private pilots acting as pilot in command, or in any other capacity as a required pilot flight crewmember, must have in their personal possession while aboard the aircraft a current

A—logbook endorsement to show that a flight review has been satisfactorily accomplished.
B—medical certificate and an appropriate pilot certificate.
C—endorsement on the pilot certificate to show that a flight review has been satisfactorily accomplished.

3019. Each person who holds a pilot certificate or a medical certificate shall present it for inspection upon the request of the Administrator, the National Transportation Safety Board, or any

A—authorized representative of the Department of Transportation.
B—person in a position of authority.
C—federal, state, or local law enforcement officer.

3020. A Third-Class Medical Certificate is issued on August 10, this year. To exercise the privileges of a Private Pilot Certificate, the medical certificate will be valid until midnight on

A—August 10, 2 years later.
B—August 31, 2 years later.
C—August 31, 3 years later.

3021. A Third-Class Medical Certificate is issued on May 3, this year. To exercise the privileges of a Private Pilot Certificate, the medical certificate will be valid until midnight on

A—May 3, 1 year later.
B—May 31, 1 year later.
C—May 31, 2 years later.

3022. For private pilot operations, a Second-Class Medical Certificate issued on July 15, this year, will expire at midnight on

A—July 15, 2 years later.
B—July 31, 1 year later.
C—July 31, 2 years later.

3023. For private pilot operations, a First-Class Medical Certificate issued on October 21, this year, will expire at midnight on

A—October 21, 2 years later.
B—October 31, next year.
C—October 31, 2 years later.

3024. The pilot in command is required to hold a type rating in which aircraft?

A—Aircraft operated under an authorization issued by the Administrator.
B—Aircraft having a gross weight of more than 12,500 pounds.
C—Aircraft involved in ferry flights, training flights, or test flights.

3025. What is the definition of a high-performance airplane?

A—An airplane with 180 horsepower, or retractable landing gear, flaps, and a fixed-pitch propeller.
B—An airplane with more than 200 horsepower, or retractable landing gear, flaps, and a controllable propeller.
C—An airplane with a normal cruise speed in excess of 200 knots, flaps, and a controllable propeller.

3026. Before a person holding a Private Pilot Certificate may act as pilot in command of a high-performance airplane, that person must have

A—passed a flight test in that airplane from an FAA inspector.
B—an endorsement in that person's logbook that he/she is competent to act as pilot in command.
C—received flight instruction from an authorized flight instructor who then endorses that person's logbook.

3027. In order to act as pilot in command of a high-performance airplane, a pilot must have

A—made three solo takeoffs and landings in a high-performance airplane.
B—received flight instruction in an airplane that has more than 200 horsepower, or retractable landing gear, flaps, and a controllable propeller.
C—passed a flight test in a high-performance airplane.

3028. To act as pilot in command of an aircraft carrying passengers, a pilot must show by logbook endorsement the satisfactory completion of a flight review or completion of a pilot proficiency check within the preceding

A—6 calendar months.
B—12 calendar months.
C—24 calendar months.

3029. If recency of experience requirements for night flight are not met and official sunset is 1830, the latest time passengers may be carried is

A—1829.
B—1859.
C—1929.

3030. To act as pilot in command of an aircraft carrying passengers, the pilot must have made at least three takeoffs and three landings in an aircraft of the same category, class, and if a type rating is required, of the same type, within the preceding

A—90 days.
B—12 calendar months.
C—24 calendar months.

3031. To act as pilot in command of an aircraft carrying passengers, the pilot must have made three takeoffs and three landings within the preceding 90 days in an aircraft of the same

A—make and model.
B—category and class, but not type.
C—category, class, and type, if a type rating is required.

3032. The takeoffs and landings required to meet the recency of experience requirements for carrying passengers in a tailwheel airplane

A—may be touch and go or full stop.
B—must be touch and go.
C—must be to a full stop.

3033. The three takeoffs and landings that are required to act as pilot in command at night must be done during the time period from

A—sunset to sunrise.
B—1 hour after sunset to 1 hour before sunrise.
C—the end of evening civil twilight to the beginning of morning civil twilight.

3034. To meet the recency of experience requirements to act as pilot in command carrying passengers at night, a pilot must have made at least three takeoffs and three landings to a full stop within the preceding 90 days in

A—the same category and class of aircraft to be used.
B—the same type of aircraft to be used.
C—any aircraft.

3035. If a certificated pilot changes permanent mailing address and fails to notify the FAA Airmen Certification Branch of the new address, the pilot is entitled to exercise the privileges of the pilot certificate for a period of only

A—30 days after the date of the move.
B—60 days after the date of the move.
C—90 days after the date of the move.

3036. A certificated private pilot may not act as pilot in command of an aircraft towing a glider unless there is entered in the pilot's logbook a minimum of

A—100 hours of pilot flight time in any aircraft.
B—100 hours of pilot flight time in powered aircraft.
C—200 hours of pilot flight time in powered aircraft.

3037. To act as pilot in command of an aircraft towing a glider, a person is required to have made within the preceding 12 months

A—at least three flights as observer in a glider being towed by an aircraft.
B—at least three flights in a powered glider.
C—at least three actual or simulated glider tows while accompanied by a qualified pilot.

3038. A recreational pilot acting as pilot in command must have in his/her personal possession while aboard the aircraft

A—a current logbook endorsement to show that a flight review has been satisfactorily accomplished.
B—the current and appropriate pilot and medical certificates.
C—the pilot logbook to show recent experience requirements to serve as pilot in command have been met.

3039. A Third-Class Medical Certificate was issued on August 10, this year. To exercise the privileges of a Recreational Pilot Certificate, the medical certificate will expire at midnight on

A—August 10, 2 years later.
B—August 31, 2 years later.
C—August 31, 3 years later.

3040. If a recreational pilot had a flight review on August 8, this year, when is the next flight review required?

A—August 8, 2 years later.
B—August 31, next year.
C—August 31, 2 years later.

3041. Each recreational pilot is required to have

A—a biennial flight review.
B—an annual flight review.
C—a semiannual flight review.

3042. If a recreational pilot had a flight review on August 8, this year, when is the next flight review required?

A—August 8, next year.
B—August 31, next year.
C—August 31, 2 years later.

3043. How many passengers is a recreational pilot allowed to carry on board?

A—One.
B—Two.
C—Three.

3044. According to regulations pertaining to privileges and limitations, a recreational pilot may

A—be paid for the operating expenses of a flight.
B—share the operating expenses of a flight with a passenger.
C—not be paid in any manner for the operating expenses of a flight.

3045. In regard to privileges and limitations, a recreational pilot may

A—fly for compensation or hire.
B—share the operating expenses of the flight with the passenger.
C—not be paid in any manner for the operating expenses of a flight.

3046. What is the maximum distance recreational pilots may fly from the airport/heliport at which they received instruction?

A—25 nautical miles.
B—50 nautical miles.
C—100 nautical miles.

3047. A recreational pilot may act as pilot in command of an aircraft that is certificated for a maximum of how many occupants?

A—Two.
B—Three.
C—Four.

3048. A recreational pilot may act as pilot in command of an aircraft with a maximum engine horsepower of

A—160.
B—180.
C—200.

3049. What exception, if any, permits a recreational pilot to act as pilot in command of an aircraft carrying a passenger for hire?

A—If the passenger pays no more than the operating expenses.
B—If a donation is made to a charitable organization for the flight.
C—There is no exception.

3050. May a recreational pilot act as pilot in command of an aircraft in furtherance of a business?

A—Yes, if the flight is only incidental to that business.
B—Yes, providing the aircraft does not carry a person or property for compensation or hire.
C—No, it is not allowed.

3051. With respect to daylight hours, what is the earliest time a recreational pilot may take off?

A—One hour before sunrise.
B—At sunrise.
C—At the beginning of morning civil twilight.

3052. If sunset is 2021 and the end of evening civil twilight is 2043, when must a recreational pilot terminate the flight?

A—2021.
B—2043.
C—2121.

3053. When may a recreational pilot operate to or from an airport that lies within Class C airspace?

A—Anytime the control tower is in operation.
B—When the ceiling is at least 1,000 feet and the surface visibility is at least 3 miles.
C—For the purpose of obtaining an additional certificate or rating while under the supervision of an authorized flight instructor.

3054. Under what conditions may a recreational pilot operate at an airport that lies within Class D airspace and that has a part-time control tower in operation?

A—When the tower is in operation, the ceiling is at least 2,500 feet, and the visibility is at least 3 miles.
B—When the tower is in operation, the ceiling is at least 3,000 feet, and the visibility is more than 1 mile.
C—When the tower is closed, the ceiling is at least 1,000 feet, and the visibility is at least 3 miles.

3055. When may a recreational pilot fly above 10,000 feet MSL?

A—When 2,000 feet AGL or below.
B—When 2,500 feet AGL or below.
C—When outside of controlled airspace.

3056. During daytime, what is the minimum flight or surface visibility required for recreational pilots in Class G airspace below 10,000 feet MSL?

A—1 mile.
B—3 miles.
C—5 miles.

3057. During daytime, what is the minimum flight visibility required for recreational pilots in controlled airspace below 10,000 feet MSL?

A—1 mile.
B—3 miles.
C—5 miles.

3058. Under what conditions, if any, may a recreational pilot demonstrate an aircraft in flight to a prospective buyer?

A—The buyer pays all the operating expenses.
B—The flight is not outside the United States.
C—None.

3059. When, if ever, may a recreational pilot act as pilot in command in an aircraft towing a banner?

A—If the pilot has logged 100 hours of flight time in powered aircraft.
B—If the pilot has an endorsement in his/her pilot logbook from an authorized flight instructor.
C—It is not allowed.

3060. When must a recreational pilot have a pilot-in-command flight check?

A—Every 400 hours.
B—Every 180 days.
C—If the pilot has less than 400 total flight hours and has not flown as pilot in command in an aircraft within the preceding 180 days.

3061. A recreational pilot may fly as sole occupant of an aircraft at night while under the supervision of a flight instructor provided the flight or surface visibility is at least

A—3 miles.
B—4 miles.
C—5 miles.

3062. Prior to becoming certified as a private pilot with a glider rating, the pilot must have at least

A—passed a third-class medical exam.
B—obtained a statement from a designated medical examiner.
C—made a statement certifying that he/she has no known medical deficiency that would make him/her unable to act as pilot.

3063. Prior to becoming certified as a private pilot with a balloon rating, the pilot must have at least

A—passed a third-class medical exam.
B—obtained a statement from a designated medical examiner.
C—made a statement certifying that he/she has no known medical deficiency that would make him/her unable to act as pilot.

3064. In regard to general privileges and limitations, a private pilot may

A—act as pilot in command of an aircraft carrying a passenger for compensation if the flight is in connection with a business or employment.
B—share the operating expenses of a flight with a passenger.
C—not be paid in any manner for the operating expenses of a flight.

3065. According to regulations pertaining to general privileges and limitations, a private pilot may

A—be paid for the operating expenses of a flight if at least three takeoffs and three landings were made by the pilot within the preceding 90 days.
B—share the operating expenses of a flight with the passengers.
C—not be paid in any manner for the operating expenses of a flight.

3066. What exception, if any, permits a private pilot to act as pilot in command of an aircraft carrying passengers who pay for the flight?

A—If the passengers pay all the operating expenses.
B—If a donation is made to a charitable organization for the flight.
C—There is no exception.

3067. The width of a Federal Airway from either side of the centerline is

A—4 nautical miles.
B—6 nautical miles.
C—8 nautical miles.

3068. Unless otherwise specified, Federal Airways include that Class E airspace extending upward from

A—700 feet above the surface up to and including 17,999 feet MSL.
B—1,200 feet above the surface up to and including 17,999 feet MSL.
C—the surface up to and including 18,000 feet MSL.

3069. Normal VFR operations in Class D airspace with an operating control tower require the ceiling and visibility to be at least

A—1,000 feet and 1 mile.
B—1,000 feet and 3 miles.
C—2,500 feet and 3 miles.

3070. The final authority as to the operation of an aircraft is the

A—Federal Aviation Administration.
B—pilot in command.
C—aircraft manufacturer.

3071. The person directly responsible for the pre-launch briefing of passengers for a flight is the

A—safety officer.
B—pilot in command.
C—ground crewmember.

3072. If an in-flight emergency requires immediate action, the pilot in command may

A—deviate from the FAR's to the extent required to meet the emergency, but must submit a written report to the Administrator within 24 hours.
B—deviate from the FAR's to the extent required to meet that emergency.
C—not deviate from the FAR's unless prior to the deviation approval is granted by the Administrator.

3073. When must a pilot who deviates from a regulation during an emergency send a written report of that deviation to the Administrator?

A—Within 7 days.
B—Within 10 days.
C—Upon request.

3074. Who is responsible for determining if an aircraft is in condition for safe flight?

A—A certificated aircraft mechanic.
B—The pilot in command.
C—The owner or operator.

3075. Where may an aircraft's operating limitations be found?

A—On the Airworthiness Certificate.
B—In the current, FAA-approved flight manual, approved manual material, markings, and placards, or any combination thereof.
C—In the aircraft airframe and engine logbooks.

3076. Under what conditions may objects be dropped from an aircraft?

A—Only in an emergency.
B—If precautions are taken to avoid injury or damage to persons or property on the surface.
C—If prior permission is received from the Federal Aviation Administration.

3077. A person may not act as a crewmember of a civil aircraft if alcoholic beverages have been consumed by that person within the preceding

A—8 hours.
B—12 hours.
C—24 hours.

3078. Under what condition, if any, may a pilot allow a person who is obviously under the influence of drugs to be carried aboard an aircraft?

A—In an emergency or if the person is a medical patient under proper care.
B—Only if the person does not have access to the cockpit or pilot's compartment.
C—Under no condition.

3079. No person may attempt to act as a crewmember of a civil aircraft with

A—.008 percent by weight or more alcohol in the blood.
B—.004 percent by weight or more alcohol in the blood.
C—.04 percent by weight or more alcohol in the blood.

3080. Which preflight action is specifically required of the pilot prior to each flight?

A—Check the aircraft logbooks for appropriate entries.
B—Become familiar with all available information concerning the flight.
C—Review wake turbulence avoidance procedures.

3081. Preflight action, as required for all flights away from the vicinity of an airport, shall include

A—the designation of an alternate airport.
B—a study of arrival procedures at airports/heliports of intended use.
C—an alternate course of action if the flight cannot be completed as planned.

3082. In addition to other preflight actions for a VFR flight away from the vicinity of the departure airport, regulations specifically require the pilot in command to

A—review traffic control light signal procedures.
B—check the accuracy of the navigation equipment and the emergency locator transmitter (ELT).
C—determine runway lengths at airports of intended use and the aircraft's takeoff and landing distance data.

3083. Flight crewmembers are required to keep their safety belts and shoulder harnesses fastened during

A—takeoffs and landings.
B—all flight conditions.
C—flight in turbulent air.

3084. Which best describes the flight conditions under which flight crewmembers are specifically required to keep their safety belts and shoulder harnesses fastened?

A—Safety belts during takeoff and landing; shoulder harnesses during takeoff and landing.
B—Safety belts during takeoff and landing; shoulder harnesses during takeoff and landing and while en route.
C—Safety belts during takeoff and landing and while en route; shoulder harnesses during takeoff and landing.

3085. With respect to passengers, what obligation, if any, does a pilot in command have concerning the use of safety belts?

A—The pilot in command must instruct the passengers to keep their safety belts fastened for the entire flight.
B—The pilot in command must brief the passengers on the use of safety belts and notify them to fasten their safety belts during taxi, takeoff, and landing.
C—The pilot in command has no obligation in regard to passengers' use of safety belts.

3086. With certain exceptions, safety belts are required to be secured about passengers during

A—taxi, takeoffs, and landings.
B—all flight conditions.
C—flight in turbulent air.

3087. Safety belts are required to be properly secured about which persons in an aircraft and when?

A—Pilots only, during takeoffs and landings.
B—Passengers, during taxi, takeoffs, and landings only.
C—Each person on board the aircraft during the entire flight.

3088. No person may operate an aircraft in formation flight

A—over a densely populated area.
B—in Class D airspace under special VFR.
C—except by prior arrangement with the pilot in command of each aircraft.

3089. Which aircraft has the right-of-way over all other air traffic?

A—A balloon.
B—An aircraft in distress.
C—An aircraft on final approach to land.

3090. What action is required when two aircraft of the same category converge, but not head-on?

A—The faster aircraft shall give way.
B—The aircraft on the left shall give way.
C—Each aircraft shall give way to the right.

3091. Which aircraft has the right-of-way over the other aircraft listed?

A—Glider.
B—Airship.
C—Aircraft refueling other aircraft.

3092. An airplane and an airship are converging. If the airship is left of the airplane's position, which aircraft has the right-of-way?

A—The airship.
B—The airplane.
C—Each pilot should alter course to the right.

3093. Which aircraft has the right-of-way over the other aircraft listed?

A—Airship.
B—Aircraft towing other aircraft.
C—Gyroplane.

3094. What action should the pilots of a glider and an airplane take if on a head-on collision course?

A—The airplane pilot should give way to the left.
B—The glider pilot should give way to the right.
C—Both pilots should give way to the right.

3095. When two or more aircraft are approaching an airport for the purpose of landing, the right-of-way belongs to the aircraft

A—that has the other to its right.
B—that is the least maneuverable.
C—at the lower altitude, but it shall not take advantage of this rule to cut in front of or to overtake another.

3096. A seaplane and a motorboat are on crossing courses. If the motorboat is to the left of the seaplane, which has the right-of-way?

A—The motorboat.
B—The seaplane.
C—Both should alter course to the right.

3097. Unless otherwise authorized, what is the maximum indicated airspeed at which a person may operate an aircraft below 10,000 feet MSL?

A—200 knots.
B—250 knots.
C—288 knots.

3098. Unless otherwise authorized, the maximum indicated airspeed at which aircraft may be flown when at or below 2,500 feet AGL and within 4 nautical miles of the primary airport of Class C airspace is

A—200 knots.
B—230 knots.
C—250 knots.

3099. When flying in the airspace underlying Class B airspace, the maximum speed authorized is

A—200 knots.
B—230 knots.
C—250 knots.

3100. When flying in a VFR corridor designated through Class B airspace, the maximum speed authorized is

A—180 knots.
B—200 knots.
C—250 knots.

3101. Except when necessary for takeoff or landing, what is the minimum safe altitude for a pilot to operate an aircraft anywhere?

A—An altitude allowing, if a power unit fails, an emergency landing without undue hazard to persons or property on the surface.
B—An altitude of 500 feet above the surface and no closer than 500 feet to any person, vessel, vehicle, or structure.
C—An altitude of 500 feet above the highest obstacle within a horizontal radius of 1,000 feet.

3102. Except when necessary for takeoff or landing, what is the minimum safe altitude required for a pilot to operate an aircraft over congested areas?

A—An altitude of 1,000 feet above any person, vessel, vehicle, or structure.
B—An altitude of 500 feet above the highest obstacle within a horizontal radius of 1,000 feet of the aircraft.
C—An altitude of 1,000 feet above the highest obstacle within a horizontal radius of 2,000 feet of the aircraft.

3103. Except when necessary for takeoff or landing, what is the minimum safe altitude required for a pilot to operate an aircraft over other than a congested area?

A—An altitude allowing, if a power unit fails, an emergency landing without undue hazard to persons or property on the surface.
B—An altitude of 500 feet AGL, except over open water or a sparsely populated area, which requires 500 feet from any person, vessel, vehicle, or structure.
C—An altitude of 500 feet above the highest obstacle within a horizontal radius of 1,000 feet.

3104. Except when necessary for takeoff or landing, an aircraft may not be operated closer than what distance from any person, vessel, vehicle, or structure?

A—500 feet.
B—700 feet.
C—1,000 feet.

3105. If an altimeter setting is not available before flight, to which altitude should the pilot adjust the altimeter?

A—The elevation of the nearest airport corrected to mean sea level.
B—The elevation of the departure area.
C—Pressure altitude corrected for nonstandard temperature.

3106. Prior to takeoff, the altimeter should be set to which altitude or altimeter setting?

A—The current local altimeter setting, if available, or the departure airport elevation.
B—The corrected density altitude of the departure airport.
C—The corrected pressure altitude for the departure airport.

3107. At what altitude shall the altimeter be set to 29.92, when climbing to cruising flight level?

A—14,500 feet MSL.
B—18,000 feet MSL.
C—24,000 feet MSL.

3108. When an ATC clearance has been obtained, no pilot in command may deviate from that clearance, unless that pilot obtains an amended clearance. The one exception to this regulation is

A—when the clearance states "at pilot's discretion."
B—an emergency.
C—if the clearance contains a restriction.

3109. When would a pilot be required to submit a detailed report of an emergency which caused the pilot to deviate from an ATC clearance?

A—When requested by ATC.
B—Immediately.
C—Within 7 days.

3110. What action, if any, is appropriate if the pilot deviates from an ATC instruction during an emergency and is given priority?

A—Take no special action since you are pilot in command.
B—File a detailed report within 48 hours to the chief of the appropriate ATC facility, if requested.
C—File a report to the FAA Administrator, as soon as possible.

3111. A steady green light signal directed from the control tower to an aircraft in flight is a signal that the pilot

A—is cleared to land.
B—should give way to other aircraft and continue circling.
C—should return for landing.

3112. Which light signal from the control tower clears a pilot to taxi?

A—Flashing green.
B—Steady green.
C—Flashing white.

3113. If the control tower uses a light signal to direct a pilot to give way to other aircraft and continue circling, the light will be

A—flashing red.
B—steady red.
C—alternating red and green.

3114. A flashing white light signal from the control tower to a taxiing aircraft is an indication to

A—taxi at a faster speed.
B—taxi only on taxiways and not cross runways.
C—return to the starting point on the airport.

3115. An alternating red and green light signal directed from the control tower to an aircraft in flight is a signal to

A—hold position.
B—exercise extreme caution.
C—not land; the airport is unsafe.

3116. While on final approach for landing, an alternating green and red light followed by a flashing red light is received from the control tower. Under these circumstances, the pilot should

A—discontinue the approach, fly the same traffic pattern and approach again, and land.
B—exercise extreme caution and abandon the approach, realizing the airport is unsafe for landing.
C—abandon the approach, circle the airport to the right, and expect a flashing white light when the airport is safe for landing.

3117. A blue segmented circle on a Sectional Chart depicts which class airspace?

A—Class B.
B—Class C.
C—Class D.

3118. Airspace at an airport with a part-time control tower is classified as Class D airspace only

A—when the weather minimums are below basic VFR.
B—when the associated control tower is in operation.
C—when the associated Flight Service Station is in operation.

3119. Unless otherwise authorized, two-way radio communications with Air Traffic Control are required for landings or takeoffs

A—at all tower controlled airports regardless of weather conditions.
B—at all tower controlled airports only when weather conditions are less than VFR.
C—at all tower controlled airports within Class D airspace only when weather conditions are less than VFR.

3120. Each pilot of an aircraft approaching to land on a runway served by a visual approach slope indicator (VASI) shall

A—maintain a 3° glide to the runway.
B—maintain an altitude at or above the glide slope.
C—stay high until the runway can be reached in a power-off landing.

3121. When approaching to land on a runway served by a visual approach slope indicator (VASI), the pilot shall

A—maintain an altitude that captures the glide slope at least 2 miles downwind from the runway threshold.
B—maintain an altitude at or above the glide slope.
C—remain on the glide slope and land between the two-light bar.

3122. Which is appropriate for a helicopter approaching an airport for landing?

A—Remain below the airplane traffic pattern altitude.
B—Avoid the flow of fixed-wing traffic.
C—Fly right-hand traffic.

3123. Which is the correct traffic pattern departure procedure to use at a noncontrolled airport?

A—Depart in any direction consistent with safety, after crossing the airport boundary.
B—Make all turns to the left.
C—Comply with any FAA traffic pattern established for the airport.

3124. Two-way radio communication must be established with the Air Traffic Control facility having jurisdiction over the area prior to entering which class airspace?

A—Class C.
B—Class E.
C—Class G.

3125. What minimum radio equipment is required for operation within Class C airspace?

A—Two-way radio communications equipment and a 4096-code transponder.
B—Two-way radio communications equipment, a 4096-code transponder, and DME.
C—Two-way radio communications equipment, a 4096-code transponder, and an encoding altimeter.

3126. What minimum pilot certification is required for operation within Class B airspace?

A—Recreational Pilot Certificate.
B—Private Pilot Certificate or Student Pilot Certificate with appropriate logbook endorsements.
C—Private Pilot Certificate with an instrument rating.

3127. What minimum pilot certification is required for operation within Class B airspace?

A—Private Pilot Certificate or Student Pilot Certificate with appropriate logbook endorsements.
B—Commercial Pilot Certificate.
C—Private Pilot Certificate with an instrument rating.

3128. What minimum radio equipment is required for VFR operation within Class B airspace?

A—Two-way radio communications equipment and a 4096-code transponder.
B—Two-way radio communications equipment, a 4096-code transponder, and an encoding altimeter.
C—Two-way radio communications equipment, a 4096-code transponder, an encoding altimeter, and a VOR or TACAN receiver.

3129. An operable 4096-code transponder and Mode C encoding altimeter are required in

A—Class B airspace and within 30 miles of the Class B primary airport.
B—Class D airspace.
C—Class E airspace below 10,000 feet MSL.

3130. In which type of airspace are VFR flights prohibited?

A—Class A.
B—Class B.
C—Class C.

3131. What is the specific fuel requirement for flight under VFR during daylight hours in an airplane?

A—Enough to complete the flight at normal cruising speed with adverse wind conditions.
B—Enough to fly to the first point of intended landing and to fly after that for 30 minutes at normal cruising speed.
C—Enough to fly to the first point of intended landing and to fly after that for 45 minutes at normal cruising speed.

3132. What is the specific fuel requirement for flight under VFR at night in an airplane?

A—Enough to complete the flight at normal cruising speed with adverse wind conditions.
B—Enough to fly to the first point of intended landing and to fly after that for 30 minutes at normal cruising speed.
C—Enough to fly to the first point of intended landing and to fly after that for 45 minutes at normal cruising speed.

3133. No person may begin a flight in a rotorcraft under VFR unless there is enough fuel to fly to the first point of intended landing and, assuming normal cruising speed, to fly thereafter for at least

A—20 minutes.
B—30 minutes.
C—1 hour.

3134. What minimum visibility and clearance from clouds are required for a recreational pilot in Class G airspace at 1,200 feet AGL or below during daylight hours?

A—1 mile visibility and clear of clouds.
B—3 miles visibility and clear of clouds.
C—3 miles visibility, 500 feet below the clouds.

3135. Outside controlled airspace, the minimum flight visibility requirement for a recreational pilot flying VFR above 1,200 feet AGL and below 10,000 feet MSL during daylight hours is

A—1 mile.
B—3 miles.
C—5 miles.

3136. During operations within controlled airspace at altitudes of less than 1,200 feet AGL, the minimum horizontal distance from clouds requirement for VFR flight is

A—1,000 feet.
B—1,500 feet.
C—2,000 feet.

3137. What minimum visibility and clearance from clouds are required for VFR operations in Class G airspace at 700 feet AGL or below during daylight hours?

A—1 mile visibility and clear of clouds.
B—1 mile visibility, 500 feet below, 1,000 feet above, and 2,000 feet horizontal clearance from clouds.
C—3 miles visibility and clear of clouds.

3138. What minimum flight visibility is required for VFR flight operations on an airway below 10,000 feet MSL?

A—1 mile.
B—3 miles.
C—4 miles.

3139. The minimum distance from clouds required for VFR operations on an airway below 10,000 feet MSL is

A—remain clear of clouds.
B—500 feet below, 1,000 feet above, and 2,000 feet horizontally.
C—500 feet above, 1,000 feet below, and 2,000 feet horizontally.

3140. During operations within controlled airspace at altitudes of more than 1,200 feet AGL, but less than 10,000 feet MSL, the minimum distance above clouds requirement for VFR flight is

A—500 feet.
B—1,000 feet.
C—1,500 feet.

3141. VFR flight in controlled airspace above 1,200 feet AGL and below 10,000 feet MSL requires a minimum visibility and vertical cloud clearance of

A—3 miles, and 500 feet below or 1,000 feet above the clouds in controlled airspace.
B—5 miles, and 1,000 feet below or 1,000 feet above the clouds at all altitudes.
C—5 miles, and 1,000 feet below or 1,000 feet above the clouds only in Class A airspace.

3142. During operations outside controlled airspace at altitudes of more than 1,200 feet AGL, but less than 10,000 feet MSL, the minimum flight visibility for VFR flight at night is

A—1 mile.
B—3 miles.
C—5 miles.

3143. Outside controlled airspace, the minimum flight visibility requirement for VFR flight above 1,200 feet AGL and below 10,000 feet MSL during daylight hours is

A—1 mile.
B—3 miles.
C—5 miles.

3144. During operations outside controlled airspace at altitudes of more than 1,200 feet AGL, but less than 10,000 feet MSL, the minimum distance below clouds requirement for VFR flight at night is

A—500 feet.
B—1,000 feet.
C—1,500 feet.

3145. The minimum flight visibility required for VFR flights above 10,000 feet MSL and more than 1,200 feet AGL in controlled airspace is

A—1 mile.
B—3 miles.
C—5 miles.

3146. For VFR flight operations above 10,000 feet MSL and more than 1,200 feet AGL, the minimum horizontal distance from clouds required is

A—1,000 feet.
B—2,000 feet.
C—1 mile.

3147. During operations at altitudes of more than 1,200 feet AGL and at or above 10,000 feet MSL, the minimum distance above clouds requirement for VFR flight is

A—500 feet.
B—1,000 feet.
C—1,500 feet.

3148. No person may take off or land an aircraft under basic VFR at an airport that lies within Class D airspace unless the

A—flight visibility at that airport is at least 1 mile.
B—ground visibility at that airport is at least 1 mile.
C—ground visibility at that airport is at least 3 miles.

3149. The basic VFR weather minimums for operating an aircraft within Class D airspace are

A—500-foot ceiling and 1 mile visibility.
B—1,000-foot ceiling and 3 miles visibility.
C—clear of clouds and 2 miles visibility.

3150. A special VFR clearance authorizes the pilot of an aircraft to operate VFR while within Class D airspace when the visibility is

A—less than 1 mile and the ceiling is less than 1,000 feet.
B—at least 1 mile and the aircraft can remain clear of clouds.
C—at least 3 miles and the aircraft can remain clear of clouds.

3151. What is the minimum weather condition required for airplanes operating under special VFR in Class D airspace?

A—1 mile flight visibility.
B—1 mile flight visibility and 1,000-foot ceiling.
C—3 miles flight visibility and 1,000-foot ceiling.

3152. Under what conditions, if any, may a private pilot operate a helicopter under special VFR at night within Class D airspace?

A—The helicopter must be fully instrument equipped and the pilot must be instrument rated.
B—The flight visibility must be at least 1 mile.
C—There are no conditions; regulations permit this.

3153. What are the minimum requirements for airplane operations under special VFR in Class D airspace at night?

A—The airplane must be under radar surveillance at all times while in Class D airspace.
B—The airplane must be equipped for IFR with an altitude reporting transponder.
C—The pilot must be instrument rated, and the airplane must be IFR equipped.

3154. No person may operate an airplane within Class D airspace at night under special VFR unless the

A—flight can be conducted 500 feet below the clouds.
B—airplane is equipped for instrument flight.
C—flight visibility is at least 3 miles.

3155. Which cruising altitude is appropriate for a VFR flight on a magnetic course of 135°?

A—Even thousandths.
B—Even thousandths plus 500 feet.
C—Odd thousandths plus 500 feet.

3156. Which VFR cruising altitude is acceptable for a flight on a Victor Airway with a magnetic course of 175°? The terrain is less than 1,000 feet.

A—4,500 feet.
B—5,000 feet.
C—5,500 feet.

3157. Which VFR cruising altitude is appropriate when flying above 3,000 feet AGL on a magnetic course of 185°?

A—4,000 feet.
B—4,500 feet.
C—5,000 feet.

3158. Each person operating an aircraft at a VFR cruising altitude shall maintain an odd-thousand plus 500-foot altitude while on a

A—magnetic heading of 0° through 179°.
B—magnetic course of 0° through 179°.
C—true course of 0° through 179°.

3159. In addition to a valid Airworthiness Certificate, what documents or records must be aboard an aircraft during flight?

A—Aircraft engine and airframe logbooks, and owner's manual.
B—Radio operator's permit, and repair and alteration forms.
C—Operating limitations and Registration Certificate.

3160. When must batteries in an emergency locator transmitter (ELT) be replaced or recharged, if rechargeable?

A—After any inadvertent activation of the ELT.
B—When the ELT has been in use for more than 1 cumulative hour.
C—When the ELT can no longer be heard over the airplane's communication radio receiver.

3161. When are non-rechargeable batteries of an emergency locator transmitter (ELT) required to be replaced?

A—Every 24 months.
B—When 50 percent of their useful life expires.
C—At the time of each 100-hour or annual inspection.

3162. Except in Alaska, during what time period should lighted position lights be displayed on an aircraft?

A—End of evening civil twilight to the beginning of morning civil twilight.
B—1 hour after sunset to 1 hour before sunrise.
C—Sunset to sunrise.

3163. When operating an aircraft at cabin pressure altitudes above 12,500 feet MSL up to and including 14,000 feet MSL, supplemental oxygen shall be used during

A—the entire flight time at those altitudes.
B—that flight time in excess of 10 minutes at those altitudes.
C—that flight time in excess of 30 minutes at those altitudes.

3164. Unless each occupant is provided with supplemental oxygen, no person may operate a civil aircraft of U.S. registry above a maximum cabin pressure altitude of

A—12,500 feet MSL.
B—14,000 feet MSL.
C—15,000 feet MSL.

3165. An operable 4096-code transponder with an encoding altimeter is required in which airspace?

A—Class A, Class B (and within 30 miles of the Class B primary airport), and Class C.
B—Class D and Class E (below 10,000 feet MSL).
C—Class D and Class G (below 10,000 feet MSL).

3166. With certain exceptions, all aircraft within 30 miles of a Class B primary airport from the surface upward to 10,000 feet MSL must be equipped with

A—an operable VOR or TACAN receiver and an ADF receiver.
B—instruments and equipment required for IFR operations.
C—an operable transponder having either Mode S or 4096-code capability with Mode C automatic altitude reporting capability.

3167. No person may operate an aircraft in acrobatic flight when

A—flight visibility is less than 5 miles.
B—over any congested area of a city, town, or settlement.
C—less than 2,500 feet AGL.

3168. In which controlled airspace is acrobatic flight prohibited?

A—Class D airspace, Class E airspace designated for Federal Airways.
B—All Class E airspace below 1,500 feet AGL.
C—All Class G airspace.

3169. What is the lowest altitude permitted for acrobatic flight?

A—1,000 feet AGL.
B—1,500 feet AGL.
C—2,000 feet AGL.

3170. No person may operate an aircraft in acrobatic flight when the flight visibility is less than

A—3 miles.
B—5 miles.
C—7 miles.

3171. A chair-type parachute must have been packed by a certificated and appropriately rated parachute rigger within the preceding

A—60 days.
B—90 days.
C—120 days.

3172. An approved chair-type parachute may be carried in an aircraft for emergency use if it has been packed by an appropriately rated parachute rigger within the preceding

A—120 days.
B—180 days.
C—365 days.

3173. With certain exceptions, when must each occupant of an aircraft wear an approved parachute?

A—When a door is removed from the aircraft to facilitate parachute jumpers.
B—When intentionally pitching the nose of the aircraft up or down 30° or more.
C—When intentionally banking in excess of 30°.

3174. The minimum allowable strength of a towline used for an aerotow of a glider having a certificated gross weight of 700 pounds is

A—560 pounds.
B—700 pounds.
C—1,000 pounds.

3175. The minimum allowable strength of a towline used for an aerotow of a glider having a certificated gross weight of 1,040 pounds is

A—502 pounds.
B—832 pounds.
C—1,040 pounds.

3176. For the aerotow of a glider that weighs 700 pounds, which towrope tensile strength would require the use of safety links at each end of the rope?

A—850 pounds.
B—1,040 pounds.
C—1,450 pounds.

3177. When using a towline having a breaking strength more than twice the maximum certificated operating weight of the glider, an approved safety link must be installed at what point(s)?

A—Only the point where the towline is attached to the glider.
B—The point where the towline is attached to the glider and the point of attachment of the towline to the towplane.
C—Only the point where the towline is attached to the towplane.

3178. Which is normally prohibited when operating a restricted category civil aircraft?

A—Flight under instrument flight rules.
B—Flight over a densely populated area.
C—Flight within Class D airspace.

3179. Unless otherwise specifically authorized, no person may operate an aircraft that has an experimental certificate

A—beneath the floor of Class B airspace.
B—over a densely populated area or in a congested airway.
C—from the primary airport within Class D airspace.

3180. The responsibility for ensuring that an aircraft is maintained in an airworthy condition is primarily that of the

A—pilot in command.
B—owner or operator.
C—mechanic who performs the work.

3181. The responsibility for ensuring that maintenance personnel make the appropriate entries in the aircraft maintenance records indicating the aircraft has been approved for return to service lies with the

A—owner or operator.
B—pilot in command.
C—mechanic who performed the work.

3182. Completion of an annual inspection and the return of the aircraft to service should always be indicated by

A—the relicensing date on the Registration Certificate.
B—an appropriate notation in the aircraft maintenance records.
C—an inspection sticker placed on the instrument panel that lists the annual inspection completion date.

3183. If an alteration or repair substantially affects an aircraft's operation in flight, that aircraft must be test flown by an appropriately-rated pilot and approved for return to service prior to being operated

A—by any private pilot.
B—with passengers aboard.
C—for compensation or hire.

3184. Before passengers can be carried in an aircraft that has been altered in a manner that may have appreciably changed its flight characteristics, it must be flight tested by an appropriately-rated pilot who holds at least a

A—Commercial Pilot Certificate with an instrument rating.
B—Private Pilot Certificate.
C—Commercial Pilot Certificate and a mechanic's certificate.

3185. An aircraft's annual inspection was performed on July 12, this year. The next annual inspection will be due no later than

A—July 1, next year.
B—July 13, next year.
C—July 31, next year.

3186. To determine the expiration date of the last annual aircraft inspection, a person should refer to the

A—Airworthiness Certificate.
B—Registration Certificate.
C—aircraft maintenance records.

3187. How long does the Airworthiness Certificate of an aircraft remain valid?

A—As long as the aircraft has a current Registration Certificate.
B—Indefinitely, unless the aircraft suffers major damage.
C—As long as the aircraft is maintained and operated as required by Federal Aviation Regulations.

3188. What aircraft inspections are required for rental aircraft that are also used for flight instruction?

A—Annual and 100-hour inspections.
B—Biannual and 100-hour inspections.
C—Annual and 50-hour inspections.

3189. An aircraft had a 100-hour inspection when the tachometer read 1259.6. When is the next 100-hour inspection due?

A—1349.6 hours.
B—1359.6 hours.
C—1369.6 hours.

3190. A 100-hour inspection was due at 3302.5 hours on the tachometer. The 100-hour inspection was actually done at 3309.5 hours. When is the next 100-hour inspection due?

A—3312.5 hours.
B—3402.5 hours.
C—3409.5 hours.

3191. No person may use an ATC transponder unless it has been tested and inspected within at least the preceding

A—6 calendar months.
B—12 calendar months.
C—24 calendar months.

3192. Maintenance records show the last transponder inspection was performed on September 1, 1993. The next inspection will be due no later than

A—September 30, 1994.
B—September 1, 1995.
C—September 30, 1995.

3193. Which records or documents shall the owner or operator of an aircraft keep to show compliance with an applicable Airworthiness Directive?

A—Aircraft maintenance records.
B—Airworthiness Certificate and Pilot's Operating Handbook.
C—Airworthiness and Registration Certificates.

3194. If an aircraft is involved in an accident which results in substantial damage to the aircraft, the nearest NTSB field office should be notified

A—immediately.
B—within 48 hours.
C—within 7 days.

3195. Which incident requires an immediate notification to the nearest NTSB field office?

A—A forced landing due to engine failure.
B—Landing gear damage, due to a hard landing.
C—Flight control system malfunction or failure.

3196. Which incident would necessitate an immediate notification to the nearest NTSB field office?

A—An in-flight generator/alternator failure.
B—An in-flight fire.
C—An in-flight loss of VOR receiver capability.

3197. Which incident requires an immediate notification be made to the nearest NTSB field office?

A—An overdue aircraft that is believed to be involved in an accident.
B—An in-flight radio communications failure.
C—An in-flight generator or alternator failure.

3198. May aircraft wreckage be moved prior to the time the NTSB takes custody?

A—Yes, but only if moved by a federal, state, or local law enforcement officer.
B—Yes, but only to protect the wreckage from further damage.
C—No, it may not be moved under any circumstances.

3199. The operator of an aircraft that has been involved in an accident is required to file an accident report within how many days?

A—5.
B—7.
C—10.

3200. The operator of an aircraft that has been involved in an incident is required to submit a report to the nearest field office of the NTSB

A—within 7 days.
B—within 10 days.
C—when requested.

3201. The four forces acting on an airplane in flight are

A—lift, weight, thrust, and drag.
B—lift, weight, gravity, and thrust.
C—lift, gravity, power, and friction.

3202. When are the four forces that act on an airplane in equilibrium?

A—During unaccelerated flight.
B—When the aircraft is accelerating.
C—When the aircraft is at rest on the ground.

3203. (Refer to Figure 1.) The acute angle A is the angle of

A—incidence.
B—attack.
C—dihedral.

3204. The term "angle of attack" is defined as the angle

A—between the wing chord line and the relative wind.
B—between the airplane's climb angle and the horizon.
C—formed by the longitudinal axis of the airplane and the chord line of the wing.

3205. What is the relationship of lift, drag, thrust, and weight when the airplane is in straight-and-level flight?

A—Lift equals weight and thrust equals drag.
B—Lift, drag, and weight equal thrust.
C—Lift and weight equal thrust and drag.

3206. How will frost on the wings of an airplane affect takeoff performance?

A—Frost will disrupt the smooth flow of air over the wing, adversely affecting its lifting capability.
B—Frost will change the camber of the wing, increasing its lifting capability.
C—Frost will cause the airplane to become airborne with a higher angle of attack, decreasing the stall speed.

3207. In what flight condition is torque effect the greatest in a single-engine airplane?

A—Low airspeed, high power, high angle of attack.
B—Low airspeed, low power, low angle of attack.
C—High airspeed, high power, high angle of attack.

3208. The left turning tendency of an airplane caused by P-factor is the result of the

A—clockwise rotation of the engine and the propeller turning the airplane counter-clockwise.
B—propeller blade descending on the right, producing more thrust than the ascending blade on the left.
C—gyroscopic forces applied to the rotating propeller blades acting 90° in advance of the point the force was applied.

3209. When does P-factor cause the airplane to yaw to the left?

A—When at low angles of attack.
B—When at high angles of attack.
C—When at high airspeeds.

3210. An airplane said to be inherently stable will

A—be difficult to stall.
B—require less effort to control.
C—not spin.

3211. What determines the longitudinal stability of an airplane?

A—The location of the CG with respect to the center of lift.
B—The effectiveness of the horizontal stabilizer, rudder, and rudder trim tab.
C—The relationship of thrust and lift to weight and drag.

3212. What causes an airplane (except a T-tail) to pitch nosedown when power is reduced and controls are not adjusted?

A—The CG shifts forward when thrust and drag are reduced.
B—The downwash on the elevators from the propeller slipstream is reduced and elevator effectiveness is reduced.
C—When thrust is reduced to less than weight, lift is also reduced and the wings can no longer support the weight.

3213. What is the purpose of the rudder on an airplane?

A—To control yaw.
B—To control overbanking tendency.
C—To control roll.

3214. (Refer to Figure 2.) If an airplane weighs 2,300 pounds, what approximate weight would the airplane structure be required to support during a 60° banked turn while maintaining altitude?

A—2,300 pounds.
B—3,400 pounds.
C—4,600 pounds.

3215. (Refer to Figure 2.) If an airplane weighs 3,300 pounds, what approximate weight would the airplane structure be required to support during a 30° banked turn while maintaining altitude?

A—1,200 pounds.
B—3,100 pounds.
C—3,960 pounds.

3216. (Refer to Figure 2.) If an airplane weighs 4,500 pounds, what approximate weight would the airplane structure be required to support during a 45° banked turn while maintaining altitude?

A—4,500 pounds.
B—6,750 pounds.
C—7,200 pounds.

3217. The amount of excess load that can be imposed on the wing of an airplane depends upon the

A—position of the CG.
B—speed of the airplane.
C—abruptness at which the load is applied.

3218. Which basic flight maneuver increases the load factor on an airplane as compared to straight-and-level flight?

A—Climbs.
B—Turns.
C—Stalls.

3219. One of the main functions of flaps during approach and landing is to

A—decrease the angle of descent without increasing the airspeed.
B—permit a touchdown at a higher indicated airspeed.
C—increase the angle of descent without increasing the airspeed.

3220. What is one purpose of wing flaps?

A—To enable the pilot to make steeper approaches to a landing without increasing the airspeed.
B—To relieve the pilot of maintaining continuous pressure on the controls.
C—To decrease wing area to vary the lift.

3221. Excessively high engine temperatures will

A—cause damage to heat-conducting hoses and warping of the cylinder cooling fins.
B—cause loss of power, excessive oil consumption, and possible permanent internal engine damage.
C—not appreciably affect an aircraft engine.

3222. If the engine oil temperature and cylinder head temperature gauges have exceeded their normal operating range, the pilot may have been operating with

A—the mixture set too rich.
B—higher-than-normal oil pressure.
C—too much power and with the mixture set too lean.

3223. One purpose of the dual ignition system on an aircraft engine is to provide for

A—improved engine performance.
B—uniform heat distribution.
C—balanced cylinder head pressure.

3224. On aircraft equipped with fuel pumps, the practice of running a fuel tank dry before switching tanks is considered unwise because

A—the engine-driven fuel pump or electric fuel boost pump may draw air into the fuel system and cause vapor lock.
B—the engine-driven fuel pump is lubricated by fuel and operating on a dry tank may cause pump failure.
C—any foreign matter in the tank will be pumped into the fuel system.

3225. The operating principle of float-type carburetors is based on the

A—automatic metering of air at the venturi as the aircraft gains altitude.
B—difference in air pressure at the venturi throat and the air inlet.
C—increase in air velocity in the throat of a venturi causing an increase in air pressure.

3226. The basic purpose of adjusting the fuel/air mixture at altitude is to

A—decrease the amount of fuel in the mixture in order to compensate for increased air density.
B—decrease the fuel flow in order to compensate for decreased air density.
C—increase the amount of fuel in the mixture to compensate for the decrease in pressure and density of the air.

3227. During the run-up at a high-elevation airport, a pilot notes a slight engine roughness that is not affected by the magneto check but grows worse during the carburetor heat check. Under these circumstances, what would be the most logical initial action?

A—Check the results obtained with a leaner setting of the mixture.
B—Taxi back to the flight line for a maintenance check.
C—Reduce manifold pressure to control detonation.

3228. While cruising at 9,500 feet MSL, the fuel/air mixture is properly adjusted. What will occur if a descent to 4,500 feet MSL is made without readjusting the mixture?

A—The fuel/air mixture may become excessively lean.
B—There will be more fuel in the cylinders than is needed for normal combustion, and the excess fuel will absorb heat and cool the engine.
C—The excessively rich mixture will create higher cylinder head temperatures and may cause detonation.

3229. Which condition is most favorable to the development of carburetor icing?

A—Any temperature below freezing and a relative humidity of less than 50 percent.
B—Temperature between 32 and 50°F and low humidity.
C—Temperature between 20 and 70°F and high humidity.

3230. The possibility of carburetor icing exists even when the ambient air temperature is as

A—high as 70°F and the relative humidity is high.
B—high as 95°F and there is visible moisture.
C—low as 0°F and the relative humidity is high.

3231. If an aircraft is equipped with a fixed-pitch propeller and a float-type carburetor, the first indication of carburetor ice would most likely be

A—a drop in oil temperature and cylinder head temperature.
B—engine roughness.
C—loss of RPM.

3232. Applying carburetor heat will

A—result in more air going through the carburetor.
B—enrich the fuel/air mixture.
C—not affect the fuel/air mixture.

3233. What change occurs in the fuel/air mixture when carburetor heat is applied?

A—A decrease in RPM results from the lean mixture.
B—The fuel/air mixture becomes richer.
C—The fuel/air mixture becomes leaner.

3234. Generally speaking, the use of carburetor heat tends to

A—decrease engine performance.
B—increase engine performance.
C—have no effect on engine performance.

3235. The presence of carburetor ice in an aircraft equipped with a fixed-pitch propeller can be verified by applying carburetor heat and noting

A—an increase in RPM and then a gradual decrease in RPM.
B—a decrease in RPM and then a constant RPM indication.
C—a decrease in RPM and then a gradual increase in RPM.

3236. With regard to carburetor ice, float-type carburetor systems in comparison to fuel injection systems are generally considered to be

A—more susceptible to icing.
B—equally susceptible to icing.
C—susceptible to icing only when visible moisture is present.

3237. If the grade of fuel used in an aircraft engine is lower than specified for the engine, it will most likely cause

A—a mixture of fuel and air that is not uniform in all cylinders.
B—lower cylinder head temperatures.
C—detonation.

3238. Detonation occurs in a reciprocating aircraft engine when

A—the spark plugs are fouled or shorted out or the wiring is defective.
B—hot spots in the combustion chamber ignite the fuel/air mixture in advance of normal ignition.
C—the unburned charge in the cylinders explodes instead of burning normally.

3239. If a pilot suspects that the engine (with a fixed-pitch propeller) is detonating during climb-out after takeoff, the initial corrective action to take would be to

A—lean the mixture.
B—lower the nose slightly to increase airspeed.
C—apply carburetor heat.

3240. The uncontrolled firing of the fuel/air charge in advance of normal spark ignition is known as

A—combustion.
B—pre-ignition.
C—detonation.

3241. Which would most likely cause the cylinder head temperature and engine oil temperature gauges to exceed their normal operating ranges?

A—Using fuel that has a lower-than-specified fuel rating.
B—Using fuel that has a higher-than-specified fuel rating.
C—Operating with higher-than-normal oil pressure.

3242. What type fuel can be substituted for an aircraft if the recommended octane is not available?

A—The next higher octane aviation gas.
B—The next lower octane aviation gas.
C—Unleaded automotive gas of the same octane rating.

3243. Filling the fuel tanks after the last flight of the day is considered a good operating procedure because this will

A—force any existing water to the top of the tank away from the fuel lines to the engine.
B—prevent expansion of the fuel by eliminating airspace in the tanks.
C—prevent moisture condensation by eliminating airspace in the tanks.

3244. For internal cooling, reciprocating aircraft engines are especially dependent on

A—a properly functioning thermostat.
B—air flowing over the exhaust manifold.
C—the circulation of lubricating oil.

3245. An abnormally high engine oil temperature indication may be caused by

A—the oil level being too low.
B—operating with a too high viscosity oil.
C—operating with an excessively rich mixture.

3246. What effect does high density altitude, as compared to low density altitude, have on propeller efficiency and why?

A—Efficiency is increased due to less friction on the propeller blades.
B—Efficiency is reduced because the propeller exerts less force at high density altitudes than at low density altitudes.
C—Efficiency is reduced due to the increased force of the propeller in the thinner air.

3247. If the pitot tube and outside static vents become clogged, which instruments would be affected?

A—The altimeter, airspeed indicator, and turn-and-slip indicator.
B—The altimeter, airspeed indicator, and vertical speed indicator.
C—The altimeter, attitude indicator, and turn-and-slip indicator.

3248. Which instrument will become inoperative if the pitot tube becomes clogged?

A—Altimeter.
B—Vertical speed.
C—Airspeed.

3249. Which instrument(s) will become inoperative if the static vents become clogged?

A—Airspeed only.
B—Altimeter only.
C—Airspeed, altimeter, and vertical speed.

3250. (Refer to Figure 3.) Altimeter 1 indicates

A—500 feet.
B—1,500 feet.
C—10,500 feet.

3251. (Refer to Figure 3.) Altimeter 2 indicates

A—1,500 feet.
B—4,500 feet.
C—14,500 feet.

3252. (Refer to Figure 3.) Altimeter 3 indicates

A—9,500 feet.
B—10,950 feet.
C—15,940 feet.

3253. (Refer to Figure 3.) Which altimeter(s) indicate(s) more than 10,000 feet?

A—1, 2, and 3.
B—1 and 2 only.
C—1 only.

3254. Altimeter setting is the value to which the barometric pressure scale of the altimeter is set so the altimeter indicates

A—calibrated altitude at field elevation.
B—absolute altitude at field elevation.
C—true altitude at field elevation.

3255. How do variations in temperature affect the altimeter?

A—Pressure levels are raised on warm days and the indicated altitude is lower than true altitude.
B—Higher temperatures expand the pressure levels and the indicated altitude is higher than true altitude.
C—Lower temperatures lower the pressure levels and the indicated altitude is lower than true altitude.

3256. What is true altitude?

A—The vertical distance of the aircraft above sea level.
B—The vertical distance of the aircraft above the surface.
C—The height above the standard datum plane.

3257. What is absolute altitude?

A—The altitude read directly from the altimeter.
B—The vertical distance of the aircraft above the surface.
C—The height above the standard datum plane.

3258. What is density altitude?

A—The height above the standard datum plane.
B—The pressure altitude corrected for nonstandard temperature.
C—The altitude read directly from the altimeter.

3259. What is pressure altitude?

A—The indicated altitude corrected for position and installation error.
B—The altitude indicated when the barometric pressure scale is set to 29.92.
C—The indicated altitude corrected for nonstandard temperature and pressure.

3260. Under what condition is indicated altitude the same as true altitude?

A—If the altimeter has no mechanical error.
B—When at sea level under standard conditions.
C—When at 18,000 feet MSL with the altimeter set at 29.92.

3261. If it is necessary to set the altimeter from 29.15 to 29.85, what change occurs?

A—70-foot increase in indicated altitude.
B—70-foot increase in density altitude.
C—700-foot increase in indicated altitude.

3262. The pitot system provides impact pressure for which instrument?

A—Altimeter.
B—Vertical-speed indicator.
C—Airspeed indicator.

3263. As altitude increases, the indicated airspeed at which a given airplane stalls in a particular configuration will

A—decrease as the true airspeed decreases.
B—decrease as the true airspeed increases.
C—remain the same regardless of altitude.

3264. What does the red line on an airspeed indicator represent?

A—Maneuvering speed.
B—Turbulent or rough-air speed.
C—Never-exceed speed.

3265. (Refer to Figure 4.) What is the full flap operating range for the airplane?

A—60 to 100 MPH.
B—60 to 208 MPH.
C—65 to 165 MPH.

3266. (Refer to Figure 4.) What is the caution range of the airplane?

A—0 to 60 MPH.
B—100 to 165 MPH.
C—165 to 208 MPH.

3267. (Refer to Figure 4.) The maximum speed at which the airplane can be operated in smooth air is

A—100 MPH.
B—165 MPH.
C—208 MPH.

3268. (Refer to Figure 4.) Which color identifies the never-exceed speed?

A—Lower limit of the yellow arc.
B—Upper limit of the white arc.
C—The red radial line.

3269. (Refer to Figure 4.) Which color identifies the power-off stalling speed in a specified configuration?

A—Upper limit of the green arc.
B—Upper limit of the white arc.
C—Lower limit of the green arc.

3270. (Refer to Figure 4.) What is the maximum flaps-extended speed?

A—65 MPH.
B—100 MPH.
C—165 MPH.

3271. (Refer to Figure 4.) Which color identifies the normal flap operating range?

A—The lower limit of the white arc to the upper limit of the green arc.
B—The green arc.
C—The white arc.

3272. (Refer to Figure 4.) Which color identifies the power-off stalling speed with wing flaps and landing gear in the landing configuration?

A—Upper limit of the green arc.
B—Upper limit of the white arc.
C—Lower limit of the white arc.

3273. (Refer to Figure 4.) What is the maximum structural cruising speed?

A—100 MPH.
B—165 MPH.
C—208 MPH.

3274. What is an important airspeed limitation that is not color coded on airspeed indicators?

A—Never-exceed speed.
B—Maximum structural cruising speed.
C—Maneuvering speed.

3275. (Refer to Figure 5.) A turn coordinator provides an indication of the

A—movement of the aircraft about the yaw and roll axes.
B—angle of bank up to but not exceeding 30°.
C—attitude of the aircraft with reference to the longitudinal axis.

3276. (Refer to Figure 6.) To receive accurate indications during flight from a heading indicator, the instrument must be

A—set prior to flight on a known heading.
B—calibrated on a compass rose at regular intervals.
C—periodically realigned with the magnetic compass as the gyro precesses.

3277. (Refer to Figure 7.) The proper adjustment to make on the attitude indicator during level flight is to align the

A—horizon bar to the level-flight indication.
B—horizon bar to the miniature airplane.
C—miniature airplane to the horizon bar.

3278. (Refer to Figure 7.) How should a pilot determine the direction of bank from an attitude indicator such as the one illustrated?

A—By the direction of deflection of the banking scale (A).
B—By the direction of deflection of the horizon bar (B).
C—By the relationship of the miniature airplane (C) to the deflected horizon bar (B).

3279. Deviation in a magnetic compass is caused by the

A—presence of flaws in the permanent magnets of the compass.
B—difference in the location between true north and magnetic north.
C—magnetic fields within the aircraft distorting the lines of magnetic force.

3280. In the Northern Hemisphere, a magnetic compass will normally indicate initially a turn toward the west if

A—a left turn is entered from a north heading.
B—a right turn is entered from a north heading.
C—an aircraft is accelerated while on a north heading.

3281. In the Northern Hemisphere, a magnetic compass will normally indicate initially a turn toward the east if

A—an aircraft is decelerated while on a south heading.
B—an aircraft is accelerated while on a north heading.
C—a left turn is entered from a north heading.

3282. In the Northern Hemisphere, a magnetic compass will normally indicate a turn toward the north if

A—a right turn is entered from an east heading.
B—a left turn is entered from a west heading.
C—an aircraft is accelerated while on an east or west heading.

3283. In the Northern Hemisphere, the magnetic compass will normally indicate a turn toward the south when

A—a left turn is entered from an east heading.
B—a right turn is entered from a west heading.
C—the aircraft is decelerated while on a west heading.

3284. In the Northern Hemisphere, if an aircraft is accelerated or decelerated, the magnetic compass will normally indicate

A—a turn momentarily.
B—correctly when on a north or south heading.
C—a turn toward the south.

3285. In the Northern Hemisphere, if a glider is accelerated or decelerated, the magnetic compass will normally indicate

A—a turn toward north while decelerating on an east heading.
B—correctly only when on a north or south heading.
C—a turn toward south while accelerating on a west heading.

3286. During flight, when are the indications of a magnetic compass accurate?

A—Only in straight-and-level unaccelerated flight.
B—As long as the airspeed is constant.
C—During turns if the bank does not exceed 18°

3287. An airplane has been loaded in such a manner that the CG is located aft of the aft CG limit. One undesirable flight characteristic a pilot might experience with this airplane would be

A—a longer takeoff run.
B—difficulty in recovering from a stalled condition.
C—stalling at higher-than-normal airspeed.

3288. Loading an airplane to the most aft CG will cause the airplane to be

A—less stable at all speeds.
B—less stable at slow speeds, but more stable at high speeds.
C—less stable at high speeds, but more stable at low speeds.

3289. If the outside air temperature (OAT) at a given altitude is warmer than standard, the density altitude is

A—equal to pressure altitude.
B—lower than pressure altitude.
C—higher than pressure altitude.

3290. Which combination of atmospheric conditions will reduce aircraft takeoff and climb performance?

A—Low temperature, low relative humidity, and low density altitude.
B—High temperature, low relative humidity, and low density altitude.
C—High temperature, high relative humidity, and high density altitude.

3291. What effect does high density altitude have on aircraft performance?

A—It increases engine performance.
B—It reduces climb performance.
C—It increases takeoff performance.

3292. (Refer to Figure 8.) What is the effect of a temperature increase from 25 to 50°F on the density altitude if the pressure altitude remains at 5,000 feet?

A—1,200-foot increase.
B—1,400-foot increase.
C—1,650-foot increase.

3293. (Refer to Figure 8.) Determine the pressure altitude with an indicated altitude of 1,380 feet MSL with an altimeter setting of 28.22 at standard temperature.

A—1,250 feet MSL.
B—1,373 feet MSL.
C—3,010 feet MSL.

3294. (Refer to Figure 8.) Determine the density altitude for these conditions:

Altimeter setting 29.25
Runway temperature +81°F
Airport elevation 5,250 ft MSL

A—4,600 feet MSL.
B—5,877 feet MSL.
C—8,500 feet MSL.

3295. (Refer to Figure 8.) Determine the pressure altitude at an airport that is 3,563 feet MSL with an altimeter setting of 29.96.

A—3,527 feet MSL.
B—3,556 feet MSL.
C—3,639 feet MSL.

3296. (Refer to Figure 8.) What is the effect of a temperature increase from 30 to 50°F on the density altitude if the pressure altitude remains at 3,000 feet MSL?

A—900-foot increase.
B—1,100-foot decrease.
C—1,300-foot increase.

3297. (Refer to Figure 8.) Determine the pressure altitude at an airport that is 1,386 feet MSL with an altimeter setting of 29.97.

A—1,341 feet MSL.
B—1,451 feet MSL.
C—1,562 feet MSL.

3298. (Refer to Figure 8.) Determine the density altitude for these conditions:

Altimeter setting 30.35
Runway temperature +25°F
Airport elevation 3,894 ft MSL

A—2,000 feet MSL.
B—2,900 feet MSL.
C—3,500 feet MSL.

3299. (Refer to Figure 8.) What is the effect of a temperature decrease and a pressure altitude increase on the density altitude from 90°F and 1,250 feet pressure altitude to 60°F and 1,750 feet pressure altitude?

A—500-foot increase.
B—1,300-foot decrease.
C—1,300-foot increase.

3300. What effect, if any, does high humidity have on aircraft performance?

A—It increases performance.
B—It decreases performance.
C—It has no effect on performance.

3301. What force makes an airplane turn?

A—The horizontal component of lift.
B—The vertical component of lift.
C—Centrifugal force.

3302. When taxiing with strong quartering tailwinds, which aileron positions should be used?

A—Aileron down on the downwind side.
B—Ailerons neutral.
C—Aileron down on the side from which the wind is blowing.

3303. Which aileron positions should a pilot generally use when taxiing in strong quartering headwinds?

A—Aileron up on the side from which the wind is blowing.
B—Aileron down on the side from which the wind is blowing.
C—Ailerons neutral.

3304. Which wind condition would be most critical when taxiing a nosewheel equipped high-wing airplane?

A—Quartering tailwind.
B—Direct crosswind.
C—Quartering headwind.

3305. (Refer to Figure 9, area A.) How should the flight controls be held while taxiing a tricycle-gear equipped airplane into a left quartering headwind?

A—Left aileron up, elevator neutral.
B—Left aileron down, elevator neutral.
C—Left aileron up, elevator down.

3306. (Refer to Figure 9, area B.) How should the flight controls be held while taxiing a tailwheel airplane into a right quartering headwind?

A—Right aileron up, elevator up.
B—Right aileron down, elevator neutral.
C—Right aileron up, elevator down.

3307. (Refer to Figure 9, area C.) How should the flight controls be held while taxiing a tailwheel airplane with a left quartering tailwind?

A—Left aileron up, elevator neutral.
B—Left aileron down, elevator neutral.
C—Left aileron down, elevator down.

3308. (Refer to Figure 9, area C.) How should the flight controls be held while taxiing a tricycle-gear equipped airplane with a left quartering tailwind?

A—Left aileron up, elevator neutral.
B—Left aileron down, elevator down.
C—Left aileron up, elevator down.

3309. In what flight condition must an aircraft be placed in order to spin?

A—Partially stalled with one wing low.
B—In a steep diving spiral.
C—Stalled.

3310. During a spin to the left, which wing(s) is/are stalled?

A—Both wings are stalled.
B—Neither wing is stalled.
C—Only the left wing is stalled.

3311. The angle of attack at which an airplane wing stalls will

A—increase if the CG is moved forward.
B—change with an increase in gross weight.
C—remain the same regardless of gross weight.

3312. What is ground effect?

A—The result of the interference of the surface of the Earth with the airflow patterns about an airplane.
B—The result of an alteration in airflow patterns increasing induced drag about the wings of an airplane.
C—The result of the disruption of the airflow patterns about the wings of an airplane to the point where the wings will no longer support the airplane in flight.

3313. Floating caused by the phenomenon of ground effect will be most realized during an approach to land when at

A—less than the length of the wingspan above the surface.
B—twice the length of the wingspan above the surface.
C—a higher-than-normal angle of attack.

3314. What must a pilot be aware of as a result of ground effect?

A—Wingtip vortices increase creating wake turbulence problems for arriving and departing aircraft.
B—Induced drag decreases; therefore, any excess speed at the point of flare may cause considerable floating.
C—A full stall landing will require less up elevator deflection than would a full stall when done free of ground effect.

3315. Ground effect is most likely to result in which problem?

A—Settling to the surface abruptly during landing.
B—Becoming airborne before reaching recommended takeoff speed.
C—Inability to get airborne even though airspeed is sufficient for normal takeoff needs.

3316. During an approach to a stall, an increased load factor will cause the airplane to

A—stall at a higher airspeed.
B—have a tendency to spin.
C—be more difficult to control.

3317. Angle of attack is defined as the angle between the chord line of an airfoil and the

A—direction of the relative wind.
B—pitch angle of an airfoil.
C—rotor plane of rotation.

3318. (Refer to Figure 10.) During flight, if cyclic control pressure is applied which results in a maximum increase in pitch angle of the rotor blade at position A, the rotor disc will tilt

A—forward.
B—aft.
C—left.

3319. The lift differential that exists between the advancing main rotor blade and the retreating main rotor blade is known as

A—transverse flow effect.
B—dissymmetry of lift.
C—hunting tendency.

3320. During forward cruising flight at constant airspeed and altitude, the individual rotor blades, when compared to each other, are operating

A—with increased lift on the retreating blade.
B—with a decreasing angle of attack on the advancing blade.
C—at unequal airspeed, unequal angles of attack, and equal lift moment.

3321. The upward bending of the rotor blades resulting from the combined forces of lift and centrifugal force is known as

A—coning.
B—blade slapping.
C—inertia.

3322. When a blade flaps up, the CG moves closer to its axis of rotation giving that blade a tendency to

A—decelerate.
B—accelerate.
C—stabilize its rotational velocity.

3323. During a hover, a helicopter tends to drift to the right. To compensate for this, some helicopters have the

A—tail rotor tilted to the left.
B—tail rotor tilted to the right.
C—rotor mast rigged to the left side.

3324. Which is a result of the phenomenon of ground effect?

A—The induced angle of attack of each rotor blade is increased.
B—The lift vector becomes more horizontal.
C—The angle of attack generating lift is increased.

3325. Translational lift is the result of

A—decreased rotor efficiency.
B—airspeed.
C—both airspeed and groundspeed.

3326. The primary purpose of the tail rotor system is to

A—assist in making a coordinated turn.
B—maintain heading during forward flight.
C—counteract the torque effect of the main rotor.

3327. If RPM is low and manifold pressure is high, what initial corrective action should be taken?

A—Increase the throttle.
B—Lower the collective pitch.
C—Raise the collective pitch.

3328. The purpose of the lead-lag (drag) hinge in a three-bladed, fully articulated helicopter rotor system is to compensate for

A—Coriolis effect.
B—coning.
C—geometric unbalance.

3329. High airspeeds, particularly in turbulent air, should be avoided primarily because of the possibility of

A—an abrupt pitchup.
B—retreating blade stall.
C—a low-frequency vibration developing.

3330. The maximum forward speed of a gyroplane is limited by

A—retreating blade stall.
B—the rotor RPM red line.
C—solidity ratio.

3331. When operating at high forward airspeeds, retreating blade stalls are more likely to occur under which condition?

A—Low gross weight and low density altitude.
B—High RPM and low density altitude.
C—Steep turns in turbulent air.

3332. Ground resonance is most likely to develop when

A—on the ground and harmonic vibrations develop between the main and tail rotors.
B—a series of shocks causes the rotor system to become unbalanced.
C—there is a combination of a decrease in the angle of attack on the advancing blade and an increase in the angle of attack on the retreating blade.

3333. While in level cruising flight in a helicopter, a pilot experiences low-frequency vibrations (100 to 400 cycles per minute). These vibrations are normally associated with the

A—engine.
B—cooling fan.
C—main rotor.

3334. Select the helicopter component that, if defective, would cause medium-frequency vibrations.

A—Tail rotor.
B—Main rotor.
C—Engine.

3335. The principal reason the shaded area of a Height vs. Velocity Chart should be avoided is

A—turbulence near the surface can dephase the blade dampers.
B—rotor RPM may decay before ground contact is made if an engine failure should occur.
C—insufficient airspeed would be available to ensure a safe landing in case of an engine failure.

3336. During surface taxiing, the collective pitch is used to control

A—drift during a crosswind.
B—rate of speed.
C—ground track.

3337. During surface taxiing, the cyclic pitch stick is used to control

A—forward movement.
B—heading.
C—ground track.

3338. If the pilot experiences ground resonance during rotor spin-up, what action should the pilot take?

A—Taxi to a smooth area.
B—Close the throttle and slowly raise the spin-up lever.
C—Make a normal takeoff immediately.

3339. What precaution should be taken while taxiing a gyroplane?

A—The cyclic stick should be held in the neutral position at all times.
B—Avoid abrupt control movements when blades are turning.
C—The cyclic stick should be held slightly aft of neutral at all times.

3340. What force provides the forward motion necessary to move a glider through the air?

A—Lift.
B—Centripetal force.
C—Gravity.

3341. To obtain maximum distance over the ground, the airspeed to use is the

A—minimum control speed.
B—best lift/drag speed.
C—minimum sink speed.

3342. What effect would gusts and turbulence have on the load factor of a glider with changes in airspeed?

A—Load factor decreases as airspeed increases.
B—Load factor increases as airspeed increases.
C—Load factor increases as airspeed decreases.

3343. (Refer to Figure 11.) Which yaw string and inclinometer illustrations indicate a slipping right turn?

A—3 and 6.
B—2 and 6.
C—2 and 4.

3344. (Refer to Figure 11.) Which of the illustrations depicts the excessive use of right rudder during the entry of a right turn?

A—2 only.
B—2 and 4.
C—3 and 4.

3345. A sailplane has a best glide ratio of 23:1. How many feet will the glider lose in 8 nautical miles?

A—1,840 feet.
B—2,100 feet.
C—2,750 feet.

3346. A sailplane has a best glide ratio of 30:1. How many nautical miles will the glider travel while losing 2,000 feet?

A—10 nautical miles.
B—15 nautical miles.
C—21 nautical miles.

3347. A sailplane has lost 2,000 feet in 9 nautical miles. The best glide ratio for this sailplane is approximately

A—24:1.
B—27:1.
C—30:1.

3348. How many feet will a sailplane sink in 15 nautical miles if its lift/drag ratio is 22:1?

A—2,700 feet.
B—3,600 feet.
C—4,100 feet.

3349. How many feet will a glider sink in 10 nautical miles if its lift/drag ratio is 23:1?

A—2,400 feet.
B—2,600 feet.
C—4,300 feet.

3350. What is the proper airspeed to use when flying between thermals on a cross-country flight against a headwind?

A—The best lift/drag speed increased by one-half the estimated wind velocity.
B—The minimum sink speed increased by one-half the estimated wind velocity.
C—The best lift/drag speed decreased by one-half the estimated wind velocity.

3351. The part of a balloon that bears the entire load is the

A—envelope material.
B—envelope seams.
C—load tapes (or cords).

3352. In hot air balloons, propane is preferred to butane or other hydrocarbons because it

A—is less volatile.
B—is slower to vaporize.
C—has a lower boiling point.

3353. The initial temperature at which propane boils is

A—+32°F.
B—-44°F.
C—-60°F.

3354. On cold days, it may be necessary to preheat the propane tanks because

A—the temperature of the liquid propane controls the burner pressure during combustion.
B—there may be ice in the lines to the burner.
C—the propane needs to be thawed from a solid to a liquid state.

3355. When ample liquid propane is available, propane will vaporize sufficiently to provide proper operation between the temperatures of

A—+30 to +90°F.
B—-44 to +25°F.
C—-51 to +20°F.

3356. If ample propane is available, within which temperature range will propane vaporize sufficiently to provide enough pressure for burner operation during flight?

A—0 to 30°F.
B—10 to 30°F.
C—30 to 90°F.

3357. The valve located on the top of the propane tank which opens automatically when the pressure in the tank exceeds maximum allowable pressure is the

A—pressure release valve.
B—metering valve.
C—blast valve.

3358. The valve located on each tank that indicates when the tank is filled to 80 percent capacity is the

A—main tank valve.
B—vapor-bleed valve.
C—pilot valve.

3359. The lifting forces which act on a hot air balloon are primarily the result of the interior air temperature being

A—greater than ambient temperature.
B—less than ambient temperature.
C—equal to ambient temperature.

3360. Burner efficiency of a hot air balloon decreases approximately what percent for each 1,000 feet above MSL?

A—4 percent.
B—8 percent.
C—15 percent.

3361. While in flight, ice begins forming on the outside of the fuel tank in use. This would most likely be caused by

A—water in the fuel.
B—a leak in the fuel line.
C—vaporized fuel instead of liquid fuel being drawn from the tank into the main burner.

3362. For what reason is methanol added to the propane fuel of hot air balloons?

A—To check for fuel leaks.
B—As a fire retardant.
C—As an anti-icing additive.

3363. On a balloon equipped with a blast valve, the blast valve is used for

A—climbs and descents only.
B—altitude control.
C—emergencies only.

3364. The term "weigh-off" means to determine the

A—static equilibrium of the balloon as loaded for flight.
B—amount of gas required for an ascent to a preselected altitude.
C—standard weight and balance of the balloon.

3365. What causes false lift which sometimes occurs during launch procedures?

A—Closing the maneuvering vent too rapidly.
B—Excessive temperature within the envelope.
C—Venturi effect of the wind on the envelope.

3366. What is the relationship of false lift with the wind?

A—False lift increases as the wind accelerates the balloon.
B—False lift does not exist if the surface winds are calm.
C—False lift decreases as the wind accelerates the balloon.

3367. What would cause a gas balloon to start a descent if a cold air mass is encountered and the envelope becomes cooled?

A—A density differential.
B—A barometric pressure differential.
C—The contraction of the gas.

3368. Under which condition will an airship float in the air?

A—When buoyant force equals horizontal equilibrium existing between propeller thrust and airship drag.
B—When buoyant force is less than the difference between airship weight and the weight of the air volume being displaced.
C—When buoyant force equals the difference between airship weight and the weight of the air volume being displaced.

3369. During flight in an airship, when is vertical equilibrium established?

A—When buoyancy is greater than airship weight.
B—When buoyancy equals airship weight.
C—When buoyancy is less than airship weight.

3370. An airship descending through a steep temperature inversion will

A—show no change in superheat as altitude is lost.
B—show a decrease in superheat as altitude is lost.
C—become progressively lighter, thus becoming increasingly more difficult to drive down.

3371. What is airship superheat?

A—A condition of excessive exterior temperature of the envelope.
B—The temperature of the lifting gas exceeding the red line.
C—The difference between outside air temperature and the temperature inside the envelope.

3372. In relation to the operation of an airship, what is the definition of aerostatics?

A—The gravitational factors involving equilibrium of a body freely suspended in the atmosphere.
B—The science of the dynamics involved in the expansion and contraction of hydrogen gas.
C—The expansion and contraction of the lifting gas helium.

3373. Below pressure height, each 5°F of positive superheat amounts to approximately

A—1 percent of gross lift.
B—2 percent of net lift.
C—2 percent of total lift.

3374. When the airship is at pressure height and superheat increases, constant pressure must be maintained by valving

A—gas from the envelope.
B—air from the envelope.
C—gas from the ballonets.

3375. How does the pilot know when pressure height has been reached?

A—Liquid in the gas manometer will rise and the liquid in the air manometer will fall below normal levels.
B—Liquid in the gas and air manometers will fall below the normal level.
C—Liquid in the gas manometer will fall and the liquid in the air manometer will rise above normal levels.

3376. The pressure height of an airship is the altitude at which

A—the airship would be unable to gain more altitude.
B—gas pressure would reach 3 inches of water.
C—the ballonet(s) would be empty.

3377. The maximum altitude that a rigid airship can reach (under a given atmospheric condition) and then return safely to the surface is determined by

A—the disposable load.
B—ballonet capacity.
C—pressure altitude.

3378. An unbalanced condition of an airship in flight must be overcome by

A—valving air from the ballonets.
B—valving gas from the envelope.
C—a negative or a positive dynamic force.

3379. Why should damper valves normally be kept closed during climbs? Because any air forced into the system would

A—increase the amount of gas that must be exhausted to prevent the airship from ascending at an excessively high rate.
B—increase the amount of air to be exhausted, resulting in a lower rate of ascent.
C—decrease the purity of the gas within the envelope.

3380. To check the gas pressures (pressure height) of an airship during a climb, the air damper valves should be

A—opened forward and closed aft.
B—opened aft and closed forward.
C—closed.

3381. Every physical process of weather is accompanied by, or is the result of, a

A—movement of air.
B—pressure differential.
C—heat exchange.

3382. What causes variations in altimeter settings between weather reporting points?

A—Unequal heating of the Earth's surface.
B—Variation of terrain elevation.
C—Coriolis force.

3383. A temperature inversion would most likely result in which weather condition?

A—Clouds with extensive vertical development above an inversion aloft.
B—Good visibility in the lower levels of the atmosphere and poor visibility above an inversion aloft.
C—An increase in temperature as altitude is increased.

3384. The most frequent type of ground or surface-based temperature inversion is that which is produced by

A—terrestrial radiation on a clear, relatively still night.
B—warm air being lifted rapidly aloft in the vicinity of mountainous terrain.
C—the movement of colder air under warm air, or the movement of warm air over cold air.

3385. Which weather conditions should be expected beneath a low-level temperature inversion layer when the relative humidity is high?

A—Smooth air, poor visibility, fog, haze, or low clouds.
B—Light wind shear, poor visibility, haze, and light rain.
C—Turbulent air, poor visibility, fog, low stratus type clouds, and showery precipitation.

3386. What are the standard temperature and pressure values for sea level?

A—15°C and 29.92" Hg.
B—59°C and 1013.2 millibars.
C—59°F and 29.92 millibars.

3387. If a pilot changes the altimeter setting from 30.11 to 29.96, what is the approximate change in indication?

A—Altimeter will indicate .15" Hg higher.
B—Altimeter will indicate 150 feet higher.
C—Altimeter will indicate 150 feet lower.

3388. Under which condition will pressure altitude be equal to true altitude?

A—When the atmospheric pressure is 29.92" Hg.
B—When standard atmospheric conditions exist.
C—When indicated altitude is equal to the pressure altitude.

3389. Under what condition is pressure altitude and density altitude the same value?

A—At sea level, when the temperature is 0°F.
B—When the altimeter has no installation error.
C—At standard temperature.

3390. If a flight is made from an area of low pressure into an area of high pressure without the altimeter setting being adjusted, the altimeter will indicate

A—the actual altitude above sea level.
B—higher than the actual altitude above sea level.
C—lower than the actual altitude above sea level.

3391. If a flight is made from an area of high pressure into an area of lower pressure without the altimeter setting being adjusted, the altimeter will indicate

A—lower than the actual altitude above sea level.
B—higher than the actual altitude above sea level.
C—the actual altitude above sea level.

3392. Under what condition will true altitude be lower than indicated altitude?

A—In colder than standard air temperature.
B—In warmer than standard air temperature.
C—When density altitude is higher than indicated altitude.

3393. Which condition would cause the altimeter to indicate a lower altitude than true altitude?

A—Air temperature lower than standard.
B—Atmospheric pressure lower than standard.
C—Air temperature warmer than standard.

3394. Which factor would tend to increase the density altitude at a given airport?

A—An increase in barometric pressure.
B—An increase in ambient temperature.
C—A decrease in relative humidity.

3395. The wind at 5,000 feet AGL is southwesterly while the surface wind is southerly. This difference in direction is primarily due to

A—stronger pressure gradient at higher altitudes.
B—friction between the wind and the surface.
C—stronger Coriolis force at the surface.

3396. What condition does a rising barometer indicate for balloon operations?

A—Decreasing clouds and wind.
B—Chances of thunderstorms.
C—Approaching frontal activity.

3397. What is meant by the term "dewpoint"?

A—The temperature at which condensation and evaporation are equal.
B—The temperature at which dew will always form.
C—The temperature to which air must be cooled to become saturated.

3398. The amount of water vapor which air can hold depends on the

A—dewpoint.
B—air temperature.
C—stability of the air.

3399. Clouds, fog, or dew will always form when

A—water vapor condenses.
B—water vapor is present.
C—relative humidity reaches 100 percent.

3400. What are the processes by which moisture is added to unsaturated air?

A—Evaporation and sublimation.
B—Heating and condensation.
C—Supersaturation and evaporation.

3401. Which conditions result in the formation of frost?

A—The temperature of the collecting surface is at or below freezing when small droplets of moisture fall on the surface.
B—The temperature of the collecting surface is at or below the dewpoint of the adjacent air and the dewpoint is below freezing.
C—The temperature of the surrounding air is at or below freezing when small drops of moisture fall on the collecting surface.

3402. The presence of ice pellets at the surface is evidence that there

A—are thunderstorms in the area.
B—has been cold frontal passage.
C—is a temperature inversion with freezing rain at a higher altitude.

3403. What measurement can be used to determine the stability of the atmosphere?

A—Atmospheric pressure.
B—Actual lapse rate.
C—Surface temperature.

3404. What would decrease the stability of an air mass?

A—Warming from below.
B—Cooling from below.
C—Decrease in water vapor.

3405. What is a characteristic of stable air?

A—Stratiform clouds.
B—Unlimited visibility.
C—Cumulus clouds.

3406. Moist, stable air flowing upslope can be expected to

A—produce stratus type clouds.
B—cause showers and thunderstorms.
C—develop convective turbulence.

3407. If an unstable air mass is forced upward, what type clouds can be expected?

A—Stratus clouds with little vertical development.
B—Stratus clouds with considerable associated turbulence.
C—Clouds with considerable vertical development and associated turbulence.

3408. What feature is associated with a temperature inversion?

A—A stable layer of air.
B—An unstable layer of air.
C—Chinook winds on mountain slopes.

3409. What is the approximate base of the cumulus clouds if the surface air temperature at 1,000 feet MSL is 70°F and the dewpoint is 48°F?

A—4,000 feet MSL.
B—5,000 feet MSL.
C—6,000 feet MSL.

3410. At approximately what altitude above the surface would the pilot expect the base of cumuliform clouds if the surface air temperature is 82°F and the dewpoint is 38°F?

A—9,000 feet AGL.
B—10,000 feet AGL.
C—11,000 feet AGL.

3411. What early morning weather observations indicate the possibility of good weather conditions for balloon flight most of the day?

A—Clear skies and surface winds, 10 knots or less.
B—Low moving, scattered cumulus clouds and surface winds, 5 knots or less.
C—Overcast with stratus clouds and surface winds, 5 knots or less.

3412. What are characteristics of a moist, unstable air mass?

A—Cumuliform clouds and showery precipitation.
B—Poor visibility and smooth air.
C—Stratiform clouds and showery precipitation.

3413. What are characteristics of unstable air?

A—Turbulence and good surface visibility.
B—Turbulence and poor surface visibility.
C—Nimbostratus clouds and good surface visibility.

3414. A stable air mass is most likely to have which characteristic?

A—Showery precipitation.
B—Turbulent air.
C—Smooth air.

3415. The suffix "nimbus," used in naming clouds, means

A—a cloud with extensive vertical development.
B—a rain cloud.
C—a middle cloud containing ice pellets.

3416. Clouds are divided into four families according to their

A—outward shape.
B—height range.
C—composition.

3417. An almond or lens-shaped cloud which appears stationary, but which may contain winds of 50 knots or more, is referred to as

A—an inactive frontal cloud.
B—a funnel cloud.
C—a lenticular cloud.

3418. Crests of standing mountain waves may be marked by stationary, lens-shaped clouds known as

A—mammatocumulus clouds.
B—standing lenticular clouds.
C—roll clouds.

3419. What clouds have the greatest turbulence?

A—Towering cumulus.
B—Cumulonimbus.
C—Nimbostratus.

3420. What cloud types would indicate convective turbulence?

A—Cirrus clouds.
B—Nimbostratus clouds.
C—Towering cumulus clouds.

3421. The boundary between two different air masses is referred to as a

A—frontolysis.
B—frontogenesis.
C—front.

3422. One of the most easily recognized discontinuities across a front is

A—a change in temperature.
B—an increase in cloud coverage.
C—an increase in relative humidity.

3423. One weather phenomenon which will always occur when flying across a front is a change in the

A—wind direction.
B—type of precipitation.
C—stability of the air mass.

3424. Steady precipitation preceding a front is an indication of

A—stratiform clouds with moderate turbulence.
B—cumuliform clouds with little or no turbulence.
C—stratiform clouds with little or no turbulence.

3425. Possible mountain wave turbulence could be anticipated when winds of 40 knots or greater blow

A—across a mountain ridge, and the air is stable.
B—down a mountain valley, and the air is unstable.
C—parallel to a mountain peak, and the air is stable.

3426. Where does wind shear occur?

A—Only at higher altitudes.
B—Only at lower altitudes.
C—At all altitudes, in all directions.

3427. When may hazardous wind shear be expected?

A—When stable air crosses a mountain barrier where it tends to flow in layers forming lenticular clouds.
B—In areas of low-level temperature inversion, frontal zones, and clear air turbulence.
C—Following frontal passage when stratocumulus clouds form indicating mechanical mixing.

3428. A pilot can expect a wind-shear zone in a temperature inversion whenever the windspeed at 2,000 to 4,000 feet above the surface is at least

A—10 knots.
B—15 knots.
C—25 knots.

3429. One in-flight condition necessary for structural icing to form is

A—small temperature/dewpoint spread.
B—stratiform clouds.
C—visible moisture.

3430. In which environment is aircraft structural ice most likely to have the highest accumulation rate?

A—Cumulus clouds with below freezing temperatures.
B—Freezing drizzle.
C—Freezing rain.

3431. Why is frost considered hazardous to flight?

A—Frost changes the basic aerodynamic shape of the airfoils, thereby decreasing lift.
B—Frost slows the airflow over the airfoils, thereby increasing control effectiveness.
C—Frost spoils the smooth flow of air over the wings, thereby decreasing lifting capability.

3432. How does frost affect the lifting surfaces of an airplane on takeoff?

A—Frost may prevent the airplane from becoming airborne at normal takeoff speed.
B—Frost will change the camber of the wing, increasing lift during takeoff.
C—Frost may cause the airplane to become airborne with a lower angle of attack at a lower indicated airspeed.

3433. The conditions necessary for the formation of cumulonimbus clouds are a lifting action and

A—unstable air containing an excess of condensation nuclei.
B—unstable, moist air.
C—either stable or unstable air.

3434. What feature is normally associated with the cumulus stage of a thunderstorm?

A—Roll cloud.
B—Continuous updraft.
C—Frequent lightning.

3435. Which weather phenomenon signals the beginning of the mature stage of a thunderstorm?

A—The appearance of an anvil top.
B—Precipitation beginning to fall.
C—Maximum growth rate of the clouds.

3436. What conditions are necessary for the formation of thunderstorms?

A—High humidity, lifting force, and unstable conditions.
B—High humidity, high temperature, and cumulus clouds.
C—Lifting force, moist air, and extensive cloud cover.

3437. During the life cycle of a thunderstorm, which stage is characterized predominately by downdrafts?

A—Cumulus.
B—Dissipating.
C—Mature.

3438. Thunderstorms reach their greatest intensity during the

A—mature stage.
B—downdraft stage.
C—cumulus stage.

3439. Thunderstorms which generally produce the most intense hazard to aircraft are

A—squall line thunderstorms.
B—steady-state thunderstorms.
C—warm front thunderstorms.

3440. A nonfrontal, narrow band of active thunderstorms that often develop ahead of a cold front is a known as a

A—prefrontal system.
B—squall line.
C—dry line.

3441. If there is thunderstorm activity in the vicinity of an airport at which you plan to land, which hazardous atmospheric phenomenon might be expected on the landing approach?

A—Precipitation static.
B—Wind-shear turbulence.
C—Steady rain.

3442. Upon encountering severe turbulence, which flight condition should the pilot attempt to maintain?

A—Constant altitude and airspeed.
B—Constant angle of attack.
C—Level flight attitude.

3443. What situation is most conducive to the formation of radiation fog?

A—Warm, moist air over low, flatland areas on clear, calm nights.
B—Moist, tropical air moving over cold, offshore water.
C—The movement of cold air over much warmer water.

3444. If the temperature/dewpoint spread is small and decreasing, and the temperature is 62°F, what type weather is most likely to develop?

A—Freezing precipitation.
B—Thunderstorms.
C—Fog or low clouds.

3445. In which situation is advection fog most likely to form?

A—A warm, moist air mass on the windward side of mountains.
B—An air mass moving inland from the coast in winter.
C—A light breeze blowing colder air out to sea.

3446. What types of fog depend upon wind in order to exist?

A—Radiation fog and ice fog.
B—Steam fog and ground fog.
C—Advection fog and upslope fog.

3447. Low-level turbulence can occur and icing can become hazardous in which type of fog?

A—Rain-induced fog.
B—Upslope fog.
C—Steam fog.

3448. The development of thermals depends upon

A—a counterclockwise circulation of air.
B—temperature inversions.
C—solar heating.

3449. Which is considered to be the most hazardous condition when soaring in the vicinity of thunderstorms?

A—Static electricity.
B—Lightning.
C—Wind shear and turbulence.

3450. Convective circulation patterns associated with sea breezes are caused by

A—warm, dense air moving inland from over the water.
B—water absorbing and radiating heat faster than the land.
C—cool, dense air moving inland from over the water.

3451. During which period is a sea breeze front most suitable for soaring flight?

A—Shortly after sunrise.
B—During the early forenoon.
C—During the afternoon.

3452. Which weather phenomenon is always associated with a thunderstorm?

A— Lightning.
B— Heavy rain.
C— Hail.

3453. Individual forecasts for specific routes of flight can be obtained from which weather source?

A— Transcribed Weather Broadcasts (TWEB's).
B— Terminal Forecasts.
C— Area Forecasts.

3454. Transcribed Weather Broadcasts (TWEB's) may be monitored by tuning the appropriate radio receiver to certain

A— airport advisory frequencies.
B— VOR and NDB frequencies.
C— ATIS frequencies.

3455. When telephoning a weather briefing facility for preflight weather information, pilots should state

A— the aircraft identification or the pilot's name.
B— true airspeed.
C— fuel on board.

3456. To get a complete weather briefing for the planned flight, the pilot should request

A— a general briefing.
B— an abbreviated briefing.
C— a standard briefing.

3457. Which type weather briefing should a pilot request, when departing within the hour, if no preliminary weather information has been received?

A— Outlook briefing.
B— Abbreviated briefing.
C— Standard briefing.

3458. Which type of weather briefing should a pilot request to supplement mass disseminated data?

A— An outlook briefing.
B— A supplemental briefing.
C— An abbreviated briefing.

3459. To update a previous weather briefing, a pilot should request

A— an abbreviated briefing.
B— a standard briefing.
C— an outlook briefing.

3460. A weather briefing that is provided when the information requested is 6 or more hours in advance of the proposed departure time is

A— an outlook briefing.
B— a forecast briefing.
C— a prognostic briefing.

3461. When requesting weather information for the following morning, a pilot should request

A— an outlook briefing.
B— a standard briefing.
C— an abbreviated briefing.

3462. (Refer to Figure 12.) Which of the reporting stations have VFR weather?

A— All.
B— INK, BOI, and JFK.
C— INK, BOI, and LAX.

3463. Ceiling is defined as the height above the Earth's surface of the

A— lowest reported obscuration and the highest layer of clouds reported as overcast.
B— lowest layer of clouds or obscuring phenomena reported as broken, overcast, and not classified as thin or partial.
C— lowest layer of clouds reported as scattered, broken, or thin.

3464. (Refer to Figure 12.) The wind direction and velocity at JFK is from

A— 180° true at 4 knots.
B— 180° magnetic at 4 knots.
C— 040° true at 18 knots.

3465. (Refer to Figure 12.) What are the wind conditions at Wink, Texas (INK)?

A— Calm.
B— 110° at 12 knots, peak gusts 18 knots.
C— 111° at 2 knots, peak gusts 18 knots.

3466. (Refer to Figure 12.) The remarks section for MDW has RF2 and RB12 listed. These two entries mean

A— rain and fog have reduced visibility to 2 miles and rain began at 1812Z.
B— rain and fog are obscuring two-tenths of the sky and rain began at 1812Z.
C— freezing rain has reduced visibility to 2 miles and the barometer has risen .12" Hg.

3467. (Refer to Figure 12.) What are the current conditions depicted for Chicago Midway Airport (MDW)?

A— Sky partially obscured, measured ceiling 700 overcast, visibility 1-1/2, heavy rain, fog.
B— Thin overcast, measured 700 ceiling overcast, visibility 1-1/2, heavy rain, fog.
C— Sky partially obscured, measured ceiling 700 overcast, visibility 11, occasionally 2, with rain and heavy fog.

3468. (Refer to Figure 13.) According to the weather briefing, the most ideal time to launch balloons is

A—as soon as possible after 1300Z.
B—at 1500Z when the ground will be partially shaded.
C—at 2000Z when there is enough wind for cross-country.

3469. (Refer to Figure 13.) According to the weather briefing, good balloon weather will begin to deteriorate

A—soon after 1300Z as the wind starts to increase.
B—about 1500Z when the lower scattered clouds begin to form.
C—at 2000Z due to sharp increase in wind conditions.

3470. (Refer to Figure 13.) What effect do the clouds mentioned in the weather briefing have on soaring conditions?

A—All thermals stop at the base of the clouds.
B—Thermals persist to the tops of the clouds at 25,000 feet.
C—The scattered clouds indicate thermals at least to the tops of the lower clouds.

3471. (Refer to Figure 13.) At what time will thermals begin to form?

A—Between 1300Z and 1500Z while the sky is clear.
B—By 1500Z (midmorning) when scattered clouds begin to form.
C—About 2000Z (early afternoon) when the wind begins to increase.

3472. (Refer to Figure 14.) The base and tops of the overcast layer reported by a pilot are

A—1,800 feet MSL and 5,500 feet MSL.
B—5,500 feet AGL and 7,200 feet MSL.
C—7,200 feet MSL and 8,900 feet MSL.

3473. (Refer to Figure 14.) The wind and temperature at 12,000 feet MSL as reported by a pilot are

A—009° at 121 MPH and 90°F.
B—090° at 21 knots and -9°F.
C—090° at 21 knots and -9°C.

3474. (Refer to Figure 14.) If the terrain elevation is 1,295 feet MSL, what is the height above ground level of the base of the ceiling?

A—505 feet AGL.
B—1,295 feet AGL.
C—6,586 feet AGL.

3475. (Refer to Figure 14.) The intensity of the turbulence reported at a specific altitude is

A—moderate at 5,500 feet and at 7,200 feet.
B—moderate from 5,500 feet to 7,200 feet.
C—light to moderate from 7,200 feet to 8,900 feet.

3476. (Refer to Figure 14.) The intensity and type of icing reported by a pilot is

A—light to moderate.
B—light to moderate clear.
C—moderate rime.

3477. Which weather reports and forecasts are most important for local area balloon operations?

A—Winds Aloft Forecasts and Radar Summary Charts.
B—Winds Aloft Forecasts and Surface Analysis Charts.
C—Winds Aloft Forecasts and Surface Aviation Weather Reports.

3478. From which primary source should information be obtained regarding expected weather at the estimated time of arrival if your destination has no Terminal Forecast?

A—Low-Level Prognostic Chart.
B—Weather Depiction Chart.
C—Area Forecast.

3479. (Refer to Figure 15.) What ceiling is forecast for GAG between 1600Z and 0100Z?

A—6,000 scattered, chance 10,000 broken.
B—10,000 scattered, chance 2,500 scattered.
C—10,000 broken, chance 5,000 broken.

3480. (Refer to Figure 15.) What wind conditions are expected at HBR at 1600Z?

A—Calm.
B—150° at 15 knots.
C—300° at 10 knots.

3481. (Refer to Figure 15.) What is the outlook for weather conditions at MLC?

A—Ceilings 2,000 to 3,000 feet with southerly winds.
B—Ceiling 700 feet, sky obscured, visibility 1/2 mile in thundershowers.
C—Ceilings 1,000 to 3,000 feet with thunderstorms and rain showers.

3482. (Refer to Figure 15.) The wind condition in the Terminal Forecast 6-hour categorical outlook for PNC is for

A—velocities of 25 knots or stronger.
B—a wind shift from south to northwest.
C—the wind to change from a gusty condition to calm.

3483. (Refer to Figure 15.) When is the wind forecast to shift at TUL?

A—1500Z.
B—By 2300Z.
C—Between 2300Z and 0900Z the next day.

3484. (Refer to Figure 15.) According to the Terminal Forecast for OKC, the cold front should pass through

A—between 1800Z and 2100Z.
B—by 2100Z.
C—after 2100Z.

3485. (Refer to Figure 15.) What type conditions are forecast for OKC from 1800Z to 2100Z?

A—MVFR and VFR.
B—MVFR, VFR, and IFR.
C—VFR and IFR.

3486. (Refer to Figure 15.) What is the outlook for the weather condition at TUL?

A—VFR with wind 25 knots or more with the direction not forecast.
B—Chance of ceilings 3,000 feet broken, visibility 5 miles in thunderstorms and rain showers.
C—VFR with winds 320° at 15 knots with gusts to 25 knots.

3487. To best determine general forecast weather conditions over several states, the pilot should refer to

A—Area Forecasts.
B—Weather Depiction Charts.
C—Satellite Maps.

3488. (Refer to Figure 16.) What is the forecast ceiling and visibility for Tennessee from 2300Z through 0500Z?

A—500 feet to less than 1,000 feet, and 1 mile to less than 3 miles.
B—1,000 to 3,000 feet, and 3 to 5 miles.
C—3,000 feet or greater, and 5 miles or greater.

3489. To determine the freezing level and areas of probable icing aloft, the pilot should refer to the

A—Radar Summary Chart.
B—Weather Depiction Chart.
C—Area Forecast.

3490. The section of the Area Forecast entitled "SIG CLDS AND WX" contains a summary of

A—cloudiness and weather significant to flight operations broken down by states or other geographical areas.
B—forecast sky cover, cloud tops, visibility, and obstructions to vision along specific routes.
C—weather advisories still in effect at the time of issue.

3491. (Refer to Figure 16.) What hazards are forecast in the Area Forecast for TN, AL, and the coastal waters?

A—Thunderstorms with severe or greater turbulence, severe icing, and low-level wind shear.
B—Moderate rime icing above the freezing level to 10,000 feet.
C—Moderate turbulence from 25,000 to 38,000 feet due to the jetstream.

3492. (Refer to Figure 16.) What type obstructions to vision, if any, are forecast for the entire area from 2300Z until 0500Z the next day?

A—None of any significance, VFR is forecast.
B—Visibility 3 to 5 miles in fog.
C—Visibility below 3 miles in fog over south-central Texas.

3493. (Refer to Figure 16.) What sky condition and type obstructions to vision are forecast for all the area except TN from 1040Z until 2300Z?

A—Ceilings 3,000 to 5,000 feet broken, visibility 3 to 5 miles in fog.
B—8,000 feet scattered to clear except visibility below 3 miles in fog until 1500Z over south-central Texas.
C—Generally ceilings 3,000 to 8,000 feet to clear with visibility sometimes below 3 miles in fog.

3494. To obtain a continuous transcribed weather briefing, including winds aloft and route forecasts for a cross-country flight, a pilot should monitor a

A—Transcribed Weather Broadcast (TWEB) on an ADF radio receiver.
B—VHF radio receiver tuned to an Automatic Terminal Information Service (ATIS) frequency.
C—regularly scheduled weather broadcast on a VOR frequency.

3495. What is indicated when a current CONVECTIVE SIGMET forecasts thunderstorms?

A—Moderate thunderstorms covering 30 percent of the area.
B—Moderate or severe turbulence.
C—Thunderstorms obscured by massive cloud layers.

3496. What information is contained in a CONVECTIVE SIGMET?

A—Tornadoes, embedded thunderstorms, and hail 3/4 inch or greater in diameter.
B—Severe icing, severe turbulence, or widespread dust storms lowering visibility to less than 3 miles.
C—Surface winds greater than 40 knots or thunderstorms equal to or greater than video integrator processor (VIP) level 4.

3497. SIGMET's are issued as a warning of weather conditions hazardous to which aircraft?

A—Small aircraft only.
B—Large aircraft only.
C—All aircraft.

3498. Which in-flight advisory would contain information on severe icing?

A—Convective SIGMET.
B—SIGMET.
C—AIRMET.

3499. AIRMET's are issued as a warning of weather conditions particularly hazardous to which aircraft?

A—Small single-engine aircraft.
B—Large multiengine aircraft.
C—All aircraft.

3500. (Refer to Figure 17.) What wind is forecast for STL at 6,000 feet?

A—210° magnetic at 13 knots.
B—230° true at 25 knots.
C—232° true at 5 knots.

3501. (Refer to Figure 17.) What wind is forecast for STL at 18,000 feet?

A—230° true at 56 knots.
B—235° true at 06 knots.
C—235° magnetic at 06, peak gusts to 16 knots.

3502. (Refer to Figure 17.) Determine the wind and temperature aloft forecast for DEN at 30,000 feet.

A—023° magnetic at 53 knots, temperature 47°C.
B—230° true at 53 knots, temperature -47°C.
C—235° true at 34 knots, temperature -7°C.

3503. (Refer to Figure 17.) Determine the wind and temperature aloft forecast for 3,000 feet at MKC.

A—050° true at 7 knots, temperature missing.
B—360° magnetic at 5 knots, temperature -7°C.
C—360° true at 50 knots, temperature +7°C.

3504. (Refer to Figure 17.) What wind is forecast for STL at 34,000 feet?

A—007° magnetic at 30 knots.
B—073° true at 6 knots.
C—230° true at 106 knots.

3505. What values are used for Winds Aloft Forecasts?

A—Magnetic direction and knots.
B—Magnetic direction and miles per hour.
C—True direction and knots.

3506. When the term "light and variable" is used in reference to a Winds Aloft Forecast, the coded group and windspeed is

A—0000 and less than 7 knots.
B—9900 and less than 5 knots.
C—9999 and less than 10 knots.

3507. (Refer to Figure 18.) What is the status of the front that extends from New Mexico to Indiana?

A—Stationary.
B—Occluded.
C—Retreating.

3508. (Refer to Figure 18.) The IFR weather in eastern Texas is due to

A—intermittent rain.
B—fog.
C—dust devils.

3509. (Refer to Figure 18.) Of what value is the Weather Depiction Chart to the pilot?

A—For determining general weather conditions on which to base flight planning.
B—For a forecast of cloud coverage, visibilities, and frontal activity.
C—For determining frontal trends and air mass characteristics.

3510. (Refer to Figure 18.) The marginal weather in southeast New Mexico is due to

A—reported thunderstorms.
B—600-foot overcast ceilings.
C—low visibility.

3511. (Refer to Figure 18.) What weather phenomenon is causing IFR conditions along the coast of Oregon and California?

A—Squall line activity.
B—Low ceilings.
C—Heavy rain showers.

3512. (Refer to Figure 18.) According to the Weather Depiction Chart, the weather for a flight from central Arkansas to southeast Alabama is

A—broken clouds at 2,500 feet.
B—visibility from 3 to 5 miles.
C—broken to scattered clouds at 25,000 feet.

3513. Radar weather reports are of special interest to pilots because they indicate

A—large areas of low ceilings and fog.
B—location of precipitation along with type, intensity, and trend.
C—location of broken to overcast clouds.

3514. What information is provided by the Radar Summary Chart that is not shown on other weather charts?

A—Lines and cells of hazardous thunderstorms.
B—Ceilings and precipitation between reporting stations.
C—Types of clouds between reporting stations.

3515. (Refer to Figure 19, area A.) What is the direction and speed of movement of the radar return?

A—020° at 20 knots.
B—East at 15 knots.
C—Northeast at 22 knots.

3516. (Refer to Figure 19, area C.) What type of weather is occurring in the radar return?

A—Continuous rain.
B—Heavy rain showers.
C—Rain showers increasing in intensity.

3517. (Refer to Figure 19, area D.) What is the direction and speed of movement of the radar return?

A—Southeast at 30 knots.
B—Northeast at 20 knots.
C—West at 30 knots.

3518. (Refer to Figure 19, area D.) The top of the precipitation is

A—2,000 feet.
B—20,000 feet.
C—30,000 feet.

3519. (Refer to Figure 19, area B.) What does the dashed line enclose?

A—Areas of heavy rain.
B—Severe weather watch area.
C—Areas of hail 1/4 inch in diameter.

3520. (Refer to Figure 20.) How are Significant Weather Prognostic Charts best used by a pilot?

A—For overall planning at all altitudes.
B—For determining areas to avoid (freezing levels and turbulence).
C—For analyzing current frontal activity and cloud coverage.

3521. (Refer to Figure 20.) Interpret the weather symbol depicted in southern California on the 12-hour Significant Weather Prognostic Chart.

A—Moderate turbulence, surface to 18,000 feet.
B—Thunderstorm tops at 18,000 feet.
C—Base of clear air turbulence, 18,000 feet.

3522. (Refer to Figure 20.) What weather is forecast for the Gulf Coast area just ahead of the cold front during the first 12 hours?

A—Ceiling 1,000 to 3,000 feet and/or visibility 3 to 5 miles with intermittent thundershowers and rain showers.
B—IFR with moderate or greater turbulence over the coastal areas.
C—Rain and thunderstorms moving northeastward ahead of the front.

3523. (Refer to Figure 20.) The low pressure associated with the cold front in the western states is forecast to move

A—east at 30 knots.
B—northeast at 12 knots.
C—southeast at 30 knots.

3524. (Refer to Figure 20.) At what altitude is the freezing level over northeastern Oklahoma on the 24-hour Significant Weather Prognostic Chart?

A—4,000 feet.
B—8,000 feet.
C—10,000 feet.

3525. In addition to the standard briefing, what additional information should be asked of the weather briefer in order to evaluate soaring conditions?

A—The upper soundings to determine the thermal index at all soaring levels.
B—Dry adiabatic rate of cooling to determine the height of cloud bases.
C—Moist adiabatic rate of cooling to determine the height of cloud tops.

3526. When telephoning a weather briefing facility for preflight weather information, pilots should

A—identify themselves as pilots.
B—tell the number of hours they have flown within the preceding 90 days.
C—state the number of occupants on board and the color of the aircraft.

3527. When telephoning a weather briefing facility for preflight weather information, pilots should state

A—the full name and address of the pilot in command.
B—the intended route, destination, and type of aircraft.
C—the radio frequencies to be used.

3528. When telephoning a weather briefing facility for preflight weather information, pilots should state

A—the full name and address of the formation commander.
B—that they possess a current pilot certificate.
C—whether they intend to fly VFR only.

3529. (Refer to Figure 21.) En route to First Flight Airport (area 5), your flight passes over Hampton Roads Airport (area 2) at 1456 and then over Chesapeake Municipal at 1501. At what time should your flight arrive at First Flight?

A—1516.
B—1521.
C—1526.

3530. (Refer to Figure 21, area 3.) Determine the approximate latitude and longitude of Currituck County Airport.

A—36°24'N – 76°01'W.
B—36°48'N – 76°01'W.
C—47°24'N – 75°58'W.

3531. (Refer to Figure 21.) Determine the magnetic course from First Flight Airport (area 5) to Hampton Roads Airport (area 2).

A—312°.
B—321°.
C—330°.

3532. (Refer to Figure 21.) What is your approximate position on low altitude airway Victor 1, southwest of Norfolk (area 1), if the VOR receiver indicates you are on the 340° radial of Elizabeth City VOR (area 3)?

A—15 nautical miles from Norfolk VORTAC.
B—18 nautical miles from Norfolk VORTAC.
C—23 nautical miles from Norfolk VORTAC.

3533. (Refer to Figure 21, area 3; and Figure 29.) The VOR is tuned to Elizabeth City VOR, and the aircraft is positioned over Shawboro. Which VOR indication is correct?

A—5.
B—6.
C—8.

3534. (Refer to Figure 22.) What is the estimated time en route from Mercer County Regional Airport (area 3) to Minot International (area 1)? The wind is from 330° at 25 knots and the true airspeed is 100 knots. Add 3-1/2 minutes for departure and climb-out.

A—44 minutes.
B—48 minutes.
C—52 minutes.

3535. (Refer to Figure 22, area 2.) Which airport is located at approximately 47°39'30"N latitude and 100°53'00"W longitude?

A—Linrud.
B—Crooked Lake.
C—Johnson.

3536. (Refer to Figure 22, area 3.) Which airport is located at approximately 47°21'N latitude and 101°01'W longitude?

A—Underwood.
B—Evenson.
C—Washburn.

3537. (Refer to Figure 22.) An airship crosses over Minot VORTAC (area 1) at 1056 and over the creek 8 nautical miles south-southeast on Victor 15 at 1108. What should be the approximate position on Victor 15 at 1211?

A—Over Lake Nettie National Wildlife Refuge.
B—Crossing the road east of Underwood.
C—Over the powerlines east of Washburn Airport.

3538. (Refer to Figure 22.) Determine the magnetic heading for a flight from Mercer County Regional Airport (area 3) to Minot International (area 1). The wind is from 330° at 25 knots, the true airspeed is 100 knots, and the magnetic variation is 11° east.

A—002°.
B—012°.
C—351°.

3539. (Refer to Figure 22.) What course should be selected on the omnibearing selector (OBS) to make a direct flight from Mercer County Regional Airport (area 3) to the Minot VORTAC (area 1) with a TO indication?

A—001°.
B—012°.
C—181°.

3540. (Refer to Figure 23.) What is the estimated time en route from Dave Wall Field (area 1) to St. Maries Airport (area 4)? The wind is from 215° at 25 knots and the true airspeed is 125 knots.

A—27 minutes.
B—30 minutes.
C—34 minutes.

3541. (Refer to Figure 23.) Determine the estimated time en route for a flight from Priest River Airport (area 1) to Shoshone County Airport (area 3). The wind is from 030 at 12 knots and the true airspeed is 95 knots. Add 2 minutes for climb-out.

A—23 minutes.
B—27 minutes.
C—31 minutes.

3542. (Refer to Figure 23.) What is the estimated time en route for a flight from St. Maries Airport (area 4) to Priest River Airport (area 1)? The wind is from 300° at 14 knots and the true airspeed is 90 knots. Add 3 minutes for climb-out.

A—38 minutes.
B—43 minutes.
C—48 minutes.

3543. (Refer to Figure 23, area 3.) Determine the approximate latitude and longitude of Shoshone County Airport.

A—47°02'N – 116°11'W.
B—47°32'N – 116°11'W.
C—47°32'N – 116°41'W.

3544. (Refer to Figure 23, area 2.) If a balloon is launched at Ranch Aero (Pvt) Airport with a reported wind from 220° at 5 knots, what should be its approximate position after 2 hours of flight?

A—Near Hackney (Pvt) Airport.
B—Crossing the railroad southwest of Granite Airport.
C—3-1/2 miles southwest of Rathdrum.

3545. (Refer to Figure 23.) Determine the magnetic heading for a flight from Dave Wall Field (area 1) to St. Maries Airport (area 4). The wind is from 215° at 25 knots and the true airspeed is 125 knots.

A— 161°.
B— 167°.
C— 181°.

3546. (Refer to Figure 23.) What is the magnetic heading for a flight from Priest River Airport (area 1) to Shoshone County Airport (area 3)? The wind is from 030° at 12 knots and the true airspeed is 95 knots.

A— 116°.
B— 123°.
C— 130°.

3547. (Refer to Figure 23.) Determine the magnetic heading for a flight from St. Maries Airport (area 4) to Priest River Airport (area 1). The wind is from 300° at 14 knots and the true airspeed is 90 knots.

A— 319°.
B— 325°.
C— 331°.

3548. (Refer to Figure 24.) What is the estimated time en route for a flight from Allendale County Airport (area 1) to Claxton-Evans County Airport (area 2)? The wind is from 090° at 16 knots and the true airspeed is 90 knots. Add 2 minutes for climb-out.

A— 33 minutes.
B— 37 minutes.
C— 41 minutes.

3549. (Refer to Figure 24.) What is the estimated time en route for a flight from Claxton-Evans County Airport (area 2) to Hampton Varnville Airport (area 1)? The wind is from 290° at 18 knots and the true airspeed is 85 knots. Add 2 minutes for climb-out.

A— 35 minutes.
B— 39 minutes.
C— 44 minutes.

3550. (Refer to Figure 24.) Determine the compass heading for a flight from Allendale County Airport (area 1) to Claxton-Evans County Airport (area 2). The wind is from 090° at 16 knots and the true airspeed is 90 knots.

A— 200°.
B— 205°.
C— 211°.

3551. (Refer to Figure 24.) Determine the compass heading for a flight from Claxton-Evans County Airport (area 2) to Hampton Varnville Airport (area 1). The wind is from 290° at 18 knots and the true airspeed is 85 knots.

A— 034°.
B— 038°.
C— 042°.

3552. (Refer to Figure 24.) What is the approximate position of the aircraft if the VOR receivers indicate the 310° radial of Savannah VORTAC (area 3) and the 190° radial of Allendale VOR (area 1)?

A— Town of Guyton.
B— Town of Springfield.
C— 3 miles east of Marlow.

3553. (Refer to Figure 24.) On what radial should the VOR receiver (OBS) be set to navigate direct from Hampton Varnville Airport (area 1) to Savannah VORTAC (area 3)?

A— 005°.
B— 185°.
C— 200°.

3554. (Refer to Figure 24.) While en route on Victor 185, a flight crosses the 248° radial of Allendale VOR at 0951 and then crosses the 216° radial of Allendale VOR at 1000. What is the estimated time of arrival at Savannah VORTAC?

A— 1023.
B— 1028.
C— 1036.

3555. (Refer to Figure 25.) Estimate the time en route from Majors Airport (area 1) to Winnsboro Airport (area 2). The wind is from 340° at 12 knots and the true airspeed is 36 knots.

A— 55 minutes.
B— 59 minutes.
C— 63 minutes.

3556. (Refer to Figure 25). Determine the magnetic course from Airpark East Airport (area 1) to Winnsboro Airport (area 2). Magnetic variation is 6°30'E.

A— 075°.
B— 082°.
C— 091°.

3557. (Refer to Figure 25.) An airship passes over the Quitman VORTAC at 0940 and then over the intersection of the powerline and Victor 114 at 0948. Approximately what time should the flight arrive over the Blue Ridge VORTAC?

A— 1104.
B— 1109.
C— 1117.

3558. (Refer to Figure 25.) Determine the magnetic heading for a flight from Majors Airport (area 1) to Winnsboro Airport (area 2). The wind is from 340° at 12 knots, the true airspeed is 36 knots, and the magnetic variation is 6°30'E.

A— 078°.
B— 091°.
C— 101°.

3559. (Refer to Figure 25.) What is the approximate position of the aircraft if the VOR receivers indicate the 250° radial of Sulphur Springs VORTAC (area 2) and the 130° radial of Blue Ridge VORTAC (area 1)?

A—Caddo Mills Airport.
B—Meadowview Airport.
C—3 miles southeast of Caddo Mills Airport.

3560. (Refer to Figure 25.) On what course should the VOR receiver (OBS) be set in order to navigate direct from Majors Airport (area 1) to Quitman VORTAC (area 2)?

A—101°.
B—108°.
C—281°.

3561. (Refer to Figure 25, area 1; and Figure 29.) The VOR is tuned to Blue Ridge VORTAC, and the aircraft is positioned over the town of Lone Oak, southeast of Majors Airport. Which VOR indication is correct?

A—1.
B—4.
C—7.

3562. (Refer to Figure 26.) What is the estimated time en route for a flight from Denton Muni (area 1) to Addison (area 2)? The wind is from 200° at 20 knots, the true airspeed is 110 knots, and the magnetic variation is 7° east.

A—13 minutes.
B—16 minutes.
C—19 minutes.

3563. (Refer to Figure 26.) Estimate the time en route from Addison (area 2) to Redbird (area 3). The wind is from 300° at 15 knots, the true airspeed is 120 knots, and the magnetic variation is 7° east.

A—8 minutes.
B—11 minutes.
C—14 minutes.

3564. (Refer to Figure 26.) Determine the magnetic heading for a flight from Redbird (area 3) to Fort Worth Meacham (area 4). The wind is from 030° at 10 knots, the true airspeed is 35 knots, and the magnetic variation is 7° east.

A—266°.
B—298°.
C—312°.

3565. (Refer to Figure 26.) Determine the magnetic heading for a flight from Fort Worth Meacham (area 4) to Denton Muni (area 1). The wind is from 330° at 25 knots, the true airspeed is 110 knots, and the magnetic variation is 7° east.

A—003°.
B—017°.
C—023°.

3566. (Refer to Figure 26, area 5.) The VOR is tuned to the Dallas/Fort Worth VORTAC. The omnibearing selector (OBS) is set on 253°, with a TO indication, and a right course deviation indicator (CDI) deflection. What is the aircraft's position from the VORTAC?

A—East-northeast.
B—North-northeast.
C—West-southwest.

3567. (Refer to Figure 27, area 2.) What is the approximate latitude and longitude of Cooperstown Airport?

A—47°25'N – 98°06'W.
B—47°25'N – 99°54'W.
C—47°55'N – 98°06'W.

3568. (Refer to Figure 27.) Determine the magnetic course from Breckheimer (Pvt) Airport (area 1) to Jamestown Airport (area 4).

A—013°.
B—021°.
C—181°.

3569. (Refer to Figure 27, area 5.) A balloon drifts over the town of Eckelson on a magnetic course of 282° at 10 MPH. If wind conditions remain constant, where will the balloon be after 2 hours 30 minutes?

A—3 miles south-southwest of Buchanan.
B—Over Buchanan.
C—Over the tower southwest of Fried.

3570. (Refer to Figure 27, areas 4 and 3; and Figure 29.) The VOR is tuned to Jamestown VOR, and the aircraft is positioned over the town of Wimbledon. Which VOR indication is correct?

A—1.
B—4.
C—6.

3571. (Refer to Figure 28.) An aircraft departs an airport in the eastern daylight time zone at 0945 EDT for a 2-hour flight to an airport located in the central daylight time zone. The landing should be at what coordinated universal time?

A—1345Z.
B—1445Z.
C—1545Z.

3572. (Refer to Figure 28.) An aircraft departs an airport in the central standard time zone at 0930 CST for a 2-hour flight to an airport located in the mountain standard time zone. The landing should be at what time?
A—0930 MST.
B—1030 MST.
C—1130 MST.

3573. (Refer to Figure 28.) An aircraft departs an airport in the central standard time zone at 0845 CST for a 2-hour flight to an airport located in the mountain standard time zone. The landing should be at what coordinated universal time?
A—1345Z.
B—1445Z.
C—1645Z.

3574. (Refer to Figure 28.) An aircraft departs an airport in the mountain standard time zone at 1615 MST for a 2-hour 15-minute flight to an airport located in the Pacific standard time zone. The estimated time of arrival at the destination airport should be
A—1630 PST.
B—1730 PST.
C—1830 PST.

3575. (Refer to Figure 28.) An aircraft departs an airport in the Pacific standard time zone at 1030 PST for a 4-hour flight to an airport located in the central standard time zone. The landing should be at what coordinated universal time?
A—2030Z.
B—2130Z.
C—2230Z.

3576. (Refer to Figure 28.) An aircraft departs an airport in the mountain standard time zone at 1515 MST for a 2-hour 30-minute flight to an airport located in the Pacific standard time zone. What is the estimated time of arrival at the destination airport?
A—1645 PST.
B—1745 PST.
C—1845 PST.

3577. (Refer to Figure 29, illustration 1.) The VOR receiver has the indications shown. What is the aircraft's position relative to the station?
A—North.
B—East.
C—South.

3578. (Refer to Figure 29, illustration 3.) The VOR receiver has the indications shown. What is the aircraft's position relative to the station?
A—East.
B—Southeast.
C—West.

3579. (Refer to Figure 29, illustration 8.) The VOR receiver has the indications shown. What radial is the aircraft crossing?
A—030°.
B—210°.
C—300°.

3580. (Refer to Figure 30, illustration 1.) Determine the magnetic bearing TO the station.
A—030°.
B—180°.
C—210°.

3581. (Refer to Figure 30, illustration 2.) What magnetic bearing should the pilot use to fly TO the station?
A—010°.
B—145°.
C—190°.

3582. (Refer to Figure 30, illustration 2.) Determine the approximate heading to intercept the 180° bearing TO the station.
A—040°.
B—160°.
C—220°.

3583. (Refer to Figure 30, illustration 3.) What is the magnetic bearing FROM the station?
A—025°.
B—115°.
C—295°.

3584. (Refer to Figure 30.) Which ADF indication represents the aircraft tracking TO the station with a right crosswind?
A—1.
B—2.
C—4.

3585. (Refer to Figure 30, illustration 1.) What outbound bearing is the aircraft crossing?
A—030°.
B—150°.
C—180°.

3586. (Refer to Figure 30, illustration 1.) What is the relative bearing TO the station?
A—030°.
B—210°.
C—240°.

3587. (Refer to Figure 30, illustration 2.) What is the relative bearing TO the station?
A—190°.
B—235°.
C—315°.

3588. (Refer to Figure 30, illustration 4.) What is the relative bearing TO the station?

A—020°.
B—060°.
C—340°.

3589. (Refer to Figure 31, illustration 1.) The relative bearing TO the station is

A—045°.
B—180°.
C—315°.

3590. (Refer to Figure 31, illustration 2.) The relative bearing TO the station is

A—090°.
B—180°.
C—270°.

3591. (Refer to Figure 31, illustration 3.) The relative bearing TO the station is

A—090°.
B—180°.
C—270°.

3592. (Refer to Figure 31, illustration 4.) On a magnetic heading of 320°, the magnetic bearing TO the station is

A—005°.
B—185°.
C—225°.

3593. (Refer to Figure 31, illustration 5.) On a magnetic heading of 035°, the magnetic bearing TO the station is

A—035°.
B—180°.
C—215°.

3594. (Refer to Figure 31, illustration 6.) On a magnetic heading of 120°, the magnetic bearing TO the station is

A—045°.
B—165°.
C—270°.

3595. (Refer to Figure 31, illustration 6.) If the magnetic bearing TO the station is 240°, the magnetic heading is

A—045°.
B—105°.
C—195°.

3596. (Refer to Figure 31, illustration 7.) If the magnetic bearing TO the station is 030°, the magnetic heading is

A—060°.
B—120°.
C—270°.

3597. (Refer to Figure 31, illustration 8.) If the magnetic bearing TO the station is 135°, the magnetic heading is

A—135°.
B—270°.
C—360°.

3598. When the course deviation indicator (CDI) needle is centered during an omnireceiver check using a VOR test signal (VOT), the omnibearing selector (OBS) and the TO/FROM indicator should read

A—180° FROM, only if the pilot is due north of the VOT.
B—0° TO or 180° FROM, regardless of the pilot's position from the VOT.
C—0° FROM or 180° TO, regardless of the pilot's position from the VOT.

3599. (Refer to Figure 26, area 4.) The floor of Class B airspace overlying Hicks Airport (T67) north-northwest of Fort Worth Meacham Field is

A—at the surface.
B—3,200 feet MSL.
C—4,000 feet MSL.

3600. (Refer to Figure 26, area 2.) The floor of Class B airspace at Addison Airport is

A—at the surface.
B—3,000 feet MSL.
C—3,100 feet MSL.

3601. (Refer to Figure 21.) What hazards to aircraft may exist in warning areas such as Warning W-50B?

A—Unusual, often invisible, hazards such as aerial gunnery or guided missiles over international waters.
B—High volume of pilot training or unusual type of aerial activity.
C—Heavy military aircraft traffic in the approach and departure area of the North Atlantic Control Area.

3602. (Refer to Figure 27.) What hazards to aircraft may exist in areas such as Devils Lake East MOA?

A—Unusual, often invisible, hazards to aircraft such as artillery firing.
B—High density military training activities.
C—Parachute jump operations.

3603. (Refer to Figure 22.) What type military flight operations should a pilot expect along IR 644?

A—IFR training flights above 1,500 feet AGL at speeds in excess of 250 knots.
B—VFR training flights above 1,500 feet AGL at speeds less than 250 knots.
C—Instrument training flights below 1,500 feet AGL at speeds in excess of 150 knots.

3604. (Refer to Figure 21, area 3.) What is the recommended communications procedure for a landing at Currituck County Airport?

A—Transmit intentions on 122.9 MHz when 10 miles out and give position reports in the traffic pattern.
B—Contact Elizabeth City FSS for airport advisory service.
C—Contact New Bern FSS for area traffic information.

3605. (Refer to Figure 22, area 2.) The CTAF/MULTICOM frequency for Garrison Municipal is

A—122.8 MHz.
B—122.9 MHz.
C—123.0 MHz.

3606. (Refer to Figure 23, area 2; and Figure 32.) If Coeur D'Alene Tower is not in operation, which frequency should be used as a Common Traffic Advisory Frequency (CTAF) to self-announce position and intentions?

A—119.1 MHz.
B—122.1/108.8 MHz.
C—122.8 MHz.

3607. (Refer to Figure 23, area 2; and Figure 32.) If Coeur D'Alene Tower is not in operation, which frequency should be used as a Common Traffic Advisory Frequency (CTAF) to monitor airport traffic?

A—119.1 MHz.
B—122.1/108.8 MHz.
C—122.8 MHz.

3608. (Refer to Figure 23, area 2; and figure 32.) What is the correct UNICOM frequency to be used at Coeur D'Alene to request fuel?

A—119.1 MHz.
B—122.1/108.8 MHz.
C—122.8 MHz.

3609. (Refer to Figure 26, area 3.) If Redbird Tower is not in operation, which frequency should be used as a Common Traffic Advisory Frequency (CTAF) to monitor airport traffic?

A—120.3 MHz.
B—122.95 MHz.
C—126.35 MHz.

3610. (Refer to Figure 27, area 2.) What is the recommended communication procedure when inbound to land at Cooperstown Airport?

A—Broadcast intentions when 10 miles out on the CTAF/MULTICOM frequency, 122.9 MHz.
B—Contact UNICOM when 10 miles out on 122.8 MHz.
C—Circle the airport in a left turn prior to entering traffic.

3611. (Refer to Figure 27, area 4.) The CTAF/UNICOM frequency at Jamestown Airport is

A—122.0 MHz.
B—123.0 MHz.
C—123.6 MHz.

3612. (Refer to Figure 27, area 6.) What is the CTAF/UNICOM frequency at Barnes County Airport?

A—122.0 MHz.
B—122.8 MHz.
C—123.6 MHz.

3613. When flying HAWK N666CB, the proper phraseology for initial contact with McAlester AFSS is

A—"MC ALESTER RADIO, HAWK SIX SIX SIX CHARLIE BRAVO, RECEIVING ARDMORE VORTAC, OVER."
B—"MC ALESTER STATION, HAWK SIX SIX SIX CEE BEE, RECEIVING ARDMORE VORTAC, OVER."
C—"MC ALESTER FLIGHT SERVICE STATION, HAWK NOVEMBER SIX CHARLIE BRAVO, RECEIVING ARDMORE VORTAC, OVER."

3614. The correct method of stating 4,500 feet MSL to ATC is

A—"FOUR THOUSAND FIVE HUNDRED."
B—"FOUR POINT FIVE."
C—"FORTY-FIVE HUNDRED FEET MSL."

3615. The correct method of stating 10,500 feet MSL to ATC is

A—"TEN THOUSAND, FIVE HUNDRED FEET."
B—"TEN POINT FIVE."
C—"ONE ZERO THOUSAND, FIVE HUNDRED."

3616. How should contact be established with an En Route Flight Advisory Service (EFAS) station, and what service would be expected?

A—Call EFAS on 122.2 for routine weather, current reports on hazardous weather, and altimeter settings.
B—Call flight assistance on 122.5 for advisory service pertaining to severe weather.
C—Call Flight Watch on 122.0 for information regarding actual weather and thunderstorm activity along proposed route.

3617. What service should a pilot normally expect from an En Route Flight Advisory Service (EFAS) station?

A—Actual weather information and thunderstorm activity along the route.
B—Preferential routing and radar vectoring to circumnavigate severe weather.
C—Severe weather information, changes to flight plans, and receipt of routine position reports.

3618. (Refer to Figure 27, area 3.) When flying over Arrowwood National Wildlife Refuge, a pilot should fly no lower than

A—2,000 feet AGL.
B—2,500 feet AGL.
C—3,000 feet AGL.

3619. (Refer to Figure 23, area 2 and legend 1.) For information about the parachute jumping and glider operations at Silverwood Airport, refer to

A—notes on the border of the chart.
B—the Airport/Facility Directory.
C—the Notices to Airmen (NOTAM) publication.

3620. (Refer to Figure 23, area 1.) The visibility and cloud clearance requirements to operate VFR during daylight hours over Dave Wall Field at less than 1,200 feet AGL are

A—1 mile and clear of clouds.
B—1 mile and 1,000 feet above, 500 feet below, and 2,000 feet horizontally from each cloud.
C—3 miles and 1,000 feet above, 500 feet below, and 2,000 feet horizontally from each cloud.

3621. (Refer to Figure 27, area 2.) The visibility and cloud clearance requirements to operate VFR during daylight hours over the town of Cooperstown between 1,200 feet AGL and 10,000 feet MSL are

A—1 mile and clear of clouds.
B—1 mile and 1,000 feet above, 500 feet below, and 2,000 feet horizontally from clouds.
C—3 miles and 1,000 feet above, 500 feet below, and 2,000 feet horizontally from clouds.

3622. (Refer to Figure 27, area 1.) Identify the airspace over Lowe Airport that exists from the surface to 14,500 feet MSL.

A—Class G airspace – surface to 14,500 feet MSL.
B—Class G airspace – surface to 3,500 feet MSL; Class E airspace – 3,500 feet MSL to 14,500 feet MSL.
C—Class G airspace – surface to 3,500 feet MSL; Class E airspace – 3,500 feet MSL to 10,000 feet MSL; Class G airspace – 10,000 feet MSL to 14,500 feet MSL.

3623. (Refer to Figure 27, area 6.) The airspace overlying and within 5 miles of Barnes County Airport is

A—Class D airspace from the surface to the floor of the overlying Class E airspace.
B—Class E airspace from the surface to 1,200 feet MSL.
C—Class G airspace from the surface to 700 feet AGL.

3624. (Refer to Figure 26, area 7.) The airspace overlying McKinney Muni is uncontrolled from the surface to

A—700 feet AGL.
B—1,700 feet MSL.
C—4,000 feet AGL.

3625. (Refer to Figure 26, area 4.) The airspace directly overlying Fort Worth Meacham is

A—Class B airspace to 10,000 feet MSL.
B—Class C airspace to 5,000 feet MSL.
C—Class D airspace to 3,200 feet MSL.

3626. (Refer to Figure 24, area 3.) What is the floor of the Savannah Class C airspace at the outer circle?

A—1,200 feet AGL.
B—1,300 feet MSL.
C—1,700 feet MSL.

3627. (Refer to Figure 21, area 1.) What minimum radio equipment is required to land and take off at Norfolk International?

A—Mode C transponder and omnireceiver.
B—Mode C transponder and two-way radio.
C—Mode C transponder, omnireceiver, and DME.

3628. (Refer to Figure 26.) At which airports is fixed-wing Special VFR not authorized?

A—Fort Worth Meacham and Fort Worth Spinks.
B—Dallas-Fort Worth International and Dallas Love Field.
C—Addison and Redbird.

3629. (Refer to Figure 23, area 3.) The vertical limits of that portion of Class E airspace designated as a Federal Airway over Magee Airport are

A—1,200 feet AGL to 10,000 feet MSL.
B—7,500 feet MSL to 12,500 feet MSL.
C—7,500 feet MSL to 17,999 feet MSL.

3630. (Refer to Figure 22.) On what frequency can a pilot receive Hazardous Inflight Weather Advisory Service (HIWAS) in the vicinity of area 1?

A—117.1 MHz.
B—118.0 MHz.
C—122.0 MHz.

3631. (Refer to Figure 21, area 5.) The CAUTION box denotes what hazard to aircraft?

A—Guy wires extending from radio or TV towers.
B—Tall bridge over the inlet to the body of water.
C—Cable extending from radar-outfitted balloons.

3632. (Refer to Figure 21, area 2.) The flag symbol at Lake Drummond represents a

A—compulsory reporting point for Norfolk Class C airspace.
B—compulsory reporting point for Hampton Roads Airport.
C—visual checkpoint used to identify position for initial callup to Norfolk Approach Control.

3633. (Refer to Figure 21, area 2.) The elevation of the Chesapeake Municipal Airport is

A—20 feet.
B—36 feet.
C—360 feet.

3634. (Refer to Figure 22.) The terrain elevation of the light tan area between Minot (area 1) and Audubon Lake (area 2) varies from

A—sea level to 2,000 feet MSL.
B—2,000 feet to 2,500 feet MSL.
C—2,000 feet to 2,700 feet MSL.

3635. (Refer to Figure 22.) Which public use airports depicted are indicated as having fuel?

A—Minot and Mercer County Regional Airport.
B—Minot and Garrison.
C—Mercer County Regional Airport and Garrison.

3636. (Refer to Figure 24.) The flag symbols at Statesboro Airport, Claxton-Evans County Airport, and Ridgeland Airport are

A—outer boundaries of Savannah Class C airspace.
B—airports with special traffic patterns.
C—visual checkpoints to identify position for initial callup prior to entering Savannah Class C airspace.

3637. (Refer to Figure 24, area 3.) What is the height of the lighted obstacle approximately 7 nautical miles southwest of Savannah International?

A—1,500 feet AGL.
B—1,532 feet AGL.
C—1,549 feet AGL.

3638. (Refer to Figure 24, area 3.) The top of the lighted stack approximately 12 nautical miles from the Savannah VORTAC on the 350° radial is

A—305 feet AGL.
B—400 feet AGL.
C—430 feet AGL.

3639. (Refer to Figure 25, area 1.) What minimum altitude is necessary to vertically clear the obstacle on the northeast side of Airpark East Airport by 500 feet?

A—1,010 feet MSL.
B—1,273 feet MSL.
C—1,283 feet MSL.

3640. (Refer to Figure 25, area 2.) What minimum altitude is necessary to vertically clear the obstacle on the southeast side of Winnsboro Airport by 500 feet?

A—823 feet MSL.
B—1,013 feet MSL.
C—1,403 feet MSL.

3641. (Refer to Figure 26, area 2.) The control tower frequency for Addison Airport is

A—122.95 MHz.
B—126.0 MHz.
C—133.4 MHz.

3642. (Refer to Figure 26, area 8.) What minimum altitude is required to fly over the Cedar Hill TV towers in the congested area south of NAS Dallas?

A—2,533 feet MSL.
B—2,849 feet MSL.
C—3,349 feet MSL.

3643. (Refer to Figure 26, area 5.) The navigation facility at Dallas-Ft. Worth International (DFW) is a

A—VOR.
B—VORTAC.
C—VOR/DME.

3644. (Refer to Figure 21, area 4.) A balloon launched at the town of Edenton drifts northeasterly along the railroad. What minimum altitude must it maintain to clear all of the obstacles in the vicinity of Hertford by at least 500 feet?

A—805 feet MSL.
B—1,000 feet MSL.
C—1,015 feet MSL.

3645. (Refer to Figure 22, area 1.) A balloon launched at Flying S Ranch Airport drifts southward towards the lighted obstacle. If the altimeter was set at 0 feet upon launch, what should it indicate if the balloon is to clear the obstacle at 500 feet above the top?

A—1,531 feet AGL.
B—1,809 feet AGL.
C—2,340 feet AGL.

3646. (Refer to Figure 23, area 1.) A balloon, launched at CX Airport located near the east end of Lake Pend Oreille, drifts south-southwest. What is the approximate elevation of the highest terrain for 20 miles along its path?

A—2,000 – 4,000 feet MSL.
B—4,000 – 6,000 feet MSL.
C—6,000 – 7,000 feet MSL.

3647. (Refer to Figure 21.) Over which area should a glider pilot expect to find the best lift under normal conditions?

A—6.
B—7.
C—8.

3648. (Refer to Figure 27.) If a glider is launched over Barnes County Airport (area 6) with sufficient altitude to glide to Jamestown Airport (area 4), how long will it take for the flight at an average of 40 MPH groundspeed?

A—20 minutes.
B—27 minutes.
C—46 minutes.

3649. (Refer to Figure 25, area 1.) A glider is launched over Caddo Mills Airport with sufficient altitude to glide to Airpark East Airport, south of Caddo Mills. How long will it take for the flight at an average of 35 MPH groundspeed?

A—27 minutes.
B—29 minutes.
C—31 minutes.

3650. (Refer to Figure 27, areas 5 and 6.) What minimum altitude should be used for a go-ahead point at Eckelson in order to arrive at Barnes County Airport at 1,000 feet AGL if the glide ratio is 22:1 in no wind conditions? Use the recommended safety factor.

A—5,959 feet MSL.
B—7,960 feet MSL.
C—9,359 feet MSL.

3651. What action can a pilot take to aid in cooling an engine that is overheating during a climb?

A—Reduce rate of climb and increase airspeed.
B—Reduce climb speed and increase RPM.
C—Increase climb speed and increase RPM.

3652. What is one procedure to aid in cooling an engine that is overheating?

A—Enrich the fuel mixture.
B—Increase the RPM.
C—Reduce the airspeed.

3653. How is engine operation controlled on an engine equipped with a constant-speed propeller?

A—The throttle controls power output as registered on the manifold pressure gauge and the propeller control regulates engine RPM.
B—The throttle controls power output as registered on the manifold pressure gauge and the propeller control regulates a constant blade angle.
C—The throttle controls engine RPM as registered on the tachometer and the mixture control regulates the power output.

3654. What is an advantage of a constant-speed propeller?

A—Permits the pilot to select and maintain a desired cruising speed.
B—Permits the pilot to select the blade angle for the most efficient performance.
C—Provides a smoother operation with stable RPM and eliminates vibrations.

3655. A precaution for the operation of an engine equipped with a constant-speed propeller is to

A—avoid high RPM settings with high manifold pressure.
B—avoid high manifold pressure settings with low RPM.
C—always use a rich mixture with high RPM settings.

3656. What should be the first action after starting an aircraft engine?

A—Adjust for proper RPM and check for desired indications on the engine gauges.
B—Place the magneto or ignition switch momentarily in the OFF position to check for proper grounding.
C—Test each brake and the parking brake.

3657. Should it become necessary to handprop an airplane engine, it is extremely important that a competent pilot

A—call "contact" before touching the propeller.
B—be at the controls in the cockpit.
C—be in the cockpit and call out all commands.

3658. In regard to preflighting an aircraft, what is the minimum expected of a pilot prior to every flight?

A—Drain fuel from each quick drain.
B—Perform a walk-around inspection of the aircraft.
C—Check the required documents aboard the aircraft.

3659. Why is the use of a written checklist recommended for preflight inspection and engine start?

A—To ensure that all necessary items are checked in a logical sequence.
B—For memorizing the procedures in an orderly sequence.
C—To instill confidence in the passengers.

3660. What special check should be made on an aircraft during preflight after it has been stored an extended period of time?

A—ELT batteries and operation.
B—Condensation in the fuel tanks.
C—Damage or obstructions caused by animals, birds, or insects.

3661. Which items are included in the empty weight of an aircraft?

A—Unusable fuel and undrainable oil.
B—Only the airframe, powerplant, and optional equipment.
C—Full fuel tanks and engine oil to capacity.

3662. An aircraft is loaded 110 pounds over maximum certificated gross weight. If fuel (gasoline) is drained to bring the aircraft weight within limits, how much fuel should be drained?

A—15.7 gallons.
B—16.2 gallons.
C—18.4 gallons.

3663. If an aircraft is loaded 90 pounds over maximum certificated gross weight and fuel (gasoline) is drained to bring the aircraft weight within limits, how much fuel should be drained?

A—10 gallons.
B—12 gallons.
C—15 gallons.

3664. GIVEN:

	WEIGHT (LB)	ARM (IN)	MOMENT (LB-IN)
Empty weight	1,495.0	101.4	151,593.0
Pilot and passengers	380.0	64.0	—
Fuel (30 gal usable – no reserve)	—	96.0	—

The CG is located how far aft of datum?

A—CG 92.44.
B—CG 94.01.
C—CG 119.8.

3665. (Refer to Figures 33 and 34.) Determine if the airplane weight and balance is within limits.

Front seat occupants .... 340 lb
Rear seat occupants .... 295 lb
Fuel (main wing tanks) .... 44 gal
Baggage .... 56 lb

A—20 pounds overweight, CG aft of aft limits.
B—20 pounds overweight, CG within limits.
C—20 pounds overweight, CG forward of forward limits.

3666. (Refer to Figures 33 and 34.) What is the maximum amount of baggage that can be carried when the airplane is loaded as follows?

Front seat occupants .... 387 lb
Rear seat occupants .... 293 lb
Fuel .... 35 gal

A—45 pounds.
B—63 pounds.
C—220 pounds.

3667. (Refer to Figures 33 and 34.) Calculate the weight and balance and determine if the CG and the weight of the airplane are within limits.

Front seat occupants .... 350 lb
Rear seat occupants .... 325 lb
Baggage .... 27 lb
Fuel .... 35 gal

A—CG 81.7, out of limits forward.
B—CG 83.4, within limits.
C—CG 84.1, within limits.

3668. (Refer to Figures 33 and 34.) Determine if the airplane weight and balance is within limits.

Front seat occupants .... 415 lb
Rear seat occupants .... 110 lb
Fuel, main tanks .... 44 gal
Fuel, aux. tanks .... 19 gal
Baggage .... 32 lb

A—19 pounds overweight, CG within limits.
B—19 pounds overweight, CG out of limits forward.
C—Weight within limits, CG out of limits.

3669. (Refer to Figure 35.) What is the maximum amount of baggage that may be loaded aboard the airplane for the CG to remain within the moment envelope?

	WEIGHT (LB)	MOM/1000
Empty weight	1,350	51.5
Pilot and front passenger	250	—
Rear passengers	400	—
Baggage	—	—
Fuel, 30 gal	—	—
Oil, 8 qt	—	-0.2

A—105 pounds.
B—110 pounds.
C—120 pounds.

3670. (Refer to Figure 35.) Calculate the moment of the airplane and determine which category is applicable.

	WEIGHT (LB)	MOM/1000
Empty weight	1,350	51.5
Pilot and front passenger	310	—
Rear passengers	96	—
Fuel, 38 gal	—	—
Oil, 8 qt	—	-0.2

A—79.2, utility category.
B—80.8, utility category.
C—81.2, normal category.

3671. (Refer to Figure 35.) What is the maximum amount of fuel that may be aboard the airplane on takeoff if loaded as follows?

	WEIGHT (LB)	MOM/1000
Empty weight	1,350	51.5
Pilot and front passenger	340	—
Rear passengers	310	—
Baggage	45	—
Oil, 8 qt	—	—

A—24 gallons.
B—32 gallons.
C—40 gallons.

3672. (Refer to Figure 35.) Determine the moment with the following data:

	WEIGHT (LB)	MOM/1000
Empty weight	1,350	51.5
Pilot and front passenger	340	—
Fuel (std tanks)	Capacity	—
Oil, 8 qt	—	—

A—69.9 pound-inches.
B—74.9 pound-inches.
C—77.6 pound-inches.

3673. (Refer to Figure 35.) Determine the aircraft loaded moment and the aircraft category.

	WEIGHT (LB)	MOM/1000
Empty weight	1,350	51.5
Pilot and front passenger	380	—
Fuel, 48 gal	288	—
Oil, 8 qt	—	—

A—78.2, normal category.
B—79.2, normal category.
C—80.4, utility category.

3674. (Refer to Figures 33 and 34.) Upon landing, the front passenger (180 pounds) departs the airplane. A rear passenger (204 pounds) moves to the front passenger position. What effect does this have on the CG if the airplane weighed 2,690 pounds and the MOM/100 was 2,260 just prior to the passenger transfer?

A—The CG moves forward approximately 3 inches.
B—The weight changes, but the CG is not affected.
C—The CG moves forward approximately 0.1 inch.

3675. (Refer to Figures 33 and 34.) Which action can adjust the airplane's weight to maximum gross weight and the CG within limits for takeoff?

Front seat occupants	425 lb
Rear seat occupants	300 lb
Fuel, main tanks	44 gal

A—Drain 12 gallons of fuel.
B—Drain 9 gallons of fuel.
C—Transfer 12 gallons of fuel from the main tanks to the auxiliary tanks.

3676. (Refer to Figures 33 and 34.) What effect does a 35-gallon fuel burn (main tanks) have on the weight and balance if the airplane weighed 2,890 pounds and the MOM/100 was 2,452 at takeoff?

A—Weight is reduced by 210 pounds and the CG is aft of limits.
B—Weight is reduced by 210 pounds and the CG is unaffected.
C—Weight is reduced to 2,680 pounds and the CG moves forward.

3677. (Refer to Figures 33 and 34.) With the airplane loaded as follows, what action can be taken to balance the airplane?

Front seat occupants	411 lb
Rear seat occupants	100 lb
Main wing tanks	44 gal

A—Fill the auxiliary wing tanks.
B—Add a 100-pound weight to the baggage compartment.
C—Transfer 10 gallons of fuel from the main tanks to the auxiliary tanks.

3678. (Refer to Figure 36.) Approximately what true airspeed should a pilot expect with 65 percent maximum continuous power at 9,500 feet with a temperature of 36°F below standard?

A—178 MPH.
B—181 MPH.
C—183 MPH.

3679. (Refer to Figure 36.) What is the expected fuel consumption for a 1,000-nautical mile flight under the following conditions?

Pressure altitude	8,000 ft
Temperature	22°C
Manifold pressure	20.8" Hg
Wind	Calm

A—60.2 gallons.
B—70.1 gallons.
C—73.2 gallons.

3680. (Refer to Figure 36.) What is the expected fuel consumption for a 500-nautical mile flight under the following conditions?

Pressure altitude	4,000 ft
Temperature	+29°C
Manifold pressure	21.3" Hg
Wind	Calm

A—31.4 gallons.
B—36.1 gallons.
C—40.1 gallons.

3681. (Refer to Figure 36.) What fuel flow should a pilot expect at 11,000 feet on a standard day with 65 percent maximum continuous power?

A—10.6 gallons per hour.
B—11.2 gallons per hour.
C—11.8 gallons per hour.

3682. (Refer to Figure 36.) Determine the approximate manifold pressure setting with 2,450 RPM to achieve 65 percent maximum continuous power at 6,500 feet with a temperature of 36°F higher than standard.

A—19.8" Hg.
B—20.8" Hg.
C—21.0" Hg.

3683. (Refer to Figure 37.) What is the headwind component for a landing on Runway 18 if the tower reports the wind as 220° at 30 knots?

A—19 knots.
B—23 knots.
C—26 knots.

3684. (Refer to Figure 37.) Determine the maximum wind velocity for a 45° crosswind if the maximum crosswind component for the airplane is 25 knots.

A—25 knots.
B—29 knots.
C—35 knots.

3685. (Refer to Figure 37.) What is the maximum wind velocity for a 30° crosswind if the maximum crosswind component for the airplane is 12 knots?

A—16 knots.
B—20 knots.
C—24 knots.

3686. (Refer to Figure 37.) With a reported wind of north at 20 knots, which runway (6, 29, or 32) is acceptable for use for an airplane with a 13-knot maximum crosswind component?

A—Runway 6.
B—Runway 29.
C—Runway 32.

3687. (Refer to Figure 37.) With a reported wind of south at 20 knots, which runway (10, 14, or 24) is appropriate for an airplane with a 13-knot maximum crosswind component?

A—Runway 10.
B—Runway 14.
C—Runway 24.

3688. (Refer to Figure 37.) What is the crosswind component for a landing on Runway 18 if the tower reports the wind as 220° at 30 knots?

A—19 knots.
B—23 knots.
C—30 knots.

3689. (Refer to Figure 38.) Determine the total distance required to land.

OAT	32°F
Pressure altitude	8,000 ft
Weight	2,600 lb
Headwind component	20 kts
Obstacle	50 ft

A—850 feet.
B—1,400 feet.
C—1,750 feet.

3690. (Refer to Figure 38.) Determine the total distance required to land.

OAT	Std
Pressure altitude	2,000 ft
Weight	2,300 lb
Wind component	Calm
Obstacle	None

A—850 feet.
B—1,250 feet.
C—1,450 feet.

3691. (Refer to Figure 38.) Determine the total distance required to land.

OAT	90°F
Pressure altitude	3,000 ft
Weight	2,900 lb
Headwind component	10 kts
Obstacle	50 ft

A—1,450 feet.
B—1,550 feet.
C—1,725 feet.

3692. (Refer to Figure 38.) Determine the approximate ground roll distance after landing.

OAT	90°F
Pressure altitude	4,000 ft
Weight	2,800 lb
Tailwind component	10 kts

A—1,575 feet.
B—1,725 feet.
C—1,950 feet.

3693. (Refer to Figure 39.) Determine the approximate landing ground roll distance.

Pressure altitude .... Sea level
Headwind .... 4 kts
Temperature .... Std

A—356 feet.
B—401 feet.
C—490 feet.

3694. (Refer to Figure 39.) Determine the total distance required to land over a 50-foot obstacle.

Pressure altitude .... 7,500 ft
Headwind .... 8 kts
Temperature .... Std
Runway .... Dry grass

A—1,004 feet.
B—1,205 feet.
C—1,506 feet.

3695. (Refer to Figure 39.) Determine the total distance required to land over a 50-foot obstacle.

Pressure altitude .... 5,000 ft
Headwind .... 8 kts
Temperature .... 41°F
Runway .... Hard surface

A—837 feet.
B—956 feet.
C—1,076 feet.

3696. (Refer to Figure 39.) Determine the total distance required to land over a 50-foot obstacle.

Pressure altitude .... 5,000 ft
Headwind .... Calm
Temperature .... 101°F

A—1,076 feet.
B—1,291 feet.
C—1,314 feet.

3697. (Refer to Figure 39.) Determine the approximate landing ground roll distance.

Pressure altitude .... 3,750 ft
Headwind .... 12 kts
Temperature .... Std

A—338 feet.
B—425 feet.
C—483 feet.

3698. (Refer to Figure 39.) Determine the approximate landing ground roll distance.

Pressure altitude .... 1,250 ft
Headwind .... 8 kts
Temperature .... Std

A—275 feet.
B—366 feet.
C—470 feet.

3699. (Refer to Figure 40.) Determine the total landing distance to clear a 50-foot obstacle in a gyroplane. The outside air temperature (OAT) is 75°F and the pressure altitude at the airport is 2,500 feet.

A—521 feet.
B—525 feet.
C—529 feet.

3700. (Refer to Figure 40.) Approximately how much additional landing distance will be required for a gyroplane to clear a 50-foot obstacle with an increase in temperature from 40 to 60°F at 3,200 feet pressure altitude?

A—4 feet.
B—8 feet.
C—12 feet.

3701. (Refer to Figure 40.) Determine the total landing distance to clear a 50-foot obstacle in a gyroplane. The outside air temperature (OAT) is 80°F and the pressure altitude is 3,500 feet.

A—521 feet.
B—526 feet.
C—531 feet.

3702. (Refer to Figure 40.) Determine the total takeoff distance required for a gyroplane to clear a 50-foot obstacle if the temperature is 95°F and the pressure altitude is 1,700 feet.

A—1,825 feet.
B—1,910 feet.
C—2,030 feet.

3703. (Refer to Figure 40.) Determine the total takeoff distance required for a gyroplane to clear a 50-foot obstacle if the temperature is standard at sea level pressure altitude.

A—950 feet.
B—1,090 feet.
C—1,200 feet.

3704. (Refer to Figure 40.) Approximately how much additional takeoff distance will be required for a gyroplane to clear a 50-foot obstacle if the temperature increases from 75 to 90°F at a pressure altitude of 2,300 feet?

A—160 feet.
B—200 feet.
C—2,020 feet.

3705. (Refer to Figure 41.) Determine the total distance required for takeoff to clear a 50-foot obstacle.

OAT .... Std
Pressure altitude .... 4,000 ft
Takeoff weight .... 2,800 lb
Headwind component .... Calm

A— 1,500 feet.
B— 1,750 feet.
C— 2,000 feet.

3706. (Refer to Figure 41.) Determine the total distance required for takeoff to clear a 50-foot obstacle.

OAT .... Std
Pressure altitude .... Sea level
Takeoff weight .... 2,700 lb
Headwind component .... Calm

A— 1,000 feet.
B— 1,400 feet.
C— 1,700 feet.

3707. (Refer to Figure 41.) Determine the approximate ground roll distance required for takeoff.

OAT .... 100°F
Pressure altitude .... 2,000 ft
Takeoff weight .... 2,750 lb
Headwind component .... Calm

A— 1,150 feet.
B— 1,300 feet.
C— 1,800 feet.

3708. (Refer to Figure 41.) Determine the approximate ground roll distance required for takeoff.

OAT .... 90°F
Pressure altitude .... 2,000 ft
Takeoff weight .... 2,500 lb
Headwind component .... 20 kts

A— 650 feet.
B— 850 feet.
C— 1,000 feet.

3709. FAA advisory circulars (some free, others at cost) are available to all pilots and are obtained by

A— distribution from the nearest FAA district office.
B— ordering those desired from the Government Printing Office.
C— subscribing to the Federal Register.

3710. Prior to starting each maneuver, pilots should

A— check altitude, airspeed, and heading indications.
B— visually scan the entire area for collision avoidance.
C— announce their intentions on the nearest CTAF.

3711. The most important rule to remember in the event of a power failure after becoming airborne is to

A— immediately establish the proper gliding attitude and airspeed.
B— quickly check the fuel supply for possible fuel exhaustion.
C— determine the wind direction to plan for the forced landing.

3712. What is the most effective way to use the eyes during night flight?

A— Look only at far away, dim lights.
B— Scan slowly to permit offcenter viewing.
C— Concentrate directly on each object for a few seconds.

3713. The best method to use when looking for other traffic at night is to

A— look to the side of the object and scan slowly.
B— scan the visual field very rapidly.
C— look to the side of the object and scan rapidly.

3714. The most effective method of scanning for other aircraft for collision avoidance during nighttime hours is to use

A— regularly spaced concentration on the 3-, 9-, and 12-o'clock positions.
B— a series of short, regularly spaced eye movements to search each 30-degree sector.
C— peripheral vision by scanning small sectors and utilizing offcenter viewing.

3715. During a night flight, you observe a steady red light and a flashing red light ahead and at the same altitude. What is the general direction of movement of the other aircraft?

A— The other aircraft is crossing to the left.
B— The other aircraft is crossing to the right.
C— The other aircraft is approaching head-on.

3716. During a night flight, you observe a steady white light and a flashing red light ahead and at the same altitude. What is the general direction of movement of the other aircraft?

A— The other aircraft is flying away from you.
B— The other aircraft is crossing to the left.
C— The other aircraft is crossing to the right.

3717. During a night flight, you observe steady red and green lights ahead and at the same altitude. What is the general direction of movement of the other aircraft?

A— The other aircraft is crossing to the left.
B— The other aircraft is flying away from you.
C— The other aircraft is approaching head-on.

3718. Airport taxiway edge lights are identified at night by

A—white directional lights.
B—blue omnidirectional lights.
C—alternate red and green lights.

3719. VFR approaches to land at night should be accomplished

A—at a higher airspeed.
B—with a steeper descent.
C—the same as during daytime.

3720. (Refer to Figure 44.) What action, if any, should be taken for lateral balance if the helicopter is loaded as follows?

Gross weight .... 1,800 lb
Pilot .... 140 lb, 13.5 in. left of "0" MOM arm
Copilot .... 180 lb, 13.5 in. right of "0" MOM arm

A—Add 10 pounds of weight to the pilot's side.
B—Decrease the gross weight 50 pounds.
C—No action is required.

3721. (Refer to Figure 44.) What action should be taken for lateral balance if the helicopter is loaded as follows?

Gross weight .... 1,800 lb
Pilot .... 100 lb, 13.5 in. left of "0" MOM arm
Copilot .... 200 lb, 13.5 in. right of "0" MOM arm

A—Add 50 pounds of weight to the pilot's side.
B—Decrease the gross weight 50 pounds.
C—No action is required.

3722. (Refer to Figure 42.) Determine the weight and balance of the helicopter.

	WEIGHT (LB)	ARM (IN)	MOMENT (LB-IN)
Empty weight	1,495.0	101.4	151,593.0
Pilot and one passenger	350.0	64.0	—
Fuel (40 gal usable)	—	96.0	—

A—Over gross weight limit, but within CG limit.
B—Within gross weight limit and at the aft CG limit.
C—Over gross weight limit and exceeds the aft CG limit.

3723. (Refer to Figure 43.) Determine if the helicopter's CG is within limits.

	WEIGHT (LB)	MOMENT (1000)
Empty weight (including oil)	1,025	102,705
Pilot and passenger	345	—
Fuel, 35 gal	—	—

A—Out of limits forward.
B—Within limits.
C—Out of limits aft.

3724. (Refer to Figure 43.) What effect does adding a 185-pound passenger have on the CG, if prior to boarding the passenger, the helicopter weighed 1,380 pounds and the moment is 136,647.5 pound-inches?

A—The CG is moved forward 1.78 inches.
B—The CG is moved aft 1.78 inches.
C—The CG is moved forward 2.36 inches.

3725. How is the CG of the helicopter affected after a fuel burn of 20 gallons?

Gross weight prior to fuel burn .... 2,050 lb
Moment .... 195,365 lb-in
Fuel arm .... 96.9 in

A—CG shifts forward 1.0 inch.
B—CG shifts forward 0.1 inch.
C—CG shifts aft 1.0 inch.

3726. (Refer to Figure 43.) How is the CG of the helicopter affected when all of the auxiliary fuel is burned off?

Gross weight prior to fuel burn .... 1,660 lb
Moment .... 159,898.5 lb-in

A—CG moves aft 0.12 inch.
B—CG moves forward 0.78 inch.
C—CG moves forward 1.07 inches.

3727. (Refer to Figure 44.) Calculate the weight and balance of the helicopter, and determine if the CG is within limits.

	WEIGHT (LB)	ARM (IN)	MOMENT (100)
Empty weight	1,495.0	101.4	1,515.93
Oil, 8 qt	—	100.5	—
Fuel, 40 gal	—	96.0	—
Pilot	160.0	64.0	—

A—CG 90.48 inches, out of limits forward.
B—CG 95.32 inches, within limits.
C—CG 97.58 inches, within limits.

3728. (Refer to Figure 44.) Determine if the helicopter weight and balance is within limits.

	WEIGHT (LB)	ARM (IN)	MOMENT (100)
Empty weight	1,495.0	101.4	1,515.93
Oil, 8 qt	—	100.5	—
Fuel, 40 gal	—	96.0	—
Pilot and copilot	300.0	64.0	—

A—CG 95.2 inches, within limits.
B—CG 95.3 inches, weight and CG out of limits.
C—CG 95.4 inches, within limits.

3729. (Refer to Figures 45 and 46.) What is the new CG of the gyroplane after a 10-gallon fuel burn if the original weight was 1,450 pounds and the MOM/1000 was 108 pound-inches?

A—Out of limits forward.
B—Out of limits aft.
C—Within limits near the forward limit.

3730. (Refer to Figures 45 and 46.) What is the condition of the weight and balance of the gyroplane as loaded?

	WEIGHT (LB)	MOMENT (1000)
Empty weight	1,074	85.6
Oil, 6 qt	—	1.0
Pilot and passenger	247	—
Fuel, 12 gal	—	—
Baggage	95	—

A—Within limits.
B—Overweight.
C—Out of limits aft.

3731. (Refer to Figures 45 and 46.) Approximately how much baggage, if any, may be carried in the gyroplane, without exceeding weight and balance limits?

	WEIGHT (LB)	MOMENT (1000)
Empty weight	1,074	85.6
Oil, 6 qt	—	1.0
Fuel, Full	—	—
Pilot (FWD)	224	—

A—None, overweight.
B—70 pounds.
C—100 pounds.

3732. (Refer to Figure 47.) What is the best rate-of-climb speed for the helicopter?

A—24 MPH.
B—40 MPH.
C—57 MPH.

3733. With calm wind conditions, which flight operation would require the most power?

A—A right-hovering turn.
B—A left-hovering turn.
C—Hovering out of ground effect.

3734. If the pilot were to make a near-vertical power approach into a confined area with the airspeed near zero, what hazardous condition may develop?

A—Ground resonance when ground contact is made.
B—A settling-with-power condition.
C—Blade stall vibration could develop.

3735. (Refer to Figure 47.) The airspeed range to avoid while flying in ground effect is

A—25 – 40 MPH.
B—25 – 57 MPH.
C—40 MPH and above.

3736. (Refer to Figure 47.) Which airspeed/altitude combination should be avoided during helicopter operations?

A—30 MPH/200 feet AGL.
B—50 MPH/300 feet AGL.
C—60 MPH/20 feet AGL.

3737. (Refer to Figure 47.) Which airspeed/altitude combination should be avoided during helicopter operations?

A—20 MPH/200 feet AGL.
B—35 MPH/175 feet AGL.
C—40 MPH/75 feet AGL.

3738. If anti-torque failure occurred during the landing touchdown, what could be done to help straighten out a left yaw prior to touchdown?

A—A flare to zero airspeed and a vertical descent to touchdown should be made.
B—Apply available throttle to help swing the nose to the right just prior to touchdown.
C—A normal running landing should be made.

3739. Which flight technique is recommended for use during hot weather?

A—Use minimum allowable RPM and maximum allowable manifold pressure during all phases of flight.
B—During hovering flight, maintain minimum engine RPM during left pedal turns, and maximum engine RPM during right pedal turns.
C—During takeoff, accelerate slowly into forward flight.

3740. Under what condition should a helicopter pilot consider using a running takeoff?

A—When gross weight or density altitude prevents a sustained hover at normal hovering altitude.
B—When a normal climb speed is assured between 10 and 20 feet.
C—When the additional airspeed can be quickly converted to altitude.

3741. What action should the pilot take if engine failure occurs at altitude?

A—Open the throttle as the collective pitch is raised.
B—Reduce cyclic back stick pressure during turns.
C—Lower the collective pitch control, as necessary, to maintain rotor RPM.

3742. Which is a precaution to be observed during an autorotative descent?

A—Normally, the airspeed is controlled with the collective pitch.
B—Normally, only the cyclic control is used to make turns.
C—Do not allow the rate of descent to get too low at zero airspeed.

3743. The proper action to initiate a quick stop is to apply

A—forward cyclic and lower the collective pitch.
B—aft cyclic and raise the collective pitch.
C—aft cyclic and lower the collective pitch.

3744. What is the procedure for a slope landing?

A—When the downslope skid is on the ground, hold the collective pitch at the same position.
B—Minimum RPM shall be held until the full weight of the helicopter is on the skid.
C—When parallel to the slope, slowly lower the upslope skid to the ground prior to lowering the downslope skid.

3745. Takeoff from a slope is normally accomplished by

A—moving the cyclic in a direction away from the slope.
B—bringing the helicopter to a level attitude before completely leaving the ground.
C—moving the cyclic stick to a full up position as the helicopter nears a level attitude.

3746. Which action would be appropriate for confined area operations?

A—Takeoffs and landings must be made into the wind.
B—Plan the flightpath over areas suitable for a forced landing.
C—A very steep angle of descent should be used to land on the selected spot.

3747. If possible, when departing a confined area, what type of takeoff is preferred?

A—A normal takeoff from a hover.
B—A vertical takeoff.
C—A normal takeoff from the surface.

3748. Which is a correct general rule for pinnacle and ridgeline operations?

A—Gaining altitude on takeoff is more important than gaining airspeed.
B—The approach path to a ridgeline is usually perpendicular to the ridge.
C—A climb to a pinnacle or ridgeline should be performed on the upwind side.

3749. Before beginning a confined area or pinnacle landing, the pilot should first

A—execute a high reconnaissance.
B—execute a low reconnaissance.
C—fly around the area to discover areas of turbulence.

3750. What minimum upward current must a glider encounter to maintain altitude?

A—At least 2 feet per second.
B—The same as the glider's sink rate.
C—The same as the adjacent down currents.

3751. On which side of a rocky knoll, that is surrounded by vegetation, should a pilot find the best thermals?

A—On the side facing the Sun.
B—On the downwind side.
C—Exactly over the center.

3752. What is one recommended method for locating thermals?

A—Fly an ever increasing circular path.
B—Maintain a straight track downwind.
C—Look for converging streamers of dust or smoke.

3753. What is a recommended procedure for entering a dust devil for soaring?

A—Enter above 500 feet and circle the edge in the same direction as the rotation.
B—Enter below 500 feet and circle the edge opposite the direction of rotation.
C—Enter at or above 500 feet and circle the edge opposite the direction of rotation.

3754. What is an important precaution when soaring in a dust devil?

A—Avoid the eye of the vortex.
B—Avoid the clear area at the outside edge of the dust.
C—Maintain the same direction as the rotation of the vortex.

3755. What is the best visual indication of a thermal?

A—Fragmented cumulus clouds with concave bases.
B—Smooth cumulus clouds with concave bases.
C—Scattered to broken sky with cumulus clouds.

3756. How can a pilot locate bubble thermals?

A—Look for wet areas where recent showers have occurred.
B—Look for birds that are soaring in areas of intermittent heating.
C—Fly the area just above the boundary of a temperature inversion.

3757. Where may the most favorable type thermals for cross-country soaring be found?

A—Just ahead of a warm front.
B—Along thermal streets.
C—Under mountain waves.

3758. Where and under what condition can enough lift be found for soaring when the weather is generally stable?

A—On the upwind side of hills or ridges with moderate winds present.
B—In mountain waves that form on the upwind side of the mountains.
C—Over isolated peaks when strong winds are present.

3759. To use VHF/DF facilities for assistance in locating an aircraft's position, the aircraft must have a

A—VHF transmitter and receiver.
B—4096-code transponder.
C—VOR receiver and DME.

3760. A slightly high glide slope indication from a precision approach path indicator is

A—four white lights.
B—three white lights and one red light.
C—two white lights and two red lights.

3761. A below glide slope indication from a tri-color VASI is a

A—red light signal.
B—pink light signal.
C—green light signal.

3762. An above glide slope indication from a tri-color VASI is

A—a white light signal.
B—a green light signal.
C—an amber light signal.

3763. An on glide slope indication from a tri-color VASI is

A—a white light signal.
B—a green light signal.
C—an amber light signal.

3764. A below glide slope indication from a pulsating approach slope indicator is a

A—pulsating white light.
B—steady white light.
C—pulsating red light.

3765. (Refer to Figure 48.) Illustration A indicates that the aircraft is

A—below the glide slope.
B—on the glide slope.
C—above the glide slope.

3766. (Refer to Figure 48.) VASI lights as shown by illustration C indicate that the airplane is

A—off course to the left.
B—above the glide slope.
C—below the glide slope.

3767. (Refer to Figure 48.) While on final approach to a runway equipped with a standard 2-bar VASI, the lights appear as shown by illustration D. This means that the aircraft is

A—above the glide slope.
B—below the glide slope.
C—on the glide slope.

3768. To set the high intensity runway lights on medium intensity, the pilot should click the microphone seven times, then click it

A—one time.
B—three times.
C—five times.

3769. An airport's rotating beacon operated during daylight hours indicates

A—there are obstructions on the airport.
B—that weather at the airport located in Class D airspace is below basic VFR weather minimums.
C—the Air Traffic Control tower is not in operation.

3770. A lighted heliport may be identified by a

A—green, yellow, and white rotating beacon.
B—flashing yellow light.
C—blue lighted square landing area.

3771. A military air station can be identified by a rotating beacon that emits

A—white and green alternating flashes.
B—two quick, white flashes between green flashes.
C—green, yellow, and white flashes.

3772. How can a military airport be identified at night?

A—Alternate white and green light flashes.
B—Dual peaked (two quick) white flashes between green flashes.
C—White flashing lights with steady green at the same location.

3773. (Refer to Figure 49.) That portion of the runway identified by the letter A may be used for

A—landing.
B—taxiing and takeoff.
C—taxiing and landing.

3774. (Refer to Figure 49.) According to the airport diagram, which statement is true?

A—Runway 30 is equipped at position E with emergency arresting gear to provide a means of stopping military aircraft.
B—Takeoffs may be started at position A on Runway 12, and the landing portion of this runway begins at position B.
C—The takeoff and landing portion of Runway 12 begins at position B.

3775. (Refer to Figure 49.) What is the difference between area A and area E on the airport depicted?

A—"A" may be used for taxi and takeoff; "E" may be used only as an overrun.
B—"A" may be used for all operations except heavy aircraft landings; "E" may be used only as an overrun.
C—"A" may be used only for taxiing; "E" may be used for all operations except landings.

3776. (Refer to Figure 49.) Area C on the airport depicted is classified as a

A—stabilized area.
B—multiple heliport.
C—closed runway.

3777. (Refer to Figure 50.) The arrows that appear on the end of the north/south runway indicate that the area

A—may be used only for taxiing.
B—is usable for taxiing, takeoff, and landing.
C—cannot be used for landing, but may be used for taxiing and takeoff.

3778. The numbers 9 and 27 on a runway indicate that the runway is oriented approximately

A—009° and 027° true.
B—090° and 270° true.
C—090° and 270° magnetic.

3779. The vertical limit of Class C airspace above the primary airport is normally

A—1,200 feet AGL.
B—3,000 feet AGL.
C—4,000 feet AGL.

3780. The normal radius of the outer area of Class C airspace is

A—5 nautical miles.
B—15 nautical miles.
C—20 nautical miles.

3781. All operations within Class C airspace must be in

A—accordance with instrument flight rules.
B—compliance with ATC clearances and instructions.
C—an aircraft equipped with a 4096-code transponder with Mode C encoding capability.

3782. Under what condition may an aircraft operate from a satellite airport within Class C airspace?

A—The pilot must file a flight plan prior to departure.
B—The pilot must monitor ATC until clear of the Class C airspace.
C—The pilot must contact ATC as soon as practicable after takeoff.

3783. Under what condition, if any, may pilots fly through a restricted area?

A—When flying on airways with an ATC clearance.
B—With the controlling agency's authorization.
C—Regulations do not allow this.

3784. A balloon flight through a restricted area is

A—permitted at certain times, but only with prior permission by the appropriate authority.
B—permitted anytime, but caution should be exercised because of high-speed military aircraft.
C—never permitted.

3785. What action should a pilot take when operating under VFR in a Military Operations Area (MOA)?

A—Obtain a clearance from the controlling agency prior to entering the MOA.
B—Operate only on the airways that transverse the MOA.
C—Exercise extreme caution when military activity is being conducted.

3786. Responsibility for collision avoidance in an alert area rests with

A—the controlling agency.
B—all pilots.
C—Air Traffic Control.

3787. The lateral dimensions of Class D airspace are based on

A—the number of airports that lie within the Class D airspace.
B—5 statute miles from the geographical center of the primary airport.
C—the instrument procedures for which the controlled airspace is established.

3788. A non-tower satellite airport, within the same Class D airspace as that designated for the primary airport, requires radio communications be established and maintained with the

A—satellite airport's UNICOM.
B—associated Flight Service Station.
C—primary airport's control tower.

3789. Prior to entering an Airport Advisory Area, a pilot should

A—monitor ATIS for weather and traffic advisories.
B—contact approach control for vectors to the traffic pattern.
C—contact the local FSS for airport and traffic advisories.

3790. Select the UNICOM frequencies normally assigned to stations at landing areas used exclusively as heliports.

A—122.75 and 123.65 MHz.
B—123.0 and 122.95 MHz.
C—123.05 and 123.075 MHz.

3791. Automatic Terminal Information Service (ATIS) is the continuous broadcast of recorded information concerning

A—pilots of radar-identified aircraft whose aircraft is in dangerous proximity to terrain or to an obstruction.
B—nonessential information to reduce frequency congestion.
C—noncontrol information in selected high-activity terminal areas.

3792. An ATC radar facility issues the following advisory to a pilot flying on a heading of 090°:

"TRAFFIC 3 O'CLOCK, 2 MILES, WESTBOUND..."

Where should the pilot look for this traffic?

A—East.
B—South.
C—West.

3793. An ATC radar facility issues the following advisory to a pilot flying on a heading of 360°:

"TRAFFIC 10 O'CLOCK, 2 MILES, SOUTHBOUND..."

Where should the pilot look for this traffic?

A—Northwest.
B—Northeast.
C—Southwest.

3794. An ATC radar facility issues the following advisory to a pilot during a local flight:

"TRAFFIC 2 O'CLOCK, 5 MILES, NORTHBOUND..."

Where should the pilot look for this traffic?

A—Between directly ahead and 90° to the left.
B—Between directly behind and 90° to the right.
C—Between directly ahead and 90° to the right.

3795. An ATC radar facility issues the following advisory to a pilot flying north in a calm wind:

"TRAFFIC 9 O'CLOCK, 2 MILES, SOUTHBOUND..."

Where should the pilot look for this traffic?

A—South.
B—North.
C—West.

3796. Basic radar service in the terminal radar program is best described as

A—traffic advisories and limited vectoring to VFR aircraft.
B—mandatory radar service provided by the Automated Radar Terminal System (ARTS) program.
C—wind-shear warning at participating airports.

3797. From whom should a departing VFR aircraft request Stage II Terminal Radar Advisory Service during ground operations?

A—Clearance delivery.
B—Tower, just before takeoff.
C—Ground control, on initial contact.

3798. Stage III Service in the terminal radar program provides

A—IFR separation (1,000 feet vertical and 3 miles lateral) between all aircraft.
B—warning to pilots when their aircraft are in unsafe proximity to terrain, obstructions, or other aircraft.
C—sequencing and separation for participating VFR aircraft.

3799. Which initial action should a pilot take prior to entering Class C airspace?

A—Contact approach control on the appropriate frequency.
B—Contact the tower and request permission to enter.
C—Contact the FSS for traffic advisories.

3800. When making routine transponder code changes, pilots should avoid inadvertent selection of which codes?

A—0700, 1700, 7000.
B—1200, 1500, 7000.
C—7500, 7600, 7700.

3801. When operating under VFR below 18,000 feet MSL, unless otherwise authorized, what transponder code should be selected?

A—1200.
B—7600.
C—7700.

3802. Unless otherwise authorized, if flying a transponder equipped aircraft, a recreational pilot should squawk which VFR code?

A—1200.
B—7600.
C—7700.

3803. If Air Traffic Control advises that radar service is terminated when the pilot is departing Class C airspace, the transponder should be set to code

A—0000.
B—1200.
C—4096.

3804. If the aircraft's radio fails, what is the recommended procedure when landing at a controlled airport?

A—Observe the traffic flow, enter the pattern, and look for a light signal from the tower.
B—Enter a crosswind leg and rock the wings.
C—Flash the landing lights and cycle the landing gear while circling the airport.

3805. (Refer to Figure 50.) Select the proper traffic pattern and runway for landing.

A—Left-hand traffic and Runway 18.
B—Right-hand traffic and Runway 18.
C—Left-hand traffic and Runway 22.

3806. (Refer to Figure 50.) If the wind is as shown by the landing direction indicator, the pilot should land on

A—Runway 18 and expect a crosswind from the right.
B—Runway 22 directly into the wind.
C—Runway 36 and expect a crosswind from the right.

3807. (Refer to Figure 51.) The segmented circle indicates that the airport traffic is

A—left-hand for Runway 35 and right-hand for Runway 17.
B—left-hand for Runway 17 and right-hand for Runway 35.
C—right-hand for Runway 9 and left-hand for Runway 27.

3808. (Refer to Figure 51.) The traffic patterns indicated in the segmented circle have been arranged to avoid flights over an area to the

A—south of the airport.
B—north of the airport.
C—southeast of the airport.

3809. (Refer to Figure 51.) The segmented circle indicates that a landing on Runway 26 will be with a

A—right-quartering headwind.
B—left-quartering headwind.
C—right-quartering tailwind.

3810. (Refer to Figure 51.) Which runway and traffic pattern should be used as indicated by the wind cone in the segmented circle?

A—Right-hand traffic on Runway 8.
B—Right-hand traffic on Runway 17.
C—Left-hand traffic on Runway 35.

3811. After landing at a tower-controlled airport, when should the pilot contact ground control?

A—When advised by the tower to do so.
B—Prior to turning off the runway.
C—After reaching a taxiway that leads directly to the parking area.

3812. If instructed by ground control to taxi to Runway 9, the pilot may proceed

A—via taxiways and across runways to, but not onto, Runway 9.
B—to the next intersecting runway where further clearance is required.
C—via taxiways and across runways to Runway 9, where an immediate takeoff may be made.

3813. What ATC facility should the pilot contact to receive a special VFR departure clearance in Class D airspace?

A—Automated Flight Service Station.
B—Air Traffic Control Tower.
C—Air Route Traffic Control Center.

3814. What procedure is recommended when climbing or descending VFR on an airway?

A—Execute gentle banks, left and right for continuous visual scanning of the airspace.
B—Advise the nearest FSS of the altitude changes.
C—Fly away from the centerline of the airway before changing altitude.

3815. (Refer to Figure 52.) If more than one cruising altitude is intended, which should be entered in block 7 of the flight plan?

A—Initial cruising altitude.
B—Highest cruising altitude.
C—Lowest cruising altitude.

3816. (Refer to Figure 52.) What information should be entered in block 9 for a VFR day flight?

A—The name of the airport of first intended landing.
B—The name of destination airport if no stopover for more than 1 hour is anticipated.
C—The name of the airport where the aircraft is based.

3817. (Refer to Figure 52.) What information should be entered in block 12 for a VFR day flight?

A—The estimated time en route plus 30 minutes.
B—The estimated time en route plus 45 minutes.
C—The amount of usable fuel on board expressed in time.

3818. How should a VFR flight plan be closed at the completion of the flight at a controlled airport?

A—The tower will automatically close the flight plan when the aircraft turns off the runway.
B—The pilot must close the flight plan with the nearest FSS or other FAA facility upon landing.
C—The tower will relay the instructions to the nearest FSS when the aircraft contacts the tower for landing.

3819. When activated, an emergency locator transmitter (ELT) transmits on

A—118.0 and 118.8 MHz.
B—121.5 and 243.0 MHz.
C—123.0 and 119.0 MHz.

3820. When must the battery in an emergency locator transmitter (ELT) be replaced (or recharged if the battery is rechargeable)?

A—After one-half the battery's useful life.
B—During each annual and 100-hour inspection.
C—Every 24 calendar months.

3821. When may an emergency locator transmitter (ELT) be tested?

A—Anytime.
B—At 15 and 45 minutes past the hour.
C—During the first 5 minutes after the hour.

3822. Which procedure is recommended to ensure that the emergency locator transmitter (ELT) has not been activated?

A—Turn off the aircraft ELT after landing.
B—Ask the airport tower if they are receiving an ELT signal.
C—Monitor 121.5 before engine shutdown.

3823. Below FL180, en route weather advisories should be obtained from an FSS on

A—122.0 MHz.
B—122.1 MHz.
C—123.6 MHz.

3824. Wingtip vortices are created only when an aircraft is

A—operating at high airspeeds.
B—heavily loaded.
C—developing lift.

3825. The greatest vortex strength occurs when the generating aircraft is

A—light, dirty, and fast.
B—heavy, dirty, and fast.
C—heavy, clean, and slow.

3826. Wingtip vortices created by large aircraft tend to

A—sink below the aircraft generating turbulence.
B—rise into the traffic pattern.
C—rise into the takeoff or landing path of a crossing runway.

3827. When taking off or landing at an airport where heavy aircraft are operating, one should be particularly alert to the hazards of wingtip vortices because this turbulence tends to

A—rise from a crossing runway into the takeoff or landing path.
B—rise into the traffic pattern area surrounding the airport.
C—sink into the flightpath of aircraft operating below the aircraft generating the turbulence.

3828. The wind condition that requires maximum caution when avoiding wake turbulence on landing is a

A—light, quartering headwind.
B—light, quartering tailwind.
C—strong headwind.

3829. When landing behind a large aircraft, the pilot should avoid wake turbulence by staying

A—above the large aircraft's final approach path and landing beyond the large aircraft's touchdown point.
B—below the large aircraft's final approach path and landing before the large aircraft's touchdown point.
C—above the large aircraft's final approach path and landing before the large aircraft's touchdown point.

3830. When departing behind a heavy aircraft, the pilot should avoid wake turbulence by maneuvering the aircraft

A—below and downwind from the heavy aircraft.
B—above and upwind from the heavy aircraft.
C—below and upwind from the heavy aircraft.

3831. Pilots flying over a national wildlife refuge are requested to fly no lower than

A—1,000 feet AGL.
B—2,000 feet AGL.
C—3,000 feet AGL.

3832. Large accumulations of carbon monoxide in the human body result in

A—tightness across the forehead.
B—loss of muscular power.
C—an increased sense of well-being.

3833. What effect does haze have on the ability to see traffic or terrain features during flight?

A—Haze causes the eyes to focus at infinity.
B—The eyes tend to overwork in haze and do not detect relative movement easily.
C—All traffic or terrain features appear to be farther away than their actual distance.

3834. The most effective method of scanning for other aircraft for collision avoidance during daylight hours is to use

A—regularly spaced concentration on the 3-, 9-, and 12-o'clock positions.
B—a series of short, regularly spaced eye movements to search each 10-degree sector.
C—peripheral vision by scanning small sectors and utilizing offcenter viewing.

3835. Which technique should a pilot use to scan for traffic to the right and left during straight-and-level flight?

A—Systematically focus on different segments of the sky for short intervals.
B—Concentrate on relative movement detected in the peripheral vision area.
C—Continuous sweeping of the windshield from right to left.

3836. How can you determine if another aircraft is on a collision course with your aircraft?

A—The other aircraft will always appear to get larger and closer at a rapid rate.
B—The nose of each aircraft is pointed at the same point in space.
C—There will be no apparent relative motion between your aircraft and the other aircraft.

3837. An ATC clearance provides

A—priority over all other traffic.
B—adequate separation from all traffic.
C—authorization to proceed under specified traffic conditions in controlled airspace.

3838. (Refer to Figure 53.) When approaching Lincoln Municipal from the west at noon for the purpose of landing, initial communications should be with

A—Lincoln Approach Control on 124.0 MHz.
B—Minneapolis Center on 128.75 MHz.
C—Lincoln Tower on 118.5 MHz.

3839. (Refer to Figure 53.) Which type radar service is provided to VFR aircraft at Lincoln Municipal?

A—Sequencing to the primary Class C airport and standard separation.
B—Sequencing to the primary Class C airport and conflict resolution so that radar targets do not touch, or 1,000 feet vertical separation.
C—Sequencing to the primary Class C airport, traffic advisories, conflict resolution, and safety alerts.

3840. (Refer to Figure 53.) What is the recommended communications procedure for landing at Lincoln Municipal during the hours when the tower is not in operation?

A—Monitor airport traffic and announce your position and intentions on 118.5 MHz.
B—Contact UNICOM on 122.95 MHz for traffic advisories.
C—Monitor ATIS for airport conditions, then announce your position on 122.95 MHz.

3841. (Refer to Figure 53.) Where is Loup City Municipal located with relation to the city?

A—Northeast approximately 3 miles.
B—Northwest approximately 1 mile.
C—East approximately 10 miles.

3842. (Refer to Figure 53.) Traffic patterns in effect at Lincoln Municipal are

A—to the right on Runway 17L and Runway 35L; to the left on Runway 17R and Runway 35R.
B—to the left on Runway 17L and Runway 35L; to the right on Runway 17R and Runway 35R.
C—to the right on Runways 14 – 32.

3843. The letters VHF/DF appearing in the Airport/Facility Directory for a certain airport indicate that

A—this airport is designated as an airport of entry.
B—the Flight Service Station has equipment with which to determine your direction from the station.
C—this airport has a direct-line phone to the Flight Service Station.

3844. Which statement best defines hypoxia?

A—A state of oxygen deficiency in the body.
B—An abnormal increase in the volume of air breathed.
C—A condition of gas bubble formation around the joints or muscles.

3845. Rapid or extra deep breathing while using oxygen can cause a condition known as

A—hyperventilation.
B—aerosinusitis.
C—aerotitis.

3846. Which would most likely result in hyperventilation?

A—Emotional tension, anxiety, or fear.
B—The excessive consumption of alcohol.
C—An extremely slow rate of breathing and insufficient oxygen.

3847. A pilot should be able to overcome the symptoms or avoid future occurrences of hyperventilation by

A—closely monitoring the flight instruments to control the airplane.
B—slowing the breathing rate, breathing into a bag, or talking aloud.
C—increasing the breathing rate in order to increase lung ventilation.

3848. Susceptibility to carbon monoxide poisoning increases as

A—altitude increases.
B—altitude decreases.
C—air pressure increases.

3849. What preparation should a pilot make to adapt the eyes for night flying?

A—Wear sunglasses after sunset until ready for flight.
B—Avoid red lights at least 30 minutes before the flight.
C—Avoid bright white lights at least 30 minutes before the flight.

3850. The danger of spatial disorientation during flight in poor visual conditions may be reduced by

A—shifting the eyes quickly between the exterior visual field and the instrument panel.
B—having faith in the instruments rather than taking a chance on the sensory organs.
C—leaning the body in the opposite direction of the motion of the aircraft.

3851. A state of temporary confusion resulting from misleading information being sent to the brain by various sensory organs is defined as

A—spatial disorientation.
B—hyperventilation.
C—hypoxia.

3852. Pilots are more subject to spatial disorientation if

A—they ignore the sensations of muscles and inner ear.
B—body signals are used to interpret flight attitude.
C—eyes are moved often in the process of cross-checking the flight instruments.

3853. If a pilot experiences spatial disorientation during flight in a restricted visibility condition, the best way to overcome the effect is to

A—rely upon the aircraft instrument indications.
B—concentrate on yaw, pitch, and roll sensations.
C—consciously slow the breathing rate until symptoms clear and then resume normal breathing rate.

3854. FAA advisory circulars containing subject matter specifically related to Airmen are issued under which subject number?

A—60.
B—70.
C—90.

3855. FAA advisory circulars containing subject matter specifically related to Airspace are issued under which subject number?

A—60.
B—70.
C—90.

3856. FAA advisory circulars containing subject matter specifically related to Air Traffic Control and General Operations are issued under which subject number?

A—60.
B—70.
C—90.

3857. Which is an advantage of using a CG hook for a winch tow rather than the nose hook?

A—A greater percent of the line length can be used to reach altitude.
B—Maximum release altitude is limited.
C—It is the safest method of launching.

3858. To stop pitch oscillation (porpoising) during a winch launch, the pilot should

A—release back pressure and then pull back against the cycle of pitching oscillation to get in phase with the undulations.
B—signal the ground crew to increase the speed of the tow.
C—relax the back pressure on the control stick and shallow the angle of climb.

3859. A pilot plans to fly solo in the front seat of a two-place glider which displays the following placards on the instrument panel:

MINIMUM PILOT WEIGHT: 135 LB
MAXIMUM PILOT WEIGHT: 220 LB

NOTE: Seat ballast should be used as necessary.

The recommended towing speed for all tows is 55 – 65 knots. What action should be taken if the pilot's weight is 115 pounds?

A—Add 20 pounds of seat ballast to the rear seat.
B—Add 55 pounds of seat ballast to obtain the average pilot weight of 170 pounds.
C—Add 20 pounds of seat ballast.

3860. A pilot plans to fly solo in the front seat of a two-place glider which displays the following placards on the instrument panel:

MINIMUM PILOT WEIGHT: 135 LB
MAXIMUM PILOT WEIGHT: 220 LB

NOTE: Seat ballast should be used as necessary.

The recommended towing speed for all tows is 55 - 65 knots. What action should be taken if the pilot's weight is 125 pounds?

A—Add 10 pounds of seat ballast to the rear seat.
B—Add 10 pounds of seat ballast.
C—Add 45 pounds of seat ballast to obtain the average pilot weight of 170 pounds.

3861. (Refer to Figure 54.) Calculate the weight and balance of the glider, and determine if the CG is within limits.

Pilot (fwd seat) .... 160 lb
Passenger (aft seat) .... 185 lb

A—CG 71.65 inches aft of datum – out of limits forward.
B—CG 79.67 inches aft of datum – within limits.
C—CG 83.43 inches aft of datum – within limits.

3862. (Refer to Figure 54.) How is the CG affected if radio and oxygen equipment weighing 35 pounds is added at station 43.8? The glider weighs 945 pounds with a moment of 78,000.2 pound-inches prior to adding the equipment.

A—CG shifts forward 0.79 inch – out of limits forward.
B—CG shifts forward 1.38 inches – within limits.
C—CG shifts aft 1.38 inches – out of limits aft.

3863. (Refer to Figure 54.) What is the CG of the glider if the pilot and passenger each weigh 215 pounds?

A—74.69 inches aft of datum – out of limits forward.
B—81.08 inches aft of datum – within limits.
C—81.08 inches aft of datum – over maximum gross weight.

3864. (Refer to Figure 55.) How many feet will the glider sink in 1 statute mile at 53 MPH in still air?

A—144 feet.
B—171 feet.
C—211 feet.

3865. (Refer to Figure 55.) At what speed will the glider attain a sink rate of 5 feet per second in still air?

A—75 MPH.
B—79 MPH.
C—84 MPH.

3866. (Refer to Figure 55.) How many feet will the glider descend at minimum sink speed for 1 statute mile in still air?

A—132 feet.
B—170 feet.
C—180 feet.

3867. (Refer to Figure 55.) At what speed will the glider gain the most distance while descending 1,000 feet in still air?

A—44 MPH.
B—53 MPH.
C—83 MPH.

3868. (Refer to Figure 55.) What approximate lift/drag ratio will the glider attain at 68 MPH in still air?

A—10.5:1.
B—21.7:1.
C—28.5:1.

3869. (Refer to Figure 56.) Illustration 2 means

A—release towline.
B—ready to tow.
C—hold position.

3870. (Refer to Figure 56.) Illustration 3 means

A—stop operations.
B—release towline.
C—take up slack.

3871. (Refer to Figure 56.) Which illustration is a signal to stop operation?

A—2.
B—3.
C—7.

3872. (Refer to Figure 56.) Which illustration is a signal from the sailplane for the towplane to turn right?

A—5.
B—6.
C—11.

3873. (Refer to Figure 56.) Which illustration is a signal that the glider is unable to release?

A—8.
B—10.
C—11.

3874. (Refer to Figure 56.) Which illustration is a signal to the towplane to reduce airspeed?

A—7.
B—10.
C—12.

3875. (Refer to Figure 56.) Which illustration means the towplane cannot release?

A—6.
B—8.
C—9.

3876. What corrective action should the sailplane pilot take during takeoff if the towplane is still on the ground and the sailplane is airborne and drifting to the left?

A—Crab into the wind by holding upwind (right) rudder pressure.
B—Crab into the wind so as to maintain a position directly behind the towplane.
C—Establish a right wing low drift correction to remain in the flightpath of the towplane.

3877. An indication that the glider has begun a turn too soon on aerotow is that the

A—glider's nose is pulled to the outside of the turn.
B—towplane's nose is pulled to the outside of the turn.
C—towplane will pitch up.

3878. The sailplane has become airborne and the towplane loses power before leaving the ground. The sailplane should release immediately,

A—and maneuver to the right of the towplane.
B—extend the spoilers, and land straight ahead.
C—and maneuver to the left of the towplane.

3879. What should a glider pilot do if a towline breaks below 200 feet AGL?

A—Turn into the wind, then back to the runway for a downwind landing.
B—Turn away from the wind, then back to the runway for a downwind landing.
C—Land straight ahead or make slight turns to reach a suitable landing area.

3880. A pilot unintentionally enters a steep diving spiral to the left. What is the proper way to recover from this attitude without overstressing the glider?

A—Apply up-elevator pressure to raise the nose.
B—Apply more up-elevator pressure and then use right aileron pressure to control the overbanking tendency.
C—Relax the back pressure and shallow the bank; then apply up-elevator pressure until the nose has been raised to the desired position.

3881. What corrective action should be taken if, while thermalling at minimum sink speed in turbulent air, the left wing drops while turning to the left?

A—Apply more opposite (right) aileron pressure than opposite (right) rudder pressure to counteract the overbanking tendency.
B—Apply opposite (right) rudder pressure to slow the rate of turn.
C—Lower the nose before applying opposite (right) aileron pressure.

3882. A sailplane pilot can differentiate between a spin and a spiral dive because in a spiral dive,

A—the speed remains constant.
B—the G loads increase.
C—there is a small loss of altitude in each rotation.

3883. How are forward slips normally performed?

A—With the direction of the slip away from any crosswind that exists.
B—With dive brakes or spoilers fully open.
C—With rudder and aileron deflection on the same side.

3884. What would be a proper action or procedure to use if the pilot is getting too low on a cross-country flight in a sailplane?

A—Continue on course until descending to 1,000 feet above the ground and then plan the landing approach.
B—Fly directly into the wind and make a straight-in approach at the end of the glide.
C—Have a suitable landing area selected upon reaching 2,000 feet AGL, and a specific field chosen upon reaching 1,500 feet AGL.

3885. Why should propane tanks not be refueled in a closed trailer or truck?

A—Propane vapor is one and one-half times heavier than air and will linger in the floor of the truck or trailer.
B—The propane vapor is odorless and the refuelers may be overcome by the fumes.
C—Propane is very cold and could cause damage to the truck or trailer.

3886. Why should special precautions be taken when filling the propane bottles?

A—Propane is transferred from the storage tanks to the propane bottles under high pressure.
B—During transfer, propane reaches a high temperature and can cause severe burns.
C—Propane is super-cold and may cause severe freeze burns.

3887. What constitutes the payload of a balloon?

A—Total gross weight.
B—Total weight of passengers, cargo, and fuel.
C—Weight of the aircraft and equipment.

3888. (Refer to Figure 57.) The gross weight of the balloon is 1,350 pounds and the outside air temperature (OAT) is +51°F. The maximum height would be

A—5,000 feet.
B—8,000 feet.
C—10,000 feet.

3889. (Refer to Figure 57.) The gross weight of the balloon is 1,200 pounds and the maximum height the pilot needs to attain is 5,000 feet. The maximum temperature to achieve this performance is

A—+37°F.
B—+70°F.
C—+97°F.

3890. (Refer to Figure 58.) Determine the maximum payload for a balloon flying at 2,500 feet at an ambient temperature of 91°F.

A—420 pounds.
B—465 pounds.
C—505 pounds.

3891. (Refer to Figure 58.) What is the maximum altitude for the balloon if the gross weight is 1,100 pounds and standard temperature exists at all altitudes?

A—1,000 feet.
B—4,000 feet.
C—5,500 feet.

3892. (Refer to Figure 58.) What is the maximum altitude for the balloon if the gross weight is 1,000 pounds and standard temperature exists at all altitudes?

A—4,000 feet.
B—5,500 feet.
C—11,000 feet.

3893. (Refer to Figure 58.) Determine the maximum weight allowable for pilot and passenger for a flight at approximately 1,000 feet with a temperature of 68°F. Launch with 20 gallons of propane.

A—580 pounds.
B—620 pounds.
C—720 pounds.

3894. (Refer to Figure 58.) What is the maximum weight allowed for pilot and passengers for a flight at 5,000 feet with a standard temperature? Launch with 20 gallons of propane.

A—670 pounds.
B—760 pounds.
C—1,095 pounds.

3895. All fuel tanks should be fired during preflight to determine

A—the burner pressure and condition of the valves.
B—that the pilot light functions properly on each tank.
C—if there are any leaks in the tank.

3896. What is a recommended ascent upon initial launch?

A—Maximum ascent to altitude to avoid low-level thermals.
B—Shallow ascent to avoid flashbacks of flames as the envelope is cooled.
C—A moderate-rate ascent to determine wind directions at different levels.

3897. What is a potential hazard when climbing at maximum rate?

A—The envelope may collapse.
B—Deflation ports may be forced open.
C—The rapid flow of air may extinguish the burner and pilot light.

3898. How should a roundout from a moderate-rate ascent to level flight be made?

A—Reduce the amount of heat gradually as the balloon is approaching altitude.
B—Cool the envelope by venting and add heat just before arriving at altitude.
C—Vent at altitude and add heat upon settling back down to altitude.

3899. What is one procedure for relighting the burner while in flight?

A—Open the regulator or blast valve full open and light the pilot light.
B—Close the tank valves, vent the fuel lines, reopen the tank valves, and light the pilot light.
C—Open another tank valve, open the regulator or blast valve, and light the main jets with reduced flow.

3900. The windspeed is such that it is necessary to deflate the envelope as rapidly as possible during a landing. When should the deflation port (rip panel) be opened?

A—The instant the gondola contacts the surface.
B—As the balloon skips off the surface the first time and the last of the ballast has been discharged.
C—Just prior to ground contact.

3901. When landing a free balloon, what should the occupants do to minimize landing shock?

A— Be seated on the floor of the basket.
B— Stand with knees slightly bent, in the center of the gondola, facing the direction of movement.
C— Stand back-to-back and hold onto the load ring.

3902. Prior to a high-wind landing, the pilot in command should brief the passengers to prepare for the landing by

A— kneeling on the floor and facing aft.
B— crouching on the floor and jumping out of the basket upon contact with the ground.
C— crouching while hanging on in two places, and remaining in the basket until advised otherwise.

3903. Which precaution should be exercised if confronted with the necessity of having to land a balloon when the air is turbulent?

A— Land in any available lake close to the upwind shore.
B— Land in the center of the largest available field.
C— Land in the trees to absorb shock forces, thus cushioning the landing.

3904. What action is most appropriate when an envelope over-temperature condition occurs?

A— Throw all unnecessary equipment overboard.
B— Descend; hover in ground effect until the envelope cools.
C— Land as soon as practical.

3905. In addition to the required documents, what carry-on equipment should be accounted for during preflight?

A— Flotation gear.
B— Emergency locator transmitter.
C— Two means of burner ignition.

3906. How should a balloon fuel system be checked for leaks prior to flight?

A— Listen and smell.
B— Check all connections with a lighted match.
C— Cover all connections and tubing with soapy water.

3907. In a balloon, best fuel economy in level flight can be accomplished by

A— riding the haze line in a temperature inversion.
B— short blasts of heat at high frequency.
C— long blasts of heat at low frequency.

3908. The minimum size a launch site should be is at least

A— twice the height of the balloon.
B— 100 feet for every 1 knot of wind.
C— 500 feet on the downwind side.

3909. What is a hazard of rapid descents?

A— Wind shear can cavitate one side of the envelope, forcing air out of the mouth.
B— The pilot light cannot remain lit with the turbulent air over the basket.
C— Aerodynamic forces may collapse the envelope.

3910. It may be possible to make changes in the direction of flight in a hot air balloon by

A— flying a constant atmospheric pressure gradient.
B— operating at different flight altitudes.
C— operating above the friction level, if there is no gradient wind.

3911. What action should be taken if a balloon encounters unforecast weather and shifts direction abruptly while in the vicinity of a thunderstorm?

A— Land immediately.
B— Descend to and maintain the lowest altitude possible.
C— Ascend to an altitude which will ensure adequate obstacle clearance in all directions.

3912. To land an airship that is 250 pounds heavy when the wind is calm, the best landing can usually be made if the airship is

A— in trim.
B— nose heavy approximately 20°.
C— tail heavy approximately 20°.

3913. Which takeoff procedure is considered to be most hazardous for an airship?

A— Maintaining only 50 percent of the maximum permissible positive angle of inclination.
B— Failing to apply full engine power properly on all takeoffs, regardless of wind.
C— Maintaining a negative angle of inclination during takeoff after elevator response is adequate for controllability.

3914. Which action is necessary in order to perform a normal descent in an airship?

A— Valve gas.
B— Valve air.
C— Take air into the aft ballonets.

3915. If an airship should experience failure of both engines during flight and neither engine can be restarted, what initial immediate action must the pilot take?

A— The airship must be driven down to a landing before control and envelope shape are lost.
B— The emergency auxiliary power unit must be started for electrical power to the airscoop blowers so that ballonet inflation can be maintained.
C— Immediate preparations to operate the airship as a free balloon are necessary.

Answers, References & Explanations

ALL
3001 [B] — (A01) — FAR §1.1
With respect to the certification of airmen, "category" means a broad classification of aircraft such as airplane, rotorcraft, glider, and lighter-than-air.

ALL
3002 [B] — (A01) — FAR §1.1
With respect to the certification of airmen, a "class" refers to aircraft with similar operating characteristics such as single-engine land/sea and multi-engine land/sea, gyroplane, helicopter, airship, and free balloon.

ALL
3003 [A] — (A01) — FAR §1.1
With respect to the certification of aircraft, "a category of aircraft" means a grouping of aircraft based upon intended use or operating limitations. Examples include normal, utility, acrobatic, transport, limited, restricted, and provisional.

ALL
3004 [A] — (A01) — FAR §1.1
With respect to the certification of aircraft, "class" is a broad grouping of aircraft having similar means of propulsion, flight, or landing. Examples include airplane, helicopter, glider, balloon, landplane, and seaplane.

ALL
3005 [C] — (A01) — FAR §1.1
Night is the time between the end of evening civil twilight and the beginning of morning civil twilight converted to local time, as published in the American Air Almanac.

ALL
3006 [A] — (A02) — FAR §1.2
V_A is design maneuvering speed.

AIR, GLI
3007 [A] — (A02) — FAR §1.2
V_{FE} is the highest calibrated airspeed permissible with the wing flaps in a prescribed extended position.

AIR, GLI
3008 [A] — (A02) — FAR §1.2
V_{LE} is the maximum calibrated airspeed at which the airplane can be safely flown with the landing gear extended.

AIR, GLI
3009 [C] — (A02) — FAR §1.2
V_{NO} is the maximum calibrated airspeed for normal operation, or the maximum structural cruising speed.

AIR, GLI
3010 [A] — (A02) — FAR §1.2
V_{SO} is the calibrated power-off stalling speed or the minimum steady-flight speed at which the aircraft is controllable in the landing configuration.

AIR
3011 [C] — (A02) — FAR §1.2
V_X (best angle) is the calibrated airspeed at which the aircraft will attain the highest altitude in a given horizontal distance.

AIR
3012 [A] — (A02) — FAR §1.2
V_Y (best rate) is the calibrated airspeed at which the airplane will obtain the maximum increase in altitude per unit of time (feet per minute) after takeoff.

ALL
3013 [C] — (A15) — FAR §91.417(a)
Each registered owner or operator shall keep records of preventative maintenance. The records must include:

1. A description of the work performed;
2. The date of completion of the work performed; and
3. The signature and certificate number of the person approving the aircraft for return to service (could be pilot certificate number for Part 43 when you are doing your own preventative maintenance).

ALL
3014 [A] — (A16) — FAR Part 43
Preventative maintenance items which can be performed by the pilot are listed in Part 43 and include such basic items as oil changes, wheel bearing lubrication, and hydraulic fluid (brakes, landing gear system) refills.

ALL
3015 [B] — (A16) — FAR Part 43
Preventative maintenance items which can be performed by the pilot are listed in Part 43 and include such basic items as oil changes, wheel bearing lubrication, and hydraulic fluid (brakes, landing gear system) refills.

ALL
3016 [C] — (A20) — FAR §61.3(a), (c)
No person may act as pilot-in-command (PIC), or in any other capacity as a required pilot flight crewmember, of a civil aircraft of United States registry unless he/she has in possession a current pilot certificate. Except for free balloon pilots piloting balloons and glider pilots piloting gliders, no person may act as pilot-in-command or in any other capacity as a required pilot flight crewmember of an aircraft unless he/she has in possession an appropriate current medical certificate.

ALL
3017 [C] — (A20) — FAR §61.3(a)
No person may act as pilot-in-command (PIC), or in any other capacity as a required pilot flight crewmember, of a civil aircraft of United States registry unless he/she has in possession a current pilot certificate.

ALL
3018 [B] — (A20) — FAR §61.3(a), (c)
No person may act as pilot-in-command (PIC), or in any other capacity as a required pilot flight crewmember, of a civil aircraft of United States registry unless he/she has in possession a current pilot certificate. Except for free balloon pilots piloting balloons and glider pilots piloting gliders, no person may act as pilot-in-command or in any other capacity as a required pilot flight crewmember of an aircraft unless he/she has in possession an appropriate current medical certificate.

ALL
3019 [C] — (A20) — FAR §61.3(h)
Each person who holds a pilot or medical certificate shall present it for inspection upon the request of the FAA Administrator, an NTSB representative, or any Federal, State, or local law enforcement officer.

AIR, RTC, REC, LTA
3020 [B] — (A20) — FAR §61.23(c)
A Third-Class Medical Certificate expires at the end of the **last day** of the 24th month after the month of the date of examination shown on the certificate, for operations requiring a Private or Student Pilot Certificate.

AIR, RTC, REC, LTA
3021 [C] — (A20) — FAR §61.23(c)
A Third-Class Medical Certificate expires at the end of the **last day** of the 24th month after the month of the date of examination shown on the certificate, for operations requiring a Private or Student Pilot Certificate.

AIR, RTC, REC, LTA
3022 [C] — (A20) — FAR §61.23(b)(2)
A Second-Class Medical Certificate expires at the end of the **last day** of the 24th month after the month of the date of examination shown on the certificate, for operations requiring a Private or Student Pilot Certificate.

AIR, RTC, REC, LTA
3023 [C] — (A20) — FAR §61.23(a)(3)
A First-Class Medical Certificate expires at the end of the **last day** of the 24th month after the month of the date of examination shown on the certificate, for operations requiring a Private or Student Pilot Certificate.

AIR, RTC
3024 [B] — (A20) — FAR §61.31(a)(1)
A type rating is required in order for a pilot to act as pilot-in-command of a large aircraft (except lighter-than-air) which is further defined as more than 12,500 pounds maximum certificated takeoff weight or a turbojet-powered aircraft.

AIR
3025 [B] — (A20) — FAR §61.31
A high-performance airplane is one with more than 200 horsepower, or that has a retractable landing gear, flaps, and a controllable propeller.

AIR
3026 [C] — (A20) — FAR §61.31
No person holding a Private or Commercial pilot certificate may pilot a high-performance aircraft unless he/she has received instruction and has been certified competent in his/her logbook.

AIR
3027 [B] — (A20) — FAR §61.31
A high-performance airplane is one with more than 200 horsepower, or that has a retractable landing gear, flaps, and a controllable propeller. No person holding a Private or Commercial pilot certificate may pilot a high-performance aircraft unless he/she has received instruction and has been certified competent in his/her logbook.

ALL
3028 [C] — (A20) — FAR §61.56(c)(1)
Each pilot must complete a flight review every 24 calendar months.

ALL
3029 [C] — (A20) — FAR §61.57(d)
No person may act as pilot-in-command of an aircraft carrying passengers during the period beginning one hour after sunset and ending one hour before sunrise (as published in the American Air Almanac) unless, within the preceding 90 days, he/she has made at least three takeoffs and three landings to a full stop during that period in the category and class of aircraft to be used. 1830 + 59 minutes = 1929

ALL
3030 [A] — (A20) — FAR §61.57(c)
No person may act as pilot-in-command of an aircraft carrying passengers, unless, within the preceding 90 days, he/she has made three takeoffs and three landings as the sole manipulator of the flight controls in an aircraft of the same category and class and, if a type rating is required, of the same type. If the aircraft is a tailwheel airplane, the landings must have been made to a full stop.

ALL
3031 [C] — (A20) — FAR §61.57(c)
No person may act as pilot-in-command of an aircraft carrying passengers, unless, within the preceding 90 days, he/she has made three takeoffs and three landings as the sole manipulator of the flight controls in an aircraft of the same category and class and, if a type rating is required, of the same type. If the aircraft is a tailwheel airplane, the landings must have been made to a full stop.

AIR
3032 [C] — (A20) — FAR §61.57(c)
No person may act as pilot-in-command of an aircraft carrying passengers, unless, within the preceding 90 days, he/she has made three takeoffs and three landings as the sole manipulator of the flight controls in an aircraft of the same category and class and, if a type rating is required, of the same type. If the aircraft is a tailwheel airplane, the landings must have been made to a full stop.

AIR, RTC
3033 [B] — (A20) — FAR §61.57(d)
No person may act as pilot-in-command of an aircraft carrying passengers during the period beginning one hour after sunset and ending one hour before sunrise (as published in the American Air Almanac) unless, within the preceding 90 days, he/she has made at least three takeoffs and three landings to a full stop during that period in the category and class of aircraft to be used.

ALL
3034 [A] — (A20) — FAR §61.57(d)
No person may act as pilot-in-command of an aircraft carrying passengers during the period beginning one hour after sunset and ending one hour before sunrise (as published in the American Air Almanac) unless, within the preceding 90 days, he/she has made at least three takeoffs and three landings to a full stop during that period in the category and class of aircraft to be used.

ALL
3035 [A] — (A20) — FAR §61.60
The holder of a Pilot or Flight Instructor Certificate who has made a change in his/her permanent mailing address may not, after 30 days from the date moved, exercise the privileges of his/her certificate unless he/she has notified in writing the Department of Transportation, Federal Aviation Administration, Airman Certification Branch, Box 25082, Oklahoma City, OK 73125, of the new address.

AIR, GLI
3036 [B] — (A21) — FAR §61.69(d)
With a Private pilot certificate, no person may act as PIC of an aircraft towing a glider unless he/she has had, and entered in his/her logbook, at least:

1. 100 hours of pilot flight time in powered aircraft, or
2. 200 hours of pilot flight time in powered or other aircraft.

AIR, GLI
3037 [C] — (A21) — FAR §61.69(e)
No person may act a pilot-in-command of an aircraft towing a glider unless within the preceding 12 months he/she has—

1. Made at least three actual or simulated glider tows while accompanied by a qualified pilot who meets the requirements of this FAR § 61.69, or
2. Made at least three flights as pilot-in-command of a glider towed by an aircraft.

REC
3038 [B] — (A29) — FAR §61.3(a)(c) and FAR §61.101(a)(3)(iii), (d)
All pilots are required to carry their current and appropriate pilot and medical certificates.

REC
3039 [B] — (A29) — FAR §61.23(c)
A Third-Class Medical Certificate expires at the end of the 24th month after the month of the date of the examination shown on the certificate, for operations requiring a Private, Recreational, or Student Pilot Certificate. A calendar month always ends on the last day of the month. A Third-Class Medical Certificate issued to a recreational pilot on August 10 will expire on August 31, two years later.

REC
3040 [C] — (A29) — FAR §61.56
Each pilot must have completed a biennial flight review since the beginning of the 24th calendar month before the month in which that pilot acts as pilot-in-command. A calendar month always ends at midnight of the last day of the month. If a recreational pilot had a flight review on August 8, the next flight review would be due on August 31, two years later.

REC
3041 [A] — (A29) — FAR §61.56(d)
Each pilot must have completed a biennial flight review since the beginning of the 24th calendar month before the month in which that pilot acts as pilot-in-command.

REC
3042 [C] — (A29) — FAR §61.56(d)
Each pilot must have completed a biennial flight review since the beginning of the 24th calendar month before the month in which that pilot acts as pilot-in-command. A calendar month always ends at midnight of the last day of the month. If a recreational pilot had a flight review on August 8, the next flight review would be due on August 31, two years later.

REC
3043 [A] — (A29) — FAR §61.101(a)(1)
A recreational pilot may not carry more than one passenger.

REC
3044 [B] — (A29) — FAR §61.101(a)(2)
A recreational pilot may share the operating expenses of the flight with the passenger.

REC
3045 [B] — (A29) — FAR §61.101(a)(2)
A recreational pilot may share the operating expenses of the flight with the passenger.

REC
3046 [B] — (A29) — FAR §101(a)(3)(i)
A recreational pilot may act as pilot-in-command of an aircraft only when the flight is within 50 NM of an airport at which the pilot has received ground and flight instruction from an authorized instructor.

REC
3047 [C] — (A29) — FAR §61.101(b)(i)
A recreational pilot may not act as pilot-in-command of an aircraft that is certificated for more than four occupants.

REC
3048 [B] — (A29) — FAR §61.101(b)(iii)
A recreational pilot may not act as pilot-in-command of an aircraft that is certificated with a powerplant of more than 180 horsepower.

REC
3049 [C] — (A29) — FAR §61.101(b)(3)(4)(5)
A recreational pilot may not act as pilot-in-command of an aircraft that is carrying a passenger or property for compensation or hire, in furtherance of a business, or for a charitable organization.

REC
3050 [C] — (A29) — FAR §61.101(b)(5)
A recreational pilot may not act as pilot-in-command of an aircraft in furtherance of a business.

REC
3051 [B] — (A29) — FAR §61.101(b)(6)
A recreational pilot may not act as pilot-in-command of an aircraft between sunset and sunrise. The earliest a recreational pilot may takeoff is at sunrise.

REC
3052 [A] — (A29) — FAR §61.101(b)(6)
A recreational pilot may not act as pilot-in-command of an aircraft between sunset and sunrise. A recreational pilot must land by sunset.

REC
3053 [C] — (A29) — FAR §61.101(f)(2)
A recreational pilot may not operate in airspace where air traffic control is required, unless under the supervision of an authorized instructor in airspace with air traffic control for the purpose of obtaining an additional certificate or rating.

REC
3054 [C] — (A29) — FAR §61.101(b)(7)(9)
A recreational pilot may not act as pilot-in-command of an aircraft in airspace in which communication with ATC is required. If the tower is closed, no communication is required and it reverts to Class E airspace. The visibility and cloud clearances for Class E airspace require a ceiling at least 1,000 feet and the visibility at least 3 miles.

REC
3055 [A] — (A29) — FAR 61.101(b)(8)
A recreational pilot may not act as pilot-in-command of an aircraft at an altitude of more than 10,000 feet MSL or 2,000 feet AGL, whichever is higher.

REC
3056 [B] — (A29) — FAR §61.101(b)(9)
A recreational pilot may not act as pilot-in-command of an aircraft when the flight or surface visibility is less than 3 statute miles.

REC
3057 [B] — (A29) — FAR §61.101(b)(9)
A recreational pilot may not act as pilot-in-command of an aircraft when the flight or surface visibility is less than 3 statute miles.

REC
3058 [C] — (A29) — FAR §61.101(b)(12)
A recreational pilot may not act as pilot-in-command of an aircraft to demonstrate that aircraft in flight to a prospective buyer.

REC
3059 [C] — (A29) — FAR §61.101(b)(14)
A recreational pilot may not act as pilot-in-command of an aircraft that is towing any object.

REC
3060 [C] — (A29) — FAR §61.101(d)
A recreational pilot who has logged fewer than 400 flight hours and who has not logged pilot-in-command time in an aircraft within the preceding 180 days may not act as pilot-in-command of an aircraft until flight instruction is received from an authorized flight instructor who certifies in the pilot's logbook that the pilot is competent to act as pilot-in-command of the aircraft. This requirement can be met in combination with the requirements of flight reviews, at the discretion of the instructor.

REC
3061 [C] — (A29) — FAR §61.101(f)(3)
For the purpose of obtaining additional certificates or ratings, while under the supervision of an authorized flight instructor, a recreational pilot may fly as sole occupant of an aircraft between sunset and sunrise, provided the flight or surface visibility is at least 5 statute miles.

GLI
3062 [C] — (A23) — FAR §61.3, FAR §61.103(c)
If a glider pilot does not hold a current Third-Class Medical Certificate, he/she must certify (on the application for certification) that he/she has no known medical defect that makes him/her unable to pilot a glider.

LTA
3063 [C] — (A23) — FAR §61.103(c)
If a balloon pilot does not hold a current Third-Class Medical Certificate, he/she must certify that he/she has no known medical defect that makes him/her unable to pilot a balloon.

ALL
3064 [B] — (A23) — FAR §61.118(b)
A private pilot may share the operating expenses of a flight with passengers.

ALL
3065 [B] — (A23) — FAR §61.118(b)
A private pilot may share the operating expenses of a flight with passengers.

AIR, RTC
3066 [B] — (A23) — FAR §61.118(d)
A private pilot may act as pilot-in-command of an aircraft used in a passenger-carrying airlift sponsored by a charitable organization, and for which the passengers make a donation to the organization. This can be done if the sponsor of the airlift notifies the FAA General Aviation District Office having jurisdiction over the area concerned, at least 7 days before the flight, and furnishes any essential information that the office requests.

ALL
3067 [A] — (A60) — FAR §71.5(b)(1)
Federal airways are part of Class B, C, D, or E airspace. They are eight miles wide, four miles either side of centerline. They usually begin at 1,200 AGL and continue up to but not including 18,000 feet MSL, or FL180.

ALL
3068 [B] — (A60) — FAR §71.5(c)(1)
Federal airways are part of Class B, C, D, or E airspace. They are eight miles wide, four miles either side of centerline. They usually begin at 1,200 AGL and continue up to but not including 18,000 feet MSL, or FL180.

ALL
3069 [B] — (A60) — FAR §91.155(a),(c)
Except as provided in FAR §91.157, no person may operate an aircraft, under VFR, within the lateral boundaries of the surface areas of Class B, Class C, Class D, or Class E airspace designated for an airport when the ceiling is less than 1,000 feet. The flight visibility and cloud clearance for VFR operations in Class D airspace is 3 statute miles visibility, and 500 feet below, 1,000 feet above, 2,000 feet horizontal from all clouds.

ALL
3070 [B] — (B07) — FAR §91.3(a)
The pilot-in-command of an aircraft is directly responsible for, and is the final authority as to the operation of that aircraft.

LTA
3071 [B] — (B07) — FAR §91.3(a)
The pilot-in-command is responsible for briefing crewmembers and occupants in all areas of the flight, including inflation, tether, in-flight, landing, emergency, and recovery procedures.

ALL
3072 [B] — (B07) — FAR §91.3(b)
In an emergency requires immediate action, the pilot-in-command may deviate from the operating rules of Part 91 to the extent necessary to meet that emergency. No report of such deviation is required unless the FAA requests one.

ALL
3073 [C] — (B07) — FAR §91.3(c)
Each pilot-in-command who deviates from a rule in an emergency shall, **upon request**, send a written report of that deviation to the Administrator.

ALL
3074 [B] — (B07) — FAR §91.7(b)
The pilot-in-command of an aircraft is responsible for determining whether that aircraft is in condition for safe flight. The pilot shall discontinue the flight when unairworthy mechanical, electrical or structural conditions occur.

ALL
3075 [B] — (B07) — FAR §91.9(a)
No person may operate a civil aircraft without complying with the limitations found in the approved flight manual, markings, and placards.

ALL
3076 [B] — (B07) — FAR §91.15
No pilot-in-command of a civil aircraft may allow any object to be dropped from an aircraft in flight that creates a hazard to persons or property. However, this does not prohibit the dropping of any object if reasonable precautions are taken to avoid injury or damage to persons or property.

ALL
3077 [A] — (B07) — FAR §91.17(a)(1)
No person may act or attempt to act as a crewmember of a civil aircraft within 8 hours after the consumption of any alcoholic beverage. Remember "8 hours bottle to throttle."

ALL
3078 [A] — (B07) — FAR §91.17(b)
Except in an emergency, or a medical patient under proper care, no pilot of a civil aircraft may allow a person who appears to be intoxicated, or who demonstrates by manner or physical indications that the individual is under the influence of drugs, to be carried in that aircraft.

ALL
3079 [C] — (B07) — FAR §91.17(a)(4)
No persons may act, or attempt to act, as a crewmember of a civil aircraft while having .04 percent or more, by weight, alcohol in the blood.

ALL
3080 [B] — (B07) — FAR §91.103
Each pilot-in-command shall, before each flight, become familiar with all available information concerning that flight. This information must include:

(a) For a flight under IFR or a flight not in the vicinity of an airport, weather reports and forecasts, fuel requirements, alternatives available if the planned flight cannot be completed, and any known traffic delays of which the pilot has been advised by ATC;

(b) For any flight, runway lengths of airports of intended use, and the following takeoff and landing distance information:

1. For civil aircraft for which an approved airplane or rotorcraft flight manual containing takeoff and landing distance data is required, the takeoff and landing distance data contained therein; and

2. For civil aircraft other than those specified in paragraph (b)(1) of this section, other reliable information appropriate to the aircraft, relating to aircraft performance under expected values of airport elevation and runway slope, aircraft gross weight, and wind and temperature.

ALL
3081 [C] — (B07) — FAR §91.103(a)
Each pilot-in-command shall, before each flight, become familiar with all available information concerning that flight. This information must include:

(a) For a flight under IFR or a flight not in the vicinity of an airport, weather reports and forecasts, fuel requirements, alternatives available if the planned flight cannot be completed, and any known traffic delays of which the pilot has been advised by ATC;

(b) For any flight, runway lengths of airports of intended use, and the following takeoff and landing distance information:

1. For civil aircraft for which an approved airplane or rotorcraft flight manual containing takeoff and landing distance data is required, the takeoff and landing distance data contained therein; and

2. For civil aircraft other than those specified in paragraph (b)(1) of this section, other reliable information appropriate to the aircraft, relating to aircraft performance under expected values of airport elevation and runway slope, aircraft gross weight, and wind and temperature.

ALL
3082 [C] — (B07) — FAR §91.103(b)
Each pilot-in-command shall, before each flight, become familiar with all available information concerning that flight. This information must include:

(a) For a flight under IFR or a flight not in the vicinity of an airport, weather reports and forecasts, fuel requirements, alternatives available if the planned flight cannot be completed, and any known traffic delays of which the pilot has been advised by ATC;

(b) For any flight, runway lengths of airports of intended use, and the following takeoff and landing distance information:

1. For civil aircraft for which an approved airplane or rotorcraft flight manual containing takeoff and landing distance data is required, the takeoff and landing distance data contained therein; and

2. For civil aircraft other than those specified in paragraph (b)(1) of this section, other reliable information appropriate to the aircraft, relating to aircraft performance under expected values of airport elevation and runway slope, aircraft gross weight, and wind and temperature.

ALL
3083 [A] — (B07) — FAR §91.105
During takeoff and landing, and while en route, each required flight crewmember shall keep his/her seatbelt fastened while at the station. During takeoff and landing this includes shoulder harness (if installed) unless it interferes with required duties.

ALL
3084 [C] — (B07) — FAR §91.105
During takeoff and landing, and while en route, each required flight crewmember shall keep his/her seatbelt fastened while at his/her station. During takeoff and landing this includes shoulder harness (if installed) unless it interferes with required duties.

AIR, GLI, RTC, REC
3085 [B] — (B07) — FAR §91.107(a)
Unless otherwise authorized by the Administrator, no pilot may takeoff in a civil aircraft unless the pilot-in-command of that aircraft ensures that each person on board is briefed on how to fasten and unfasten that person's seatbelt, and that each person has been notified to fasten the seatbelt during taxi, takeoff and landing.

AIR, GLI, RTC, REC
3086 [A] — (B07) — FAR §91.107(b)
During taxi, takeoff and landing, each person on board the aircraft must occupy a seat or berth with a seatbelt and shoulder harness, properly secured if installed.

AIR, GLI, RTC, REC
3087 [B] — (B07) — FAR §91.107(b)
During taxi, takeoff and landing, each person on board the aircraft must occupy a seat or berth with a safety belt and shoulder harness, properly secured if installed. However, a person who has not reached his/her second birthday may be held by an adult who is occupying a seat or a berth, and a person on board for the purpose of engaging in sport parachuting may use the floor of the aircraft as a seat.

ALL
3088 [C] — (B08) — FAR §91.111
No person may operate an aircraft in formation flight except by arrangement with the pilot-in-command of each aircraft in the formation. The only restriction to formation flight is when carrying passengers for hire.

ALL
3089 [B] — (B08) — FAR §91.113(c)
An aircraft in distress has the right-of-way over all other air traffic.

ALL
3090 [B] — (B08) — FAR §91.113(d)
When two aircraft of the same "right-of-way" category converge at approximately the same altitude, the aircraft to the other's right has the right-of-way.

ALL
3091 [A] — (B08) — FAR §91.113(d)(2)
A glider has the right-of-way over an airship, airplane, rotorcraft, or an aircraft refueling another.

ALL
3092 [A] — (B08) — FAR §91.113(d)(3)
An airship has the right-of-way over an airplane or rotorcraft.

ALL
3093 [B] — (B08) — FAR §91.113(d)(3)
An aircraft towing or refueling other aircraft has the right-of-way over all other engine driven aircraft.

AIR, GLI, REC
3094 [C] — (B08) — FAR §91.113(e)
When two aircraft are approaching each other from head-on, or nearly so, each pilot must alter course to the right. This rule does not give right-of-way by categories.

ALL
3095 [C] — (B08) — FAR §91.113(f)
When two aircraft are approaching an airport for landing, the lower aircraft has the right-of-way. A pilot shall not take advantage of that rule to overtake or cut in front of another aircraft.

AIR
3096 [B] — (B08) — FAR §91.115(b)
For water operation, when aircraft, or an aircraft and a vessel, are on crossing courses, the aircraft or vessel to the other's right has the right-of-way.

AIR, RTC
3097 [B] — (B08) — FAR §91.117(a)
Maximum speed below 10,000 feet MSL is 250 knots.

AIR, RTC
3098 [A] — (B08) — FAR §91.117(b)
Unless otherwise authorized or required by ATC, no person may operate an aircraft at or below 2,500 feet AGL within 4 NM of the primary airport of a Class C or Class D airspace area at an indicated airspeed of more than 200 knots.

AIR, RTC
3099 [A] — (B08) — FAR §91.117(b)
No person may operate an aircraft in the airspace underlying Class B airspace at a speed of more than 200 knots.

AIR, RTC
3100 [B] — (B08) — FAR §91.117(b)
Maximum speed in a VFR corridor through Class B airspace is 200 KIAS.

ALL
3101 [A] — (B08) — FAR §91.119(a)(b)(c)
Except when necessary for takeoff or landing, no person may operate an aircraft anywhere below an altitude allowing, if a power unit fails, an emergency landing without undue hazard to persons or property on the surface.

AIR, GLI, LTA, REC
3102 [C] — (B08) — FAR §91.119(a)(b)(c)
Except when necessary for takeoff or landing, no person may operate an aircraft over any congested area of a city, town, or settlement, or over any open air assembly of persons, below an altitude of 1,000 feet above the highest obstacle within a horizontal radius of 2,000 feet of the aircraft.

AIR, GLI, LTA, REC
3103 [B] — (B08) — FAR §91.119(a)(b)(c)
Except when necessary for takeoff or landing, no person may operate an aircraft over other than congested areas below an altitude of 500 feet above the surface except over open water or sparsely populated areas. In that case, the aircraft may not be operated closer than 500 feet to any person, vessel, vehicle, or structure.

AIR, GLI, LTA, REC
3104 [A] — (B08) — FAR §91.119(a)(b)(c)
Except when necessary for takeoff or landing, no person may operate an aircraft closer than 500 feet to any person, vessel, vehicle, or structure.

ALL
3105 [B] — (B08) — FAR §91.121(a)(1)(iii)
The altimeter should be set to the elevation of the departure airport for airplanes, and the departure area for other aircraft.

ALL
3106 [A] — (B08) — FAR §91.121(a)(1)
The altimeter should be set to the elevation of the departure airport for airplanes, and the departure area for other aircraft.

ALL
3107 [B] — (B08) — FAR §91.121(2)
The altimeter should be set to 29.92" Hg at 18,000 feet MSL and above.

ALL
3108 [B] — (B08) — FAR §91.123
Except in an emergency, no person may operate an aircraft contrary to an ATC clearance or instruction.

ALL
3109 [A] — (B08) — FAR §91.123(d)
Each pilot-in-command who deviated from an ATC clearance during an emergency must submit a detailed report when requested by ATC.

ALL
3110 [B] — (B08) — FAR §91.123
Each pilot-in-command who (though not deviating from a rule of FAR Part 91) is given priority by ATC in an emergency shall, if requested by ATC, submit a detailed report of that emergency within 48 hours to the chief of that ATC facility.

ALL
3111 [A] — (B08) — FAR §91.125
A steady green light signal directed to an aircraft in flight means that the pilot is cleared to land.

AIR, RTC
3112 [A] — (B08) — FAR §91.125
A flashing green light signal clears a pilot to taxi.

AIR, RTC
3113 [B] — (B08) — FAR §91.125
A steady red signal directed to an aircraft in flight indicates the pilot should give way to other aircraft and continue circling.

AIR, RTC
3114 [C] — (B08) — FAR §91.125
A flashing white light signal to a taxiing aircraft is an indication to return to the starting point on the airport.

ALL
3115 [B] — (B08) — FAR §91.125
An alternating red and green light signal means to exercise extreme caution.

AIR, RTC
3116 [B] — (B08) — FAR §91.125
An alternating red and green light means to exercise extreme caution. A flashing red light means the airport is unsafe, do not land.

ALL
3117 [C] — (B08) — FAR §1.1
A blue segmented circle on a sectional chart depicts Class D airspace which means a control tower is in operation.

ALL
3118 [B] — (B08) — FAR §1.1
Class D airspace means a control tower is in operation. If the tower closes, it reverts to Class E airspace.

ALL
3119 [A] — (B08) — FAR §91.126, FAR §91.127, and FAR §91.129(b)
No person may operate an aircraft to, from, or on an airport having a control tower operated by the United States unless two-way radio communications are maintained between that aircraft and the control tower.

AIR, RTC
3120 [B] — (B08) — FAR §91.129(d)(3)
An airplane approaching to land on a runway served by a visual approach indicator, shall maintain an altitude at or above the glide slope until a lower altitude is necessary for a safe landing.

AIR, RTC
3121 [B] — (B08) — FAR §91.129(d)(3)
An airplane approaching to land on a runway served by a visual approach indicator, shall maintain an altitude at or above the glide slope until a lower altitude is necessary for a safe landing.

RTC
3122 [B] — (B08) — FAR §91.129(e)(2) and FAR §91.127(a)(2)
Helicopters must avoid the flow of fixed-wing aircraft.

ALL
3123 [C] — (B08) — FAR §91.127
In the case of an aircraft departing an airport without an operating control tower, comply with any FAA traffic pattern for that airport.

ALL
3124 [A] — (B08) — FAR §91.130
Two-way radio communication must be established with the ATC facility having jurisdiction over the Class C airspace prior to entry and thereafter as instructed by ATC.

ALL
3125 [C] — (B08) — FAR §91.130(c)(d)(f) and FAR §91.215(b)(4)
Class C requires two-way radio communications equipment, a transponder, and an encoding altimeter.

ALL
3126 [B] — (B08) — FAR §91.131(b)(1)(2)
It is generally true that no person may operate a civil aircraft within Class B airspace unless the pilot-in-command holds at least a Private Pilot Certificate or is a student pilot that has the proper logbook endorsements. However, there are certain Class B airports which never permit students, even if they have the proper endorsements.

ALL
3127 [A] — (B08) — FAR §61.95 and FAR §91.131(b)(1),(2)
It is generally true that no person may operate a civil aircraft within Class B airspace unless the pilot-in-command holds at least a Private Pilot Certificate or a student pilot has the proper logbook endorsements. However, there are some Class B airports which never permit students, even if they have the proper endorsements.

ALL
3128 [B] — (B08) — FAR §91.131(c)(d)
Unless otherwise authorized by ATC, no person may operate an aircraft within Class B airspace unless that aircraft is equipped with an operable two-way radio capable of communications with ATC, a transponder with applicable altitude reporting equipment, and an encoding altimeter.

ALL
3129 [A] — (B08) — FAR §91.131(a), FAR §91.215
Encoding transponders are required within all Class B Airspace and within 30 miles of the primary airport even if you are below a Class B airspace layer.

AIR, GLI
3130 [A] — (B08) — FAR §91.135(a)(1)
No person may operate an aircraft within Class A airspace unless that aircraft is operated under IFR at a specific flight level assigned by ATC.

AIR, REC
3131 [B] — (B09) — FAR §91.151(a)(1)
No person may begin a flight in an airplane under VFR unless (considering wind and forecast weather conditions) there is enough fuel to fly to the first point of intended landing and, assuming normal cruising speed, and day operations, to fly after that for at least 30 minutes.

AIR
3132 [C] — (B09) — FAR §91.151(a)(2)
No person may begin a flight in an airplane under VFR unless (considering wind and forecast weather conditions) there is enough fuel to fly to the first point of intended landing and, assuming normal cruising speed, and night operations, to fly after that for at least 45 minutes.

RTC
3133 [A] — (B09) — FAR §91.151(b)
No person may begin a flight in a rotorcraft under VFR unless (considering wind and forecast weather conditions) there is enough fuel to fly to the first point of intended landing and, assuming normal cruising speed, to fly after that for at least 20 minutes.

REC
3134 [B] — (B09) — FAR §61.101(b)(9)
Minimum flight or surface visibility for recreational pilots is 3 miles and minimum cloud clearance for all pilots in Class G airspace, below 1,200 AGL, is clear of clouds.

REC
3135 [B] — (B09) — FAR §61.101(b)(9)
Minimum flight or surface visibility for recreational pilots is 3 miles.

ALL
3136 [C] — (B09) — FAR §91.155
Minimum horizontal distance from clouds within Class C, D, or E airspace below 10,000 feet is 2,000 feet. *See the following figure.*

Airspace	Flight Visibility	Distance from Clouds
Class A	Not Applicable	Not Applicable
Class B	3 statute miles	Clear of clouds
Class C	3 statute miles	500 feet below 1,000 feet above 2,000 feet horizontal
Class D	3 statute miles	500 feet below 1,000 feet above 2,000 feet horizontal
Class E Less than 10,000 feet MSL	3 statute miles	500 feet below 1,000 feet above 2,000 feet horizontal
At or above 10,000 feet MSL	5 statute miles	1,000 feet below 1,000 feet above 1 statute mile horizontal
Class G 1,200 feet or less above the surface (regardless of MSL altitude) Day, except as provided in § 91.155(b)	1 statute mile	Clear of clouds
Night, except as provided in § 91.155(b)	3 statute miles	500 feet below 1,000 feet above 2,000 feet horizontal
More than 1,200 feet above the surface but less than 10,000 feet MSL Day	1 statute mile	500 feet below 1,000 feet above 2,000 feet horizontal
Night	3 statute miles	500 feet below 1,000 feet above 2,000 feet horizontal
More than 1,200 feet above the surface and at or above 10,000 feet MSL	5 statute miles	1,000 feet below 1,000 feet above 1 statute mile horizontal

Questions 3136 through 3147

AIR, GLI, LTA
3137 [A] — (B09) — FAR §91.155
Minimum visibility and cloud clearance for Class G airspace at 700 feet AGL or below during daylight hours is 1 mile visibility and clear of clouds. *See* the previous figure.

ALL
3138 [B] — (B09) — FAR §91.155
An airway below 10,000 feet MSL is in either Class B, C, or D, or E airspace, and requires 3 miles flight visibility. *See* the previous figure.

ALL
3139 [B] — (B09) — FAR §91.155
An airway below 10,000 feet MSL is in either Class B, C, or D, or E airspace, and requires a cloud clearance of 500 feet below, 1,000 feet above, and 2,000 feet horizontally. *See* the previous figure.

ALL
3140 [B] — (B09) — FAR §91.155
Class B, C, D, and E airspace are all controlled airspace in which VFR flight is allowed, and requires a cloud clearance of 1,000 feet above at altitudes of more than 1,200 feet AGL, but less than 10,000 feet MSL. *See* the previous figure.

ALL
3141 [A] — (B09) — FAR §91.155
Class B, C, D, and E airspace are all controlled airspace in which VFR flight is allowed, and requires 3 miles visibility and cloud clearance of 500 feet below or 1,000 feet above when operating above 1,200 feet AGL and below 10,000 feet MSL. *See* the previous figure.

AIR, GLI, RTC, LTA
3142 [B] — (B09) — FAR §91.155
At altitudes of more than 1,200 feet AGL but less than 10,000 feet MSL, Class G airspace requires 3 miles visibility at night. *See* the previous figure.

AIR, GLI, LTA, REC
3143 [A] — (B09) — FAR §91.155
At altitudes of more than 1,200 feet AGL but less than 10,000 feet MSL, Class G airspace requires 1 mile visibility during the day. *See* the previous figure.

AIR, GLI, LTA
3144 [A] — (B09) — FAR §91.155
At altitudes of more than 1,200 feet AGL but less than 10,000 feet MSL, Class G airspace requires a cloud clearance of 500 feet below, 1,000 feet above, and 2,000 feet horizontal, during the day. *See* the previous figure.

ALL
3145 [C] — (B09) — FAR §91.155
Controlled airspace above 10,000 feet which allows VFR is Class E airspace, and requires 5 miles visibility above 10,000 feet MSL and more than 1,200 feet AGL. *See* the previous figure.

ALL
3146 [C] — (B09) — FAR §91.155
Controlled airspace above 10,000 feet which allows VFR is Class E airspace, and requires cloud clearance of 1,000 feet below, 1,000 feet above, and 1 SM horizontal during operations above 10,000 feet MSL and more than 1,200 feet AGL. *See* the previous figure.

ALL
3147 [B] — (B09) — FAR §91.155
Controlled airspace above 10,000 feet which allows VFR is Class E airspace, and requires cloud clearance of 1,000 feet below, 1,000 feet above, and 1 SM horizontal during operations above 10,000 feet MSL and more than 1,200 feet AGL. *See* the previous figure.

AIR, GLI, RTC, LTA
3148 [C] — (B09) — FAR §91.155(d)(1)
Except for Special VFR procedures, no person may operate an aircraft under VFR within Class D airspace, beneath the ceiling when the ceiling is less than 1,000 feet. No person may takeoff or land an aircraft, or enter the traffic pattern of an airport under VFR, within Class D airspace unless ground visibility at that airport is at least 3 statute miles.

AIR, GLI, RTC, LTA
3149 [B] — (B09) — FAR §91.155(c), (d)(1)
Except for Special VFR procedures, no person may operate an aircraft under VFR within Class D airspace, beneath the ceiling when the ceiling is less than 1,000 feet. No person may takeoff or land an aircraft, or enter the traffic pattern of an airport under VFR, within Class D airspace unless ground visibility at that airport is at least 3 statute miles.

AIR
3150 [B] — (B09) — FAR §91.157(b)(c)
No person may operate an aircraft (other than a helicopter) in a Class D airspace under Special VFR unless clear of clouds and flight visibility is at least 1 statute mile.

AIR
3151 [A] — (B09) — FAR §91.157(b)(c)
No person may operate an aircraft (other than a helicopter) in a Class D airspace under special VFR unless clear of clouds and flight visibility is at least 1 statute mile.

RTC
3152 [C] — (B09) — FAR §91.157(e).
There are no restrictions on helicopters for Special VFR operations within Class D airspace.

AIR
3153 [C] — (B09) — FAR §61.3(e), FAR §91.157(e), FAR §91.205(d)
No person may operate an aircraft (other than a helicopter) in a Class D airspace under special weather minimums between sunset and sunrise unless the pilot and airplane are certified for instrument flight.

AIR
3154 [B] — (B09) — FAR §91.155(d)(1)(2)
No person may operate an aircraft (other than a helicopter) in a Class D airspace under special weather minimums between sunset and sunrise unless the airplane and pilot are certified for instrument flight.

AIR, RTC
3155 [C] — (B09) — FAR §91.159(a)
When operating below 18,000 feet MSL in VFR cruising flight more than 3,000 feet above the surface and on a magnetic course of 0° through 179°, any odd thousand-foot MSL altitude plus 500 feet (i.e., 3,500, 5,500, etc.) is appropriate. On a course of 180° through 359°, even thousands plus 500 feet (4,500, 6,500, etc.) is appropriate.

AIR, RTC
3156 [C] — (B09) — FAR §91.159
When operating below 18,000 feet MSL in VFR cruising flight more than 3,000 feet above the surface and on a magnetic course of 0° through 179°, any odd thousand-foot MSL altitude plus 500 feet (i.e., 3,500, 5,500, etc.) is appropriate. On a course of 180° through 359°, even thousands plus 500 feet (4,500, 6,500, etc.) is appropriate.

AIR, RTC
3157 [B] — (B09) — FAR §91.159
When operating below 18,000 feet MSL in VFR cruising flight more than 3,000 feet above the surface and on a magnetic course of 0° through 179°, any odd thousand-foot MSL altitude plus 500 feet (i.e., 3,500, 5,500, etc.) is appropriate. On a course of 180° through 359°, even thousands plus 500 feet (4,500, 6,500, etc.) is appropriate.

AIR, RTC
3158 [B] — (B09) — FAR §91.159
When operating below 18,000 feet MSL in VFR cruising flight more than 3,000 feet above the surface and on a magnetic course of 0° through 179°, any odd thousand-foot MSL altitude plus 500 feet (i.e., 3,500, 5,500, etc.) is appropriate. On a course of 180° through 359°, even thousands plus 500 feet (4,500, 6,500, etc.) is appropriate.

ALL
3159 [C] — (B11) — FAR §91.203
No person may operate an aircraft unless it has within it:

1. An appropriate and current Airworthiness Certificate, displayed at the cabin or cockpit entrance so that it is legible to passengers or crew.
2. A Registration Certificate issued to its owner.
3. An approved flight manual, manual material, markings and placards or any combination thereof, which show the operating limitations of the aircraft.

AIR
3160 [B] — (B11) — FAR §91.207(c)(1)(2)
ELT batteries must be replaced after 1 hour of cumulative use or when 50% of their useful life has expired, whichever comes first.

AIR
3161 [B] — (B11) — FAR §91.207(c)(1)(2)
ELT batteries must be replaced after 1 hour of cumulative use or when 50% of their useful life has expired, whichever comes first.

ALL
3162 [C] — (B11) — FAR §91.209(a)
An aircraft must display lighted position lights from sunset to sunrise.

ALL
3163 [C] — (B11) — FAR §91.211(1)
No person may operate civil aircraft at cabin pressure altitudes above 12,500 feet MSL up to and including 14,000 feet MSL, unless the required minimum flight crew is uses supplemental oxygen for that part of the flight at those altitudes that is more than 30 minutes duration.

ALL
3164 [C] — (B11) — FAR §91.211(a)(3)
No person may operate a civil aircraft at cabin pressure altitudes above 15,000 feet MSL unless each occupant is provided with supplemental oxygen.

ALL
3165 [A] — (B11) — FAR §91.215(b)(1)(3)(4)
Class A, B (and within 30 miles of the Class B primary airport), and C airspace require a Mode C transponder.

AIR, RTC
3166 [C] — (B11) — FAR §91.215(b)
With certain exceptions, all aircraft need encoding transponders under the 30-mile veil of Class B airspace.

AIR, GLI, REC
3167 [B] — (B12) — FAR §91.303
No person may operate an aircraft in acrobatic flight—

1. Over any congested area of a city, town, or settlement;
2. Over an open-air assembly of persons;
3. Within the lateral boundaries of Class B, C, D or E airspace designated for an airport;
4. Within 4 nautical miles of the centerline of a Federal airway;
5. Below an altitude of 1,500 feet above the surface; or
6. When flight visibility is less than 3 statute miles.

AIR, GLI, REC
3168 [A] — (B12) — FAR §91.303
No person may operate an aircraft in acrobatic flight—
1. Over any congested area of a city, town, or settlement;
2. Over an open-air assembly of persons;
3. Within the lateral boundaries of Class B, C, D or E airspace designated for an airport;
4. Within 4 nautical miles of the centerline of a Federal airway;
5. Below an altitude of 1,500 feet above the surface; or
6. When flight visibility is less than 3 statute miles.

AIR, GLI, REC
3169 [B] — (B12) — FAR §91.303
No person may operate an aircraft in acrobatic flight—
1. Over any congested area of a city, town, or settlement;
2. Over an open-air assembly of persons;
3. Within the lateral boundaries of Class B, C, D or E airspace designated for an airport;
4. Within 4 nautical miles of the centerline of a Federal airway;
5. Below an altitude of 1,500 feet above the surface; or
6. When flight visibility is less than 3 statute miles.

AIR, GLI, REC
3170 [A] — (B12) — FAR §91.303
No person may operate an aircraft in acrobatic flight—
1. Over any congested area of a city, town, or settlement;
2. Over an open-air assembly of persons;
3. Within the lateral boundaries of Class B, C, D or E airspace designated for an airport;
4. Within 4 nautical miles of the centerline of a Federal airway;
5. Below an altitude of 1,500 feet above the surface; or
6. When flight visibility is less than 3 statute miles.

AIR, GLI, REC, RTC
3171 [C] — (B12) — FAR §91.307(a)(1)
No pilot of a civil aircraft may allow a parachute that is available for emergency use to be carried in that aircraft unless, if a chair type, it has been packed by a certified and appropriately-rated parachute rigger within the preceding 120 days.

AIR, GLI, REC, RTC
3172 [A] — (B12) — FAR §91.307(a)(1)
No pilot of a civil aircraft may allow a parachute that is available for emergency use to be carried in that aircraft unless, if a chair type, it has been packed by a certified and appropriately-rated parachute rigger within the preceding 120 days.

AIR, GLI, REC, RTC
3173 [B] — (B12) — FAR §91.307(c)(2)
Unless each occupant of the aircraft is wearing an approved parachute, no pilot of a civil aircraft, carrying any person (other than a crewmember) may execute an intentional maneuver that exceeds 60° bank or 30° nose up or down, relative to the horizon.

GLI
3174 [A] — (B12) — FAR §91.309(a)(3)
No person may operate a civil aircraft towing a glider unless the towline used has a breaking strength not less than 80% of the maximum certificated operating weight of the glider, and not greater than twice this operating weight unless safety links are used.

```
  700 lbs
x 0.80
─────────
  560 lbs
```

GLI
3175 [B] — (B12) — FAR §91.309(a)(3)
No person may operate a civil aircraft towing a glider unless the towline used has a breaking strength not less than 80% of the maximum certificated operating weight of the glider, and not greater than twice this operating weight unless safety links are used.

```
1,040 lbs
x 0.80
─────────
  832 lbs
```

GLI
3176 [C] — (B12) — FAR §91.309(a)(3)
No person may operate a civil aircraft towing a glider unless the towline used has a breaking strength not less than 80% of the maximum certificated operating weight of the glider, and not greater than twice this operating weight unless safety links are used.

```
  700 lbs
    x 2
─────────
1,400 lbs
```

GLI
3177 [B] — (B12) — FAR §91.309(a)(3)
The towline may have a breaking strength of more than twice the maximum certificated operating weight of the glider if a safety link is installed at the point of attachment of the towline to the glider and a safety link is installed at the point of attachment of the towline to the towing aircraft.

AIR, GLI, RTC
3178 [B] — (B12) — FAR §91.313(e)
No person may operate a restricted category civil aircraft within the United States:
1. Over a densely populated area.
2. In a congested airway.
3. Near a busy airport where passenger transport operations are conducted.

ALL
3179 [B] — (B12) — FAR §91.319(2)(c)
Unless otherwise authorized by the Administrator in special operating limitations, no person may operate an aircraft that has an experimental certificate over a densely populated area or in a congested airway.

ALL
3180 [B] — (B13) — FAR §91.403(a)
The owner or operator of an aircraft is primarily responsible for maintaining the aircraft in an airworthy condition. The pilot-in-command of a civil aircraft is responsible for determining whether that aircraft is in condition for safe flight.

ALL
3181 [A] — (B13) — FAR §91.417(a)(1)(i-iii)
The registered owner or operator shall ensure that the aircraft maintenance records include the signature and the certificate number of the person approving the aircraft for return to service.

ALL
3182 [B] — (B13) — FAR §91.417(a)
Each registered owner or operator shall keep records of the maintenance and alteration, and records of the 100-hour, annual, progressive, and other required or approved inspections, as appropriate, for each aircraft (including the airframe) and each engine, propeller, rotor, and appliance of an aircraft. The records must include:
1. A description (or reference to data acceptable to the Administrator) of the work performed;
2. The date of completion of the work performed; and
3. The signature and certificate number of the person approving the aircraft for return to service.

ALL
3183 [B] — (B13) — FAR §91.407(b)
No person may carry any person (other than crewmembers) in an aircraft that has been maintained, rebuilt, or altered in a manner that may have appreciably changed its flight characteristics or substantially affected its operation in flight until an appropriately-rated pilot with at least a Private Pilot Certificate flies the aircraft, makes an operational check of the maintenance performed or alteration made, and logs the flight in the aircraft records.

ALL
3184 [B] — (B13) — FAR §91.407
No person may carry any person (other than crewmembers) in an aircraft that has been maintained, rebuilt, or altered in a manner that may have appreciably changed its flight characteristics or substantially affected its operation in flight until an appropriately-rated pilot with at least a Private Pilot Certificate flies the aircraft, makes an operational check of the maintenance performed or alteration made, and logs the flight in the aircraft records.

ALL
3185 [C] — (B13) — FAR §91.409
No person may operate an aircraft unless, within the preceding 12 calendar months, it has had an annual inspection in accordance with Part 43 and has been approved for return to service by an authorized person.

ALL
3186 [C] — (B13) — FAR §91.417(a)
Each registered owner or operator shall keep records of the maintenance and alteration, and records of the 100-hour, annual, progressive, and other required or approved inspections, as appropriate, for each aircraft (including the airframe) and each engine, propeller, rotor, and appliance of an aircraft.

ALL
3187 [C] — (B13) — FAR §21.181
Unless sooner surrendered, suspended, revoked, or a termination date is otherwise established by the Administrator, Standard Airworthiness Certificates and Airworthiness Certificates issued for restricted or limited category aircraft are effective as long as the maintenance, preventive maintenance, and alterations are performed in accordance with Parts 43 and 91 and the aircraft are registered in the United States.

ALL
3188 [A] — (B13) — FAR §91.409(b)
No person may operate an aircraft carrying any person for hire, and no person may give flight instruction for hire in an aircraft which that person provides, unless within the preceding 100 hours of time in service it has received an annual or 100-hour inspection and been approved for return to service.

AIR, RTC
3189 [B] — (B13) — FAR §91.409(b)
The 100-hour limitation may be exceeded by not more than 10 hours if necessary to reach a place at which the inspection can be done. The excess time, however, is included in computing the next 100 hours in service.

```
1259.6  time at 100-hour inspection
+100.0  time in service
1359.6  time next inspection due
```

AIR, RTC
3190 [B] — (B13) — FAR §91.409(b)
The 100-hour limitation may be exceeded by not more than 10 hours if necessary to reach a place at which the inspection can be done. The excess time, however, is included in computing the next 100 hours in service.

```
3302.5  time inspection was due
+100.0  time in service
3402.5  time next inspection due
```

ALL
3191 [C] — (B13) — FAR §91.413(a)
No person may use an ATC transponder unless within the preceding 24 calendar months, the ATC transponder has been tested and inspected and found to comply with Appendix F of Part 43.

ALL
3192 [C] — (B13) — FAR §91.413(a)
No person may use an ATC transponder unless within the preceding 24 calendar months, the ATC transponder has been tested and inspected and found to comply with Appendix F of Part 43.

ALL
3193 [A] — (B13) — FAR §91.417
Each registered owner or operator shall keep records of the maintenance and alteration, and records of the 100-hour, annual, progressive, and other required or approved inspections, as appropriate, for each aircraft (including the airframe) and each engine, propeller, rotor, and appliance of an aircraft.

ALL
3194 [A] — (G11) — NTSB §830.5
The operator of an aircraft shall immediately, and by the most expeditious means available, notify the nearest NTSB field office when an aircraft accident occurs.

ALL
3195 [C] — (G11) — NTSB §830.5
A flight control system malfunction or failure requires immediate NTSB notification.

ALL
3196 [B] — (G11) — NTSB §830.5
Immediate notification of the NTSB is necessary if an in-flight fire occurs.

ALL
3197 [A] — (G11) — NTSB §830.5
When an aircraft is overdue and believed to have been involved in an accident, the NTSB must be notified immediately.

ALL
3198 [B] — (G12) — NTSB §830.10
Prior to the time the Board and its authorized representative takes custody of aircraft wreckage, it may not be disturbed or moved except to remove persons injured or trapped, to protect the wreckage from further damage, or to protect the public from injury.

ALL
3199 [C] — (G13) — NTSB §830.15
The operator of an aircraft shall file a report on Board Form 6120.1 or 6120.2 within 10 days of an accident.

ALL
3200 [C] — (G13) — NTSB §830.15
A report on an incident for which notification is required shall be filed only as requested by an authorized representative of the Board.

ALL
3201 [A] — (H01) — AC 61-23B, Chapter 1
Lift, weight, thrust, and drag are the four basic aerodynamic forces acting on an aircraft in flight.

AIR, GLI
3202 [A] — (H01) — AC 61-23B, Chapter 1
In unaccelerated (steady state) flight the opposing forces are in equilibrium.

ALL
3203 [B] — (H01) — AC 61-23B, Chapter 1
The angle of attack is the acute angle between the relative wind and the chord line of the wing.

ALL
3204 [A] — (H01) — AC 61-23B, Chapter 1
The angle of attack is the acute angle between the relative wind and the chord line of the wing.

AIR
3205 [A] — (H01) — AC 61-23B, Chapter 1
Lift and thrust are considered positive forces, while weight and drag are considered negative forces and the sum of the opposing forces is zero. That is, lift = weight and thrust = drag.

AIR, GLI
3206 [A] — (H01) — AC 00-6A, Chapter 10
The roughness of the surface of frost spoils the smooth flow of air, thus causing a slowing of the airflow. This slowing of the air causes early air flow separation over the affected airfoil, resulting in a loss of lift. Even a small amount of frost on airfoils may prevent an aircraft from becoming airborne at normal takeoff speed.

AIR
3207 [A] — (H01) — AC 61-23B, Chapter 1
The effect of torque increases in direct proportion to the engine power, airspeed, and airplane attitude. If the power setting is high, the airspeed slow, and the angle of attack high, the effect of torque is greater.

AIR
3208 [B] — (H01) — AC 61-23B, Chapter 1
The downward-moving blade on the right side of the propeller has a higher angle of attack and greater action and reaction than the upward moving blade on the left. This results in a tendency for the airplane to yaw around the vertical axis to the left.

AIR
3209 [B] — (H01) — AC 61-23B, Chapter 1
The effects of P-factor, or asymmetric propeller loading, usually occur when the airplane is flown at high angles of attack and at high power settings.

AIR, GLI
3210 [B] — (H01) — AC 61-23B, Chapter 1
A stable airplane will tend to return to the original condition of flight if disturbed by a force such as turbulent air. This means that a stable airplane is easy to fly.

AIR, GLI
3211 [A] — (H01) — AC 61-23B, Chapter 1
The location of the center of gravity with respect to the center of lift determines to a great extent the longitudinal stability of an airplane. Center of gravity aft of the center of lift will result in an undesirable pitch-up moment during flight. An airplane with the center of gravity forward of the center of lift will pitch down when power is reduced. This will increase the airspeed and the downward force on the elevators. This increased downward force on the elevators will bring the nose up, providing positive stability. The farther forward the CG is, the more stable the airplane.

AIR, GLI
3212 [B] — (H01) — AC 61-23B, Chapter 1
The location of the center of gravity with respect to the center of lift determines to a great extent the longitudinal stability of an airplane. Center of gravity aft of the center of lift will result in an undesirable pitch-up moment during flight. An airplane with the center of gravity forward of the center of lift will pitch down when power is reduced. This will increase the airspeed and the downward force on the elevators. This increased downward force on the elevators will bring the nose up, providing positive stability. The farther forward the CG is, the more stable the airplane.

AIR
3213 [A] — (H01) — AC 61-23B, Chapter 1
The purpose of the rudder is to control yaw.

AIR
3214 [C] — (H01) — AC 61-23B, Chapter 1
Referencing FAA Figure 2, use the following steps:
1. Enter the chart at a 60° angle of bank and proceed upward to the curved reference line. From the point of intersection, move to the left side of the chart and read a load factor of 2 Gs.
2. Multiply the aircraft weight by the load factor:
   2,300 x 2 = 4,600 lbs

AIR
3215 [C] — (H01) — AC 61-23B, Chapter 1
Referencing FAA Figure 2, use the following steps:
1. Enter the chart at a 30° angle of bank and proceed upward to the curved reference line. From the point of intersection, move to the left side of the chart and read an approximate load factor of 1.2 Gs.
2. Multiply the aircraft weight by the load factor:
   3,300 x 1.2 = 3,960 lbs

AIR
3216 [B] — (H01) — AC 61-23B, Chapter 1
Referencing FAA Figure 2, use the following steps:
1. Enter the chart at a 45° angle of bank and proceed upward to the curved reference line. From the point of intersection, move to the left side of the chart and read a load factor of 1.5 Gs.
2. Multiply the aircraft weight by the load factor.
   4,500 x 1.5 = 6,750 lbs

AIR
3217 [B] — (H01) — AC 61-23B, Chapter 1
At slow speeds, the maximum available lifting force of the wing is only slightly greater than the amount necessary to support the weight of the airplane. However, at high speeds, the capacity of the elevator controls, or a strong gust, may increase the load factor beyond safe limits.

AIR
3218 [B] — (H01) — AC 61-23B, Chapter 1
A change in speed during straight flight will not produce any appreciable change in load, but when a change is made in the airplane's flight path, an additional load is imposed upon the airplane structure. This is particularly true if a change in direction is made at high speeds with rapid, forceful control movements.

AIR, GLI
3219 [C] — (H02) — AC 61-23B, Chapter 2
Flaps increase drag, allowing the pilot to make steeper approaches without increasing airspeed.

AIR, GLI
3220 [A] — (H02) — AC 61-23B, Chapter 2
Flaps increase drag, allowing the pilot to make steeper approaches without increasing airspeed.

AIR, RTC
3221 [B] — (H02) — AC 61-23B, Chapter 2
Operating an engine at a higher temperature than it was designed for will cause loss of power, excessive oil consumption, and detonation. It will also lead to serious permanent injury to the engine including scoring of cylinder walls, damage to pistons and rings, and burning and warping of valves.

AIR, RTC
3222 [C] — (H02) — AC 61-23B, Chapter 2
Excessively high engine temperatures can result from insufficient cooling caused by too lean a mixture, too low a grade of fuel, low oil, or insufficient airflow over the engine.

AIR
3223 [A] — (H02) — AC 61-23B, Chapter 2
The dual ignition system has two magnetos to supply the electrical current to two spark plugs for each combustion chamber. This provides both a redundancy of ignition and an improvement of engine performance.

AIR
3224 [A] — (H02) — AC 61-23B, Chapter 2
Running out of fuel would cause air to be pumped into the fuel lines.

AIR, RTC
3225 [B] — (H02) — AC 61-23, Chapter 2
In a carburetor system, outside air flows into the carburetor and through a venturi (a narrow throat in the carburetor). When air flows rapidly through the venturi, a low pressure area is created. This low pressure allows the fuel to flow through the main fuel jet (located within the throat) and into the airstream where it mixes with the flowing air.

AIR, RTC
3226 [B] — (H02) — AC 61-23B, Chapter 2
The mixture becomes richer as the airplane gains altitude, because the carburetor meters the same amount of fuel as at sea level. Leaning the mixture control prevents this by decreasing the rate of fuel discharge to compensate for the decrease in air density.

AIR
3227 [A] — (H02) — AC 61-23B, Chapter 2
When carburetor heat is applied, the air/fuel mixture of an engine will be enriched because any given volume of hot air is less dense than cold air of the same volume. This condition would be aggravated at high altitude where, because of decreased air density, the mixture is already richer than at sea level.

AIR, RTC
3228 [A] — (H02) — AC 61-23B, Chapter 2
Air density increases in the descent, but the amount of fuel drawn into the carburetor remains the same. To re-establish a balanced fuel/air mixture in a descent, the mixture control must be adjusted toward "rich."

AIR, RTC
3229 [C] — (H02) — AC 61-23B, Chapter 2
If the temperature is between -7°C (20°F) and 21°C (70°F) with visible moisture or high humidity, the pilot should be constantly on the alert for carburetor ice.

AIR, RTC
3230 [A] — (H02) — AC 61-23B, Chapter 2
If the temperature is between -7°C (20°F) and 21°C (70°F) with visible moisture or high humidity, the pilot should be constantly on the alert for carburetor ice.

AIR
3231 [C] — (H02) — AC 61-23B, Chapter 2
For airplanes with a fixed-pitch propeller, the first indication of carburetor ice is loss of RPM.

AIR, RTC
3232 [B] — (H02) — AC 61-23B, Chapter 2
Carburetors are normally calibrated at sea level pressure to meter the correct fuel/air mixture. As altitude increases, air density decreases and the amount of fuel is too great for the amount of air—the mixture is "too rich." This same result may be brought about by the application of carburetor heat. The heated air entering the carburetor has less density than unheated air and the fuel/air mixture is enriched.

AIR, RTC
3233 [B] — (H02) — AC 61-23B, Chapter 2
Carburetors are normally calibrated at sea level pressure to meter the correct fuel/air mixture. As altitude increases, air density decreases and the amount of fuel is too great for the amount of air—the mixture is "too rich." This same result may be brought about by the application of carburetor heat. The heated air entering the carburetor has less density than unheated air and the fuel/air mixture is enriched.

AIR, RTC
3234 [A] — (H02) — AC 61-23, Chapter 2
Use of carburetor heat tends to reduce the output of the engine and also to increase the operating temperature.

AIR
3235 [C] — (H02) — AC 61-23B, Chapter 2
When heat is applied there will be a drop in RPM in airplanes equipped with fixed-pitch propellers. If carburetor ice is present, there will normally be a rise in RPM after the initial drop. Then, when the carburetor heat is turned off, the RPM will rise to a setting greater than that before application of the heat. The engine should also run more smoothly after the ice has been removed.

AIR, RTC
3236 [A] — (H02) — AC 61-23B, Chapter 2
Fuel injection systems are less susceptible to icing than carburetor systems because of the lack of the temperature drop caused by the venturi in a carburetor. Be aware that one can acquire carburetor ice even without easily visible moisture and, in the right circumstances, even at full power.

AIR, RTC
3237 [C] — (H02) — AC 61-23B, Chapter 2
Using aviation fuel of a lower rating is harmful under any circumstances because it may cause loss of power, excessive heat, burned spark plugs, burned and sticky valves, high oil consumption, and detonation.

AIR, RTC
3238 [C] — (H02) — AC 61-23B, Chapter 2
Using low-grade fuel or too lean a mixture can cause detonation. Detonation is a sudden explosion or shock to a small area of the piston top, similar to striking it with a hammer.

AIR
3239 [B] — (H02) — AC 61-23B, Chapter 2
To prevent detonation, the pilot should use the correct grade of fuel, maintain a sufficiently rich mixture, open the throttle smoothly, and keep the temperature of the engine within recommended operating limits. Some aircraft have an automatically enriched mixture for enhanced cooling in takeoff and climb-out at full throttle. Lowering the nose will allow the aircraft to gain airspeed, which eventually lowers the engine temperature.

AIR, RTC
3240 [B] — (H02) — AC 61-21A, Chapter 2
Preignition is defined as ignition of the fuel prior to normal ignition.

AIR, RTC
3241 [A] — (H02) — AC 61-23B, Chapter 2
Excessively high engine temperatures result from insufficient cooling caused by too lean a mixture, too low a grade of fuel, low oil, or insufficient airflow over the engine.

AIR, RTC
3242 [A] — (H02) — AC 61-23B, Chapter 2
If the proper grade of fuel is not available, it is possible (but not desirable), to use the next higher (aviation) grade as a substitute.

AIR, RTC
3243 [C] — (H02) — AC 61-23B, Chapter 2
Water in the fuel system is dangerous and the pilot must prevent contamination. The fuel tanks should be filled after each flight, or at least after the last flight of the day. This will prevent moisture condensation within the tank, since no air space will be left inside.

AIR, RTC
3244 [C] — (H02) — AC 61-23B, Chapter 2
Oil, used primarily to lubricate the moving parts of the engine, also cools the internal parts of the engine as it circulates.

AIR, RTC
3245 [A] — (H02) — AC 61-23B, Chapter 2
Oil, used primarily to lubricate the moving parts of the engine, also helps reduce engine temperature by removing some of the heat from the cylinders. Therefore, if the oil level is too low, the transfer of heat to less oil would cause the oil temperature to rise.

AIR, LTA, RTC
3246 [B] — (H02) — AC 61-23B, Chapter 4
The propeller produces thrust in proportion to the mass of air being accelerated through the rotating blades. If the air is less dense, propeller efficiency is decreased.

AIR, GLI, RTC
3247 [B] — (H03) — AC 61-23B, Chapter 3
Airspeed, altimeter and vertical speed all receive static input and would indicate inaccurately if the static sources became plugged.

ALL
3248 [C] — (H03) — AC 61-23B, Chapter 3
The pitot tube provides input for the airspeed indicator only.

ALL
3249 [C] — (H03) — AC 61-23B, Chapter 3
Airspeed, altimeter and vertical speed all receive static input and would indicate inaccurately if the static sources became plugged.

ALL
3250 [C] — (H03) — AC 61-27C, Chapter 4
On altimeter #1 the 10,000-foot pointer (shortest hand) is just above 10,000 feet, the 1,000-foot pointer (fat hand) is between 0 and 1,000 feet, and the 100-foot pointer is on 500 feet.

ALL
3251 [C] — (H03) — AC 61-27C, Chapter 4
On altimeter #2 the 10,000-foot pointer is between 10,000 feet and 20,000 feet. The 1,000-foot pointer is between 4,000 feet and 5,000 feet, and the 100-foot pointer is on 500 feet.

ALL
3252 [A] — (H03) — AC 61-27C, Chapter 4
On altimeter #3 the 10,000-foot pointer is not quite to 10,000 feet. The 1,000-foot pointer is halfway between 9,000 and 10,000 feet, and the 100-foot pointer is on 500 feet.

ALL
3253 [B] — (H03) — AC 61-27C, Chapter 4
The shortest hand (10,000 foot) in #1 is between 1 and 2, indicating 10,000 feet plus. The shortest hand in #2 also indicates 10,000 feet plus. The shortest hand in #3 indicates less than 10,000 feet.

ALL
3254 [C] — (H03) — AC 61-27C, Chapter 4
The local altimeter setting corrects for the difference between existing pressure and standard atmospheric pressure. Whether local pressure is higher or lower than standard, it will indicate true altitude (MSL) at ground level, when the aircraft altimeter is set to the local altimeter setting (assuming no setting scale error).

ALL
3255 [A] — (H03) — AC 61-23B, Chapter 3
On a warm day, the expanded air is lighter than on a cold day, and consequently the pressure levels are raised. For example, the pressure level where the altimeter indicates 10,000 feet will be higher on a warm day than under standard conditions. On a cold day the reverse is true.

ALL
3256 [A] — (H03) — AC 61-27C, Chapter 4
True altitude is height above sea level. Airport terrain and obstacle elevations found on aeronautical charts are true altitudes.

ALL
3257 [B] — (H03) — AC 61-27C, Chapter 4
Absolute altitude is height above the surface. This height may be indicated directly on a radar altimeter. Absolute altitude may be approximately computed from indicated altitude and chart elevation data.

ALL
3258 [B] — (H03) — AC 61-21A, Chapter 2
Under standard atmospheric conditions, each level of air in the atmosphere has a specific density, and under standard conditions, pressure altitude and density altitude identify the same level. Under conditions higher or lower than standard, density altitude cannot be determined directly from the altimeter.

ALL
3259 [B] — (H03) — AC 61-21A, Chapter 17
The pressure altitude can be determined by either of two methods:
1. Setting the barometric scale of the altimeter to 29.92 and reading the indicated altitude, or
2. Applying a correction factor to the elevation (true altitude) according to the reported "altimeter setting."

ALL
3260 [B] — (H03) — AC 61-27C, Chapter 4
On a standard day (29.92" Hg and +15°C) at sea level, pressure altitude, indicated altitude, and density altitude are all equal. Any variation from standard temperature or pressure will have an effect on the altimeter.

ALL
3261 [C] — (H03) — AC 61-23B, Chapter 3
When the knob on the altimeter is rotated, the pressure scale moves simultaneously with the altimeter pointers. The numerical values of pressure indicated in the window increase while the altimeter indicates an increase in altitude; or decrease while the altimeter indicates a decrease in altitude. This is contrary to the reaction on the pointers when air pressure changes, and is based solely on the mechanical makeup of the altimeter. The difference between the two settings is equal to 0.70" Hg (28.85 – 29.15). At the standard pressure lapse rate of 1" Hg = 1,000 feet in altitude, the amount of change equals 700 feet.

AIR, GLI, RTC
3262 [C] — (H03) — AC 61-23B, Chapter 3
The pitot tube provides input for the airspeed indicator only.

AIR, GLI
3263 [C] — (H03) — AC 61-23B, Chapter 3
An increase in altitude has no effect on the indicated airspeed at which an airplane stalls at altitudes normally used by general aviation aircraft. This means that the same indicated airspeed should be maintained during the landing approach regardless of the elevation or the density altitude at the airport of landing.

ALL
3264 [C] — (H03) — AC 61-23B, Chapter 3
The upper end of the arc is marked by a red radial line which is the "never exceed" speed (V_{NE}).

AIR
3265 [A] — (H03) — AC 61-23B, Chapter 3
The flap operating range is marked by the white arc. The low end is V_{SO} (stall speed in a landing configuration), and the high end is V_{FE} (maximum flap extended speed).

AIR, GLI
3266 [C] — (H03) — AC 61-23B, Chapter 3
The caution range (yellow arc) includes speeds which should only be flown in smooth air, and is 165 to 208 MPH for this airplane.

AIR
3267 [C] — (H03) — AC 61-23B, Chapter 3
The caution range (yellow arc) includes speeds which should only be flown in smooth air; the maximum speed in the caution range is 208 MPH for this airplane.

ALL
3268 [C] — (H03) — AC 61-23B, Chapter 3
The upper end of the arc is marked by a red radial line which is the "never exceed" speed (V_{NE}).

ALL
3269 [C] — (H03) — AC 61-23B, Chapter 3
The green arc is the normal operating range. The lower end of the arc (V_{S1}) is the stalling speed in a specified configuration.

AIR
3270 [B] — (H03) — AC 61-23B, Chapter 3
The flap operating range is marked by the white arc. The high end is V_{FE} (maximum flap extended speed), which is 100 MPH for this airplane.

AIR
3271 [C] — (H03) — AC 61-23B, Chapter 3
The flap operating range is marked by the white arc. The low end is V_{SO} (stall speed in a landing configuration), and the high end is V_{FE} (maximum flap extended speed).

AIR
3272 [C] — (H03) — AC 61-23B, Chapter 3
The flap operating range is marked by the white arc. The low end is V_{SO} (stall speed in a landing configuration).

AIR
3273 [B] — (H03) — AC 61-23B, Chapter 3
The green arc is the normal operating range. The upper end of the arc (V_{NO}) is defined as the "maximum structural cruising speed."

AIR
3274 [C] — (H03) — AC 61-23B, Chapter 3
Maneuvering speed (V_A) is not displayed on the airspeed indicator.

AIR
3275 [A] — (H03) — AC 61-23B, Chapter 3
The movement of the miniature airplane on the instrument is proportional to the roll rate of the airplane. When the roll rate is reduced to zero, i.e., the bank is held constant, the instrument provides an indication of the rate of turn. This design features a realignment of the gyro in such a manner that it senses airplane movement about the yaw and roll axis.

AIR, RTC
3276 [C] — (H03) — AC 61-23B, Chapter 3
Because the heading indicator is run by a gyroscope instead of a magnetic source, precession will cause creep or drift from a heading to which it is set. It is important to check the indications frequently and reset the heading indicator to align it with the magnetic compass when required.

AIR, RTC
3277 [C] — (H03) — AC 61-23B, Chapter 3
The miniature airplane "C" is adjusted so that the wings overlap the horizon bar "B" when the airplane is in straight-and-level cruising flight.

ALL
3278 [C] — (H03) — AC 61-23B, Chapter 3
The relationship of the miniature aircraft C to the horizon bar B is the same as the relationship of the real aircraft to the actual horizon.

ALL
3279 [C] — (H03) — AC 61-23B, Chapter 3
Magnetic disturbances from magnetic fields produced by metals and electrical accessories in an aircraft disturb the compass card and produce an additional error which is referred to as deviation.

AIR, GLI, RTC
3280 [B] — (H03) — AC 61-23B, Chapter 3
If on a northerly heading and a turn is made toward east or west, the initial indication of the compass lags, or indicates a turn in the opposite direction.

AIR, GLI, RTC
3281 [C] — (H03) — AC 61-23B, Chapter 3
If on a northerly heading and a turn is made toward east or west, the initial indication of the compass lags, or indicates a turn in the opposite direction.

ALL
3282 [C] — (H03) — AC 61-23B, Chapter 3
While on an east or west heading, an increase in airspeed or acceleration will cause the compass to indicate a turn toward the north and a deceleration will cause the compass to indicate a turn to the south. If on a north or south heading, no error will be apparent because of acceleration or deceleration. (Remember **ANDS** = Accelerate North Decelerate South)

ALL
3283 [C] — (H03) — AC 61-23B, Chapter 3
While on an east or west heading, an increase in airspeed or acceleration will cause the compass to indicate a turn toward the north and a deceleration will cause the compass to indicate a turn to the south. If on a north or south heading, no error will be apparent because of acceleration or deceleration. (Remember **ANDS** = Accelerate North Decelerate South)

ALL
3284 [B] — (H03) — AC 61-23B, Chapter 3
While on an east or west heading, an increase in airspeed or acceleration will cause the compass to indicate a turn toward the north and a deceleration will cause the compass to indicate a turn to the south. If on a north or south heading, no error will be apparent because of acceleration or deceleration. (Remember **ANDS** = Accelerate North Decelerate South)

GLI
3285 [B] — (H03) — AC 61-23B, Chapter 3
While on an east or west heading, an increase in airspeed or acceleration will cause the compass to indicate a turn toward the north and a deceleration will cause the compass to indicate a turn to the south. If on a north or south heading, no error will be apparent because of acceleration or deceleration. (Remember **ANDS** = Accelerate North Decelerate South)

AIR, GLI, RTC
3286 [A] — (H03) — AC 61-23B, Chapter 3
The magnetic compass should be read only when the aircraft is flying straight-and-level at a constant speed. This will help reduce errors to the minimum.

AIR, GLI
3287 [B] — (H04) — AC 61-23B, Chapter 3
Loading in a tail-heavy condition can reduce the airplane's ability to recover from stalls and spins. Tail-heavy loading also produces very light stick forces, making it easy for the pilot to inadvertently overstress the airplane.

AIR, GLI
3288 [A] — (H04) — AC 61-23B, Chapter 3
Loading in a tail-heavy condition can reduce the airplane's ability to recover from stalls and spins. Tail-heavy loading also produces very light stick forces at all speeds, making it easy for the pilot to inadvertently overstress the airplane.

ALL
3289 [C] — (H04) — AC 61-23B, Chapter 3
If the temperature is above standard, the density altitude will be higher than pressure altitude.

AIR, RTC
3290 [C] — (H04) — AC 61-23B, Chapter 4
An increase in air temperature or humidity, or a decrease in air pressure (which results in a higher density altitude), will significantly decrease both power output and propeller efficiency.

AIR, RTC
3291 [B] — (H04) — AC 61-23B, Chapter 4
An increase in air temperature or humidity, or a decrease in air pressure (which results in a higher density altitude), will significantly decrease both power output and propeller efficiency.

AIR, RTC
3292 [C] — (H04) — AC 61-23B, Chapter 4
Referencing FAA Figure 8, use the following steps:

1. Enter the density altitude chart at 25°F. Proceed upward to intersect the 5,000-foot pressure altitude line. From the point of intersection, move left to the edge of the chart and read a density altitude of 3,850 feet.

2. Enter the density altitude chart at 50°F. Proceed upward to the 5,000-foot pressure altitude line. From the point of intersection, move left to the edge of the chart and read a density altitude of 5,500 feet.

3. Determine the change in density altitude:

    5,500 − 3,850 = 1,650 feet (increase)

AIR, RTC
3293 [C] — (H04) — AC 61-23B, Chapter 4
Referencing FAA Figure 8, use the following steps:

1. Since the altimeter setting that is given is not shown in FAA Figure 8, interpolation is necessary. Locate the settings immediately above and below the given value of 28.22" Hg:

Altimeter Setting	Conversion Factor
28.2	1,630 feet
28.3	1,533 feet

2. Determine the difference in the two conversion factors:

    1,630 − 1,533 = 97 feet

3. Determine the amount of the difference to be subtracted from the 28.20" Hg conversion factor (2/10 of 97).

    97.0 × .2 = 19.4

4. Subtract the amount of difference from the amount shown for the 28.20" Hg conversion factor:

    1,630.0 − 19.4 = 1,610.6

5. Add the correction factor to the indicated altitude to find the pressure altitude:

    1,610.6
    + 1,380.0
    2,990.6 feet MSL (pressure altitude)

ALL
3294 [C] — (H04) — AC 61-23B, Chapter 4
Referencing FAA Figure 4, use the following steps:

1. Since the altimeter setting that is given is not shown in FAA Figure 8, interpolation is necessary. Locate the settings immediately above and below the given value of 29.25" Hg:

Altimeter Setting	Conversion Factor
29.20	673 feet
29.30	579 feet

2. Determine the difference between the two conversion factors:

    673 − 579 = 94 feet

3. Determine the amount of difference to be added to the 29.30" Hg conversion factor:

    94 × .5 = 47 feet

4. Add the amount of difference to the amount shown for the 29.30" Hg conversion factor:

    579 + 47 = 626 feet

5. Add the correction factor to the airport elevation to find pressure altitude:

    5,250
    + 626
    5,876 feet MSL (pressure altitude)

6. Determine the density altitude by entering the chart at +81°F; move upward to the 5,876 pressure altitude line; from the point of intersection, move to the left and read a density altitude of 8,500 feet.

ALL
3295 [A] — (H04) — AC 61-23B, Chapter 4
Referencing FAA Figure 8, use the following steps:

1. Since the altimeter setting that is given is not shown in FAA Figure 8, interpolation is necessary. Locate the settings immediately above and below the given value of 29.96" Hg:

Altimeter Setting	Conversion Factor
29.92	0 feet
30.00	-73 feet

2. Determine the difference between the two conversion factors:

    0 − 73 = -73 feet

    The setting 29.96 is halfway between the two values, so:

    -73 ÷ 2 = -36.5 feet

3. Determine the amount of difference to be subtracted from the 30.00" Hg conversion factor.

4. Subtract the correction factor from the airport elevation to find pressure altitude:

    3,563.0
    − 36.5
    3,526.5 feet MSL (pressure altitude)

AIR, RTC
3296 [C] — (H04) — AC 61-23B, Chapter 4
Referencing FAA Figure 8, use the following steps:

1. Enter the density altitude chart at 30°F. Proceed upward to the 3,000-foot pressure altitude line. From the point of intersection, move left to the edge of the chart and read a density altitude of 1,650 feet.

2. Enter the density altitude chart at 50°F. Proceed upward to the 3,000-foot pressure altitude line. From the point of intersection, move left to the edge of the chart and read a density altitude of 3,000 feet.

3. Find the difference between the two values:

    3,000 – 1,650 = 1,350 foot (increase)

AIR, RTC
3297 [A] — (H04) — AC 61-23B, Chapter 4
Referencing FAA Figure 8, use the following steps:

1. Since the altimeter setting that is given is not shown in FAA Figure 8, interpolation is necessary. Locate the settings immediately above and below the given value of 29.97" Hg:

Altimeter Setting	Conversion Factor
29.92	0 feet
30.00	-73 feet

2. Determine the difference between the two conversion factors:

    0 – 73 = -73 feet

3. Determine the amount of the difference to be subtracted from the 29.92" Hg conversion factor: (-73 ÷ 8) x 5 = -45.6 or 46 feet

4. Subtract the conversion factor from the airport elevation to determine the pressure altitude:

    1,386
    – 46
    ―――
    1,340 feet MSL (pressure altitude)

ALL
3298 [A] — (H04) — AC 61-23B, Chapter 4
Referencing FAA Figure 8, use the following steps:

1. Since the altimeter setting that is given is not shown in FAA Figure 8, interpolation is necessary. Locate the settings immediately above and below the given value of 30.35" Hg:

Altimeter Setting	Conversion Factor
30.30	-348 feet
30.40	-440 feet

2. Determine the difference between the two factors:

    -440 + 348 = -92 feet

3. Determine amount of difference to be added to the 30.30" Hg conversion factor:

    -92.0 x .5 = -46.0 feet

4. Add the amount of difference to the amount shown for the 30.30" Hg conversion factor:

    -348 + (-46) = -394 feet

5. Subtract the correction factor from the airport elevation to find pressure altitude:

    3,894
    – 394
    ―――
    3,500 feet MSL (pressure altitude)

6. Determine the density altitude by entering the chart at +25°F; proceed upward to the 3,500-foot pressure altitude line; from the point of intersection move to the left edge of the chart and read a density altitude of 2,000 feet.

ALL
3299 [B] — (H04) — AC 61-23B, Chapter 4
Referencing FAA Figure 8, use the following steps:

1. Determine the density altitude when the temperature is +90°F and the pressure altitude is 1,250 feet. Enter the density altitude chart at +90°F and proceed upward to the 1,250-foot pressure altitude line. From the point of intersection move to the left edge of the chart and read a density altitude of 3,600 feet.

2. Determine the density altitude when the temperature is +60°F and the pressure altitude is 1,750 feet. Enter the density altitude chart at +60°F and proceed upward to the 1,750-foot pressure altitude line. From the point of intersection move to the left edge of the chart. Read a density altitude of 2,300 feet.

3. Determine the change in density altitude:

    3,600 – 2,300 = 1,300 foot (decrease)

AIR, RTC
3300 [B] — (H05) — AC 61-23B, Chapter 4
An increase in air temperature or humidity, or a decrease in air pressure (which results in a higher density altitude) will significantly decrease both power output and propeller efficiency. If an air mass is humid, there is more water in it, therefore, less oxygen.

AIR, GLI
3301 [A] — (H52) — AC 61-23B, Chapter 1
As the airplane is banked, lift acts horizontally as well as vertically and the airplane is pulled around the turn.

AIR
3302 [C] — (H54) — AC 61-21A
Taxiing with a quartering tailwind provides the most hazardous conditions. In this case, the elevator should be in the down position and the aileron on the upwind side should also be in the down position to keep the wing from lifting.

AIR
3303 [A] — (H54) — AC 61-21A
When taxiing a nosewheel aircraft in the presence of moderate to strong winds, extra caution should be taken. For a quartering headwind, the elevator should be held in the neutral position, and the aileron on the upwind side should be in the up position.

AIR
3304 [A] — (H54) — AC 61-21A
When taxiing a nosewheel aircraft in the presence of moderate to strong winds, extra caution should be taken. Taxiing with a quartering tailwind produces the most hazardous conditions.

AIR
3305 [A] — (H54) — AC 61-21A
When taxiing a nosewheel aircraft in the presence of moderate to strong winds, extra caution should be taken. For a quartering headwind, the elevator should be held in the neutral position, and the aileron on the upwind side should be in the up position.

AIR
3306 [A] — (H54) — AC 61-21A
When taxiing a tailwheel airplane with a quartering headwind, the aileron on the upwind side should be up, and the elevator held in the up position to hold the tail down.

AIR
3307 [C] — (H54) — AC 61-21A
When taxiing a tailwheel aircraft with a quartering tailwind, the upwind aileron should be down to keep that wing from lifting, and the elevator should also be down.

AIR
3308 [B] — (H54) — AC 61-21A
Taxiing with a quartering tailwind produces the most hazardous conditions. In this case, the elevator should be in the down position, and the aileron on the upwind side should also be in the down position to keep the wing from lifting.

AIR, GLI
3309 [C] — (H60) — AC 61-21A, Chapter 2
A spin results when a sufficient degree of rolling or yawing control input is imposed on an airplane in the stalled condition. If the wing is not stalled, a spin cannot occur.

AIR, GLI
3310 [A] — (H60) — Flight Theory for Pilots
One wing is less stalled than the other but both wings are stalled in a spin.

AIR, GLI
3311 [C] — (H66) — AC 61-23B, Chapter 1
When the angle of attack is increased to between 18° and 20° (critical angle of attack) on most airfoils, the airstream can no longer follow the upper curvature of the wing because of the excessive change in direction. The airplane will stall if the critical angle of attack is exceeded. The indicated airspeed at which stall occurs will be determined by weight and load factor, but the stall angle of attack is the same.

AIR, GLI, RTC
3312 [A] — (H66) — AC 61-21A, Chapter 17
Ground effect is the result of the interference of the surface of the Earth with the airflow patterns about an airplane.

AIR, GLI, RTC
3313 [A] — (H66) — AC 61-21A, Chapter 17
When the wing is at a height equal to its span, the reduction in induced drag is only 1.4%. However, when the wing is at a height equal to one-fourth its span, the reduction in induced drag is 23.5% and when the wing is at a height equal to one-tenth its span, the reduction in induced drag is 47.6%.

AIR, GLI, RTC
3314 [B] — (H66) — AC 61-21A, Chapter 17
The reduction of the wing-tip vortices, due to ground effect, alters the spanwise lift distribution and reduces the induced angle of attack, and induced drag causing floating.

ALL
3315 [B] — (H66) — AC 61-21A, Chapter 17
Due to the reduced drag in ground effect, the airplane may seem capable of takeoff well below the recommended speed. It is important that no attempt be made to force the airplane to become airborne with a deficiency of speed. The recommended takeoff speed is necessary to provide adequate initial climb performance.

AIR, GLI
3316 [A] — (H66) — AC 61-23B, Chapter 1
Stall speed increases in proportion to the square root of the load factor. Thus, with a load factor of 4, an aircraft will stall at a speed which is double the normal stall speed.

RTC
3317 [A] — (H70) — AC 61-13B, Chapter 1
The angle of attack is the angle between the chord line of the airfoil and the direction of the relative wind.

RTC
3318 [A] — (H71) — AC 61-13B, Chapter 2
Gyroscopic precession is the resultant action of a spinning object when a force is applied to the object. The action occurs approximately 90° later in the direction of rotation. Thus, if the maximum increase in angle of attack occurs at point A, maximum deflection takes place 90° later. This is maximum upward deflection at the rear, and the tip-path plane tips forward.

RTC
3319 [B] — (H71) — AC 61-13B, Chapter 2
The difference in lift that exists between the advancing blade half of the disc and retreating blade half, created by horizontal flight or by wind during hovering flight, is called dissymmetry of lift.

RTC
3320 [C] — (H71) — AC 61-13B, Chapter 2
As the helicopter moves into forward flight, the relative wind moving over each rotor blade becomes a combination of the rotational speed of the rotor and the forward movement of the helicopter. Increased lift on the advancing blade will cause the blade to flap, decreasing the angle of attack. Decreased lift on the retreating blade will cause the blade to flap down, increasing the angle of attack. The combination of decreased angle of attack on the advancing blade and increased angle of attack on the retreating blade through blade flapping action tends to equalize lift over the two halves of the rotor disc.

RTC
3321 [A] — (H71) — AC 61-13B, Chapter 2
As a vertical takeoff is made, two major forces are acting at the same time—centrifugal force acting outward, perpendicular to the rotor mast, and lift, acting upward and parallel to the mast. The result of these two forces is that the blades assume a conical path instead of remaining in the plane perpendicular to the mast.

RTC
3322 [B] — (H71) — AC 61-13B, Chapter 2
When a rotor blade flaps up, the center of mass of that blade moves closer to the axis of rotation and blade acceleration takes place.

RTC
3323 [C] — (H71) — AC 61-13B, Chapter 2
To counteract drift, the rotor mast in some helicopters is rigged slightly to the left side so that the tip-path plane has a built-in tilt to the left, thus producing a small sideward thrust.

RTC
3324 [C] — (H71) — AC 61-13B, Chapter 2
In ground effect, as downwash velocity is reduced, the induced angle of attack is reduced and the lift vector becomes more vertical. Simultaneously, a reduction in induced drag occurs. In addition, as the induced angle of attack is reduced, the angle of attack generating lift is increased. The net result of these actions is a beneficial increase in lift and a lower power requirement to support a given weight.

RTC
3325 [B] — (H71) — AC 61-13B, Chapter 2
Translational lift is that additional lift obtained when entering horizontal flight due to the increased efficiency of the rotor system. Translational lift depends upon airspeed rather than ground speed.

RTC
3326 [C] — (H73) — AC 61-13B, Chapter 2
The force that compensates for torque and keeps the fuselage from turning in the direction opposite to the main rotor is produced by means of an auxiliary rotor located on the end of the tail boom.

RTC
3327 [B] — (H73) — AC 61-13B, Chapter 4
Lowering the collective pitch will reduce the manifold pressure, decrease drag on the rotor, and therefore increase the RPM.

RTC
3328 [A] — (H74) — AC 61-13B, Chapter 5
In a fully-articulated rotor system, each rotor blade is attached to the hub by a vertical hinge called a drag or lag hinge that permits each blade, independently of the others, to move back and forth in the plane of the rotor disc. This movement is called dragging, lead-lag, or hunting. The purpose of the drag hinge and dampers is to absorb the acceleration and deceleration of the rotor blades caused by Coriolis effect.

RTC
3329 [B] — (H78) — AC 61-13, Chapter 9
A tendency for the retreating blade to stall in forward flight is a major factor in limiting a helicopter's forward airspeed. When operating at high airspeeds, stalls are more liable to occur under conditions of high gross weight, low RPM, high density altitude, steep or abrupt turns, and/or turbulent flight.

RTC
3330 [A] — (H78) — AC 61-13, Chapter 9
A tendency for the retreating blade to stall in forward flight is a major factor in limiting a helicopter's forward airspeed. When operating at high airspeeds, stalls are more liable to occur under conditions of high gross weight, low RPM, high density altitude, steep or abrupt turns, and/or turbulent flight.

RTC
3331 [C] — (H78) — AC 61-13, Chapter 9
A tendency for the retreating blade to stall in forward flight is a major factor in limiting a helicopter's forward airspeed. When operating at high airspeeds, stalls are more liable to occur under conditions of high gross weight, low RPM, high density altitude, steep or abrupt turns, and/or turbulent flight.

RTC
3332 [B] — (H78) — AC 61-13B, Chapter 9
When one landing gear of the helicopter strikes the surface first, a shock is transmitted through the fuselage to the rotor. This shock may cause the blades straddling the contact point to be forced closer together. When one of the other landing gears strikes, the unbalance could be aggravated. This sets up a resonance of the fuselage.

RTC
3333 [C] — (H78) — AC 61-13B, Chapter 9
Low-frequency vibrations are always associated with the main rotor.

RTC
3334 [A] — (H78) — AC 61-13B, Chapter 9
Medium-frequency vibrations are a result of trouble with the tail rotor in most helicopters.

RTC
3335 [C] — (H78) — AC 61-13B, Chapter 9
The chart can be used to determine those altitude-airspeed combinations from which it would be impossible to successfully complete an autorotative landing. The altitude-airspeed combinations that should be avoided are represented by the shaded areas of the chart.

RTC
3336 [B] — (H79) — AC 61-13B, Chapter 11
Collective pitch is used to control rate of speed during taxi. The higher the collective pitch, the faster will be the taxi speed.

RTC
3337 [C] — (H80) — AC 61-13B, Chapter 11
Cyclic pitch is used to control ground track during surface taxi.

RTC
3338 [B] — (H91) — AC 61-13B, Chapter 9
Corrective action for ground resonance could be an immediate takeoff if RPM is in proper range, or an immediate closing of the throttle and placing the blades in low pitch if RPM is low. "During rotor spin-up" implies low RPM.

RTC
3339 [B] — (H94) — Flight Manual, McCulloch J-2 Gyroplane, ¶2-7, D
Avoid abrupt control motions while taxiing.

GLI
3340 [C] — (N20) — Soaring Flight Manual, Chapter 1
The pull of gravity provides the forward motion necessary to move the wings through the air.

GLI
3341 [B] — (N21) — Soaring Flight Manual, Chapter 2
If the maximum distance over the ground is desired, the airspeed for best L/D should be used.

GLI
3342 [B] — (N21) — Soaring Flight Manual, Chapter 2
Both positive and negative gust load factors increase with increasing airspeed.

GLI
3343 [B] — (N22) — Soaring Flight Manual, Chapter 3
In the case of a slipping right turn, the yaw string moves outside left and the ball moves inside, or right, as illustrated by 2 and 6 of FAA Figure 11.

GLI
3344 [C] — (N22) — Soaring Flight Manual, Chapter 3
In the case of a skidding right turn, the yaw string moves outside left and the ball moves inside, or right, as illustrated by 3 and 4 of FAA Figure 11.

GLI
3345 [B] — (N27) — Soaring Flight Manual, Chapter 9
L/D is lift divided by drag. This significant ratio is numerically the same as glide ratio, the ratio of forward to downward motion. Hence, 23 to 1 glide ratio would indicate:

1. $\dfrac{23}{1} = \dfrac{6{,}000 \ (\text{feet/NM} - \text{forward})}{X \ (\text{feet/NM} - \text{downward})}$

2. $\dfrac{23}{1} \times X = 6{,}000$

3. $X = 261$ feet downward for each 6,000 feet (1 NM) forward.

4. The total sink is 8 NM x 261 feet/NM or about 2,100 feet in 8 NM in calm air.

GLI
3346 [A] — (N27) — Soaring Flight Manual, Chapter 9
L/D is lift divided by drag. This significant ratio is numerically the same as glide ratio, the ratio of forward to downward motion. Hence, 30 to 1 glide ratio would indicate:

1. $\dfrac{30}{1} = \dfrac{X \ (\text{feet/NM} - \text{forward})}{2{,}000 \ (\text{feet/NM} - \text{downward})}$

2. $\dfrac{30}{1} \times 2{,}000 = X$

3. $X = 60{,}000$ feet (10 NM) forward for each 2,000 feet downward.

GLI
3347 [B] — (N27) — Soaring Flight Manual, Chapter 9
L/D is lift divided by drag. This significant ratio is numerically the same as glide ratio, the ratio of forward to downward motion. Assuming that 1 NM is approximately 6,000 feet, the glide ratio and L/D may be expressed as:

$$\dfrac{9 \times 6{,}000 \text{ feet forward}}{2{,}000 \text{ feet downward}} = \dfrac{54{,}000}{2{,}000} = \dfrac{54}{2} = \dfrac{27}{1} \text{ or } 27{:}1$$

GLI
3348 [C] — (N27) — Soaring Flight Manual, Chapter 9
L/D is lift divided by drag. This significant ratio is numerically the same as glide ratio, the ratio of forward to downward motion. Hence, 22 to 1 glide ratio would indicate:

1. $\dfrac{22}{1} = \dfrac{6{,}000 \ (\text{feet/NM} - \text{forward})}{X \ (\text{feet/NM} - \text{downward})}$

2. $\dfrac{22}{1} \times X = 6{,}000$

3. $X = 273$ feet downward for each 6,000 feet (1 NM) forward.

4. The total sink is 15 NM x 273 feet/NM, or about 4,095 feet in 15 NM in calm air.

GLI
3349 [B] — (N27) — Soaring Flight Manual, Chapter 9
L/D is lift divided by drag. This significant ratio is numerically the same as glide ratio, the ratio of forward to downward motion. Hence, 23 to 1 glide ratio would indicate:

1. $\dfrac{23}{1} = \dfrac{6{,}000 \text{ (feet/NM} - \text{forward)}}{X \text{ (feet/NM} - \text{downward)}}$

2. $\dfrac{23}{1} \times X = 6{,}000$

3. X = 261 feet downward for each 6,000 feet (1 NM) forward.

4. The total sink is 10 NM x 261 feet/NM, or about 2,610 feet in 10 NM in calm air.

GLI
3350 [A] — (N34) — Soaring Flight Manual, Chapter 2
When gliding into a headwind, maximum distance will be achieved by adding approximately one-half the estimated headwind velocity to the best L/D speed.

LTA
3351 [C] — (O01) — Taming the Gentle Giant
The load tape supports the weight of the balloon and minimizes the strain on the envelope fabric.

LTA
3352 [C] — (O02) — Propane Systems, IV C2-4
Propane is preferred over butane and other hydrocarbons in balloon design because propane has a lower boiling point (-44°F).

LTA
3353 [B] — (O02) — Propane Systems, IV C2-4
Propane is preferred over butane and other hydrocarbons in balloon design because propane has a lower boiling point (-44°F).

LTA
3354 [A] — (O02) — Taming the Gentle Giant, page 19
On very cold days, it may be necessary to preheat the propane tanks since the temperature of the liquid propane controls the burner pressure during combustion.

LTA
3355 [A] — (O02) — Taming the Gentle Giant, page 19
When ample liquid propane is available, propane will vaporize sufficiently to provide proper operation between 30°F and 90°F.

LTA
3356 [C] — (O02) — Taming the Gentle Giant, page 19
When ample liquid propane is available, propane will vaporize sufficiently to provide proper operation between 30°F and 90°F.

LTA
3357 [A] — (O02) — Taming the Gentle Giant, page 20
The pressure release valve is located on top of the fuel tank and opens automatically when the pressure in the tank exceeds the maximum allowable pressure.

LTA
3358 [B] — (O02) — Taming the Gentle Giant, page 20
A vapor-bleed valve, or "spit tube," is located on each tank and indicates when the tank is filled to 80% of capacity.

LTA
3359 [A] — (O05) — Taming the Gentle Giant, page 104
A hot air balloon derives lift from the fact that air inside the envelope is warmer and therefore, "lighter" than the air around the balloon.

LTA
3360 [A] — (O05) — Taming the Gentle Giant, page 104
Burner efficiency of a hot air balloon system decreases at approximately 4% per 1,000 feet above MSL.

LTA
3361 [C] — (O05) — Taming the Gentle Giant, page 104
If large quantities of vapor are withdrawn rapidly from a propane cylinder, the cooling effect of the vaporization in the tank cools the propane and lowers the vapor pressure and the rate of vaporization.

LTA
3362 [C] — (O22) — Propane Systems, IV C2-23
Since propane holds little water in solution, there is a tendency for free water to collect in the bottom of the tanks where it may reach the dip tube, be piped into the burner system, and freeze up the regulators. If water contamination is suspected, methyl alcohol (methanol) should be added to the system.

LTA
3363 [B] — (O24) — Taming the Gentle Giant, pages 20 and 104
The blast valve is located on the burner and controls ascent or descent by use of short bursts of power. When reaching the desired altitude, the pilot should reduce the frequency of blasts. As the envelope cools, the desired altitude can be maintained by using short blasts of heat evenly spaced.

LTA
3364 [A] — (O30) — Powerline Excerpts, page 4
A weigh-off is used to determine the static equilibrium of the balloon.

LTA
3365 [C] — (O30) — Taming the Gentle Giant, page 104
False lift is caused by the venturi effect produced by the wind blowing across an inflated but stationary envelope. This is "dynamic lift" created by relative air movement. If the balloon is released, the relative wind decreases as the balloon accelerates to the speed of the wind and false lift decreases.

LTA
3366 [C] — (O30) — Taming the Gentle Giant, page 104
False lift is caused by the venturi effect produced by the wind blowing across an inflated but stationary envelope. This is "dynamic lift" created by relative air movement. If the balloon is released, the relative wind decreases as the balloon accelerates to the speed of the wind and false lift decreases.

LTA
3367 [C] — (O30) — Taming the Gentle Giant, page 9
As the gas is cooled, it contracts and becomes more dense and so displaces less air.

LTA
3368 [C] — (P01) — Goodyear Airship Operations Manual
A lighter-than-air craft is in equilibrium when buoyancy equals weight. The buoyant force is equal to the weight of the air volume displaced.

LTA
3369 [B] — (P01) — Goodyear Airship Operations Manual
A lighter-than-air craft is in equilibrium when buoyancy equals weight. The buoyant force is equal to the weight of the air volume displaced.

LTA
3370 [C] — (P01) — Goodyear Airship Operations Manual
As the airship descends into the colder temperature of the inversion, the weight of the displaced air volume is increasing, thereby increasing buoyancy.

LTA
3371 [C] — (P01) — Goodyear Airship Operations Manual
Superheat is the difference between outside air temperature and the temperature in the airship envelope.

LTA
3372 [A] — (P04) — Goodyear Airship Operations Manual
Aerostatics are the gravitational factors involving equilibrium of a body freely suspended in the atmosphere.

LTA
3373 [A] — (P04) — Goodyear Airship Operations Manual
Each 5°F amounts to about 1% of gross lift.

LTA
3374 [A] — (P04) — Goodyear Airship Operations Manual
Expansion of the gas will cause the ballonets to completely deflate at pressure height. Gas must be valved from the envelope to maintain constant pressure.

LTA
3375 [A] — (P04) — Goodyear Airship Operations Manual
When pressure height has been reached, the liquid in the gas manometer will rise and the liquid in the air manometer will fall below normal levels.

LTA
3376 [C] — (P04) — Goodyear Airship Operations Manual
Expansion of the gas will cause the ballonets to completely deflate at pressure height. Thus, no further increase in displaced air volume is possible.

LTA
3377 [C] — (P04) — Goodyear Airship Operations Manual
Expansion of the gas will cause the ballonets to completely deflate at pressure height. Thus, no further increase in displaced air volume is possible.

LTA
3378 [C] — (P04) — Goodyear Airship Operations Manual
Dynamic force, created by movement through the air, must be used to overcome any out-of-equilibrium condition.

LTA
3379 [B] — (P09) — Goodyear Airship Operations Manual
Any air entering the ballonets through the damper valves will have to be exhausted overboard as the gas expands. This slows the rate of ascent.

LTA
3380 [C] — (P09) — Goodyear Airship Operations Manual
If damper valves are open, ram air pressure will keep the ballonets inflated longer than they should be inflated.

ALL
3381 [C] — (I21) — AC 00-6A, Chapter 5
Every physical process of weather is accompanied by, or is a result of, unequal heating of the Earth's surface.

ALL
3382 [A] — (I21) — AC 00-6A, Chapter 3
All altimeter settings are corrected to sea level. Unequal heating of the Earth's surface causes pressure differences.

ALL
3383 [C] — (I21) — AC 00-6A, Chapter 2
An increase in temperature with altitude is defined as an inversion. An inversion often develops near the ground on clear, cool nights when wind is light. The ground radiates heat and cools much faster than the overlying air. Air in contact with the ground becomes cold while the temperature a few hundred feet above changes very little. Thus, the temperature increases with height. A ground-based inversion usually means poor visibility.

ALL
3384 [A] — (I21) — AC 00-6A, Chapter 2
An inversion often develops near the ground on clear, cool nights when wind is light. The ground radiates heat and cools much faster than the overlying air. Air in contact with the ground becomes cold while the temperature a few hundred feet above changes very little. Thus, the temperature increases with height.

ALL
3385 [A] — (I21) — AC 00-6A, Chapters 2 and 6
A ground-based inversion leads to poor visibility by trapping fog, smoke, and other restrictions into low levels of the atmosphere. The layer is stable and convection is suppressed.

ALL
3386 [A] — (I21) — AC 61-23B, Chapter 3
Standard sea level pressure is 29.92 inches of mercury. Standard sea level temperature is 15°C.

AIR, GLI, RTC
3387 [C] — (I22) — AC 61-23B, Chapter 3
When the knob on the altimeter is rotated, the altimeter setting pressure scale moves simultaneously with the altimeter pointers. The numerical values of pressure indicated in the window increase while the altimeter indicates an increase in altitude, or decrease while the altimeter indicates a decrease in altitude. This is contrary to the reaction on the pointers when air pressure changes and is based solely on the mechanical makeup of the altimeter. The difference between the two settings is equal to 0.15" Hg (30.11 − 29.96 = 0.15). At the standard pressure lapse rate of 1" Hg = 1,000 feet in altitude, the amount of change equals 150 feet.

ALL
3388 [B] — (I22) — AC 00-6A, Chapter 3
Pressure altitude is equal to true altitude under standard atmospheric conditions.

ALL
3389 [C] — (I22) — AC 61-23B, Chapter 3
When conditions are standard, pressure altitude and density altitude are the same.

ALL
3390 [C] — (I22) — AC 61-23B, Chapter 3
If a flight is made from a high-pressure area to a low-pressure area without adjusting the altimeter, the actual altitude of the airplane will be lower than the indicated altitude, and when flying from a low-pressure area to high-pressure area, the actual altitude of the airplane will be higher than the indicated altitude.

ALL
3391 [B] — (I22) — AC 61-23B, Chapter 3
If a flight is made from a high-pressure area to a low-pressure area without adjusting the altimeter, the actual altitude of the airplane will be lower than the indicated altitude, and when flying from a low-pressure area to high-pressure area, the actual altitude of the airplane will be higher than the indicated altitude.

ALL
3392 [A] — (I22) — AC 00-6A, Chapter 3
True altitude will be lower than indicated altitude in colder than standard air temperature, even with an accurate altimeter set to 29.92.

ALL
3393 [C] — (I22) — AC 00-6A, Chapter 3
The altimeter will indicate a lower altitude than actually flown, in air temperature warmer than standard.

ALL
3394 [B] — (I22) — AC 61-23B, Chapter 3
On a hot day, the air becomes "thinner" or lighter, and its density is equivalent to a higher altitude in the standard atmosphere, thus the term "high density altitude."

ALL
3395 [B] — (I23) — AC 00-6A, Chapter 4
Friction between the wind and the surface slows the wind. The Coriolis force has less affect on slower winds, therefore there will be less deflection with surface winds than with winds at 5,000 feet AGL.

LTA
3396 [A] — (I23) — Taming the Gentle Giant, page 68
Within a high-pressure system, flying conditions are generally more favorable than in low-pressure areas because there are normally fewer clouds, better visibility, calm or light winds, and less turbulence.

ALL
3397 [C] — (I24) — AC 00-6A, Chapter 5
Dew point is the temperature to which air must be cooled to become saturated by the water vapor already present in the air.

ALL
3398 [B] — (I24) — AC 00-6A, Chapter 5
Temperature largely determines the maximum amount of water vapor air can hold.

ALL
3399 [A] — (I24) — AC 00-6A, Chapter 5
As water vapor condenses or sublimates on condensation nuclei, liquid or ice particles begin to grow. Some condensation nuclei have an affinity for water and can induce condensation or sublimation even when air is almost, but not completely, saturated.

ALL
3400 [A] — (I24) — AC 00-6A, Chapter 5
Evaporation is the changing of liquid water to invisible water vapor. Sublimation is the changing of liquid water directly to ice, or vice versa.

ALL
3401 [B] — (I24) — AC 00-6A, Chapter 5
Frost forms in much the same way as dew. The difference is that the dew point of surrounding air must be colder than freezing.

ALL
3402 [C] — (I24) — AC 00-6A, Chapter 5
Ice pellets always indicate freezing rain at higher altitude.

ALL
3403 [B] — (I25) — AC 00-6A, Chapter 6
The difference between the existing lapse rate of a given mass of air and the adiabatic rates of cooling in upward moving air determines if the air is stable or unstable.

ALL
3404 [A] — (I25) — AC 00-6A, Chapter 6
When air near the surface is warm and moist, suspect instability. Surface heating, cooling aloft, converging or upslope winds, or an invading mass of colder air may lead to instability and cumuliform clouds.

ALL
3405 [A] — (I25) — AC 00-6A, Chapter 6
Since stable air resists convection, clouds in stable air forms in horizontal, sheet-like layers or "strata."

ALL
3406 [A] — (I25) — AC 00-6A, Chapter 6
When stable air is forced upward the air tends to retain horizontal flow and any cloudiness is flat and stratified.

ALL
3407 [C] — (I25) — AC 00-6A, Chapter 6
When unstable air is forced upward, the disturbance grows. Any resulting cloudiness shows extensive vertical development.

ALL
3408 [A] — (I25) — AC 00-6A, Chapter 6
If the temperature increases with altitude through a layer (an inversion), the layer is stable and convection is suppressed.

ALL
3409 [C] — (I25) — AC 00-6A, Chapter 6
When lifted, unsaturated air cools at approximately 5.4°F per 1,000 feet. The dew point cools at approximately 1°F per 1,000 feet. Therefore, the convergence of the temperature and dew point lapse rates is 4.4°F per 1,000 feet. The base of a cloud (AGL) that is formed by vertical currents can be roughly calculated by dividing the difference between the surface temperature and the dew point by 4.4 and multiplying the remainder by 1,000.

1. 70°F surface temperature
    − 48°F dew point
    ──────
    22

2. 22 ÷ 4.4 = 5

3. 5 x 1,000 = 5,000 feet AGL

4. 5,000 feet AGL
    + 1,000 feet field elevation
    ──────
    6,000 feet MSL

ALL
3410 [B] — (I25) — AC 00-6A, Chapter 6
When lifted, unsaturated air cools at approximately 5.4°F per 1,000 feet. The dew point cools at approximately 1°F per 1,000 feet. Therefore, the convergence of the temperature and dew point lapse rates is 4.4°F per 1,000 feet. The base of a cloud (AGL) that is formed by vertical currents can be roughly calculated by dividing the difference between the surface temperature and the dew point by 4.4 and multiplying the remainder by 1,000.

1. 82°F surface temperature
    − 38°F dew point
    ──────
    44

2. 44 ÷ 4.4 = 10

3. 10 x 1,000 = 10,000 feet AGL

LTA
3411 [C] — (I25) — Taming the Gentle Giant, page 71
Stratiform clouds indicate no turbulence and 5 knots or less winds are well within safety parameters.

ALL
3412 [A] — (I25) — AC 00-6A, Chapter 6
Characteristics of a moist, unstable air mass include cumuliform clouds, showery precipitation, rough air (turbulence), and good visibility (except in blowing obstructions).

ALL
3413 [A] — (I25) — AC 00-6A, Chapter 8
Characteristics of an unstable air mass include cumuliform clouds, showery precipitation, rough air (turbulence), and good visibility (except in blowing obstructions).

ALL
3414 [C] — (I25) — AC-00-6A, Chapter 8
Characteristics of a stable air mass include stratiform clouds and fog, continuous precipitation, smooth air, and fair to poor visibility in haze and smoke.

ALL
3415 [B] — (I26) — AC 00-6A, Chapter 7
The prefix "nimbo-" or suffix "-nimbus" means rain cloud.

ALL
3416 [B] — (I26) — AC 00-6A, Chapter 7
For identification purposes, clouds are divided into four families: high clouds, middle clouds, low clouds, and clouds with extensive vertical development.

ALL
3417 [C] — (I26) — AC 00-6A, Chapter 7
Crests of standing waves may be marked by stationary, lens-shaped clouds known as standing lenticular clouds.

ALL
3418 [B] — (I26) — AC 00-6A, Chapter 9
Crests of standing waves may be marked by stationary, lens-shaped clouds known as standing lenticular clouds.

ALL
3419 [B] — (I26) — AC 00-6A, Chapter 7
Cumulonimbus are the ultimate manifestation of instability. They are vertically-developed clouds of large dimensions with dense boiling tops, often crowned with thick veils of dense cirrus (the anvil). Nearly the entire spectrum of flying hazards are contained in these clouds including violent turbulence.

ALL
3420 [C] — (I26) — AC 00-6A, Chapter 9
Towering cumulus signifies a relatively deep layer of unstable air. They show considerable vertical development and have billowing cauliflower tops. Showers can result from these clouds. Expect very strong turbulence, and perhaps some clear icing above the freezing level.

ALL
3421 [C] — (I27) — AC 00-6A, Chapter 8
A front is the boundary between two different air masses.

ALL
3422 [A] — (I27) — AC 00-6A, Chapter 8
Temperature is one of the most easily recognized discontinuities across a front.

ALL
3423 [A] — (I27) — AC 00-6A, Chapter 8
Wind direction always changes across a front.

ALL
3424 [C] — (I27) — AC 00-6A, Chapter 8
Precipitation from stratiform clouds is usually steady and there is little or no turbulence.

ALL
3425 [A] — (I28) — AC 00-6A, Chapter 9
Always anticipate possible mountain wave turbulence when strong winds of 40 knots or greater blow across a mountain or ridge and the air is stable.

ALL
3426 [C] — (I28) — AC 00-6A, Chapters 8, 9 and 11
Wind shear may be associated with either a wind shift or a wind speed gradient at any level in the atmosphere.

ALL
3427 [B] — (I28) — AC 00-6A, Chapters 9 and 11
Hazardous wind shear can occur near the ground with either thunderstorms or a strong temperature inversion.

ALL
3428 [C] — (I28) — AC 00-6A, Chapter 9
An increase in temperature with altitude is defined as a temperature inversion. A pilot can be relatively certain of a shear zone in the inversion if the pilot knows the wind at 2,000 to 4,000 feet is 25 knots or more.

AIR, GLI, RTC
3429 [C] — (I28) — AC 00-6A, Chapter 10
Two conditions are necessary for structural icing in flight:

1. The aircraft must be flying through visible water such as rain or cloud droplets, and
2. The temperature at the point where the moisture strikes the aircraft must be 0°C (32°F) or colder.

AIR, GLI, RTC
3430 [C] — (I29) — AC 00-6A, Chapter 10
A condition favorable for rapid accumulation of clear icing is freezing rain below a frontal surface.

AIR, GLI, RTC
3431 [C] — (I29) — AC 00-6A, Chapter 10
The roughness of the surface of frost spoils the smooth flow of air, thus causing a slowing of the airflow. This slowing of the air causes early air flow separation over the affected airfoil, resulting in a loss of lift. Even a small amount of frost on airfoils may prevent an aircraft from becoming airborne at normal takeoff speed.

AIR
3432 [A] — (I29) — AC 00-6A, Chapter 10
The roughness of the surface of frost spoils the smooth flow of air, thus causing a slowing of the airflow. This slowing of the air causes early air flow separation over the affected airfoil, resulting in a loss of lift. Even a small amount of frost on airfoils may prevent an aircraft from becoming airborne at normal takeoff speed.

ALL
3433 [B] — (I30) — AC 00-6A, Chapter 11
For a cumulonimbus cloud or thunderstorm to form, the air must have:
1. Sufficient water vapor,
2. An unstable lapse rate, and
3. An initial upward boost (lifting) to start the storm process in motion.

ALL
3434 [B] — (I30) — AC 00-6A, Chapter 11
The key feature of the cumulus stage is an updraft. Precipitation beginning to fall from the cloudbase is the signal that a downdraft has developed also and a cell has entered the mature stage.

ALL
3435 [B] — (I30) — AC 00-6A, Chapter 11
The key feature of the cumulus stage is an updraft. Precipitation beginning to fall from the cloudbase is the signal that a downdraft has developed also and the cell has entered the mature stage.

ALL
3436 [A] — (I30) — AC 00-6A, Chapter 11
For a cumulonimbus cloud or thunderstorm to form, the air must have:
1. Sufficient water vapor,
2. An unstable lapse rate, and
3. An initial upward boost (lifting) to start the storm process in motion.

ALL
3437 [B] — (I30) — AC 00-6A, Chapter 11
Downdrafts characterize the dissipating stage of the thunderstorm cell and the storm dies rapidly.

ALL
3438 [A] — (I30) — AC 00-6A, Chapter 11
All thunderstorm hazards reach their greatest intensity during the mature stage.

ALL
3439 [A] — (I30) — AC 00-6A, Chapter 11
A squall line is a non-frontal, narrow band of active thunderstorms. The line may be too long to easily detour and too wide and severe to penetrate. It often contains severe steady-state thunderstorms and presents the single, most intense weather hazard to aircraft.

ALL
3440 [B] — (I30) — AC 00-6A, Chapter 11
A squall line is a non-frontal, narrow band of active thunderstorms. The line may be too long to easily detour and too wide and severe to penetrate. It often contains severe steady-state thunderstorms and presents the single, most intense weather hazard to aircraft.

ALL
3441 [B] — (I30) — AC 00-6A, Chapter 11
Wind shear is an invisible hazard associated with all thunderstorms. Shear turbulence has been encountered 20 miles laterally from a severe storm.

ALL
3442 [C] — (I30) — AC 00-6A, Chapter 11
The primary concern is to avoid undue stress on the airframe. This can best be done by attempting to maintain a constant attitude while keeping the airspeed below design maneuvering speed (V_A).

ALL
3443 [A] — (I31) — AC 00-6A, Chapter 12
Conditions favorable for radiation fog are clear sky, little or no wind, and small temperature/dew point spread (high relative humidity). Radiation fog is restricted to land because water surfaces cool little from nighttime radiation.

ALL
3444 [C] — (I31) — AC 00-6A, Chapter 2
With a small temperature/dew point spread, the air is close to saturation. This will usually result in fog or low clouds. Anticipate fog when the temperature/dew point spread is 5°F or less and decreasing.

ALL
3445 [B] — (I31) — AC 00-6A, Chapter 12
Advection fog forms when moist air moves over colder ground or water. It is most common along coastal areas. This fog frequently forms offshore as a result of cold water, then is carried inland by the wind.

ALL
3446 [C] — (I31) — AC 00-6A, Chapter 12
Advection fog forms when moist air moves over colder ground or water. It is most common along coastal areas, but often develops deep in continental areas. Advection fog deepens as wind speed increases up to about 15 knots. Wind much stronger than 15 knots lifts the fog into a layer of low stratus or stratocumulus. Upslope fog forms as a result of moist, stable air being cooled adiabatically as it moves up sloping terrain. Once upslope wind ceases, the fog dissipates.

ALL
3447 [C] — (I33) — AC 00-6A, Chapter 14
Steam fog forms in the winter when cold, dry air passes from land areas over comparatively warm ocean waters. Low-level turbulence can occur and icing can become hazardous in a steam fog.

GLI
3448 [C] — (I35) — AC 00-6A, page 173
Thermals are updrafts in convective currents dependent on solar heating. A temperature inversion would result in stable air with very little, if any, convective activity.

GLI
3449 [C] — (I35) — AC 00-6A, Chapter 11
During the mature stage of a thunderstorm, updrafts and downdrafts in close proximity create strong vertical shears and a very turbulent environment. A lightning strike can puncture the skin of an aircraft and damage communication and navigation equipment.

ALL
3450 [C] — (I35) — AC 00-6A, Chapter 4
Caused by the heating of land on warm, sunny days, the sea breeze usually begins during early forenoon, reaches a maximum during the afternoon, and subsides around dusk after the land has cooled. The leading edge of the cool sea breeze forces warmer air inland to rise. Rising air from over land returns seaward at higher altitude to complete the convective cell.

GLI
3451 [C] — (I35) — AC 00-6A, Chapter 16
A sea breeze begins during early afternoon and reaches a maximum in the afternoon, subsiding around dusk.

ALL
3452 [A] — (I36) — AC 00-6A, Chapter 11
A thunderstorm is, in general, a local storm invariably produced by a cumulonimbus cloud, and is always accompanied by lightning and thunder.

ALL
3453 [A] — (I40) — AC 00-45D, Section 4
The Transcribed Weather Broadcast (TWEB) is similar to the area forecast except information is contained in a route format; whereas a terminal forecast is a description of the surface weather expected to occur at an airport.

ALL
3454 [B] — (I40) — AC 00-45D, Section 4
Transcribed Weather Broadcasts (TWEBs) are recorded on tapes and broadcast continuously over selected low-frequency navigational aids and/or VORs.

ALL
3455 [A] — (I40) — AC 00-45D, Section 1
Although all these items would be included when filing a flight plan, when requesting a preflight weather briefing, identify yourself as a pilot or the tail number of the aircraft to be flown and provide the type of flight planned (e.g., VFR or IFR).

ALL
3456 [C] — (I40) — AC 00-45D, Section 1
You should request a standard briefing any time you are planning a flight and you have not received a previous briefing or preliminary information through mass dissemination media, e.g., TWEB, PATWAS, VRS, etc.

ALL
3457 [C] — (I40) — AC 00-45D, Section 1
You should request a standard briefing any time you are planning a flight and you have not received a previous briefing or preliminary information through mass dissemination media, e.g., TWEB, PATWAS, VRS, etc.

ALL
3458 [C] — (I40) — AC 00-45D, Section 1
Request an abbreviated briefing when you need information to supplement mass disseminated data, update a previous briefing, or when you need only one or two specific items.

ALL
3459 [A] — (I40) — AC 00-45D, Section 1
Request an abbreviated briefing when you need information to supplement mass disseminated data, update a previous briefing, or when you need only one or two specific items.

ALL
3460 [A] — (I40) — AC 00-45D, Section 1
You should request an outlook briefing whenever your proposed time of departure is 6 or more hours from the time of the briefing. This type of briefing is provided for planning purposes only. You should obtain a standard or abbreviated briefing prior to departure in order to obtain such items as current conditions, updated forecasts, winds aloft and NOTAMs.

ALL
3461 [A] — (I40) — AC 00-45D, Section 1
You should request an outlook briefing whenever your proposed time of departure is 6 or more hours from the time of the briefing. This type of briefing is provided for planning purposes only. You should obtain a standard or abbreviated briefing prior to departure in order to obtain such items as current conditions, updated forecasts, winds aloft and NOTAMs.

ALL
3462 [C] — (I41) — AC 00-45D, Section 2
IFR conditions are a ceiling less than 1,000 feet and/or visibility less than 3 miles.

- INK: No ceiling (CLR = clear) and visibility is 15 miles: VFR.
- BOI: No ceiling (SCT does not constitute a ceiling layer) and visibility is 30 miles: VFR.
- LAX: No ceiling (SCT does not constitute a ceiling layer) and visibility is 6 miles: VFR.
- MDW: Sky partially obscured, measured ceiling 700 OVC and visibility 1-1/2 miles: IFR.
- JFK: Indefinite ceiling 500 sky obscured and visibility 1/2 mile: IFR.

ALL
3463 [B] — (I41) — FAR §1.1
Ceiling means the height above the Earth's surface of the lowest layer of clouds or obscuring phenomena that is reported as "broken," "overcast," or "obscuration," and is not classified as "thin" or "partial."

ALL
3464 [A] — (I41) — AC 00-45D, Section 2
Wind follows dew point and is separated from it by a slash. The first two digits are direction from which the wind is blowing relative to true north. The second two digits are speed in knots. The group "1804" means wind from 180° true at 4 knots.

ALL
3465 [B] — (I41) — AC 00-45D, Section 2
Wind follows dew point and is separated from it by a slash. The first two digits are direction from which the wind is blowing relative to true north. The second two digits are speed in knots. The group "1112G18" means wind from 110° true at 12 knots with peak gusts to 18 knots.

ALL
3466 [B] — (I41) — AC 00-45D, Section 2
The remark for "MDW" is concerning obstructions to vision (RF2) and precipitation (RB12). MDW reported a sky partially obscured (-X) (a partial obscuration means 1/10 to 9/10 of the sky is hidden by surface-based phenomena). The "RF2" means 2/10 of the sky is hidden by rain (R) and fog (F). The "RB12" means rain (R) began (B) 12 minutes past the hour. The time of the MDW report is 1856Z, so the rain began at 1812Z.

ALL
3467 [A] — (I41) — AC 00-45D, Section 2
Chicago Midway Airport (MDW) reads:
  Sky partially obscured (-X)
  Measured (M) ceiling 700 overcast (7 OVC)
  Visibility 1-1/2 mi. (11/2)
  Heavy rain (R+), Fog (F)

The SA describes conditions as of the time of observation, not current conditions.

LTA
3468 [A] — (I41) — Taming the Gentle Giant, page 75
The telephone weather briefing given at 13Z indicates no clouds until 15Z, and no wind until after 20Z. The ideal time to launch balloons is as soon after 13Z as possible before the clouds and wind develop.

LTA
3469 [C] — (I41) — Taming the Gentle Giant, page 72
The telephone weather briefing given at 13Z indicates only a few scattered clouds at 5,000 feet AGL, with higher scattered cirrus at 25,000 feet MSL to form by 15Z. After 20Z, however, the wind should pick up to about 15 knots from the south. The marked increase of wind at 20Z indicates deteriorating ballooning weather.

GLI
3470 [C] — (I41) — AC 00-6A, Chapter 16
The telephone weather briefing indicates a few scattered clouds at 5,000 feet AGL, with higher scattered cirrus at 25,000 feet MSL. This briefing shows two different clouds bases and does not give cloud tops. Thermals are a product of instability. The height of thermals depends on the depth of the unstable layer, and their strength depends on the degree of instability. A cloud grows with a rising thermal and scattered cumulus clouds are positive signs of thermals. Whereas an abundant convective cloud cover reduces thermal activity, thermals will exist at least to the tops of the scattered clouds, especially if the outline is firm and sharp, indicating a growing cumulus.

GLI
3471 [B] — (I41) — AC 00-6A, Chapter 16
The telephone weather briefing indicates there should be a few scattered clouds at 5,000 feet AGL by 15Z. When convective clouds develop, thermal soaring usually is at its best and the problem of locating thermals is greatly simplified. Cumulus clouds are positive signs of thermals.

ALL
3472 [C] — (I42) — AC 00-45D, Section 3
Cloud layers in a PIREP are found after the "SK" heading. Height of the cloud base is given in hundreds of feet, then the cloud cover symbol (SCT, BKN, etc.) is given, followed by the height of cloud tops in hundreds of feet. A diagonal slash is used to separate cloud layers.
 The base of the broken (BKN) layer was reported by a pilot at 1,800 feet and tops at 5,500 feet (SK Ø18 BKN 055/).
 The question is asking for the overcast (OVC) layer that has a reported base at 7,200 feet and tops at 8,900 feet. All cloud heights in a PIREP are MSL (072 OVC 089).

ALL
3473 [C] — (I42) — AC 00-45D, Section 2
Winds are given after the "WV" heading. Wind direction is listed first, followed by wind speed in knots. WV 0921/ means wind from 090° at 21 knots. Air temperature is given in 2 digits, (in degrees Celsius), after the "TA" heading. Therefore, /TA -9/ means that the outside air temperature is -9°C.

ALL
3474 [A] — (I42) — AC 00-45D, Section 3
Cloud layers in a PIREP are found after the "SK" heading. Height of the cloud base is given in hundreds of feet, then the cloud cover symbol (SCT, BKN, etc.) is given, followed by the height of the cloud tops in hundreds of feet. All cloud heights in a PIREP are MSL.
 The first cloud layer was reported by a pilot to have bases at 1,800 feet and tops at 5,500 feet with broken (BKN) cloud cover (a broken cloud layer does constitute a ceiling).

If the field elevation is 1,295 feet MSL and the base of the first cloud layer (BKN) is 1,800 feet MSL, then the base of the ceiling is 505 feet AGL.

```
  1,800 MSL
− 1,295 MSL
    505 AGL
```

ALL
3475 [B] — (I42) — AC 00-45D, Section 3
Turbulence in a PIREP is found after the "TB" heading. /TB MDT 055-072/ means moderate (MDT) turbulence between 5,500 feet MSL and 7,200 feet MSL.

ALL
3476 [B] — (I42) — AC 00-45D, Section 3
The intensity and type of icing is listed in a PIREP after the "ICG" heading. /ICG LGT-MDT CLR 072-089 means light (LGT) to moderate (MDT) clear (CLR) icing from 7,200 feet MSL to 8,900 feet MSL.

LTA
3477 [C] — (I43) — AC 00-45D, Section 2
Local information is provided by the Surface Aviation Weather Report.

ALL
3478 [C] — (I43) — AC 00-45D, Section 4
An Area Forecast (FA) is used to determine forecast enroute weather and to interpolate conditions at airports which do not have Terminal Forecasts (FT) issued.

ALL
3479 [C] — (I43) — AC 00-45D, Section 4
The Terminal Forecast for Gage (GAG) shows expected changes are to occur at 16Z. By 16Z the prevailing condition will be 6,000 SCT, CEILING 10,000 BKN CHANCE CEILING 5,000 BKN (ceiling is defined as broken or overcast). The next expected change is at 01Z. The question asks for the forecast ceiling between 16Z and 01Z (midnight Z), which falls within this period.

ALL
3480 [C] — (I43) — AC 00-45D, Section 4
According to the date-time group (011515) for Hobart (HBR), the terminal forecast is valid beginning on the first day of the month at 1500Z and is valid until 1500Z the following day. The forecast begins at 1500Z with winds at 300° at 10 knots (3010). Changes are not expected until 1700Z. The question asks for wind conditions at 1600Z, which falls within this first period.

ALL
3481 [C] — (I43) — AC 00-45D, Section 4
The last time period for McAlester (MLC) is the 6-hour categorical outlook. The marginal VFR (MVFR) weather is due to low ceilings (CIG) and restrictions to visibility due to thunderstorms and rain showers (TRW).

ALL
3482 [A] — (I43) — AC 00-45D, Section 2
The last time period for Ponca City (PNC) is the 6-hour categorical outlook, which starts at 09Z. The term "WND" indicates that the wind velocity is forecast to be 25 knots or greater.

ALL
3483 [B] — (I43) — AC 00-45D, Section 4
The wind for Tulsa (TUL) is forecast to be 190°, 15 knots gusting to 22 knots by 15Z and then shifting only slightly to 180°, 15 knots gusting to 25 knots by 19Z. By 23Z, the wind should shift to 320°, 15 knots gusting to 25 knots.

ALL
3484 [B] — (I43) — AC 00-45D, Section 4
When changes are expected, preceding conditions are followed by a period (.) before time and conditions of the expected change. "21Z CFP" means by 2100Z, cold frontal passage is expected.

ALL
3485 [B] — (I43) — AC-00-45D, Section 4
The report says, from 1800Z to 2100Z, the ceiling will be 3,000 feet and be a broken layer (C30 BKN), occasionally scattered, and because there is no visibility marked, it will be 6 statute miles or greater. These are MVFR and VFR conditions. The report does indicate there is a chance of ceilings being 700 feet and obscured. (CHC C7 X). There will also be only 1/2-mile visibility with thundershower activity (1/2 TRW). These are IFR conditions.

ALL
3486 [A] — (I43) — AC 00-45D, Section 4
The last 6 hours of the terminal forecast is a categorical outlook. 09Z VFR Wind means that from 0900Z until 1500Z (the end of the forecast period), weather will be no ceiling, or ceiling more than 3,000 feet and visibility greater than 5 miles with wind forecast 25 knots or greater.

ALL
3487 [A] — (I43) — AC 00-45D, Section 4
An Area Forecast (FA) is a forecast of general conditions over an area the size of several states.

ALL
3488 [C] — (I43) — AC 00-45D, Section 4
Under the outlook portion of the report it says "VFR" which means ceilings 3,000 feet or greater and visibility 5 miles or greater.

ALL
3489 [C] — (I43) — AC 00-45D, Section 4
A forecast of non-thunderstorm-related icing of light or greater intensity for up to 12 hours is included in an Area Forecast.

ALL
3490 [A] — (I43) — AC 00-45D, Section 4
The "SIG CLDS and WX" section is a 12-hour forecast of clouds and weather significant to flight operations plus a 6-hour categorical outlook. This section may be broken down by states or geographical areas.

ALL
3491 [C] — (I43) — AC 00-45D, Section 4
Look at the flight precaution of the fourth line down from the top of the Area Forecast. It says turbulence (TURBC) for TN AL and coastal waters, icing in TN, and IFR conditions for TX. In the fourth paragraph down from the top it gives some more information about TN, AL, and the coastal waters. It forecasts occasional moderate turbulence from 25,000 to 38,000 feet due to the jet stream (OCNL MDT TURBC 250-380 DUE TO JTSTR).

ALL
3492 [A] — (I43) — AC 00-45D, Section 4
Under the last section where it says "SGFNT CLOUD AND WX VALID UNTIL 042300... OTLK 042300-050500," the entire area is covered, where it says OK AR TX LA MS AL AND CSTL WTRS and TN. The outlook for these areas is VFR.

ALL
3493 [B] — (I43) — AC 00-45D, Section 4
Look at the last section that says "SGFNT CLOUD AND WX" and find the line that reads "OK AR TX LA MS AL AND CSTL WTRS". This line refers to the entire area except for TN and is valid from 1040Z until 2300Z. The forecast is for 8,000 feet scattered to clear except visibility below 3 in fog until 1500Z over portions of south-central Texas (80 SCT TO CLR EXCP VSBY BLO 3F TIL 15Z OVER PTNS S CNTRL TX).

ALL
3494 [A] — (I43) — AC 00-45D, Section 4
A Transcribed Weather Broadcast (TWEB) contains route forecasts and winds aloft recorded on tapes and broadcast continuously over selected low-frequency navigational aids and/or VORs.

ALL
3495 [C] — (I43) — AC-00-45D, Section 4
Convective SIGMETs include: severe thunderstorms, embedded thunderstorms, line of thunderstorms, thunderstorms greater than or equal to VIP (Digital Video Interrogator and Processor) level "A" affecting 40% or more of an area of 3,000 square miles.

ALL
3496 [A] — (I43) — AC 00-45D, Section 4
Any convective SIGMET implies severe or greater turbulence, severe icing, and low-level wind shear. The forecast may be issued for any of the following: Severe thunderstorms due to—

1. Surface winds greater than or equal to 50 knots, or
2. Hail at the surface greater than or equal to 3/4 inches in diameter, or
3. Tornadoes, embedded thunderstorms, lines of thunderstorms.

ALL
3497 [C] — (I43) — AC 00-45D, Section 4
A SIGMET advises of weather potentially hazardous to all aircraft.

ALL
3498 [B] — (I43) — AC 00-45D, Section 4
A SIGMET advises of weather potentially hazardous to all aircraft other than convective activity. Some items included are severe icing, and severe or extreme turbulence.

ALL
3499 [A] — (I43) — AC 00-45D, Section 4
An AIRMET is for weather that may be hazardous to single-engine, other light aircraft and VFR pilots.

ALL
3500 [B] — (I43) — AC 00-45D, Section 4
A six-digit group shows wind directions (in reference to true north) in the first two digits, wind speed (in knots) in the second two digits, and temperature (in Celsius) in the last two digits. In this case 2325 + 07 means 230° at 25 knots, and the temperature is 7°C.

ALL
3501 [A] — (I43) — AC 00-45D, Section 4
A six-digit group shows wind directions (in reference to true north) in the first two digits, wind speed (in knots) in the second two digits, and temperature (in Celsius) in the last two digits. In this case 2356 – 16 means 230° at 56 knots, and the temperature is -16°C.

ALL
3502 [B] — (I43) — AC 00-45D, Section 4
A six-digit group shows wind directions (in reference to true north) in the first two digits, wind speed (in knots) in the second two digits, and temperature (in Celsius) in the last two digits. In this case, 235347 means winds from 230° at 53 knots and temperature -47°C (temperatures are negative above 24,000 feet).

ALL
3503 [A] — (I43) — AC 00-45D, Section 4
A six-digit group shows wind directions (in reference to true north) in the first two digits, wind speed (in knots) in the second two digits, and temperature (in Celsius) in the last two digits. In this case, 0507 means wind from 050° at 07 knots, and temperature is not reported at that altitude.

ALL
3504 [C] — (I43) — AC 00-45D, Section 4
A six-digit group shows wind direction (reference true north), wind speed knots and temperature (°C). Encoded wind speeds of 100 to 199 knots have 50 added to the direction code and 100 subtracted from the speed. Thus, a coded direction of more than "36" indicates winds of 100 knots or more. The STL forecast for 34,000 feet is "730649." To decode, 50 must be subtracted from the direction and 100 knots added to the speed. The wind direction is 230° (73 – 50 = 23), speed is 106 knots (06 + 100 knots = 106 knots), and temperature is -49°C (temperatures are negative above 24,000 feet).

ALL
3505 [C] — (I43) — AC 00-45D, Section 4
A six-digit group shows wind directions (in reference to true north) in the first two digits, wind speed (in knots) in the second two digits, and temperature (in Celsius) in the last two digits.

ALL
3506 [B] — (I43) — AC 00-45D, Section 4
When the forecast speed is less than 5 knots, the coded group is "9900" and reads "light and variable" on the Winds Aloft Forecast.

ALL
3507 [A] — (I44) — AC 00-45D, Section 6
The front shown from New Mexico to Indiana is a stationary front. *See* the following figure.

Symbols on Surface Analysis	(Surface Weather Maps)	
Color	**Symbol**	**Description**
Blue	▼▼▼	Cold front
Red	●●●	Warm front
Red/Blue	●▼●●	Stationary front
Purple	●▲●▲	Occluded front

Question 3507

ALL
3508 [B] — (I44) — AC 00-45D, Section 6
The IFR category observed weather is shown as a hatched area, outlined by a smooth line. The one station circle that was reporting IFR conditions shows the obstruction to vision to the left of the station circle as fog.

ALL
3509 [A] — (I45) — AC 00-45D, Section 6
The Weather Depiction Chart is computer-prepared from surface aviation (SA) reports to give a broad overview of observed flying category conditions as of the valid time of the chart. From it, you can determine general weather conditions more readily than any other source. Therefore, the Weather Depiction Chart is a choice place to begin the weather briefing and flight planning.

ALL
3510 [C] — (I45) — AC 00-45D, Section 6
Areas inside of contour lines without shading on a weather depiction chart indicate areas where ceilings are 1,000'-3,000' and/or visibility is 3 to 5 statute miles. These are marginal VFR conditions.

ALL
3511 [B] — (I45) — AC 00-45D, Section 6
IFR category observed weather is shown as a hatched area outlined by a smooth line. IFR conditions are defined as a ceiling less than 1,000 feet and/or visibility less than 3 miles. The visibility for the Oregon station inside the hatched area is reported as 5 miles. However, the reported ceiling for both stations is less than 1,000 feet. The cloud height is shown under the station circle in hundreds of feet. The Oregon station is reporting 300 feet OVC, and the California station is reporting a ceiling of 200 feet with sky obscured.

ALL
3512 [C] — (I45) — AC 00-45D, Section 6
The current weather from Central Arkansas to Southeast Alabama, as of the time of the chart, was VFR, since there is no outline. The cloud height is entered under the station circle in hundreds of feet. The entire route shows cloud heights at 25,000 feet. The total sky cover is shown by symbols. The chart shows a sky cover from broken to scattered along the route. *See* the following figure. The route weather was VFR at the time of the chart. If the visibility was 3 to 5 miles which is MVFR, then the area would be outlined with no hatching.

Symbol	Total Sky Cover
○	Sky clear
◐	1/10 to 5/10 inclusive (Scattered)
◕	6/10 to 9/10 inclusive (Broken)
●	10/10 (Overcast)
⊗	Sky obscured or partially obscured

Question 3512

ALL
3513 [B] — (I46) — AC 00-45D, Section 3
Radar weather reports (RAREPs) include location of precipitation along with type, intensity, and trend.

ALL
3514 [A] — (I46) — AC 00-45D, Section 3
Radar detects objects of precipitation size or greater. Based on the amount of precipitation radar detects, it can determine if it is a thunderstorm.

ALL
3515 [B] — (I46) — AC 00-45D, Section 7
Line or area movement is indicated by a shaft and barb combination with the shaft indicating the direction and the barbs the speed (knots). A whole barb is 10 knots, a half barb is 5 knots, and a pennant is 50 knots. The radar return at "A" in FAA Figure 19 shows a whole barb (10 knots) and a half barb (5 knots) indicating area movement at 15 knots towards the east.

ALL
3516 [C] — (I46) — AC 00-45D, Section 7
The radar return at "C" shows the symbol, "RW+" which means rain showers increasing in intensity.

ALL
3517 [B] — (I46) — AC 00-45D, Section 7
Individual cell movement is indicated by an arrow with the speed in knots entered as a number. The radar return at "D" shows the cell movement toward the northeast at 20 knots.

ALL
3518 [C] — (I46) — AC 00-45D, Section 7
Echo heights in locations with radar designed for weather detection are precipitation tops and bases. Tops are entered above a short line while available bases are entered below, both are in hundreds of feet MSL. The top height displayed is the highest in the indicated area. The tops in area "D" are shown to be 30,000 feet.

ALL
3519 [B] — (I46) — AC 00-45D, Section 7
Severe weather watch areas are outlined by heavy dashed lines, usually in the form of a large rectangular box.

ALL
3520 [B] — (I47) — AC 00-45D, Section 8
While Significant Weather Prognostic Charts portray forecast weather which may influence flight planning, they are most useful in identifying the freezing level and areas of turbulence.

ALL
3521 [A] — (I47) — AC 00-45D, Section 8
The area in lower California on the 12-hour prog is enclosed by a long-dashed line indicating a forecast area of moderate or greater turbulence. A single-hat symbol denotes moderate intensity. *See* the following figure. Figures below and above a short line show expected base and top of the turbulent layer in hundreds of feet MSL. Absence of a figure below the line indicates turbulence from the surface upward. In lower California, moderate turbulence is expected from the surface to 18,000 feet MSL.

Question 3521

ALL
3522 [A] — (I47) — AC 00-45D, Section 8
The two left panels are 12-hour progs. The upper left panel is the 12-hour prog of significant weather from the surface (SFC) to 400 millibars (24,000 feet). The lower left panel is the 12-hour surface prog. The gulf coast area is outlined in both a smooth line (IFR) and a scalloped line (MVFR) in the upper left panel. This is associated with the dash-dot outlined area shown in the lower left panel. The dash-dot line encloses areas of showers or thunderstorms, with symbols inside indicating both. *See* the following figure.

Question 3522

ALL
3523 [A] — (I47) — AC 00-45D, Section 8
High- and low-pressure centers are shown in the lower panels. Associated with each pressure center is an arrow showing direction of movement and a number indicating speed in knots. The area associated with the cold front and low-pressure area in the western states is forecast to move east at 30 knots.

ALL
3524 [B] — (I47) — AC 00-45D, Section 8
Freezing level height contours for freezing levels are drawn with dashes at 4,000-foot intervals for the two upper panels. Contours are labeled in hundreds of feet MSL. The dotted line shows where the freezing level is forecast to be at the surface. The upper right panel is the 24-hour significant weather prog. The freezing level height shown over northeastern Oklahoma is 8,000 feet.

GLI
3525 [A] — (I49) — AC 00-6A, Chapter 16
Since thermals depend on sinking cold air forcing warm air upward, strength of thermals depends on the temperature difference between the sinking air and the rising air—the greater the temperature difference, the stronger the thermals. To arrive at an approximation of this difference, a thermal index is computed. A thermal index may be computed for any level using upper soundings.

ALL
3526 [A] — (H05) — AC 00-45D, Section 1
When requesting a briefing, make known you are a pilot. Give clear and concise facts about your flight:

1. Type of flight: VFR or IFR
2. Aircraft identification or pilot's name
3. Aircraft type
4. Departure point
5. Route-of-flight
6. Destination
7. Altitude
8. Estimated time of departure
9. Estimated time en route or estimated time of arrival

ALL
3527 [B] — (H05) — AC 00-45D, Section 1
When requesting a briefing, make known you are a pilot. Give clear and concise facts about your flight:

1. Type of flight: VFR or IFR
2. Aircraft identification or pilot's name
3. Aircraft type
4. Departure point
5. Route-of-flight
6. Destination
7. Altitude
8. Estimated time of departure
9. Estimated time en route or estimated time of arrival

ALL
3528 [C] — (H05) — AC 00-45D, Section 1
When requesting a briefing, make known you are a pilot. Give clear and concise facts about your flight:

1. Type of flight: VFR or IFR
2. Aircraft identification or pilot's name
3. Aircraft type
4. Departure point
5. Route-of-flight
6. Destination
7. Altitude
8. Estimated time of departure
9. Estimated time en route or estimated time of arrival

ALL
3529 [C] — (H06) — AC 61-23B, Chapters 6 and 7
Use the following steps:

1. Measure the distances from Hampton Roads to Chesapeake Municipal and from Chesapeake Municipal to First Flight:

    Hampton Roads to Chesapeake = 10 NM
    Chesapeake to First Flight = 50 NM

2. Calculate the elapsed time from Hampton Roads to Chesapeake Municipal:

    1501 − 1456 = 5 minutes elapsed time

3. Determine the time required to cover the remaining 50 NM from Chesapeake to First Flight with the ratio:

    $$\frac{5}{10} = \frac{X}{50} = 25 \text{ minutes}$$

4. Add the time remaining to the actual time at Chesapeake to determine the estimated time of arrival (ETA).

    1501 + 25 = 1526 ETA

ALL
3530 [A] — (H07) — AIM ¶9-1-4
Graticules on Sectional Aeronautical Charts are the lines dividing each 30 minutes of latitude and each 30 minutes of longitude. Each tick mark represents one minute of latitude or longitude. Latitude increases northward, west longitude increases going westward. The approximate latitude and longitude of Currituck County Airport is 36°24'N, 76°01'W.

ALL
3531 [C] — (H07) — AC 61-23B, Chapter 4
Use the following steps:

1. Plot the course from First Flight Airport to Hampton Roads Airport.
2. Measure the true course angle at the approximate midpoint of the route. The true course is 321°.
3. Note that the variation is 10°W as shown on the isogonic line.
4. Using the formula:

    MC = TC ± VAR
    MC = 321° + 10°W
    MC = 331°

ALL
3532 [B] — (H07) — AC 61-23B, Chapter 7
Use the following steps:

1. Plot the 340° radial from the Elizabeth City VOR to the point of intersection with V1. Caution: the numerals "340" just inside the Elizabeth City compass rose (just to the left of the course line), refer to an obstruction height, not a VOR radial.
2. Measure the distance from Norfolk to the plotted intersection using the sectional scale of a plotter. The distance is 18 NM.

ALL
3533 [C] — (H07) — AC 61-23B, Chapter 7
1. Locate the Shawboro Airport and the Elizabeth City VOR in FAA Figure 21. Draw the radial (magnetic course "FROM") of the Elizabeth City VOR on which Ferebee Airport lies (030°).
2. When over the Shawboro Airport on the 030° radial, the CDI should be centered with a 030° FROM indication or a 210° TO indication (the reciprocal). Dials 2 and 8 satisfy these conditions. Only dial 8 is listed in the answer choices.

AIR, RTC
3534 [B] — (H06) — AC 61-23B, Chapters 6 and 7
Use the following steps:
1. Plot the course from Mercer Airport to Minot Airport.
2. Measure the true course angle at the approximate midpoint of the route. The true course (TC) is 011°.
3. Determine the ground speed using a flight computer:

    Wind direction is 330° (given in question)
    Wind speed is 25 knots (given in question)
    True course is 011° (found in Step 2)
    True airspeed is 100 knots (given in question)

    Therefore, the ground speed is 79.8 knots.
4. Measure the distance from Mercer Airport to Minot Airport (59 NM).
5. Calculate the time en route using a flight computer:

    Distance is 59 NM (found in Step 4)
    Ground speed is 80 knots (found in Step 3)

    Therefore, time en route is 44.5 minutes.
6. Add the allowance for departure and climbout (3.5 minutes) to the time en route (44.5 minutes) to obtain the estimated total time:

    44.5 + 3.5 = 48.0 minutes total time

ALL
3535 [B] — (H07) — AIM ¶9-1-4
Graticules on Sectional Aeronautical Charts are the lines dividing each 30 minutes of latitude and each 30 minutes of longitude. Each tick mark represents one minute of latitude or longitude. Latitude increases northward, west longitude increases going westward. The Crooked Lake airport is located at approximately 47°39'30"N latitude and 100°53'00"W longitude.

ALL
3536 [C] — (H07) — AIM ¶9-1-4
Graticules on Sectional Aeronautical Charts are the lines dividing each 30 minutes of latitude and each 30 minutes of longitude. Each tick mark represents one minute of latitude or longitude. Latitude increases northward, west longitude increases going westward. Washburn is located at approximately 47°21'N latitude and 101°01'W longitude.

LTA
3537 [B] — (H07) — AC 61-23B, Chapter 7
This is a time/speed/distance problem.
1. The distance is 8 NM (given in the question).
2. The time is:

    11:08 − 10:56 = 12 minutes
3. Use: $\dfrac{\text{Distance}}{\text{Time}} \times 60 = \text{Ground speed}$

    $\dfrac{8 \text{ NM}}{12 \text{ min.}} \times 60 = 40 \text{ knots}$
4. Calculate the distance traveled on the next leg at this speed by 12:11.

    12:11 − 11:08 = :63 minutes
5. Use:

    $\dfrac{\text{Speed}}{60} \times \text{Time} = \text{Distance} \quad \dfrac{40 \text{ kts}}{60 \text{ min.}} \times 63 \text{ min.} = 42 \text{ NM}$
6. Locate the 8 NM creek and measure an additional 42 NM along V15. You are east of Underwood; it is west of your position. The legs were 8 NM and 42 NM, total 50 NM.

AIR, RTC
3538 [C] — (H07) — AC 61-23B, Chapter 7
Use the following steps:
1. Plot the course from Mercer County Regional Airport to Minot Airport.
2. Measure the true course angle at the approximate midpoint of the route. The true course (TC) is 011°.
3. Find the true heading using a flight computer:

    Wind direction is 330° (given in question)
    Wind speed is 25 knots (given in question)
    True course is 011° (found in Step 2)
    True airspeed is 100 knots (given in question)

    Therefore, the true heading is 002°.
4. Calculate the magnetic heading by subtracting the easterly variation (11°) from the true heading (002°).

    MH = TH ± VAR
    MH = 002° − 11°E
    MH = 351°

AIR, RTC
3539 [A] — (H07) — AC 61-23B, Chapter 7
Use the following steps:
1. Plot a direct course from Mercer Airport to the Minot Airport VORTAC.
2. Note the radial (magnetic course FROM Minot VORTAC) on which the plotted course lies (175°).
3. Determine the course TO Minot VORTAC by finding the reciprocal:

    TO = FROM + 180°
    TO = 175° + 180°
    TO = 355° (this is closest to 001°)

AIR, RTC
3540 [C] — (H06) — AC 61-23B, Chapter 7
Use the following steps:

1. Plot the course from Dave Wall Field to St. Maries Airport.
2. Measure the true course angle at the approximate midpoint of the route (181°).
3. Determine the ground speed using a flight computer:

    Wind direction is 215° (given in question)
    Wind speed is 25 knots (given in question)
    True course is 181° (found in Step 2)
    True airspeed is 125 knots (given in question)

    Therefore, the ground speed is 103.5 knots.

4. Measure the distance from Dave Wall Field to St. Maries Airport (58 NM).
5. Calculate the time en route using a flight computer:

    Distance is 58 NM (found in Step 4)
    Ground speed is 103.5 knots (found in Step 3)

    Therefore, the time en route is 33 minutes, 37 seconds.

AIR, RTC
3541 [C] — (H06) — AC 61-23B, Chapters 6 and 7
Use the following steps:

1. Plot the course from Priest River Airport to Shoshone County Airport.
2. Measure the true course angle at the approximate midpoint of the route (144°).
3. Determine the ground speed:

    Wind direction is 030° (given in question)
    Wind speed is 12 knots (given in question)
    True course is 144° (found in Step 2)
    True airspeed is 95 knots (given in question)

    Therefore, the ground speed is 99.2 knots.

4. Measure the distance from Priest River Airport to Shoshone County Airport (49 NM).
5. Calculate the time en route using a flight computer:

    Distance is 49 NM (found in Step 4)
    Ground speed is 99.2 knots (found in Step 3)

    Therefore, the time en route is 29 minutes, 38 seconds.

6. Add the allowance for climbout (2 minutes) to the time en route (29.6 minutes) to obtain the estimated total time:

    29.6 + 2.0 = 31.6 minutes total time

AIR, RTC
3542 [B] — (H06) — AC 61-23B, Chapters 6 and 7
Use the following steps:

1. Plot the course from St. Maries Airport to Priest River Airport.
2. Measure the true course angle at the approximate midpoint of the route (345°).
3. Determine the ground speed using a flight computer:

    Wind direction is 300° (given in question)
    Wind speed is 14 knots (given in question)
    True course is 345° (found in Step 2)
    True airspeed is 90 knots (given in question)

    Therefore, the ground speed is 79.6 knots.

4. Measure the distance from St. Maries Airport to Priest River Airport (53 NM).
5. Calculate the time en route using a flight computer:

    Distance is 53 NM (found in Step 4)
    Ground speed is 79.6 knots (found in Step 3)

    Therefore, the time en route is 39 minutes, 57 seconds.

6. Add the allowance for climbout (3 minutes) to the time en route (40 minutes) to obtain the estimated total time:

    40 + 3 = 43 minutes total time

ALL
3543 [B] — (H07) — AIM ¶9-1-4
Graticules on Sectional Aeronautical Charts are the lines dividing each 30 minutes of latitude and each 30 minutes of longitude. Each tick mark represents one minute of latitude or longitude. Latitude increases northward, west longitude increases going westward. The approximate latitude and longitude of Shoshone County Airport is 47°32'N, 116°11'W.

LTA
3544 [A] — (H07) — AC 61-23B, Chapter 7
A balloon moves with the wind, so the problem asks: where do you end up if your ground speed is 5 knots and you are flying a true course of 220° for two hours?

1. Calculate the distance that will be traveled at this speed during the time given.

    Speed x Time = Distance
    5 NM x 2 hours = 10 NM total distance

2. Draw your true course line from Ranch Aero, from 220°, and measure 10 NM up the line from Ranch Aero to find you are near Hackney (Pvt) Airport.

AIR, RTC
3545 [B] — (H07) — AC 61-23B, Chapter 7
Use the following steps:

1. Plot the course from Dave Wall Field to St. Maries Airport.
2. Measure the true course angle at the approximate midpoint of the route (181°).
3. Find true heading, using a flight computer:

   Wind direction is 215° (given in question)
   Wind speed is 25 knots (given in question)
   True course is 181° (found in Step 2)
   True airspeed is 125 knots (given in question)

   Therefore, the true heading is 187°.

4. Calculate the magnetic heading by subtracting the easterly variation (19°) from the true heading (187°).

   MH = TH ± VAR
   MH = 187° – 19°E
   MH = 168°

AIR, RTC
3546 [A] — (H07) — AC 61-23B, Chapter 7
Use the following steps:

1. Plot the course from Priest River to Shoshone County Airport.
2. Measure the true course angle at the approximate midpoint of the route (144°).
3. Find the true heading using a flight computer:

   Wind direction is 030° (given in question)
   Wind speed is 12 knots (given in question)
   True course is 144° (found in Step 2)
   True airspeed is 95 knots (given in question)

   Therefore, the true heading is 137°.

4. Calculate the magnetic heading by subtracting the easterly variation (19°E, as shown on the dashed isogonic line) from the true heading (137°).

   MH = TH ± VAR
   MH = 137° – 19°E
   MH = 118° (closest answer is 116°)

AIR, RTC
3547 [A] — (H07) — AC 61-23B, Chapter 7
1. Plot the course from St. Maries Airport to Priest River Airport.
2. Measure the true course angle at the approximate midpoint of the route (345°).
3. Find the true heading using a flight computer:

   Wind direction is 300° (given in question)
   Wind speed is 14 knots (given in question)
   True course is 345° (found in Step 2)
   True airspeed is 90 knots (given in question)

   Therefore, the true heading is 339°.

4. Calculate the magnetic heading (MH) by subtracting the easterly variation (19°E, as shown on the dashed isogonic line) from the true heading (339°).

   MH = TH ± VAR
   MH = 339° – 19°E
   MH = 320°

AIR, RTC
3548 [B] — (H06) — AC 61-23B, Chapters 6 and 7
Use the following steps:

1. Plot the course from Allendale County Airport to Claxton-Evans County Airport.
2. Measure the true course angle at the approximate midpoint of the route (212°).
3. Determine the ground speed, using a flight computer:

   Wind direction is 090° (given in question)
   Wind speed is 16 knots (given in question)
   True course is 212° (found in Step 2)
   True airspeed is 90 knots (given in question)

   Therefore, the ground speed is 97.4 knots.

4. Measure the distance from Allendale County Airport to Claxton-Evans County Airport (57 NM).
5. Calculate the time en route, using a flight computer:

   Distance is 57 NM (found in Step 4)
   Ground speed is 97.4 knots (found in Step 3)

   Therefore, the time en route is 35 minutes, 7 seconds.

6. Add the allowance for climbout (2 minutes) to the time en route (35 minutes) to obtain the estimated total time.

   35 + 2 = 37 minutes total time

AIR, RTC
3549 [B] — (H06) — AC 61-23B, Chapters 6 and 7
Use the following steps:

1. Plot the true course from Claxton-Evans County Airport to Hampton Varnville Airport.
2. Measure the true course angle at the approximate midpoint of the route (044°).
3. Determine the ground speed, using a flight computer:

   Wind direction is 290° (given in question)
   Wind speed is 18 knots (given in question)
   True course is 044° (found in Step 2)
   True airspeed is 85 knots (given in question)

   Therefore, the ground speed is 90.7 knots.

4. Measure the distance from Claxton-Evans County Airport to Hampton Varnville County Airport (57 NM).
5. Calculate the time en route, using a flight computer:

   Distance is 57 NM (found in Step 4)
   Ground speed is 90.7 knots (found in Step 3)

   Therefore, the time en route is 37 minutes, 42 seconds.

6. Add the allowance for climbout (2 minutes) to the time en route (37 minutes) to obtain the estimated total time.

37 + 2 = 39 minutes total time

AIR, RTC
3550 [C] — (H07) — AC 61-23B, Chapter 7
Use the following steps:

1. Plot the course from Allendale County Airport to Claxton-Evans County Airport.
2. Measure the true course angle at the approximate midpoint of the route (212°).
3. Find true heading, using a flight computer:

   Wind direction is 090° (given in question)
   Wind speed is 16 knots (given in question)
   True course is 212° (found in Step 2)
   True airspeed is 90 knots (given in question)

   Therefore, the true heading is 203°.
4. Calculate the magnetic heading (MH) by adding the westerly variation (4°W) to the true heading (203°):

   MH = TH ± VAR
   MH = 203° + 4°W
   MH = 207°
5. Note that the compass deviation card indicates that in order to fly a magnetic course of 210°, the pilot must steer a compass heading of 214°, or a +4° compass deviation. Calculate the compass heading (CH) by adding the compass deviation (+4°) to the magnetic heading (207°).

   CH = MH ± DEV
   CH = 207° + 4°
   CH = 211°

AIR
3551 [A] — (H07) — AC 61-23B, Chapter 7
Use the following steps:

1. Plot the course from Claxton-Evans County Airport to Hampton Varnville Airport.
2. Measure the true course angle at the approximate midpoint of the route (044°).
3. Find true heading, using a flight computer:

   Wind direction is 290° (given in question)
   Wind speed is 18 knots (given in question)
   True course is 044° (found in Step 2)
   True airspeed is 85 knots (given in question)

   Therefore, the true heading is 033°.
4. Calculate the magnetic heading by adding the westerly variation (4°W) to the true heading (033°).

   MH = TH ± VAR
   MH = 033° + 4°W
   MH = 037°

5. Note that the compass deviation card indicates that in order to fly a magnetic course of 030°, the pilot must steer a compass heading of 027° or a 3° compass deviation. Calculate the compass heading (CH) by subtracting the compass deviation (3°) from the magnetic heading (037°).

   CH = MH ± DEV
   CH = 037° − 3°
   CH = 034°

ALL
3552 [A] — (H07) — AC 61-23B, Chapter 7
Use the following steps:

1. Plot the 310° radial (magnetic course FROM) of the Savannah VORTAC.
2. Plot the 190° radial of the Allendale VOR.
3. Note the intersection of the two plotted radials over the town of Guyton.

ALL
3553 [B] — (H07) — AC 61-23B, Chapter 7
1. Plot the course direct from Hampton Varnville Airport to the Savannah VORTAC.
2. Note the radial (magnetic course from Savannah) on which the plotted course lies (005°).
3. Determine the course TO the VORTAC by finding the reciprocal:

   TO = FROM + 180°
   TO = 005° + 180°
   TO = 185°

AIR, RTC
3554 [C] — (H07) — AC 61-23B, Chapters 6 and 7
Use the following steps:

1. Locate the intersection of the 248° radial of Allendale VOR with V185 (MILEN intersection).
2. Locate the intersection of the 216° radial of Allendale VOR with V185 (DOVER intersection).
3. Measure the distance between the MILEN and DOVER intersections (11 NM).
4. Compute the time it takes to fly from MILEN intersection to DOVER intersection:

   1000 − 0951 = 9 minutes elapsed time
5. Calculate the ground speed, using a flight computer (67 knots).
6. Measure the distance remaining from DOVER intersection to SAVANNAH VORTAC (41 NM).
7. Compute the time it takes to fly from DOVER intersection to SAVANNAH VORTAC, using a flight computer (41 NM at 67 knots) as 37 minutes.
8. Compute the time of arrival (ETA) at SAVANNAH VORTAC:

   1000 + 0037 = 1037 ETA

LTA
3555 [B] — (H06) — AC 21-23B, Chapter 7
Use the following steps:

1. Plot the course from Majors Airport to Winnsboro Airport.
2. Measure the true course angle at the approximate midpoint of the route (100°).
3. Determine the ground speed, using a flight computer:

    Wind direction is 340° (given in question)
    Wind speed is 12 knots (given in question)
    True course is 100° (found in Step 2)
    True airspeed is 36 knots (given in question)

    Therefore, the ground speed is 40.5 knots.

4. Measure the distance from Majors Airport to Winnsboro Airport, (40 NM).
5. Calculate the time en route, using a flight computer:

    Distance is 40 NM (found in Step 4)
    Ground speed is 40.5 knots (found in Step 3)

    Therefore, the time en route is 59 minutes, 16 seconds.

ALL
3556 [A] — (H07) — AC 61-23B, Chapter 4
Use the following steps:

1. Plot the course from Airpark East Airport to Winnsboro Airport.
2. Measure the true course angle at the approximate midpoint of the route (082°).
3. Calculate the magnetic course by subtracting the magnetic variation (6° 30') from the true course (082°).

    MC = TC ± VAR
    MC = 082° – 6°30'E
    MC = 75°30' (075° is the closest answer)

LTA
3557 [B] — (H07) — AC 61-23B, Chapter 7
Use the following steps:

1. Locate Quitman VORTAC and Blue Ridge VORTAC.
2. Measure the distance from Quitman VORTAC to the intersection of the powerline with V114 (5 NM).
3. Calculate the ground speed of the airship:

    Speed = Distance ÷ Time
    Speed = 5 NM ÷ (0948 – 0940)
    Speed = 5 NM ÷ 8 minutes or .1333 hours
    Speed = 37.5 knots

4. Measure the distance remaining from the "intersection" to Blue Ridge VORTAC (51 NM).
5. Calculate the time required to travel 51 NM at a constant 37.5 knots ground speed.

    Time = Distance ÷ Speed
    Time = 51 NM ÷ 37.5 knots
    Time = 1.36 hours or 1 hour, 21 minutes

6. Compute the arrival time by the adding estimated enroute time to the time of passing the intersection:

    0120 time en route
    + 0948 time passing intersection
    1109 ETA

LTA
3558 [A] — (H07) — AC 61-23B, Chapter 7
1. Plot the course from Majors Airport to Winnsboro Airport.
2. Measure the true course angle at the approximate midpoint of the route (100°).
3. Find true heading, using a flight computer:

    Wind direction is 340° (given in question)
    Wind speed is 12 knots (given in question)
    True course is 100° (found in Step 2)
    True airspeed is 36 knots (given in question)

    Therefore, the true heading is 083°.

4. Calculate the magnetic heading by subtracting the easterly variation (6°30'E) from the true heading (084°).

    MH = TH ± VAR
    MH = 084° – 6°30'E
    MH = 78°

LTA
3559 [B] — (H07) — AC 61-23B, Chapter 7
Use the following steps:

1. Plot the 250° radial (magnetic course FROM) of the Sulphur Springs VORTAC.
2. Plot the 130° radial (magnetic course FROM) of the Blue Ridge VORTAC.
3. Note the intersection of the two plotted radials over the Meadowview Airport (Pvt).

ALL
3560 [A] — (H07) — AC 61-23B, Chapter 7
Use the following steps:

1. Plot the course direct from Majors Airport to Quitman VORTAC.
2. Note the radial (magnetic course FROM) of Quitman VORTAC on which the plotted course lies (281°).
3. Determine the course TO the VORTAC by finding the reciprocal:

    TO = FROM + 180°
    TO = 281° + 180
    TO = 461° – 360° = 101°

ALL
3561 [C] — (H07) — AC 61-23B, Chapter 7
Use the following steps:

1. Locate Lone Oak and Blue Ridge VORTAC. Draw the magnetic course from Blue Ridge VORTAC to Lone Oak, (120°).

2. Notice that the OBS selections of all the dials in FAA Figure 29 are 030° or 210°, both of which are at 90° with respect to the 120° radial. Therefore, when over Lone Oak, the flag should indicate neither "TO" nor "FROM" and the course needle should have full deflection either side.

3. Dials 3 and 7, of FAA Figure 29, are on the 120° radial. Both provide a correct indication, but on reciprocal headings. Dial 7 is the only correct answer provided.

AIR
3562 [A] — (H06) — AC 61-23B, Chapters 6 and 7
Use the following steps:

1. Plot the course from Denton Muni (area 1) to Addison (area 2).

2. Measure the true course angle at the approximate midpoint of the route (127.5°).

3. Determine the ground speed, using a flight computer:

    Wind direction is 200° (given in question)
    Wind speed is 20 knots (given in question)
    True course is 127.5° (found in Step 2)
    True airspeed is 110 knots (given in question)

    Therefore, the ground speed is 102 knots.

4. Measure the distance from Denton Muni to Addison as 22.5 NM. For maximum precision, draw lines over your checkpoints that are perpendicular to your course line.

5. Calculate the time en route, using a flight computer:

    Distance is 22.5 NM (found in Step 4)
    Ground speed is 102 knots (found in Step 3)

    Therefore, the time en route is 13 minutes, 13 seconds.

6. All your calculations used true course and true wind, so variation is not relevant to this problem.

AIR
3563 [A] — (H06) — AC 61-23B, Chapters 6 and 7
Use the following steps:

1. Plot the course from Addison to Redbird.

2. Measure the true course angle at the approximate midpoint of the route (186°).

3. Determine the ground speed, using a flight computer:

    Wind direction is 300° (given in question)
    Wind speed is 15 knots (given in question)
    True course is 186° (found in Step 2)
    True airspeed is 120 knots (given in question)

    Therefore, the ground speed is 126 knots.

4. Measure the distance from Addison to Redbird as 17.3 NM. For maximum precision, draw lines over your checkpoints that are perpendicular to your course line.

5. Calculate the time en route, using a flight computer:

    Distance is 17.3 NM (found in Step 4)
    Ground speed is 126 knots (found in Step 3)

    Therefore, the time en route is 8.1 minutes.

6. All your calculations used true course and true wind, so variation is not relevant to this problem.

GLI
3564 [B] — (H07) — AC 61-23B, Chapter 7
Use the following steps:

1. Plot a course from Redbird to Meacham, and measure the course (289°).

2. Using the wind obtained, calculate a correction angle. This angle will be the difference between the course bearing and the heading required to maintain that course. Wind correction angle is 16° to the right.

3. Add course bearing and wind correction angle to obtain true heading.

    289° course bearing
    + 16° wind correction angle
    ─────
    305° true heading

4. Find the magnetic heading by adding the variation to the true heading.

    305° true heading
    − 007° variation (E)
    ─────
    298° magnetic heading

AIR
3565 [A] — (H07) — AC 61-23B, Chapter 7
Use the following steps:

1. Plot a course from Meacham to Denton, and measure the course (021°).

2. Using the wind obtained, calculate a correction angle. This angle will be the difference between the course bearing and the heading required to maintain that course. Wind correction angle is 10° to the left.

3. Add course bearing and wind correction angle to obtain true heading.

    021 + -010 = 011° (true heading)

4. Find the magnetic heading by adding the variation to the true heading.

    011 + -7 = 004° (magnetic heading)

Answers, References & Explanations

ALL
3566 [A] — (H07) — AC 61-21A, Chapter 12
The course selected is 253° and the TO/FROM indicator has a TO flag, which means the aircraft is north of the course. The CDI needle is deflected to the right, which means the aircraft is left (or east) of the course. Therefore, the aircraft must be to the east northeast of the station to satisfy the VOR indications.

ALL
3567 [A] — (H07) — AIM ¶9-1-4
Graticules on Sectional Aeronautical Charts are the lines dividing each 30 minutes of latitude and each 30 minutes of longitude. Each tick mark represents one minute of latitude or longitude. Latitude increases northward, west longitude increases going westward. Cooperstown airport is approximately at 47°25'N latitude, and 98°06'W longitude.

ALL
3568 [C] — (H07) — AC 61-23B, Chapter 7
Use the following steps:
1. Plot the course from Breckheimer (Pvt) Airport to Jamestown Airport.
2. Measure the true course angle at the approximate midpoint of the route (189°).
3. Note that the variation is 8° East as shown on the dashed isogonic line.
4. Using the formula:
   MC = TC ± VAR
   MC = 189 − 8° East
   MC = 181°

LTA
3569 [B] — (H07) — Soaring Flight Manual
Use the following steps:
1. Calculate the distance traveled at 10 MPH during 2-1/2 hours.
   Distance = Speed x Time
   Distance = 10 MPH x 2.5 H = 25 SM
2. Locate Eckelson in FAA Figure 27.
3. Note that the magnetic variation near Eckelson, as shown on the dashed isogonic line, is 8°E.
4. Calculate the true course from the magnetic course:
   TC ± VAR = MC
   TC − 8° = 282°
   TC = 290°
5. Plot a true course of 290° from Eckelson extending 25 statute miles. The balloon would be over Buchanan.

ALL
3570 [C] — (H07) — AC 61-23B, Chapter 7
1. Locate Wimbledon in FAA Figure 27 and note that it is on the 023° radial FROM Jamestown VOR. All OBS settings in FAA Figure 29 are set either at 030° or 210°.
2. Combine all the information above to visualize that if you were over Wimbledon:
   a. With OBS set on 030° you would have "FROM" and partial right deflection of the CDI; or
   b. With OBS set 210° you would have "TO" and partial left deflection of the CDI.

ALL
3571 [C] — (H07) — AC 61-23B, Chapter 4
Use the following steps:
1. Convert the EDT takeoff time to UTC:
   ```
     0945    EDT takeoff time
   + 0400    conversion
     1345 Z  UTC (also called "ZULU" time)
   ```
2. Add the flight time to the ZULU time of takeoff:
   ```
     1345 Z  takeoff time
   + 0200
     1545 Z  time of landing
   ```

ALL
3572 [B] — (H07) — AC 61-23, Chapter 7
Use the following steps:
1. Change the CST takeoff time to UTC:
   ```
     0930    CST takeoff time
   + 0600    conversion
     1530 Z  UTC (also called "ZULU" time)
   ```
2. Add the flight time to the time of takeoff:
   ```
     1530 Z  takeoff time
   + 0200    flight time
     1730 Z  time of landing
   ```
3. Convert UTC to MST:
   ```
     1730 Z  UTC
   − 0700    conversion
     1030    MST time of landing
   ```

ALL
3573 [C] — (H07) — AC 61-23B, Chapter 7
Use the following steps:
1. Convert the CST takeoff time to UTC:
   ```
     0845    CST takeoff time
   + 0600    conversion
     1445 Z  UTC (also called "ZULU" time)
   ```
2. Add the flight time to the ZULU time of takeoff:
   ```
     1445 Z  takeoff time
   + 0200    flight time
     1645 Z  the time of landing
   ```

ALL
3574 [B] — (H07) — AC 61-23B, Chapter 7
Use the following steps:

1. Convert the MST takeoff time to UTC:

1615	MST takeoff time
+ 0700	conversion
2315 Z	UTC (also called "ZULU" time)

2. Add the flight time to the ZULU time of takeoff:

2315 Z	takeoff time
+ 0215	flight time
0130 Z	time of landing

3. Convert UTC to PST:

0130 Z	UTC
− 0800	conversion
1730	PST time of landing

ALL
3575 [C] — (H07) — AC 61-23B, Chapter 7
Use the following steps:

1. Convert the PST takeoff time to UTC:

1030	PST takeoff time
+ 0800	conversion
1830 Z	UTC (also called "ZULU" time)

2. Add the flight time to the ZULU takeoff time:

1830 Z	takeoff time
+ 0400	flight time
2230 Z	time of landing

ALL
3576 [A] — (H07) — AC 61-23B, Chapter 7
Use the following steps:

1. Convert the MST takeoff time to UTC:

1515	MST takeoff time
+ 0700	conversion
2215 Z	UTC (also called "ZULU" time)

2. Add the flight time to the ZULU takeoff time:

2215 Z	takeoff time
+ 0230	flight time
2445 Z	(0045)Z time of landing

3. Convert UTC to PST:

2445 Z	(0045)Z
− 0800	conversion
1645	PST time of landing

ALL
3577 [C] — (H07) — AC 61-23B, Chapter 7
The course selected is 300° and the TO/FROM indicator is showing TO, which means the aircraft is south of the course. The CDI needle is deflected to the left, which means the aircraft is right of the course.

ALL
3578 [B] — (H07) — AC 61-23B, Chapter 7
Observe from illustration #3 of FAA Figure 29, that there is no TO/FROM indication and the CDI is deflected left with an OBS set on 030°. The aircraft is somewhere along the perpendicular line (120/300°). The CDI left means the 030° radial is to the left, or west, of the aircraft position. Answer B is the only one placing the aircraft on the 120° radial, or southeast of the station.

ALL
3579 [A] — (H07) — AC 61-23B, Chapter 7
The CDI is centered with the OBS set to 210° with a TO indication. Therefore, the aircraft is located on the 030° radial.

ALL
3580 [C] — (H07) — AC 61-23B, Chapter 7
The head of the needle indicates the magnetic bearing TO the station, which is 210°.

ALL
3581 [C] — (H07) — AC 61-23B, Chapter 7
The nose of the needle indicates the magnetic bearing TO the station which is 190°.

ALL
3582 [C] — (H07) — AC 61-23B, Chapter 7
To determine the intercept angle, turn to the inbound bearing and note degrees the needle is from the nose. Double this figure to get the intercept angle of 20°:

$$180° + 20° = 200°$$

The only possible answer is 220° since the other true headings would not intercept the 180° bearing to the station.

ALL
3583 [B] — (H07) — AC 61-23B, Chapter 7
The tail of the needle indicates the magnetic bearing FROM the station, which is 115°.

ALL
3584 [C] — (H07) — AC 61-23B, Chapter 7
FAA Figure 30 depicts ADF indications combined with aircraft heading information. In this case, the magnetic bearing TO can be read under the nose of the needle and the bearing FROM can be read directly under the tail of the needle. Use the following steps:

1. Note which dials, #3 and #4, of FAA Figure 30, show an aircraft proceeding toward the station.

2. A right crosswind (wind FROM the right) requires that the aircraft heading be to the right of the course to compensate for drift to the left. With the nose of the aircraft to the right of the course, the station appears to be left of the nose, as shown on dial #4.

ALL
3585 [A] — (H07) — AC 61-23B, Chapter 7
The tail of the needle indicates the magnetic bearing FROM the station, which is 030°.

ALL
3586 [C] — (H07) — AC 61-23B, Chapter 7
FAA Figure 30 depicts ADF indications combined with aircraft heading information. In this case, the magnetic bearing TO can be read under the nose of the needle and the bearing FROM can be read directly under the tail of the needle. Use the following steps:

1. The aircraft magnetic heading is 330°.
2. The magnetic bearing TO the station is 210°.
3. Calculate the relative bearing (RB):

    MB = MH + RB
    RB = 210° − 330° + 360°
    RB = 240°

ALL
3587 [B] — (H07) — AC 61-23B
FAA Figure 30 depicts ADF indications combined with aircraft heading information. In this case, the magnetic bearing TO can be read under the nose of the needle and the bearing FROM can be read directly under the tail of the needle. Use the following steps:

1. The aircraft magnetic heading is 315°.
2. The magnetic bearing TO the station is 190°.
3. Calculate the relative bearing (RB):

    MB = MH + RB
    RB = 190° − 315° + 360°
    RB = 235°

ALL
3588 [C] — (H07) — AC 61-23B, Chapter 7
FAA Figure 30 depicts ADF indications combined with aircraft heading information. In this case, the magnetic bearing TO can be read under the nose of the needle and the bearing FROM can be read directly under the tail of the needle. Use the following steps:

1. The aircraft magnetic heading is 220°.
2. The magnetic bearing TO the station is 200°.
3. Calculate the relative bearing (RB):

    MB = MH + RB
    RB = 200° − 220° + 360°
    RB = 340°

ALL
3589 [C] — (H07) — AC 61-23B, Chapter 7
On a fixed-scale (fixed-card) ADF, the nose of the aircraft is marked as 0°. The ADF indication is relative to aircraft heading, thus relative bearing may be read directly under the head of the needle, which is 315°.

ALL
3590 [A] — (H07) — AC 61-23B, Chapter 7
On a fixed-scale (fixed-card) ADF, the nose of the aircraft is marked as 0°. The ADF indication is relative to aircraft heading, thus relative bearing may be read directly under the head of the needle, which is 090°.

ALL
3591 [B] — (H07) — AC 61-23B, Chapter 7
On a fixed-scale (fixed-card) ADF, the nose of the aircraft is marked as 0°. The ADF indication is relative to aircraft heading, thus relative bearing may be read directly under the head of the needle, which is 180°.

ALL
3592 [B] — (H07) — AC 61-23B, Chapter 7
Use the following steps:

1. On a fixed-scale ADF, the aircraft heading is marked as 0°. The ADF indication is relative to the aircraft heading, thus relative bearing (RB) may be read directly under the head of the needle (225°).
2. Calculate the magnetic bearing to the station at a magnetic heading of 320°:

    MB = RB + MH
    MB = 225° + 320° = 545° − 360°
    MB = 185°

ALL
3593 [A] — (H07) — AC 61-23B, Chapter 7
Use the following steps:

1. On a fixed-scale ADF, the aircraft heading is marked as 0°. The ADF indication is relative to the aircraft heading, thus relative bearing (RB) may be read directly under the head of the needle (000°).
2. Calculate the magnetic bearing to the station for a magnetic heading of 035°:

    MB = RB + MH
    MB = 0° + 035°
    MB = 035°

ALL
3594 [B] — (H07) — AC 61-23B, Chapter 7
Use the following steps:

1. On a fixed-scale ADF, the aircraft heading is marked as 0°. The ADF indication is relative to the aircraft heading, thus relative bearing (RB) may be read directly under the head of the needle (045°).
2. Calculate the magnetic bearing to the station for a magnetic heading of 120°:

    MB = RB + MH
    MB = 045° + 120°
    MB = 165°

ALL
3595 [C] — (H07) — AC 61-23B, Chapter 7
Use the following steps:

1. On a fixed-scale ADF, the aircraft heading is marked as 0°. The ADF indication is relative to the aircraft heading and thus, relative bearing (RB) may be read directly under the head of the needle (045°).
2. Note that the magnetic bearing TO the station is 240°. Calculate the magnetic heading using:

    MB = RB + MH
    240° = 045° + MH
    MH = 240° − 045° = 195°

ALL
3596 [B] — (H07) — AC 61-23B, Chapter 7
1. On a fixed-scale ADF, the aircraft heading is marked as 0°. The ADF indication is relative to the aircraft heading, thus relative bearing (RB) may be read directly under the head of the needle (270°).
2. Note that the magnetic bearing TO the station is 030°. Calculate the magnetic heading using:

    MB = RB + MH
    030° = 270° + MH
    MH = 030° − 270° + 360°
    MH = 120°

ALL
3597 [C] — (H07) — AC 61-23B, Chapter 7
Use the following steps:

1. On a fixed-scale ADF, the aircraft heading is marked as 0°. The ADF indication is relative to the aircraft heading, thus relative bearing (RB) may be read directly under the head of the needle (135°).
2. Note that the magnetic bearing TO the station is 135°. Calculate the magnetic heading using:

    MB = RB + MH
    135° = 135° + MH
    MH = 0° or 360°

ALL
3598 [C] — (J01) — AIM ¶1-1-4
To use the VOT service, tune in the VOT frequency on the VOR receiver. With the CDI centered, the OBS should read 0° with the TO/FROM indication showing "FROM" or the OBS should read 180° with the TO/FROM indication showing "TO."

ALL
3599 [C] — (J08) — AIM ¶3-2-3
The thick blue lines on the sectional chart indicate the boundaries of the overlying Class B airspace. Within each segment, the floor and ceiling are denoted by one number over a second number or the letters SFC. The floor of the Class B airspace is 4,000 feet MSL.

ALL
3600 [B] — (J08) — AIM ¶3-2-3
The thick blue lines on the sectional chart indicate the boundaries of the overlying Class B airspace. Within each segment, the floor and ceiling are denoted by one number over a second number or the letters SFC. The floor of the Class B airspace is 3,000 feet MSL.

ALL
3601 [A] — (J09) — AIM ¶3-4-4
Warning Areas are airspace which may contain hazards to nonparticipating (non-military) aircraft in international airspace. Warning Areas are established beyond the 3-mile limit. Though the activities conducted within Warning Areas may be as hazardous as those in Restricted Areas, Warning Areas cannot be legally designated as Restricted Areas because they are over international waters. Penetration of Warning Areas during periods of activity may be hazardous to the aircraft and its occupants.

ALL
3602 [B] — (J09) — AIM ¶3-4-5
A Military Operations Area (MOA) contains military training activities such as aerobatics, and calls for extreme caution.

ALL
3603 [A] — (J10) — AIM ¶3-5-2
IR644 begins at the lower left (eastbound) and turns northeast as a thin gray line. IR644 has three digits, which mean: generally above 1,500 feet AGL (but some segments below), operations under IFR, and (as with all MTRs) may be over 250 knots.

ALL
3604 [A] — (J11) — AIM ¶4-1-9
Where there is no tower, FSS, or UNICOM station on the airport, use MULTICOM frequency 122.9 for self-announce procedures. Such airports will be identified in the appropriate aeronautical information publications.

ALL
3605 [B] — (J11) — AIM ¶4-1-9
Where there is no tower, FSS, or UNICOM station on the airport, use MULTICOM frequency 122.9 for self-announce procedures. Such airports will be identified in the appropriate aeronautical information publications.

ALL
3606 [A] — (J11) — AIM ¶4-1-9
CTAF (Common Traffic Advisory Frequency) is a frequency designed for the purpose of carrying out airport advisory practices and/or position reporting at an uncontrolled airport (which may also occur during hours when a tower is closed). The CTAF may be a UNICOM, MULTICOM, FSS, or tower frequency and is identified in the appropriate aeronautical publications. A solid dot with the letter "C" inside indicates the Common Traffic Advisory Frequency.

Answers, References & Explanations

ALL
3607 [A] — (J11) — AIM ¶4-1-9
CTAF (Common Traffic Advisory Frequency) is a frequency designed for the purpose of carrying out airport advisory practices and/or position reporting at an uncontrolled airport (which may also occur during hours when a tower is closed). The CTAF may be a UNICOM, MULTICOM, FSS, or tower frequency and is identified in the appropriate aeronautical publications. A solid dot with the letter "C" inside indicates Common Traffic Advisory Frequency.

ALL
3608 [C] — (J11) — AIM ¶4-1-11
The sectional chart and Airport Facility Directory both list the UNICOM frequency as 122.8. This is the appropriate frequency to use to contact UNICOM. The UNICOM frequency is depicted in the airport information in the lower right-hand corner.

ALL
3609 [A] — (J11) — AIM ¶4-8
A solid dot with the letter "C" inside indicates the Common Traffic Advisory Frequency.

ALL
3610 [A] — (J11) — AIM ¶4-1-9
MULTICOM frequency is always 122.9 MHz, and the correct procedure is to broadcast intentions when 10 miles from the airport.

ALL
3611 [B] — (J11) — AIM ¶4-1-9
CTAF (Common Traffic Advisory Frequency) is a frequency designed for the purpose of carrying out airport advisory practices and/or position reporting at an uncontrolled airport (which may also occur during hours when a tower is closed). The CTAF may be a UNICOM, MULTICOM, FSS, or tower frequency and is identified in the appropriate aeronautical publications. A solid dot with the letter "C" inside indicates Common Traffic Advisory Frequency; it may be a UNICOM, MULTICOM, FSS, or tower frequency.

ALL
3612 [B] — (J11) — AIM ¶4-1-9
CTAF (Common Traffic Advisory Frequency) is a frequency designed for the purpose of carrying out airport advisory practices and/or position reporting at an uncontrolled airport (which may also occur during hours when a tower is closed). The CTAF may be a UNICOM, MULTICOM, FSS, or tower frequency and is identified in the appropriate aeronautical publications. A solid dot with the letter "C" inside indicates Common Traffic Advisory Frequency.

ALL
3613 [A] — (J12) — AIM ¶4-2-3
The term "initial radio contact," or "initial callup," means the first radio call you make to a given facility, or the first call to a different controller or FSS specialist within a facility. Use the following format:

1. Name of facility being called;
2. Your full aircraft identification as filed in the flight plan;
3. Type of message to follow or your request if it is short, and
4. The word "over," if required.

Example: "New York Radio, Mooney Three One One Echo."

When the aircraft manufacturer's name or model is stated, the prefix "N" is dropped. The first two characters of the call sign may be dropped only after ATC calls you by your last three letters/numbers.

ALL
3614 [A] — (J12) — AIM ¶4-2-9
Up to but not including 18,000 feet MSL, state the separate digits of the thousands, plus the hundreds, if appropriate. Example: "4,500 — four thousand, five hundred."

ALL
3615 [C] — (J12) — AIM ¶4-2-9
Up to but not including 18,000 feet MSL, state the separate digits of the thousands, plus the hundreds, if appropriate. Example: "10,500 — one zero thousand, five hundred."

ALL
3616 [C] — (J25) — AIM ¶7-1-4
122.0 MHz is assigned nationwide as the Flight Watch which provides enroute aircraft with enroute weather reports along your route of flight. Flight Service Stations provide routine weather, current reports on hazardous weather, and altimeter settings that can be reached on 122.2, 122.4, 122.5, or 122.6. Discrete high-altitude frequencies are being implemented also.

ALL
3617 [A] — (J25) — AIM ¶7-1-4
EFAS is a service specifically designed to provide enroute aircraft with timely and meaningful weather advisories pertinent to the type of flight intended, route of flight, and altitude. EFAS is also used for exchange of PIREPs which are especially important in rural areas.

ALL
3618 [A] — (J28) — AIM ¶7-4-6
All aircraft are requested to maintain a minimum altitude of 2,000 feet above the surface of national parks, monuments, seashores, lakeshores, recreation areas, and scenic riverways administered by the National Park Service, National Wildlife Refuges, Big Game Refuges, Game Ranges and Wildlife Ranges.

ALL
3619 [B] — (J34) — AIM ¶3-5-5
Tabulations of parachute jump areas in the U.S. are contained in the Airport/Facility Directory.

ALL
3620 [A] — (J37) — AIM ¶3-2-1
Dave Wall Field is in Class G airspace, which requires 1 mile visibility and clear of clouds to operate VFR during daylight hours, at less than 1,200 feet AGL.

ALL
3621 [B] — (J37) — AIM ¶3-2-1
The town of Cooperstown lies outside any blue tint bands, i.e., Class G airspace. For VFR flight during daylight hours, between 1,200 feet AGL and 10,000 feet MSL, visibility and cloud clearances require 1 mile and 1,000 feet above, 500 feet below, and 2,000 feet horizontally.

ALL
3622 [A] — (J37) — AIM ¶3-2-1
Lowe airport lies outside any blue tint bands, i.e., Class G airspace. Class G airspace begins at the surface and continues up to but not including the overlying controlled airspace or 14,500 feet MSL, whichever occurs first.

ALL
3623 [C] — (J37) — AIM ¶3-2-1
The Barnes County Airport is depicted inside the magenta shading, which is controlled airspace from 700 feet AGL up to but not including 18,000 feet. Therefore, the airspace below 700 feet AGL is Class G.

ALL
3624 [A] — (J37) — AIM ¶3-2-1
The magenta vignette (light-magenta shaded) line indicates uncontrolled airspace (Class G) from the surface to 700 feet AGL. The outside of the magenta vignette line depicts uncontrolled airspace up to 1,200 feet AGL. Since McKinney Municipal airport is on the shaded side of the magenta vignette line, the airspace overlying it is Class G from the surface to 700 feet AGL.

ALL
3625 [C] — (J37) — AIM ¶3-2-1
A blue segmented circle depicts Class D airspace which extends from the surface to 3,200 feet MSL, in this case as shown by the blue number 32 surrounded by the blue segmented box.

ALL
3626 [B] — (J37) — AIM ¶3-31
Within the outer magenta circle of Savannah Class C airspace, there is a number 41 directly above the number 13. These depict the floor and ceiling of the Class C airspace; the floor being 1,300 feet MSL and the ceiling being 4,100 feet MSL.

ALL
3627 [B] — (J37) — AIM ¶3-2-4
Norfolk International is in Class C airspace. To operate within Class C airspace, an aircraft must have (1) two-way communications capability and (2) a Mode C transponder.

ALL
3628 [B] — (J37) — AIM ¶4-4-5
Special VFR operations by fixed-wing aircraft are prohibited in some Class B, C, and D airspaces due to the volume of IFR traffic. These airspaces are depicted by the notation "No SVFR" over the airport information.

ALL
3629 [C] — (J37) — AIM ¶3-2-6
The VOR and L/MF Airway System consists of airways designated from 1,200 feet above the surface (in some instances higher) up to, but not including, 18,000 feet MSL. This airway begins at 7,500 feet MSL, as indicated by the "7500 MSL" printed next to airway.

ALL
3630 [A] — (J37) — AIM ¶7-1-8
The block in the lower right corner indicates TWEB on the VOR frequency.

ALL
3631 [C] — (J37) — Sectional Chart Legend
Reference FAA Legend 1. The boxed caution reads, "CAUTION: STROBE LIGHTS AND UNMARKED BALLOON ON CABLE TO 3,000 MSL."

ALL
3632 [C] — (J37) — Sectional Chart Legend
Reference FAA Legend 1. The flag symbol represents a visual checkpoint used to identify position for initial callup to Norfolk Approach Control.

ALL
3633 [A] — (J37) — Sectional Chart Legend
Reference FAA Legend 1. The airport elevation is noted in the airport information, beneath the airport symbol. The elevation of Chesapeake Municipal Airport is 20 feet.

ALL
3634 [B] — (J37) — Sectional Chart Legend
Reference FAA Legend 1. The contour line which borders the tan area is labeled 2,000 feet. There are no higher contour levels depicted inside the tan area.

ALL
3635 [A] — (J37) — Sectional Chart Legend
Reference FAA Legend 1. Minot and Mercer County Regional Airport are depicted as having fuel, as indicated by the ticks around the basic airport symbol.

ALL
3636 [C] — (J37) — Sectional Chart Legend
Reference FAA Legend 1. "Visual check point" is the name for the flag symbol.

ALL
3637 [B] — (J37) — Sectional Chart Legend
Reference FAA Legend 1. The top number, printed in bold, is the height of the obstruction above mean sea level. The second number, printed in parentheses, is the height of the obstruction above ground level. The obstruction is shown as 1,549 feet MSL and 1,532 feet AGL.

ALL
3638 [B] — (J37) — Sectional Chart Legend
Reference FAA Legend 1. The top number, printed in bold, is the height of the obstruction above mean sea level. The second number, printed in parentheses, is the height of the obstruction above ground level. The obstructions are shown as 430 feet MSL and 400 feet AGL.

ALL
3639 [B] — (J37) — Sectional Chart Legend
The elevation of the top of the obstacle is shown as 773 feet above mean sea level (MSL). Add the 500-foot vertical clearance specified by the question to the height (MSL) of the obstacle:

```
   773  feet MSL
 + 500
 1,273  feet MSL minimum altitude
```

ALL
3640 [C] — (J37) — Sectional Chart Legend
The elevation of the top of the obstacle is shown as 903 feet above mean sea level (MSL). Add the 500-foot vertical clearance specified by the question to the height (MSL) of the obstacle:

```
   903  feet MSL
 + 500
 1,403  feet MSL
```

ALL
3641 [B] — (J37) — Sectional Chart Legend
The correct answer is found in the explanatory box for Addison airport in area 2: 126.0 MHz.

AIR
3642 [C] — (J37) — FAR §91.119(b)
The height of the tower is 2,349 MSL. A 1,000-foot clearance is required between obstructions and aircraft over a congested area.

```
 2,349  MSL
+1,000
 3,349  MSL
```

ALL
3643 [B] — (J37) — Sectional Chart Legend
Reference FAA Legend 1. There is a VORTAC at Dallas Love Field.

LTA
3644 [C] — (J37) — Sectional Chart Legend
Use the following steps:
1. Locate the towns of Edenton and Hertford.
2. Note the highest obstruction in the vicinity of Hertford (515 feet MSL).
3. Calculate the minimum altitude (MSL) by adding the required 500-foot clearance to the obstacle height.

```
   515  feet
 + 500  feet
 1,015  feet MSL
```

LTA
3645 [B] — (J37) — Sectional Chart Legend
Use the following steps:
1. Locate the Flying S and lighted obstacle.
2. Calculate the height of the obstacle above the Flying S field elevation:

```
 3,149  feet top of obstacle (MSL)
-1,840  feet Flying S elevation (MSL)
 1,309  feet difference in elevation
```

3. Add the required clearance to obtain the altimeter indication:

```
   500  feet required clearance
+1,309  feet difference in elevation
 1,809  feet altimeter indication
```

LTA
3646 [C] — (J37) — Sectional Chart Legend
On Sectional Aeronautical Charts, color tints are used to depict bands of elevation. These colors range from light green for the lowest elevations to brown for the higher elevations. Note the terrain height of 6,405 feet MSL within the tan shading south-southwest of CX airport.

GLI
3647 [B] — (N23) — American Soaring Handbook, page 5-10
One fundamental point is that dry areas get hotter than moist areas. Dry fields or dry ground of any nature are better thermal sources than moist areas. This applies to woods or forests, which are poor sources of thermals because of the large amount of moisture given off by the leaves.

GLI
3648 [C] — (N27) — Soaring Flight Manual, page 9-4
Use the following steps:
1. Draw a direct course line between Barnes County Airport and Jamestown Airport and determine the distance (31 SM).
2. Calculate the time required to cover 31 SM at 40 MPH ground speed using the formula:

Time = Distance ÷ Speed = 31 ÷ 40 =
0.75 hours = 46.5 minutes

GLI
3649 [B] — (N27) — Soaring Flight Manual, page 9-4
Use the following steps:

1. Draw a direct course line between Caddo Mills Airport and Airpark East Airport and determine the distance (17 SM).

2. Calculate the time required to cover 17 SM at 35 MPH ground speed using the formula:

    Time = Distance ÷ Speed = 17 ÷ 35 = .485 hours = 29.1 minutes

GLI
3650 [C] — (N34) — Soaring Flight Manual, page 16-5
Use the following steps:

1. A safety margin is provided to allow for any performance degradation. Use one-half the published L/D ratio for planning purposes. In this case use 11 to 1 (no wind).

2. Determine the distance from Eckelson to Barnes County Airport (14.5 SM).

3. If 1 SM = 5,280 feet, calculate the total sink in 14.5 SM at a glide ratio of 11:1.

    5,280 ÷11= 480 feet sink per SM
    480.0 x 14.5 = 6,960.0 feet total sink

4. Calculate the arrival altitude (MSL) by adding 1,000 feet AGL to the Barnes County elevation of 1,399 feet.

    1,399 Barnes County elevation
    + 1,000 arrival (AGL)
    2,399 arrival (MSL)

5. Determine the go-ahead minimum by adding total sink to the required arrival altitude.

    6,960 feet total sink
    + 2,399 feet MSL arrival altitude
    9,359 feet MSL go-ahead minimum attitude

AIR, RTC
3651 [A] — (H02) — AC 61-23B, Chapter 2
To avoid excessive cylinder head temperatures, a pilot can open the cowl flaps, increase airspeed, enrich the mixture, or reduce power. Any of these procedures will aid in reducing the engine temperature. Establishing a shallower climb (increasing airspeed) increases the airflow through the cooling system, preventing excessively high engine temperatures.

AIR, RTC
3652 [A] — (H02) — AC 61-23B, Chapter 2
To avoid excessive cylinder head temperatures, a pilot can open the cowl flaps, increase airspeed, enrich the mixture, or reduce power. Any of these procedures will aid in reducing the engine temperature.

AIR
3653 [A] — (H02) — AC 61-23B, Chapter 2
On aircraft equipped with a constant-speed propeller, the throttle controls the engine power output which is registered on the manifold pressure gauge. The propeller control changes the pitch angle of the propeller and governs the RPM which is indicated on the tachometer.

AIR
3654 [B] — (H02) — AC 61-23B, Chapter 2
A constant-speed propeller permits the pilot to select the blade angle that will result in the most efficient performance for a particular flight condition. A low blade angle allows higher RPM and horsepower, desirable for take-offs. An intermediate position can be used for subsequent climb. After airspeed is attained during cruising flight, the propeller blade may be changed to a higher angle for lower RPM, reduced engine noise, generally lower vibration, and greater fuel efficiency.

AIR
3655 [B] — (H02) — AC 61-23, Chapter 2
On aircraft equipped with a constant-speed propeller, the throttle controls the engine power output which is registered on the manifold pressure gauge. The propeller control changes the pitch angle of the propeller and governs the RPM which is indicated on the tachometer. On most airplanes, for any given RPM, there is a manifold pressure that should not be exceeded. If an excessive amount of manifold pressure is carried for a given RPM, the maximum allowable pressure within the engine cylinders could be exceeded, thus putting undue strain on them.

AIR, RTC
3656 [A] — (H02) — AC 61-23B, Chapter 2
As soon as the engine starts, check for unintentional movement of the aircraft and set power to the recommended warm-up RPM. The oil pressure should then be checked to determine that the oil system is functioning properly with pressure at recommended levels within the manufacturer's time limit.

AIR
3657 [B] — (H02) — AC 61-23B, Chapter 2
Because of the hazards involved in hand-starting airplane engines, it is extremely important that a competent pilot be at the controls in the cockpit and that all communications and procedures be agreed upon and rehearsed beforehand.

ALL
3658 [B] — (H02) — AC 61-23B, Chapter 2
The minimum required preflight activity is for the pilot to conduct a walk-around inspection before every flight to assure that the aircraft is safe for flight.

ALL
3659 [A] — (H02) — AC 61-23B, Chapter 2
A written checklist is the best method of ensuring all items have been covered. By following the numerically indicated route, an effective and organized preflight inspection can be accomplished.

ALL
3660 [C] — (H02) — AC 61-23B, Chapter 2
A thorough inspection is recommended for aircraft that have been tied down or stored for an extensive period of time. Inactive aircraft are frequently used for nesting by insects and animals. Birds' nests in air intake scoops impair airflow. Nests lodged between engine cylinders and engine baffles cause overheating, preignition, and detonation. Insect nests obstructing fuel tank vents cause lean mixtures and fuel starvation. Obstructions can also be present in all types of aircraft.

AIR, RTC
3661 [A] — (H04) — AC 91-23, Chapter 2
Empty weight consists of the airframe, engines, and all items of operating equipment that have fixed locations and are permanently installed in the airplane. It includes optional and special equipment, fixed ballast, hydraulic fluid, unusable (residual) fuel, and undrainable (residual) oil.

AIR, RTC
3662 [C] — (H04) — AC 91-23, Chapter 2
1. Determine the total weight to be removed (110 pounds) and the weight per gallon of gasoline (6 pounds).
2. Calculate the amount of gasoline to be drained using the formula:

$$\text{Gallons} = \frac{\text{Pounds}}{\text{Pounds/Gallon}}$$

or:

$$\frac{110}{6} = 18.33 \text{ gallons}$$

When "rounding" an answer, do so in the sense that will provide the greater flight safety. In this case, round to 18.4.

AIR, RTC
3663 [C] — (H04) — AC 91-23, Chapter 2
1. Determine the total weight to be removed (90 pounds) and the weight per gallon of gasoline (6 pounds).
2. Calculate the amount of gasoline to be drained using the formula:

$$\text{Gallons} = \frac{\text{Pounds}}{\text{Pounds/Gallon}}$$

or:

$$\frac{90}{6} = 15 \text{ gallons}$$

AIR
3664 [B] — (H04) — AC 61-23, Chapter 4
1. Compute the total weight and moment using the formula:

   Weight x Arm = Moment

   or:

Item	Weight	Arm	Moment
Empty weight	1,495.0	101.4	151,593.0
Pilot & passenger	380.0	64.0	24,320.0
Fuel (30 x 6)	180.0	96.0	17,280.0
Total	2,055.0 lbs		193,193.0

2. Compute the center of gravity using the formula:

$$CG = \frac{\text{Total Moment}}{\text{Total Weight}}$$

or:

$$CG = \frac{193,193}{2,055} = 94.01 \text{ inches aft of datum}$$

AIR
3665 [B] — (H04) — AC 61-23B, Chapter 4
When multiplying a weight by its arm you must divide by 100 to get moment index (Moment/100). Moments listed in FAA Figures 33 and 34 are already divided by 100, and are therefore moment indexes.

1. Calculate weight and moment index using the information from the question and from FAA Figures 33 and 34 and the formula:

   Weight x Arm ÷ 100 = Moment/Index

Item	Weight	Arm	Moment/100
Empty weight	2,015 lbs		1,554.0 lbs-in
Front seat	340 lbs	85	289.0 lbs-in
Rear seat	295 lbs	121	357.0 lbs-in
Fuel (44 x 6)	264 lbs	75	198.0 lbs-in
Baggage	56 lbs	140	78.4 lbs-in
Total	2,970 lbs		2,476.4 lbs-in

2. Consult the Moment Limits vs. Weight Table, FAA Figure 34. The aircraft weight is 2,970 pounds or 20 pounds in excess of the maximum weight on the chart. The moment of 2,476.4 lbs-in would be within limits if the chart went to 2,970 pounds gross weight.

---

52   ASA   Private Pilot Test Guide   Answers, References & Explanations

AIR
3666 [A] — (H04) — AC 61-23B, Chapter 4
1. When multiplying a weight times its arm you must divide by 100 to get moment index. Calculate total weight and total moment index using the information from the question and from FAA Figures 33 and 34 and the formula:

   Weight x Arm ÷ 100 = Moment/Index

Item	Weight	Arm	Moment/100
Empty weight	2,015 lbs		1,554.0 lbs-in
Front seat	387 lbs	85	329.0 lbs-in
Rear seat	293 lbs	121	354.5 lbs-in
Fuel (44 x 6)	210 lbs	75	157.5 lbs-in
Total	2,905 lbs		2,395.0 lbs-in

2. The maximum takeoff weight is 2,950 pounds. Calculate what the allowed baggage weight would be:

   2,950 − 2,905 = 45 pounds

3. Verify that the CG would remain within the allowable range with this much baggage by calculating the new weight and moment index.

Item	Weight	Arm	Moment/100
Original total	2,905 lbs		2,395.0 lbs-in
Baggage	+ 45 lbs	140	+ 63.0 lbs-in
New Total	2,950 lbs		2,458.0 lbs-in

4. Consult the Moment Limit vs. Weight Table, FAA Figure 34. For a weight of 2,950 pounds, the range of allowable moments is 2,422 to 2,499. The new total moment index of 2,458.0 is acceptable.

AIR
3667 [B] — (H04) — AC 61-23B, Chapter 4
Use the following steps:
1. Calculate weight and moment index using the information from the problem and from FAA Figures 33 and 34 and the formula:

   Weight x Arm ÷ 100 = Moment/Index

Item	Weight	Arm	Moment/100
Empty weight	2,015 lbs		1,554.0 lbs-in
Front seat	350 lbs	85	297.5 lbs-in
Rear seat	325 lbs	121	393.3 lbs-in
Baggage	27 lbs	140	37.8 lbs-in
Fuel (44 x 6)	210 lbs	75	157.5 lbs-in
Total	2,927 lbs		2,440.1 lbs-in

2. Calculate the position of CG using the formula:

   $$CG = \frac{\text{Total Mom Ind}}{\text{Total Weight}} \times \text{Reduction Factor}$$

   or:

   $$CG = \frac{2,440.1}{2,055} \times 100 = 83.4 \text{ inches aft of datum}$$

AIR
3668 [C] — (H04) — AC 61-23B, Chapter 4
Use the following steps:
1. Calculate weight and moment index using the information from the problem and from FAA Figures 33 and 34, and the formula:

   Weight x Arm ÷ 100 = Moment/Index

Item	Weight	Arm	Moment/100
Empty weight	2,015 lbs		1,554.0 lbs-in
Front seat	415 lbs	85	352.8 lbs-in
Rear seat	110 lbs	121	133.1 lbs-in
Fuel main 44 x 6	264 lbs	75	198.0 lbs-in
Fuel aux. 19 x 6	114 lbs	94	107.2 lbs-in
Baggage	32 lbs	140	44.8 lbs-in
Total	2,950 lbs		2,389.9 lbs-in

2. Calculate the CG using the formula:

   $$CG = \frac{\text{Total Mom Ind}}{\text{Total Weight}} \times \text{Reduction Factor}$$

   or:

   $$CG = \frac{2,389.9}{2,950} \times 100 = 81.0 \text{ inches aft of datum}$$

3. Consult the Moment Limits vs. Weight Table (FAA Figure 34). A CG of 81 inches is 1.1 inches forward of the forward CG limit for a weight (allowed) of 2,950 pounds.

AIR
3669 [A] — (H04) — AC 61-23B, Chapter 4
Use the following steps:
1. Find total weight and moment index (except baggage) by using the loading graphs in FAA Figure 35. Note that the reduction factor is 1,000 in this problem. The standard weight for gasoline is 6 lbs/U.S. gallon, and for oil, 7.5 lbs/U.S. gallon.

Item	Weight	Moment/1,000
B.E.W.	1,350 lbs	51.5 lbs-in
Pilot & Pax (a)	250 lbs	9.3 lbs-in
Rear Pax (b)	400 lbs	29.3 lbs-in
Fuel (30 x 6) (c)	180 lbs	8.7 lbs-in
Oil	15 lbs	-0.2 lbs
Total	2,195 lbs	98.6 lbs-in

2. Calculate the maximum allowable weight for baggage:

   2,300 − 2,195 = 105 pounds

3. Add baggage and calculate the new totals for weight and moment index.

Weight	Moment/1,000
2,195 lbs	98.6 lbs-in
+ 105 lbs	10.0 lbs-in
2,300 lbs	108.6 lbs-in

4. Plot the position of the point determined by 2,300 pounds and the moment of 108.6 lbs-in/1,000 on the center of gravity moment envelope graph. The point is in the normal category envelope.

AIR
3670 [B] — (H04) — AC 61-23B, Chapter 4
Use the following steps:

1. Find total weight and moment index by using the loading graph (FAA Figure 35). The standard weight for gasoline is 6 lbs/U.S. gallons and for oil, 7.5 lbs U.S. gallon.

Item	Weight	Moment/1,000
B.E.W.	1,350 lbs	51.5 lbs-in
Pilot & Pax (a)	310 lbs	11.5 lbs-in
Rear Pax (b)	96 lbs	7.0 lbs-in
Fuel (38 x 6) (c)	228 lbs	11.0 lbs-in
Oil	15 lbs	-0.2 lbs-in
Total	1,999 lbs	80.8 lbs-in

2. Plot the position of the point determined by 1,999 pounds and a moment of 80.8 lbs-in/1,000. The point is just inside the utility category envelope.

AIR
3671 [C] — (H04) — AC 61-23B, Chapter 4
1. Find the total weight and moment index (except fuel) by using the loading graph in FAA Figure 35.

Item	Weight	Moment/1,000
B.E.W.	1,350 lbs	51.5 lbs-in
Pilot & Pax (a)	340 lbs	12.6 lbs-in
Rear Pax (b)	310 lbs	22.6 lbs-in
Baggage (c)	45 lbs	4.2 lbs-in
Oil (d)	15 lbs	-0.2 lbs-in
Total	2,060 lbs	90.7 lbs-in

2. Calculate the additional fuel weight which can be added:

   2,300 − 2,060 = 240 lbs

3. Calculate the number of gallons of fuel at 6 lbs/gallon:

   240 ÷ 6 = 40 gallons

4. Calculate the added fuel moment index from the graph (40 gal fuel − 11.5 MOM/1,000).

5. Calculate the new total weight and moment index:

Weight	Moment/1,000
2,060 lbs	90.7 lbs-in
+ 240 lbs	11.5 lbs-in
2,300 lbs	102.2 lbs-in

6. Plot the position of the point determined by 2,300 pounds and a moment index of 102.2 lbs-in/1,000. The point lies on the normal category envelope.

AIR
3672 [B] — (H04) — AC 61-23B, Chapter 4
1. Find the total weight and moment index by using the loading graph from FAA Figure 35.

Item	Weight	Moment/1,000
B.E.W.	1,350 lbs	51.5 lbs-in
Pilot & Pax (a)	340 lbs	12.6 lbs-in
Fuel (Std. Tanks) (b)	228 lbs	11.0 lbs-in
Oil (c)	15 lbs	-0.2 lbs-in
Total	1,933 lbs	74.9 lbs-in

AIR
3673 [B] — (H04) — AC 61-23B, Chapter 4
Use the following steps:

1. Find the total weight and moment index by using the loading graph from FAA Figure 35.

Item	Weight	Moment/1,000
B.E.W.	1,350 lbs	51.5 lbs-in
Pilot & Pax (a)	380 lbs	14.0 lbs-in
Fuel (b)	288 lbs	13.8 lbs-in
Oil (c)	15 lbs	-0.2 lbs-in
Total	2,033 lbs	79.1 lbs-in

2. Plot the position of the point determined by 2,033 lbs. and a moment of 79.1 lbs-in/1,000. The point is within the normal category envelope.

AIR
3674 [A] — (H04) — AC 61-23B, Chapter 4
Use the following steps:

1. Consider the effect on the total weight.

Item	Weight
Original weight	2,690 pounds
Deplaned passenger	− 180 pounds
New Weight	2,510 pounds

2. Consider the effect on the total moment index using the arms given in FAA Figure 33, and the formula:

   Weight x Arm ÷ 100 = Moment/Index

Item	Weight	Arm	Moment/100
Original weight & Mom Ind	2,690		2,260.0 lbs-in
Passenger exiting, front	-180	85	-153.0 lbs-in
Passenger exiting, rear	-204	121	-246.8 lbs-in
Passenger into front	+ 204	85	+ 173.4 lbs-in
New Total Weight & Moment	2,510		2,033.6 lbs-in

3. Determine both the original and new CG using the formula:

$$CG = \frac{\text{Total Mom Ind}}{\text{Total Weight}} \times \text{Reduction Factor}$$

or:

a. Original CG =
$$\frac{2{,}260}{2{,}690} \times 100 = 84.0 \text{ inches aft of datum}$$

b. New CG =
$$\frac{2{,}033.6}{2{,}510} \times 100 = 81.0 \text{ inches aft of datum}$$

4. Calculate the change in CG:

   84 − 81 = 3 inches (forward)

AIR
3675 [B] — (H04) — AC 61-23B, Chapter 4
Use the following steps:

1. Calculate the original weights and moment index using the information from the problem and FAA Figures 33 and 34, and the formula:

   Weight × Arm ÷ 100 = Moment/Index

Item	Weight	Arm	Moment/100
Empty weight	2,015 lbs		1,554.0 lbs-in
Front seat	425 lbs	85	361.3 lbs-in
Rear seat	300 lbs	121	363.0 lbs-in
Fuel (44 x 6)	264 lbs	75	198.0 lbs-in
Total	3,004 lbs		2,476.3 lbs-in

2. If the aircraft has a maximum allowable takeoff weight of 2,950 lbs, compute the weight to be removed to reach an acceptable takeoff weight.

   3,004 − 2,950 = 54 pounds

3. Compute the amount of fuel (in gallons) that totals 54 lbs:

   54 ÷ 6 = 9 gallons

4. Compute the revised weight and moment index:

Item	Weight	Arm	Moment/100
Original totals	3,004 lbs		2,476.3 lbs-in
Fuel	54 lbs	75	− 40.5 lbs-in
New Total	2,950 lbs		2,435.8 lbs-in

5. Calculate the position of the CG using the formula:

$$CG = \frac{\text{Total Mom Ind}}{\text{Total Weight}} \times \text{Reduction Factor}$$

or:

$$CG = \frac{2{,}435.8}{2{,}950} \times 100 = 82.6 \text{ inches aft of datum}$$

6. Consult the Moment Limits vs. Weight Chart. A CG position of 82.6 is within limits specified for a 2,950 lbs takeoff weight.

AIR
3676 [A] — (H04) — AC 61-23B, Chapter 4
Use the following steps:

1. Calculate the change in both weight and moment index caused by a burn of 35 gallons, using the information from FAA Figures 33 and 34.

   Weight × Arm ÷ 100 = Moment/Index

Item	Weight	Arm	Moment
Fuel (35 x 6)	210 lbs	75	158 lbs-in

2. Determine the effect of burn on total weight and moment index:

Item	Weight	Arm	Moment/100
Original total	2,890 lbs		2,452.0 lbs-in
Fuel burn	− 210 lbs	140	− 158.0 lbs-in
New Total	2,680 lbs		2,294.0 lbs-in

3. Consult the Moment Limits vs. Weight Table (FAA Figure 34). The allowed range of moment indexes for a weight of 2,680 lbs is 2,123 to 2,287 lbs-in/100. Hence the new moment index exceeds the maximum allowed and the CG is aft of limits.

AIR
3677 [B] — (H04) — AC 61-23B, Chapter 4
Use the following steps:

1. Calculate the weights and moments using the information from the problem and FAA Figures 33 and 34, and the formula:

   Weight × Arm ÷ 100 = Moment/Index

Item	Weight	Arm	Moment/100
Empty weight	2,015 lbs		1,554.0 lbs-in
Front seat	411 lbs	85	349.4 lbs-in
Rear seat	100 lbs	121	121.0 lbs-in
Fuel 44 x 6	264 lbs	75	198.0 lbs-in
Total	2,790 lbs		2,222.4 lbs-in

2. Consulting the Moment Limits vs. Weight Table (FAA Figure 34), the allowed range of moments for 2,790 lbs is between 2,243 and 2,374 lbs-in/100.

3. Since the moment index is too small, add weight, and for maximum increase in moment index with minimum weight penalty, as far aft as practical. Add 100 lbs in the baggage compartment and re-compute weight and moment index:

Item	Weight	Arm	Moment/100
Original totals	2,790 lbs		2,222.4 lbs-in
Add weight	+ 100 lbs	140	+ 140.0 lbs-in
New Totals	2,890 lbs		2,362.4 lbs-in

4. Consult the Moment Limits vs. Weight Table. The allowed range of moments for 2,890 pounds is 2,354 to 2,452 lbs-in/100. The new moment is now within limits.

AIR
3678 [C] — (H04) — AC 61-23B, Chapter 4
Use the following steps:

1. Locate -36°F (ISA -20°C) on FAA Figure 36. Notice that the stated altitude of 9,500 feet does not appear on the chart so it is necessary to interpolate.

2. Read across the 8,000-foot pressure altitude line and determine the TAS (181 MPH).

3. Read across the 10,000-foot pressure altitude line and determine the TAS (184 MPH).

4. Interpolate between the values for 8,000 feet and 10,000 feet to determine a TAS for 9,500 feet.

   a. 184 MPH (10,000 feet)
       − 181 MPH (8,000 feet)
       ──────
       3 MPH difference in speed

   b. 10,000 feet   10,000 feet
       − 8,000 feet   − 9,500 feet
       ──────   ──────
       2,000 feet difference   500 feet difference

   c. .25 x 3 MPH = .75 MPH

   d. 184.00 MPH
       − .75 MPH
       ──────
       183.25 MPH or 183 MPH

AIR
3679 [B] — (H04) — AC 61-23B, page 96
Use the following steps:

1. Locate the pressure altitude of 8,000 feet on FAA Figure 36. Read to the right and identify the chart which presents an indicated outside temperature of 22°C at 8,000 feet (the chart for ISA +20°C).

2. On this chart, read across the 8,000-foot line, 22°C, 20.8" Hg manifold pressure line. The fuel flow is 11.5 GPH and the TAS is 164 knots.

3. Using a flight computer, calculate the time en route:
   Distance is 1,000 NM
   TAS is 164 knots, with no wind

   Therefore, the time en route is 6 hours, 6 minutes.

4. Using a flight computer, calculate the fuel consumption:
   Time en route is 6 hours, 6 minutes
   Fuel burn is 11.5 GPH

   Therefore, the fuel consumption is 70.1 gallons.

AIR
3680 [B] — (H04) — AC 61-23B, Chapter 4
Use the following steps:

1. Locate the pressure altitude of 4,000 feet on FAA Figure 36. Read to the right and identify the chart which presents an indicated outside temperature of +29°C at 4,000 feet (in this case, the chart for ISA +20°C).

2. On this chart, read across the 4,000-foot line, +29°C, 21.3" Hg manifold pressure line. The fuel flow is 11.5 GPH and the TAS is 159 knots.

3. Using a flight computer, calculate the time en route:
   Distance is 500 NM
   TAS is 159 knots, with no wind

   Therefore, the time en route is 3 hours, 9 minutes.

4. Using a flight computer, calculate the fuel consumption:
   Time en route is 3 hours, 9 minutes
   Fuel burn is 11.5 GPH

   Therefore, the fuel consumption is 36.2 gallons.

AIR
3681 [B] — (H04) — AC 61-23B, Chapter 4
Use the following steps:

1. Locate the Standard Day (ISA) Chart on FAA Figure 36. Notice that the stated altitude, 11,000 feet, does not appear on the chart, so it is necessary to interpolate.

2. Read across the 10,000-foot pressure altitude line and determine the fuel flow at that altitude (11.5 GPH).

3. Read across the 12,000-foot pressure altitude line and determine the fuel flow at that altitude (10.9 GPH).

4. To determine the flow at 11,000 feet, add the two flows and divide by two.

$$\text{Fuel Flow} = \frac{(11.5 + 10.9)}{2} = \frac{22.4}{2} = 11.2 \text{ gallons per hr}$$

AIR
3682 [C] — (H04) — AC 61-23B, Chapter 4
Use the following steps:

1. Locate the +36°F (ISA +20°C) Chart on FAA Figure 36. Notice that the stated altitude of 6,500 feet does not appear on the chart, so it is necessary to interpolate.

2. Read across the 6,000-foot pressure altitude line and determine the manifold pressure at that altitude (21.0" Hg).

3. Read across the 8,000-foot pressure altitude line and determine the manifold pressure at that altitude (20.8" Hg).

4. The altitude, 6,500 feet, is closer to the 6,000-foot value of 21.0" Hg. (In this instance, the FAA apparently did not interpolate.)

AIR
3683 [B] — (H04) — AC 61-23B, Chapter 4
Use the following steps:

1. Determine the relative wind angle (WA) from the difference between the runway heading (RH) and the wind direction (WD):

    WA = WD − RH
    WA = 220° − 180°
    WA = 40°

2. Locate the arc corresponding to a 30-knot wind on FAA Figure 37.

3. Find the point of intersection of the 40° line with the 30-knot wind speed arc.

4. Draw a line to the left from the intersection to the headwind component scale and read the resulting velocity of 23 knots.

AIR
3684 [C] — (H04) — AC 61-23B, Chapter 4
Use the following steps:

1. Locate the 45° wind angle in FAA Figure 37.

2. Locate the vertical line representing a 25-knot crosswind component and its point of intersection with the 45° wind angle line.

3. Interpret the intersection point as lying on an arc midway between the 30- and 40-knot wind velocity arcs, or 35 knots.

AIR
3685 [C] — (H04) — AC 61-23B, Chapter 4
Use the following steps:

1. Locate the 30° wind angle line on FAA Figure 37.

2. Locate the vertical line representing the maximum crosswind component of 12 knots and its point of intersection with the 30° wind angle line.

3. Interpret the point of intersection as lying on an arc slightly less than midway between the 20- and 30-knot wind velocity arcs or about 24 knots.

AIR
3686 [C] — (H04) — AC 61-23B, Chapter 4
Use the following steps:

1. Locate the 20-knot wind velocity arc on FAA Figure 37.

2. Draw a line upward from the 13-knot crosswind component (maximum crosswind).

3. Note that in this case, acceptable crosswind components will result anytime the relative wind angle is equal to or less than about 40° (the intersection of the 13-knot vertical line and the 20-knot wind arc).

4. Calculate the relative wind angle between the north wind (0°) and the runway headings:

RWY	Relative Angle	Landing
6	60°	Upwind
29	70°	Upwind
32	40°	Upwind

Only runway 32 provides a crosswind component that would be in acceptable limits for the airplane specified.

AIR
3687 [B] — (H04) — AC 61-23B, Chapter 4
Use the following steps:

1. Locate the 20-knot wind velocity arc on FAA Figure 37.

2. Draw a line upward from the 13-knot crosswind component (maximum crosswind).

3. Note that in this case, acceptable crosswind components will result anytime the relative wind angle is equal to or less than 43° (the intersection of the 13-knot vertical line and the 20-knot wind arc).

4. Calculate the relative wind angle between the south wind (180°) and the runway headings:

RWY	Relative Angle	Landing
6	60°	Downwind
14	40°	Upwind
24	60°	Upwind
32	40°	Downwind

While both runways 14 and 32 would limit the crosswind component to an acceptable velocity, only runway 14 provides a safer upwind landing.

ALL
3688 [A] — (H04) — AC 61-23B, Chapter 4
Use the following steps:

1. Determine the relative wind angle (WA) from the difference between the runway heading (RH) and the wind direction (WD).

    WA = WD − RH
    WA = 220° − 180°
    WA = 40°

2. Locate the arc corresponding to a 30-knot wind velocity.

3. Find the point of intersection of the 40° line with the 30-knot wind speed arc.

4. Draw a line downward from the intersection to the crosswind component scale and read the resulting velocity of 19 knots.

AIR
3689 [B] — (H04) — AC 61-23B, Chapter 4
Use the following steps:

1. Enter FAA Figure 38 at the point where the vertical 32°F temperature line intersects the 8,000-foot pressure altitude line.
2. From there, proceed to the right to the first vertical reference line.
3. From that point, proceed down and to the right (remaining proportionally between the existing lines) to the vertical line representing 2,600 pounds.
4. Then, proceed to the right to the second vertical reference line.
5. Then, proceed down and to the right (remaining proportionally between the existing headwind lines) to the vertical line representing 20 knots.
6. From that point, proceed to the right to the third reference line.
7. Finally, proceed up and to the right (remaining proportionally between the existing lines) to the 50-foot obstacle line at the end of the graph and read the landing distance (approximately 1,400 feet).

AIR
3690 [A] — (H04) — AC 61-23B, Chapter 4
Use the following steps:

1. Enter the graph at the point where the ISA line intercepts the 2,000-foot pressure altitude line.
2. From that point, proceed to the right to the first vertical reference line.
3. From there, proceed down and to the right (remaining proportionally between the existing lines), to the vertical line representing 2,300 pounds.
4. Then proceed to the right to the second vertical reference line.
5. Since the wind is calm, continue to the right to the third vertical reference line.
6. No obstacle clearance height is required by this problem. Therefore, proceed horizontally to the right to the distance scale and read the landing distance (approximately 850 feet).

AIR
3691 [C] — (H04) — AC 61-23B, Chapter 4
Use the following steps:

1. Enter FAA Figure 38 at the point where the vertical 90°F temperature line intersects the 3,000-foot pressure altitude line. (The point must be visualized midway between the 2,000- and 4,000-foot pressure altitude lines.)
2. From that point, proceed to the right to the first vertical reference line.
3. From there, proceed downward and to the right (remaining proportionally between the existing lines), to the vertical line representing 2,900 pounds.
4. Then proceed to the right to the second vertical reference line.
5. Since there is a 10-knot headwind, proceed downward and to the right (remaining proportionally between the existing lines) to the vertical line representing 10 knots.
6. From that point, proceed to the right to the third vertical reference line.
7. From there, proceed upward and to the right (remaining proportionally between the existing lines) to the vertical line representing the required 50-foot obstacle height. Read the landing distance from the vertical scale (approximately 1,725 feet).

AIR
3692 [C] — (H04) — AC 61-23B, Chapter 4
Use the following steps:

1. Enter FAA Figure 38 at the point where the vertical 90°F temperature line intersects the 4,000-foot pressure altitude line.
2. From that point, proceed to the right to the first vertical reference line.
3. From there, proceed downward and to the right (remaining proportionally between the existing lines), to the vertical line representing 2,800 pounds.
4. Then proceed to the right to the intersection with the second vertical reference line.
5. Since there is a 10-knot tailwind component, proceed upward and to the right (remaining proportionally between the existing lines) to the vertical line representing 10 knots.
6. From that point, proceed to the right to the third vertical reference line.
7. No obstacle clearance height is required by this problem. Therefore, proceed horizontally to the right to the distance scale and read the landing distance (approximately 1,950 feet).

AIR
3693 [B] — (H04) — AC 61-23B, Chapter 4
Use the following steps:

1. Locate the sea level portion of FAA Figure 39.
2. Read the landing ground roll distance (445 feet).
3. Note 1 requires that the distances shown be decreased by 10% for each 4 knots of headwind.

   445 x .10 = 44.5 feet
   445.0 − 44.5 = 400.5 or 401 feet

AIR
3694 [B] — (H04) — AC 61-23B, Chapter 4
Use the following steps:

1. Locate the portion of FAA Figure 39 that is applicable to a pressure altitude of 7,500 feet. Note: The standard temperature at 7,500 feet is approximately 32°F, based on a temperature lapse rate of 3.5°F/1,000 feet.
2. Determine from the table that the basic distance to clear a 50-foot obstacle is 1,255 feet.
3. Apply Note 1 to account for an 8-knot headwind (a 20% decrease in distance):
   1,255 x .20 = 251 feet
   1,255 − 251 = 1,004 feet
4. Now apply Note 3 to account for a dry grass runway.
   1,004 x .20 = 200.8 feet
   1,004.0 + 200.8 = 1,204.8 or 1,205 feet

AIR
3695 [B] — (H04) — AC 61-23B, Chapter 4
Use the following steps:

1. Locate the table applicable to a pressure altitude of 5,000 feet and ambient temperature of 41°F on FAA Figure 39.
2. Read the total distance required to clear a 50-foot obstacle (1,195 feet).
3. Apply Note 1 to account for an 8-knot headwind (a 20% decrease in distance):
   1,195 x .20 = 239 feet
   1,195 − 239 = 956 feet

AIR
3696 [C] — (H04) — AC 61-23B, Chapter 4
Use the following steps:

1. Locate the table which applies to a pressure altitude of 5,000 feet on FAA Figure 39.
2. Read the total distance to land over a 50-foot obstacle (1,195 feet).
3. Apply Note 2 to account for the temperature difference between 101°F ambient and the 41°F value on which the table is based.
   101°F − 41°F = 60°F
   1,195 x .10 = 119.5 feet
   1,195.0 + 119.5 = 1,314.5 feet

AIR
3697 [A] — (H04) — AC 61-23B, Chapter 4
Use the following steps:

1. Locate the 2,500-foot and 5,000-foot tables.
2. Interpolate (3,750 is midway between 2,500 feet and 5,000 feet) to obtain a landing round roll:
   (470 + 495) ÷ 2 = 482.5 feet ground roll
3. Apply Note 1 to account for the 12-knot headwind.
   12 ÷ 4 = 3
   3.00 x .10 = .30
   482.50 x .30 = 144.80
   482.50 − 144.8 = 337.70 or 338 feet

ALL
3698 [B] — (H04) — AC 61-23B, Chapter 4
Use the following steps:

1. Locate the tables for sea level and 2,500 feet. Note that 1,250 feet is midway between sea level and 2,500 feet.
2. Interpolate between charts for 2,500 feet pressure altitude and sea level to find ground roll:
   (445 + 470) ÷ 2 = 457.5 ground roll
3. Apply Note 1 to account for the 8-knot headwind (a 20% decrease in distance):
   457.5 x .20 = 91.5 feet
   457.5 − 91.5 = 366 feet

RTC
3699 [B] — (H04) — AC 61-23B, Chapter 4
Use the following steps:

1. Locate the horizontal line corresponding to 2,500 feet pressure altitude on FAA Figure 40.
2. Draw vertical lines through the points of intersection of the 2,500-foot pressure altitude line with the 75°F point. Note the landing distance of 525 feet.

RTC
3700 [A] — (H04) — AC 61-23B, Chapter 4
Use the following steps:

1. Locate the 3,200-foot pressure altitude point on FAA Figure 40.
2. Select any two adjacent temperature lines (which are separated by 20°F increments). Note the points of intersection of each line with the 3,200-foot pressure altitude.
3. Read downward from each of the two intersections to the distance scale.
4. Note the difference between the two distances (4 feet).

RTC
3701 [C] — (H04) — AC 61-23B, Chapter 4
Use the following steps:

1. Locate the horizontal line corresponding to 3,500 feet pressure altitude on FAA Figure 40.
2. Draw vertical lines through the points of intersection of the 3,500-foot pressure altitude line with the 50°F point. Note the landing distance of 531 feet.

RTC
3702 [C] — (H04) — AC 61-23B, Chapter 4
Use the following steps:

1. Locate the 1,700-foot pressure altitude on the Take-Off Distance Graph (right).
2. Draw a horizontal line from the 1,700-foot position to the 95°F OAT point.
3. Draw a vertical line downward from the point of intersection to the total Take-Off Distance Scale. Note the distance 2,030 feet.

RTC
3703 [C] — (H04) — AC 61-23B, Chapter 4
1. On the sea level line of FAA Figure 40 locate the intersection of the +59°F point.
2. Read landing distance of 1,200 feet.

RTC
3704 [A] — (H04) — AC 61-23B, Chapter 4
Use the following steps:

1. Locate the 2,300-foot pressure altitude on FAA Figure 40.
2. Draw a horizontal line from the 2,300-foot position to the 75°F and the 90°F OAT points.
3. From these points, draw vertical lines downward to the takeoff distance scale and note the distances (2,025 and 2,185, respectively).
4. The difference is the increase in takeoff distance.

    2,185 − 2,025 = 160 feet

AIR
3705 [B] — (H04) — AC 61-23B, Chapter 4
Use the following steps:

1. Locate the ISA curve on FAA Figure 41.
2. Note the intersection of the ISA curve with the pressure altitude, 4,000 feet.
3. From that point, draw a line to the right to the first reference line.
4. From there, proceed downward and to the right (remaining proportionally between the existing lines) to the vertical line representing 2,800 pounds.
5. Then proceed to the right to the second reference line.
6. In this case the reference line is also the vertical line representing the 0 MPH wind component.
7. From that point, continue to the right to the third vertical reference line.
8. From there, proceed upward and to the right (remaining proportionally between the existing lines) to the vertical line representing the obstacle height, 50 feet.
9. Read the distance (approximately 1,750 feet).

AIR
3706 [B] — (H04) — AC 61-23B, Chapter 4
Use the following steps:

1. Locate the OAT, 59°F, on FAA Figure 41.
2. From that point, draw a line upward to the line representing the pressure altitude, 0 feet (SL).
3. From that point, draw a line to the right to the first reference line.
4. From there, proceed downward and to the right (remaining proportionally between the existing lines) to the vertical line representing 2,700 pounds.
5. Then draw a line to the right to the second reference line.
6. In this case, the reference line is also the vertical line representing the 0-knot wind component.
7. From that point, continue a horizontal line to the third vertical reference line.
8. Finally, proceed upward and to the right (remaining proportionally between the existing lines) to the vertical line representing the obstacle height, 50 feet and read the distance (approximately 1,400 feet).

AIR
3707 [A] — (H04) — AC 61-23B, Chapter 4
Use the following steps:

1. Locate the OAT, 100°F, on FAA Figure 41.
2. From that point, draw a line upward to the line representing the pressure altitude, 2,000 feet.
3. From that point, draw a line to the right to the first reference line.
4. From there, proceed downward and to the right (remaining proportionally between the existing lines) to the vertical line representing 2,750 pounds.
5. Then draw a line to the right to the second reference line.
6. In this case, the reference line is also the vertical line representing the 0-knot wind component.
7. Then draw a horizontal line to the third vertical reference line.
8. In this case, the reference line is also the vertical line representing the obstacle height, 0 feet.
9. From that point, draw a horizontal line to the right and read the distance (approximately 1,150 feet).

AIR
3708 [A] — (H04) — AC 61-23B, Chapter 4
Use the following steps:

1. Locate the OAT, 90°F, on FAA Figure 41.
2. From that point, draw a line upward to the line representing the pressure altitude of 2,000 feet.
3. Form the point of intersection, draw a line to the right to the reference line and stop.
4. From that point, proceed downward and to the right (remaining proportionally between the existing guide lines) to the vertical line representing 2,500 pounds.
5. From there, draw a line to the right to the second reference line.
6. Then proceed down and to the right (remaining proportionally between the existing guide lines) to the line representing the 20-knot headwind component line.
7. From that point, draw a line to the right to the third reference line.
8. From there, move to the right and read an approximate ground roll for takeoff (650 feet).

ALL
3709 [B] — (H09) — AC 61-23B, AC 00-2
Advisory circulars which are offered for sale or free may be ordered from the Superintendent of Documents, U.S. Government Printing Office.

ALL
3710 [B] — (H50) — AIM ¶8-1-6(c)(1)
Scanning the sky for other aircraft is a key factor in collision avoidance.

AIR, RTC
3711 [A] — (H58) — AC 61-21A, Chapter 9
Maintaining the proper glide speed (safe airspeed) is the most important rule to remember in the event of a power failure.

AIR, RTC, LTA
3712 [B] — (H63) — AC 61-21A
During daylight, an object can be seen best by looking directly at it, but at night, a scanning procedure to permit "off-center" viewing of the object is more effective. In addition, the pilot should consciously practice moving the eyes more slowly than in daylight to optimize night vision. Off-center viewing must be utilized during night flying because of the distribution of rods and cones in the eye.

AIR, RTC, LTA
3713 [A] — (H63) — AC 61-21A
During daylight, an object can be seen best by looking directly at it, but at night, a scanning procedure to permit "off-center" viewing of the object is more effective. In addition, the pilot should consciously practice moving the eyes more slowly than in daylight to optimize night vision. Off-center viewing must be utilized during night flying because of the distribution of rods and cones in the eye.

AIR, RTC, LTA
3714 [C] — (H63) — AC 61-21A
During daylight, an object can be seen best by looking directly at it, but at night, a scanning procedure to permit "off-center" viewing of the object is more effective. In addition, the pilot should consciously practice moving the eyes more slowly than in daylight to optimize night vision. Off-center viewing must be utilized during night flying because of the distribution of rods and cones in the eye.

AIR, RTC, LTA
3715 [A] — (H63) — AC 61-21A
Airplanes have a red light on the left wing tip, a green light on the right wing tip and a white light on the tail. The flashing red light is the rotating beacon which can be seen from all directions around the aircraft. If the only steady light seen is red, then the airplane is crossing from right to left in relation to the observing pilot.

AIR, RTC, LTA
3716 [A] — (H63) — AC 61-21A
Airplanes have a red light on the left wing tip, a green light on the right wing tip and a white light on the tail. The flashing red light is the rotating beacon which can be seen from all directions around the aircraft. When the only steady light seen is white, then the airplane is headed away from the observing pilot.

AIR, RTC, LTA
3717 [C] — (H63) — AC 61-21A
When both a red and green light of another airplane are observed, the airplane would be flying in a general direction toward you. Airplanes have a red light on the left wing tip, a green light on the right wing tip and a white light on the tail.

AIR, RTC
3718 [B] — (H63) — AIM ¶2-1-9
A taxiway-edge lighting system consists of omnidirectional blue lights which outline the usable limits of taxi paths.

AIR, RTC
3719 [C] — (H63) — AC 61-21A
Inexperienced pilots often have a tendency to make approaches and landings at night with excessive airspeed. Every effort should be made to execute the approach and landing in the same manner as during the day.

RTC
3720 [C] — (H76) — AC 61-13B, Chapter 7
Use the following steps:

1. Compute the left and right moments using the formula:

    Weight x Arm = Moment

Item	Weight	Arm	Moment
Pilot	140 lbs	13.5	1,890 lbs-in (left)
Copilot	180 lbs	13.5	2,430 lbs-in (right)

2. Find the offset to the left or right:

    2,430.0 lbs-in (right)
    − 1,890.0 lbs-in (left)
    540.0 lbs-in offset (right)

3. Enter the bottom of the Lateral Offset Moment Graph at 540 lbs-in right of the zero point. Proceed upward until intercepting the 1,800-pound gross weight line. The point of intercept lies inside the envelope.

RTC
3721 [A] — (H76) — AC 61-13B, Chapter 7
Use the following steps:

1. Compute the left and right moments using the formula:

    Weight x Arm = Moment

Item	Weight	Arm	Moment
Copilot	200 lbs	13.5	2,700 lbs-in (right)
Pilot	100 lbs	13.5	1,350 lbs-in (left)

2. Find the offset to the right or left:

    2,700.0 lbs-in (right)
    − 1,350.0 lbs-in (left)
    1,350.0 lbs-in offset (right)

3. Enter the bottom of the Lateral Offset Moment Envelope Graph of FAA Figure 44 at 1,350 right of the zero point. Proceed upward until intercepting the 1,800-pound gross weight line. The point of intercept falls outside the envelope to the right.

4. Try adding 50 pounds to the pilot's side and do the same computations:

    Copilot 200 x 13.5 = 2,700 (right)
    Pilot 150 x 13.5 = 2,025 (left)

    2,700 (right)
    − 2,025 (left)
    675 (right)

Plot the new values on the lateral offset envelope graph of FAA Figure 44.

RTC
3722 [B] — (H76) — AC 61-23B, Chapter 4
Use the following steps:

1. Calculate the weight and moment using the information given in the problem and the formula:

    Weight x Arm = Moment

    Note: The standard weight of gasoline is 6 lbs/U.S. gallon.

Item	Weight	Arm	Moment
Empty weight	1,495 lbs		151,593.0 lbs-in
Pilot & Pax	350 lbs	64	22,400.0 lbs-in
Fuel 40 x 6	240 lbs	96	23,040.0 lbs-in
Total	2,085 lbs		197,033.0 lbs-in

2. Determine the position of the CG using the formula:

    $$CG = \frac{Total\ Moment}{Total\ Weight}$$

    or:

    $$CG = \frac{197,033}{2,085} = 94.5\ inches\ aft\ of\ datum$$

3. Locate the point on FAA Figure 42 defined by a weight of 2,085 pounds and a CG of 94.5 inches, and find the aircraft within gross weight limit and at the aft CG limit.

RTC
3723 [B] — (H76) — AC 61-23B, Chapter 4
Use the following steps:

1. Calculate the weights and moments using the information from the problem and the Loading Chart of FAA Figure 43. Use the formula:

    Weight x Arm = Moment

    Note: The standard weight of gasoline is 6 lbs/U.S gallon.

Item	Weight	Arm	Moment
Empty weight	1,025 lbs		102,705.0 lbs-in
Pilot & Pax (a)	345 lbs	83.90	28,945.0 lbs-in
Fuel 35 x 6 (b)	210 lbs	107.0	22,470.0 lbs-in
Total	1,580 lbs		154,120.5 lbs-in

2. Determine the position of the CG using the formula:

    $$CG = \frac{Total\ Moment}{Total\ Weight}$$

    or:

    $$CG = \frac{154,120.5}{1,580} = 97.54\ inches\ aft\ of\ datum$$

3. Plot the point determined by a weight of 1,580 pounds and a moment of 154,120.5 lbs-in on the CG limit graph of FAA Figure 43. The point is within the forward and aft limits.

RTC
3724 [A] — (H76) — AC 61-23B, Chapter 4
Use the following steps:
1. Calculate the original position of the CG using the formula:

   $$CG = \frac{\text{Total Moment}}{\text{Total Weight}}$$

   or:

   $$CG = \frac{136{,}647.5}{1{,}380} = 99.02 \text{ inches aft of datum}$$

2. Determine the revised weight and moment. The station for the passenger is 83.90 inches as shown on the Loading Chart of FAA Figure 43. Use the following formula:

   Weight x Arm = Moment

Item	Weight	Arm	Moment
Original total	1,380 lbs		136,647.5 lbs-in
Passenger	+185 lbs	83.9	15,521.5 lbs-in
New Total	1,565 lbs		152,169.0 lbs-in

3. Calculate the new CG:

   $$CG = \frac{152{,}169}{1{,}565} = 97.23 \text{ inches aft of datum}$$

4. Compute the change in CG:

Original CG	99.02	inches aft of datum
minus new CG	− 97.23	inches aft of datum
Movement	1.79	inches (forward)

RTC
3725 [B] — (H76) — AC 61-23B, Chapter 4
Use the following steps:
1. Calculate the original position of the CG using the formula:

   $$CG = \frac{\text{Total Moment}}{\text{Total Weight}}$$

   or:

   $$CG = \frac{195{,}365}{2{,}050} = 95.3 \text{ inches aft of datum}$$

2. Determine the revised weight and moment. The station for the fuel is 96.9 inches as shown on the question which contradicts FAA Figure 43. Use the following formula:

   Weight x Arm = Moment

Item	Weight	Arm	Moment
Original total	2,050 lbs		195,365 lbs-in
Fuel burn	− 120 lbs	96.9	11,628 lbs-in
New Total	1,930 lbs		183,737 lbs-in

3. Calculate the new CG:

   $$CG = \frac{183{,}737}{1{,}930} = 95.2 \text{ inches aft of datum}$$

4. Compute the change in CG:

Original CG	95.3	inches aft of datum
minus new CG	− 95.2	inches aft of datum
Movement	.1	inch (forward)

RTC
3726 [B] — (H76) — AC 61-23B, Chapter 4
Use the following steps:
1. Calculate the original position of the CG using the formula:

   $$CG = \frac{\text{Total Moment}}{\text{Total Weight}}$$

   or:

   $$CG = \frac{159{,}858.5}{1{,}660} = 96.3 \text{ inches aft of datum}$$

2. Determine the revised weight and moment. The station for the fuel is 106.7 inches as shown on the Loading Chart of FAA Figure 43. Use the following formula:

   Weight x Arm = Moment

Item	Weight	Arm	Moment
Original total	1,660 lbs		159,858.5 lbs-in
Fuel burn	− 54 lbs	106.8	5767.2 lbs-in
New Total	1,606 lbs		154,091.3 lbs-in

3. Calculate the new CG:

   $$CG = \frac{154{,}091}{1{,}606} = 95.94 \text{ inches aft of datum}$$

4. Compute the change in CG:

Original CG	96.30	inches aft of datum
minus new CG	− 95.94	inches aft of datum
Movement	.36	inches (forward)

Answer B is closest.

RTC
3727 [C] — (H76) — AC 61-23B, Chapter 4
This problem uses a reduction factor so we arrive at moment index instead of moment.
Use the following steps:
1. Calculate the weights and moment indexes using the information from the problem and the formula:

   Weight x Arm ÷ Reduction Factor = Moment Index

   Note: The standard weight for gasoline is 6 lbs/U.S. gallon and for oil, 7.5 lbs/U.S. gallon.

Item	Weight	Arm	Moment/100
Empty weight	1,495 lbs	101.4	1,515.93 lbs-in
Oil, 8 qts (2 x 7.5)	15 lbs	100.5	15.08 lbs-in
Fuel (40 x 6)	240 lbs	96.0	230.40 lbs-in
Pilot	160 lbs	64.0	102.40 lbs-in
Total	1,910 lbs		1,863.81 lbs-in

Continued

2. Determine the position of the CG using the formula:

$$CG = \frac{\text{Total Mom/Ind}}{\text{Total Weight}} \times \text{Reduction Factor}$$

or:

$$\frac{1{,}863.81}{1{,}910} \times 100 = 97.58 \text{ inches aft of datum}$$

3. Plot the point determined by a weight of 1,910 pounds and a CG of 97.58 inches on the longitudinal CG envelope of FAA Figure 44. The point is within the allowable limits.

RTC
3728 [B] — (H76) — AC 61-23B, Chapter 4
Use the following steps:

1. Calculate the weights and moment indexes using the information from the problem and the formula:

   Weight x Arm ÷ Reduction Factor = Moment/Index

   Note: The standard weight for gasoline is 6 lbs/U.S. gallon and for oil, 7.5 lbs/U.S. gallon.

Item	Weight	Arm	Moment/100
Empty weight	1,495 lbs	101.4	1,515.93 lbs-in
Oil, 8 qts (2 x 7.5)	15 lbs	100.5	15.08 lbs-in
Fuel (40 x 6)	240 lbs	96.0	230.40 lbs-in
Pilots	300 lbs	64.0	192 lbs-in
Total	2,050 lbs		1,953.41 lbs-in

2. Determine the position of the CG using the formula:

$$CG = \frac{\text{Total Mom/Ind}}{\text{Total Weight}} \times \text{Reduction Factor}$$

or:

$$\frac{1{,}953.41}{2{,}050} \times 100 = 95.29 \text{ inches aft of datum}$$

3. Plot the point determined by a weight of 1,910 pounds and a CG of 97.58 inches on the longitudinal CG envelope of FAA Figure 44. The point is outside the allowable limits.

RTC
3729 [A] — (H76) — The J-2 Gyroplane and How to Fly It
Use the following steps:

1. Determine the change in load moment resulting from 10 gallons of fuel burned by entering the Loading Chart at the 10 gallon point on the fuel line, drawing a line downward and reading the moment for 10 gallons of fuel (5.3 x 1,000 lbs-in).

2. Calculate the new weight and moment:

Item	Weight	Moment/1,000
Original total	1,450.0 lbs	108.0 lbs-in
Fuel (10 x 6)	– 60.0 lbs	– 5.3 lbs-in
New Total	1,390.0 lbs	102.7 lbs-in

3. Plot the point determined by 1,390 and 102.7 lbs-in/1,000 on the center of gravity moment envelope graph. The point is outside (to the left or forward) of the center of gravity moment envelope.

RTC
3730 [A] — (H76) — The J-2 Gyroplane and How to Fly It
Use the following steps:

1. Calculate the total weight and moments using the information in the problem and FAA Figure 46. The standard weight for oil is 7.5 lbs/U.S. gallon, and for gasoline it is 6 lbs/U.S. gallon.

Item	Weight	Moment/1,000
Empty weight	1,074 lbs	85.6 lbs-in
Oil, 6 qts (1.5 X 7.5)	11 lbs	1.0 lbs-in
Pilot and Pax (seat aft)	247 lbs	14.1 lbs-in
Fuel (12 x 6)	72 lbs	6.3 lbs-in
Baggage	95 lbs	5.7 lbs-in
Total	1,499 lbs	112.7 lbs-in

2. Plot the point determined by 1,499 pounds and 112.7 x 1,000 lbs-in on FAA Figure 45. The point is within the envelope (Answer A).

3. Now, consider the effect of pilot and passenger in the forward position. The moment would now be 13.3 x 1,000 lbs-in and the resulting total moment would be reduced to 111.9 x 1,000 lbs-in. When plotted on the Center of Gravity Moment Envelope Graph SEAT FWD, the weight-moment is slightly outside the envelope. Note that the manufacturer uses an aft position in presenting sample weight and balance calculations for this aircraft.

RTC
3731 [B] — (H76) — The J-2 Gyroplane and How to Fly It
Use the following steps:

1. Calculate the total weight and moment using the information in the problem and the Loading Chart. The standard weight for oil is 7.5 pounds per gallon and for gasoline is 6.0 pounds per gallon.

Item	Weight	Moment/1,000
Empty weight	1,074 lbs	85.6 lbs-in
Oil, 6 qts. (1.5 x 7.5)	11 lbs	1.0 lbs-in
Pilot (a)	224 lbs	12.1 lbs-in
Fuel (full) (b)	120 lbs	11.6 lbs-in
Totals	1,429 lbs	110.3 lbs-in

2. Consider adding enough baggage to approach the maximum takeoff weight 1,500 pounds.

   1,500 – 1,429 = 71 or about 70 pounds (Answer B)

   (This remains within the weight limit.)

3. Determine the moment of the 70 pounds of added baggage (4.2 x 1,000 lbs-in).

4. Compute the new weight and moment.

Item	Weight	Moment
Original Total	1,429	110.3
Baggage	+ 70	+ 4.2
New Total	1,499	114.2

5. Plot the point determined by 1,499.3 lbs and 114.2 x 1,000 lbs-in on the Center of Gravity Moment Envelope Graph of FAA Figure 45. The point is within the envelope.

RTC
3732 [C] — (H77) — AC 61-13B, page 68
Use the following steps:
1. Locate the recommended takeoff profile on FAA Figure 47.
2. Note that the best rate-of-climb speed at sea level is designated by the arrow pointing to the vertical line.
3. Interpret the diagram. The vertical line is most closely aligned with an IAS of about 57 MPH.

RTC
3733 [B] — (H77) — AC 61-13B, page 76
During a hovering turn to the left, the RPM will decrease if throttle is not added. In a hovering turn to the right, RPM will increase if throttle is not reduced slightly. (This is due to the amount of engine power that is being absorbed by the tail rotor, which is dependent upon the pitch angle at which the tail rotor blades are operating.)

RTC
3734 [B] — (H78) — AC 61-13B, page 66
The following combination of conditions are likely to cause settling with power:
1. A vertical, or nearly vertical, descent of at least 300 feet per minute. Actual critical rate depends on the gross weight, RPM, density altitude, and other pertinent factors.
2. The rotor system must be using some of the available engine power (from 20 to 100 percent).
3. The horizontal velocity must be no greater than approximately 10 miles per hour.

RTC
3735 [C] — (H78) — AC 61-13B, page 68
Use the following steps:
1. Locate the ground effect unsafe area on FAA Figure 47.
2. Note that the ground effect altitude in the forward flight region is 40 feet.
3. The diagram depicts that a pilot should avoid flight of 40 MPH or greater at altitudes lower than 40 feet.

RTC
3736 [C] — (H78) — AC 61-13B, page 69
Use the following steps:
1. Note the shaded "avoid operation" areas of FAA Figure 47.
2. Locate each of the three height-above-terrain and air speed points on the diagram.
3. The 60 MPH/20 feet AGL point is located within the low-altitude high airspeed area.

RTC
3737 [A] — (H78) — AC 61-13B, page 68
Use the following steps:
1. Note the shaded "avoid operation" areas of FAA Figure 47.
2. Locate each of the three height-above-terrain and air speed points on the diagram.
3. The 20 MPH/200 feet AGL point is located within the high-altitude low air speed area.

RTC
3738 [B] — (H78) — AC 61-13B, page 69
If sufficient forward speed is maintained, the fuselage remains fairly well streamlined. However, if descent is attempted at slow speeds, a continuous turning movement to the left can be expected. (Know the manufacturer's recommendations in case of tail rotor failure for each particular helicopter you fly. This information will generally be found under Emergency Procedures in the helicopter flight manual.) Directional control should be maintained primarily with cyclic control and, secondarily, by gently applying throttle momentarily, with needles joined, to swing the nose to the right.

RTC
3739 [C] — (H79) — AC 61-13B, page 72
The following techniques should be used in hot weather:
1. Make full use of wind and translational lift.
2. Hover as low as possible and no longer than necessary.
3. Maintain maximum allowable engine RPM.
4. Accelerate very slowly into forward flight.
5. Employ running takeoffs and landings when necessary.
6. Use caution in maximum performance takeoffs and steep approaches.
7. Avoid high rates of descent in all approaches.

RTC
3740 [A] — (H80) — AC 61-13B, page 89
A running takeoff is used when conditions of load and/or density altitude prevent a sustained hover at normal hovering altitude. It is often referred to as a high-altitude takeoff. With insufficient power to hover at least momentarily or at a very low altitude, a running takeoff is not advisable. No takeoff should be attempted if the helicopter cannot be lifted off the surface momentarily at full power.

RTC
3741 [C] — (H80) — AC 61-13B, page 91
By immediately lowering collective pitch (which must be done in case of engine failure), lift and drag will be reduced and the helicopter will begin an immediate descent, thus producing an upward flow of air through the rotor system. The impact of this upward flow of air provides sufficient thrust to maintain rotor RPM throughout the descent.

RTC
3742 [B] — (H80) — AC 61-13B, page 93
When making turns during an autorotative descent, generally use cyclic control only. Use of antitorque pedals to assist or speed the turn causes loss of airspeed and downward pitching of the nose. This is especially true when the left pedal is used. When the autorotation is initiated, sufficient right pedal pressure should be used to maintain straight flight and prevent yawing to the left. This pressure should not be changed to assist the turn.

RTC
3743 [C] — (H80) — AC 61-13B, page 97
A quick stop is initiated by applying aft cyclic to reduce forward speed. Simultaneously, the collective pitch should be lowered as necessary, to counteract any climbing tendency. The timing must be exact. If too little down collective is applied for the amount of aft cyclic applied, a climb will result. If too much down collective is applied for the amount of aft cyclic applied, a descent will result. A rapid application of aft cyclic requires an equally rapid application of down collective. As collective pitch is lowered, the right pedal should be increased to maintain heading, and throttle should be adjusted to maintain RPM.

RTC
3744 [C] — (H80) — AC 61-13B, page 98
A downward pressure on the collective pitch will start the helicopter descending. As the upslope skid touches the ground, apply cyclic stick in the direction of the slope. This will hold the skid against the slope while the downslope skid is continuing to be let down with the collective pitch.

RTC
3745 [B] — (H80) — AC 61-13B, page 98
Recommended slope takeoff technique is to:

1. Adjust throttle to obtain takeoff RPM and move the cyclic stick in the direction of the slope so that the rotor rotation is parallel to the true horizontal rather than the slope.

2. Apply up-collective pitch. As the helicopter becomes light on the skids, apply the pedal as needed to maintain heading.

3. As the downslope skid is rising and the helicopter approaches a level attitude, move the cyclic stick back to the neutral position, keeping the rotor disc parallel to the true horizon. Continue to apply up-collective pitch and take the helicopter straight up to a hover before moving away from the slope. In moving away from the slope, the tail should not be turned upslope because of the danger of the tail rotor striking the surface.

RTC
3746 [B] — (H81) — AC 61-13B, page 101
In any type of confined area operation, plan a flight path over areas suitable for forced landings if possible.

RTC
3747 [A] — (H81) — AC 61-13B, page 102
If possible, a normal takeoff from a hover should be made when departing a confined area.

RTC
3748 [C] — (H81) — AC 61-13B, page 102
If necessary to climb to a pinnacle or ridgeline, the climb should be performed on the upwind side, when practicable, to take advantage of any updrafts.

RTC
3749 [A] — (H81) — AC 61-13B, page 103
The purpose of the high reconnaissance is to determine the suitability of an area for landing. In a high reconnaissance, the following items should be accomplished:

1. Determine wind direction and speed.
2. Select the most suitable flight paths into and out of the area, with particular consideration being given to forced landing areas.
3. Plan the approach and select a point for touchdown.
4. Locate and determine the size of barriers, if any.

The approach path should be generally into the wind. The purpose of the low reconnaissance is to verify what was seen in the high reconnaissance.

GLI
3750 [B] — (I35) — AC 00-6A, Chapter 16
Zero sink occurs when upward currents are just strong enough to hold altitude. For a sink rate of about 2 feet per second, there must be an upward air current of at least 2 feet per second.

GLI
3751 [A] — (I35) — AC 00-6A, Chapter 16
If a rocky knoll protrudes above a grassy plane, the most likely area for thermals to occur is over the eastern slope in the forenoon and over the western slope in the afternoon.

GLI
3752 [C] — (I35) — AC 00-6A, Chapter 16
Look for converging streamers of dust and smoke.

GLI
3753 [C] — (I35) — AC 00-6A, Chapter 16
At around 500 feet, the pilot makes a circle on the outside of the dust devil against the direction of rotation.

GLI
3754 [A] — (I35) — AC 00-6A, Chapter 16
The rarefied air in the eye provides very little lift, and the wall of the hollow core is very turbulent.

GLI
3755 [B] — (I35) — AC 00-6A, Chapter 16
Look for a cumulus with a concave base, and with a firm, sharp, unfragmented outline.

GLI
3756 [B] — (I35) — AC 00-6A, Chapter 16
Birds may be soaring in a "bubble" thermal that has been pinched off and forced upward through intermittent shading.

GLI
3757 [B] — (I35) — AC 00-6A, Chapter 16
Thermal streeting is a real boon to speed and distance.

GLI
3758 [A] — (I35) — AC 00-6A, Chapter 16
An ideal slope is about 1 to 4 with an upslope wind of 15 knots or more.

ALL
3759 [A] — [J01] — AIM ¶1-1-18
The VHF/DF receiver display indicates the magnetic direction to the aircraft each time the aircraft transmits. The DF specialist will give the pilot headings to fly. Thus, the aircraft must be equipped with an operational VHF transmitter and receiver. Transponder and VOR are not necessary.

AIR, RTC
3760 [B] — (J03) — AIM ¶2-1-2(b)
The precision approach path indicator (PAPI) uses light units similar to the VASI but are installed in a single row of either two or four light units. Four white lights means you are above the glide slope, three white lights and one red light means you are slightly high, two red and two white lights means you are on the glide slope, three reds and one white light means you are slightly low and four red lights means you are below the glide slope.

AIR, RTC
3761 [A] — (J03) — AIM ¶2-1-2(c)
A tri-color VASI normally is a single light unit projecting a three-color visual approach path. Below the glidepath is red, on the glidepath is green, and above the glidepath is amber.

AIR
3762 [C] — (J03) — AIM ¶2-1-2(c)
A tri-color VASI normally is a single light unit projecting a three-color visual approach path. Below the glidepath is red, on the glidepath is green, and above the glidepath is amber.

AIR
3763 [B] — (J03) — AIM ¶2-1-2(c)
A tri-color VASI normally is a single light unit projecting a three-color visual approach path. Below the glidepath is red, on the glidepath is green, and above the glidepath is amber.

AIR
3764 [C] — (J03) — AIM ¶2-2(d)
Pulsating visual approach slope indicators normally consist of a single light unit projecting a two-color visual approach path. The below-glidepath indication is red or pulsating red. The on-glidepath indication is a steady white light for one type of system, while for another system it is an alternating red and white light.

AIR, RTC
3765 [B] — (J03) — AIM ¶2-1-2
The two-bar VASI on-glide slope indication is red over white lights.

AIR, RTC
3766 [B] — (J03) — AIM ¶2-1-2(a)
The two-bar VASI above-glide slope indication is white over white lights. VASI lights do not give horizontal direction.

AIR, RTC
3767 [B] — (J03) — AIM ¶2-1-2
The below-glide slope indication from a two-bar VASI is red over red lights.

AIR, RTC
3768 [C] — (J03) — AIM ¶2-1-7
To save money at low-usage airports, pilot-controlled lighting is installed. Key the mike seven times to set the highest level, then adjust to medium with five clicks.

ALL
3769 [B] — (J03) — AIM ¶2-1-8
In Class B, C, D or E airspace, operation of the airport beacon during the hours of daylight often indicates that the weather in the airspace is below basic VFR weather minimums (ground visibility is less than 3 miles and/or the ceiling is less than 1,000 feet).

AIR, RTC, LTA
3770 [A] — (J03) — AIM ¶2-1-8
A lighted heliport has a green, yellow and white beacon flashing 30 to 60 times per minute. A flashing yellow light identifies a lighted water port.

AIR, RTC, LTA
3771 [B] — (J03) — AIM ¶2-1-8
Military airport beacons flash alternately white and green, but are differentiated from civil beacons by dual-peaked (two quick) white flashes between the green flashes.

AIR, RTC, LTA
3772 [B] — (J03) — AIM ¶2-1-8
Military airport beacons flash alternately white and green, but are differentiated from civil beacons by dual-peaked (two quick) white flashes between the green flashes.

AIR, RTC, LTA
3773 [B] — (J05) — AIM ¶2-2-3
Thresholds are marked at the beginning of a full-strength runway surface able to endure landing impacts or at a point on the runway which will encourage pilots to avoid short approaches due to hidden noise or obstacle problems. Area A of FAA Figure 49 is marked with arrows which point towards a displaced threshold. Thus, the paved surface prior to the threshold is available for taxi, takeoff and landing rollout, but not for touchdown.

AIR, GLI, RTC, REC
3774 [B] — (J05) — AIM ¶2-2-3
Thresholds are marked at the beginning of a full-strength runway surface able to endure landing impacts or at a point on the runway which will encourage pilots to avoid short approaches due to hidden noise or obstacle problems. Area A of FAA Figure 49 is marked with arrows which point towards a displaced threshold. Thus, the paved surface prior to the threshold is available for taxi, takeoff and landing rollout, but not for touchdown.

AIR, GLI, RTC, REC
3775 [A] — (J05) — AIM ¶2-2-3
The paved area behind the displaced threshold is available for taxiing, landing rollout, and takeoff. The stopway, extending beyond the usable runway, is unusable due to the nature of its construction. Area E of FAA Figure 49, marked with chevrons, is used for overrun only.

AIR, GLI, RTC, REC
3776 [C] — (J05) — AIM ¶2-2-3
An "X" painted on the end of runway means it is closed.

AIR, GLI, RTC, REC
3777 [C] — (J05) — AIM ¶2-2-3
The paved area behind the displaced runway threshold is available for taxiing, landing rollout, and the takeoff of aircraft.

ALL
3778 [C] — (J05) — AIM ¶2-2-3
The runway number is the whole number nearest one-tenth the **magnetic** azimuth of the centerline of the runway, measured clockwise from magnetic north. For example: 272° = RWY 27; 087° = RWY 9.

ALL
3779 [C] — (J08) — AIM ¶3-2-4
Class C airspace consists of two circles, both centered on the primary/Class C airspace airport. The inner circle has a radius of 5 NM. The outer circle usually has a radius of 10 NM. The airspace of the inner circle usually extends from the surface of the Class C airspace airport up to 4,000 feet above that airport. The airspace area between the 5 and 10 NM rings usually begins at a height of 1,200 feet AGL and extends to the same altitude cap as the inner circle. These dimensions may be varied to meet individual situations.

ALL
3780 [C] — (J08) — AIM ¶3-2-4
The normal radius of the outer area will be 20 NM.

ALL
3781 [C] — (J08) — AIM ¶3-2-4
Aircraft operating in Class C airspace must have a Mode C transponder.

ALL
3782 [C] — (J08) — AIM ¶3-2-4
For aircraft departing a satellite airport, two-way radio communication must be established as soon as practicable and thereafter maintained with ATC while within the area.

ALL
3783 [B] — (J09) — AIM ¶3-4-3
Restricted areas can be penetrated but only with the permission of the controlling agency. No person may operate an aircraft within a restricted area contrary to the restrictions imposed unless he has the permission of the using or controlling agency as appropriate. Penetration of restricted areas without authorization from the using or controlling agency may be fatal to the aircraft and its occupants.

LTA
3784 [A] — (J09) — AIM ¶3-4-3
Restricted areas can be penetrated but only with the permission of the controlling agency. No person may operate an aircraft within a restricted area contrary to the restrictions imposed unless he has the permission of the using or controlling agency as appropriate. Penetration of restricted areas without authorization from the using or controlling agency may be fatal to the aircraft and its occupants.

AIR
3785 [C] — (J09) — AIM ¶3-4-5
Pilots operating under VFR should exercise extreme caution while flying within a MOA when military activity is being conducted. No clearance is necessary to enter a MOA.

ALL
3786 [B] — (J09) — AIM ¶3-4-6
All activity within an Alert Area shall be conducted in accordance with FARs, without waiver, and pilots of participating aircraft, as well as pilots transiting the area, shall be equally responsible for collision avoidance.

ALL
3787 [C] — (J10) — AIM ¶3-2-5
The dimensions of Class D airspace are as needed for each individual circumstance. The airspace may include extensions necessary for IFR arrival and departure paths.

ALL
3788 [C] — (J10) — AIM ¶3-2-5
Radio communications must be established and maintained with the primary control tower even when operating to and from a non-tower airport located within the lateral limits of Class D airspace. On takeoff from a satellite airport, communication must be established as soon as practicable after takeoff.

ALL
3789 [C] — (J10) — AIM ¶3-5-1
An Airport Advisory Area is the area within 10 statute miles of an airport where a control tower is not operating, but where a FSS is located. At such locations, the FSS provides advisory service to arriving and departing aircraft. It is not mandatory that pilots participate in the Airport Advisory Service Program, but it is strongly recommended.

ALL
3790 [C] — (J11) — AIM ¶4-1-11
Frequencies used solely for heliports are 123.050 and 123.075.

ALL
3791 [C] — (J11) — AIM ¶4-1-13
ATIS is the continuous broadcast of recorded non-control information in selected high-activity terminal areas.

ALL
3792 [B] — (J11) — AIM ¶4-1-14
Traffic information will be given in azimuth from the aircraft in terms of the 12-hour clock. Thus, each hour would constitute an angle of 30°. Picture a clock in your lap; 3 o'clock is to your right, 9 o'clock is to your left, 12 o'clock is straight ahead, and 6 o'clock is behind you. If an aircraft is proceeding on a heading of 090° (east), traffic located at the 3 o'clock position would be 90° right of the nose, south of the aircraft.

ALL
3793 [A] — (J11) — AIM ¶4-1-14
If an aircraft is proceeding on a heading of 360° (north), traffic located at the 10 o'clock position would be 60° (left) of the nose, or to the northwest.

AIR
3794 [C] — (J11) — AIM ¶4-1-14
Traffic information issued to the pilot as "2 o'clock" would mean approximately 60° right.

AIR
3795 [C] — (J11) — AIM ¶4-1-14
An aircraft flying north in calm wind would be heading 360°. When advised of traffic at the 9 o'clock position, the pilot should look 90° left of the nose, to the west.

AIR, RTC
3796 [A] — (J11) — AIM ¶4-1-17
In addition to the use of radar for the control of IFR aircraft, all commissioned radar facilities provide traffic advisories and limited vectoring (on a workload-permitting basis) to VFR aircraft. Radar facilities are not responsible for weather information and the service is not mandatory.

AIR, RTC
3797 [C] — (J11) — AIM ¶4-1-17
Pilots of departing VFR aircraft are encouraged to request radar traffic information by notifying ground control on initial contact with their request and proposed direction of flight. Note: Stage I, II and III are obsolete terms. Radar service is now classified as basic service, TRSA service, Class C service, and Class B service.

ALL
3798 [C] — (J11) — AIM ¶4-1-17
Stage III radar provides separation of participating VFR aircraft and all IFR aircraft operating within the airspace. Note: Stage I, II and III are obsolete terms. Radar service is now classified as basic service, TRSA service, Class C service, and Class B service.

ALL
3799 [A] — (J11) — AIM ¶3-2-4
Radio contact is required to operate in Class C airspace, but permission is not required.

AIR, RTC
3800 [C] — (J11) — AIM ¶4-1-19
When making routine code changes, pilots should avoid selecting codes 7500, 7600 or 7700, thereby preventing false alarms at automated ground facilities.

ALL
3801 [A] — (J11) — AIM ¶4-1-19
Unless otherwise instructed by an ATC facility, adjust the transponder to reply on Mode 3/A, code 1200, regardless of altitude.

REC
3802 [A] — (J11) — AIM ¶4-1-19
It is especially important for recreational pilots, who are typically not communicating with ATC, to operate the transponder and encoder so radar controllers will know the aircraft's position and altitude.

ALL
3803 [B] — (J11) — AIM ¶4-1-19
When VFR, unless otherwise instructed by an ATC facility, adjust transponder to reply code 1200 regardless of altitude.

AIR, RTC
3804 [A] — (J12) — AIM ¶4-2-3
When a transmitter, receiver, or both have become inoperative, an aircraft should observe the traffic flow, enter the pattern, and look for a light signal from the tower, when landing at a controlled airport.

AIR, GLI, RTC, REC
3805 [B] — (J13) — AIM ¶4-3-4
The small end of the tetrahedron points into the wind, indicating the direction of landing. The wind is coming from the southwest. However, the runway most nearly aligned into the wind is closed (X), leaving RWY 18 as the most suitable runway. The traffic pattern indicators on a segmented circle are used to indicate the direction of turns. The traffic pattern indicators, shown as extensions from the segmented circle, represent the base and final approach legs. The traffic pattern indicator shows right traffic for RWY 18.

AIR, GLI, RTC, REC
3806 [A] — (J13) — AIM ¶4-3-4
The small end of the tetrahedron points into the wind indicating the direction of landing. Landing to the south on RWY 18, the pilot could expect a right crosswind.

ALL
3807 [A] — (J13) — AIM ¶4-3-3
The traffic pattern indicators on a segmented circle are used to indicate the direction of turns. The traffic pattern indicators, shown as extensions from the segmented circle, represent the base and final approach legs.

ALL
3808 [C] — (J13) — AIM ¶4-3-3
No flights cross the southeast area of the airport.

ALL
3809 [A] — (J13) — AIM ¶4-3-3
The large end of the wind cone (wind sock) points into the wind. The wind cone in FAA Figure 51 indicates a wind from the northwest. When landing on RWY 26, this would be a right quartering headwind.

ALL
3810 [C] — (J13) — AIM ¶4-3-3
The large end of the wind cone (wind sock) points into the wind. The wind cone in FAA Figure 51 indicates a wind from the northwest. Landing into the wind can be accomplished on either Runway 26 or Runway 35. The traffic pattern indicators require right traffic to Runway 26 and left traffic to Runway 35.

AIR, RTC
3811 [A] — (J13) — AIM ¶4-3-14
A pilot who has just landed should not change from tower to ground frequency until advised to do so by the controller.

AIR, RTC
3812 [A] — (J13) — AIM ¶4-3-18
When ATC clears an aircraft to "taxi to" an assigned takeoff runway, the absence of holding instructions authorizes the aircraft to "cross" all runways which the taxi route intersects except the assigned takeoff runway. It does not include authorization to "Taxi on to" or "cross" the assigned takeoff runway at any point.

AIR
3813 [B] — (J14) — AIM ¶4-4-5
When a control tower is in operation, requests for special VFR clearances should be to the tower.

AIR, RTC
3814 [A] — (J14) — AIM ¶4-4-14
During climbs and descents in flight conditions which permit visual detection of other traffic, pilots should execute gentle banks, left and right, at a frequency which permits continuous visual scanning of the airspace about them.

AIR, RTC
3815 [A] — (J15) — AIM ¶5-1-4
Block 7 of the flight plan is the place to enter the "initial cruising altitude."

AIR, RTC
3816 [B] — (J15) — AIM ¶5-1-4
Enter the destination airport identifier code or name, or separate flight plans for each leg if a stopover will be more than one hour.

AIR, RTC
3817 [C] — (J15) — AIM ¶5-1-4
Specify the fuel on board in hours and minutes.

ALL
3818 [B] — (J15) — AIM ¶5-1-12
The pilot-in-command, upon canceling or completing the flight under the flight plan, shall notify an FAA Flight Service Station or ATC facility.

ALL
3819 [B] — (J22) — AIM ¶6-2-5
ELTs transmit an audio tone on 121.5 MHz and 243.0 MHz.

AIR
3820 [A] — (J22) — AIM ¶6-2-5
ELT batteries must be replaced after 1 hour of cumulative use or when 50% of their useful life has expired, whichever comes first.

AIR
3821 [C] — (J22) — AIM ¶6-2-5
An ELT test should be conducted only during the first 5 minutes after any hour and then only for three audible sweeps.

AIR
3822 [C] — (J22) — AIM ¶6-2-5
Immediately after hard landings and before parking, check radio frequency 121.5 MHz.

ALL
3823 [A] — (J25) — AIM ¶7-1-3
122.0 MHz is assigned nationwide as the Flight Watch frequency, which provides enroute aircraft with enroute weather reports along your route of flight.

AIR, GLI, RTC
3824 [C] — (J27) — AC 61-23B, Chapter 8
Lift is generated by the creation of a pressure differential over the wing surface. The lowest pressure occurs over the wing surface and the highest pressure occurs under the wing. This pressure differential triggers the roll up of the airflow aft of the wing, resulting in wing-tip vortices. Vortices are generated from the moment an aircraft leaves the ground, since trailing vortices are a by-product of wing lift.

AIR, GLI, RTC
3825 [C] — (J27) — AC 61-23B, Chapter 8
The strength of the vortex is governed by the weight, speed, and shape of the wing of the generating aircraft. The greatest vortex strength occurs when the generating aircraft is heavy, clean and slow.

AIR, GLI, RTC
3826 [A] — (J27) — AC 61-23B, Chapter 8
Flight tests have shown that the vortices from large aircraft sink at a rate of about 400 to 500 feet per minute. They tend to level off at a distance about 900 feet below the path of the generating aircraft.

AIR
3827 [C] — (J27) — AC 61-23B, Chapter 8
Flight tests have shown that the vortices from large aircraft sink at a rate of about 400 to 500 feet per minute. They tend to level off at a distance about 900 feet below the path of the generating aircraft.

AIR, GLI, RTC
3828 [B] — (J27) — AC 61-23B, Chapter 8
A tailwind condition can move the vortices of a preceding aircraft forward into the touchdown zone. A light quartering tailwind requires maximum caution. Pilots should be alert to large aircraft upwind from their approach and takeoff flight paths.

AIR, GLI, RTC
3829 [A] — (J27) — AC 61-23B, Chapter 8
When landing behind a large aircraft stay at or above the large aircraft's final approach path. Note its touchdown point and land beyond it.

AIR, GLI, RTC
3830 [B] — (J27) — AC 61-23B, Chapter 8
When departing behind a large aircraft, note the large aircraft's rotation point, rotate prior to it, continue to climb above it, and request permission to deviate upwind of the large aircraft's climb path until turning clear of the aircraft's wake.

ALL
3831 [B] — (J28) — AIM ¶7-4-6
All aircraft are requested to maintain a minimum altitude of 2,000 feet above the surface of the following: national parks, monuments, seashores, lakeshores, recreation areas and scenic riverways administered by the National Park Service, National Wildlife Refuges, Big Game Refuges, Game Ranges and Wildlife Ranges administered by the U.S. Fish and Wildlife Service, and Wilderness and Primitive areas administered by the U.S. Forest Service.

ALL
3832 [B] — (J31) — AC 67-2, Chapter 10
Large accumulations of carbon monoxide in the body results in loss of muscular power, vomiting, convulsions, and coma.

ALL
3833 [C] — (J31) — AIM ¶8-1-5
Atmospheric haze can create the illusion of being at a greater distance from objects on the ground and in the air.

ALL
3834 [B] — (J31) — AIM ¶8-1-6
Effective scanning is accomplished with a series of short, regularly spaced eye movements that bring successive areas of the sky into the central visual field. Each movement should not exceed 10°, and each area should be observed for at least one second to enable detection.

ALL
3835 [A] — (J31) — AIM ¶8-1-6
Effective scanning is accomplished with a series of short, regularly spaced eye movements that bring successive areas of the sky into the central visual field. Each movement should not exceed 10°, and each area should be observed for at least one second to enable detection.

ALL
3836 [C] — (J31) — AIM ¶8-1-8
Any aircraft that appears to have no relative motion and stays in one scan quadrant is likely to be on a collision course.

ALL
3837 [C] — (J33) — Pilot/Controller Glossary
An ATC Clearance is an authorization by air traffic control, for the purpose of preventing collisions between known aircraft, for an aircraft to proceed under specified traffic conditions within controlled airspace.

AIR, RTC
3838 [A] — (J34) — AIM ¶4-1-8
Arriving aircraft landing at airports within Class C airspace should contact Approach Control from outside the Class C airspace on the specified frequency.

1. Determine which of the two Approach Controls should be contacted based on the time of day. Convert noon local time by adding the appropriate UTC conversion.

    ```
      1200    local
    + 0600    UTC conversion
      1800 Z
    ```

    Lincoln Muni approach should be contacted since its hours of operation are 1200 – 0600Z.

2. Identify the appropriate frequency for the aircraft's arrival from the west, 270°. Two frequencies are available. Aircraft approaching from any direction between 170° and 349° should make contact on 124.0 MHz.

AIR, RTC
3839 [C] — (J34) — AIM ¶3-2-4
Radar service in Class C airspace consists of sequencing to the primary airport, standard IFR/IFR separation, IFR/VFR separation (so that targets do not touch or have less than 500-foot separation), and providing traffic advisories and safety alerts.

AIR, RTC, REC
3840 [A] — (J34) — AIM ¶4-1-8
At an airport where the tower is operated on a part-time basis, a pilot should self-announce on the CTAF.

ALL
3841 [B] — (J34) — A/FD Legend
Airport location is expressed as distance and direction from the center of the associated city in NM and cardinal points. The first item in parentheses is the airport identifier and the second item is the relation from the city. In this case, "1 NW."

ALL
3842 [B] — (J34) — A/FD Legend
Traffic is to the left unless otherwise stated in the Airport/Facility Directory as "Rgt tfc."

ALL
3843 [B] — (J34) — AIM ¶1-1-18
FAA facilities that provide VHF/Direction Finder (DF) service are identified in the Airport/Facility Directory. The VHF/DF receiver display indicates the magnetic direction of the aircraft from the ground station each time the aircraft transmits.

ALL
3844 [A] — (J52) — AC 67-2, Chapter 4
Hypoxia is an oxygen deficiency in the body usually caused by flight at higher altitudes. For optimum protection from hypoxia, pilots are encouraged to use supplemental oxygen above 10,000 feet during the day, and above 5,000 feet at night.

ALL
3845 [A] — (J53) — AC 67-2, Chapter 5
An abnormal increase in the volume of air breathed in and out of the lungs flushes an excessive amount of carbon dioxide from the lungs and blood, causing hyperventilation.

ALL
3846 [A] — (J53) — AC 67-2, Chapter 5
Hyperventilation is most likely to occur during periods of stress or anxiety.

ALL
3847 [B] — (J53) — AC 67-2, Chapter 5
The symptoms of hyperventilation subside within a few minutes after the rate and depth of breathing are consciously brought back under control. The buildup of carbon dioxide in the body can be hastened by controlled breathing in and out of a paper bag held over the nose and mouth. Talking aloud often helps, while normally-paced breathing at all times prevents hyperventilation.

ALL
3848 [A] — (J58) — AC 67-2, Chapter 10
Susceptibility to carbon monoxide poisoning increases with altitude. As altitude increases, air pressure decreases and the body has difficulty getting oxygen. Add carbon monoxide, which further deprives the body of oxygen, and the situation can become critical.

ALL
3849 [C] — (J60) — AIM ¶8-1-6
Exposure to total darkness for at least 30 minutes is required for complete dark adaptation. Any degree of dark adaptation is lost within a few seconds of viewing a bright light. Red lights do not affect night vision.

ALL
3850 [B] — (J61) — AC 67-2, Chapter 14
Even if the natural horizon or surface reference is clearly visible, rely on instrument indications to overcome the effects of spatial disorientation. Shifting the eyes quickly from outside to inside, and leaning, will only compound the problem.

ALL
3851 [A] — (J62) — AC 67-2, Chapter 14
Disorientation, or vertigo, is actually a state of temporary spatial confusion resulting from misleading information sent to the brain by various sensory organs.

ALL
3852 [B] — (J62) — AC 67-2, Chapter 14
Sight, supported by other senses, allows the pilot to maintain orientation. However, during periods of low visibility, the supporting senses sometimes conflict with what is seen. When this happens, a pilot is particularly vulnerable to disorientation and must rely more on flight instruments.

ALL
3853 [A] — (J62) — AC 67-2, Chapter 14
Even if the natural horizon or surface reference is clearly visible, rely on instrument indications to overcome the effects of spatial disorientation. Shifting the eyes quickly from outside to inside, and leaning, will only compound the problem.

ALL
3854 [A] — (M52) — AC 00-2.3
Appendix II of the Advisory Circular Checklist contains the Circular Numbering System wherein advisory circular numbers relate to FAR subchapter titles and correspond to the Parts and/or sections of the FARs. The four to remember are:

- 20 — Aircraft;
- 60 — Airmen;
- 70 — Airspace; and
- 90 — Air Traffic and General Operating Rules

ALL
3855 [B] — (M52) — AC 00-2.3
Appendix II of the Advisory Circular Checklist contains the Circular Numbering System wherein advisory circular numbers relate to FAR subchapter titles and correspond to the Parts and/or sections of the FARs. The four to remember are:

- 20 — Aircraft;
- 60 — Airmen;
- 70 — Airspace; and
- 90 — Air Traffic and General Operating Rules

ALL
3856 [C] — (M52) — AC 00-2.3
Appendix II of the Advisory Circular Checklist contains the Circular Numbering System wherein advisory circular numbers relate to FAR subchapter titles and correspond to the Parts and/or sections of the FARs. The four to remember are:

- 20 — Aircraft;
- 60 — Airmen;
- 70 — Airspace; and
- 90 — Air Traffic and General Operating Rules

GLI
3857 [A] — (N03) — Soaring Flight Manual, Chapter 13
A distinct advantage of a CG hook is that the sailplane can gain a greater altitude with a given line length.

GLI
3858 [C] — (N03) — Soaring Flight Manual, Chapter 13
"Porpoising" is caused by the horizontal stabilizer oscillating in and out of a stalled condition during a winch tow. The cure is to relax back pressure on the stick and shallow the climb angle.

GLI
3859 [C] — (N21) — Sailplane Aerodynamics
Two criteria must be satisfied in the loading of a glider:

1. The total weight must be within limits, and
2. Within those limits, placement of the weight with respect to the aerodynamic center of the wing must satisfy total moment conditions (Weight x Arm = Moment).

To satisfy the conditions specified in the question, first calculate the weight required:

135 − 115 = 20 lbs

In order for that weight to provide the same moment as the "pilot weight" it replaces, it will also need to be at the same (that is, the forward) seat location.

GLI
3860 [B] — (N21) — Sailplane Aerodynamics
Two criteria must be satisfied in the loading of a glider:

1. The total weight must be within limits, and
2. Within those limits, placement of the weight with respect to the aerodynamic center of the wing must satisfy total moment conditions (Weight x Arm = Moment).

To satisfy the conditions specified in the question, first calculate the weight required:

135 − 125 = 10 lbs

In order for that weight to provide the same moment as the "pilot weight" it replaces, it will also need to be at the same (that is, the forward) seat location.

GLI
3861 [C] — (N21) — Soaring Flight Manual
Use the following steps:

1. Calculate the total weight and moment using the information in the question and in FAA Figure 54, and the formula:

   Weight x Arm = Moment

Item	Weight	Arm	Moment
Empty weight	610	96.47	58,846.7 lbs-in
Pilot (fwd seat)	160	43.80	7,008.0 lbs-in
Passenger (aft seat)	185	74.70	13,819.5 lbs-in
Totals	955		79,674.2 lbs-in

2. Calculate the position of the CG using the formula:

   $$CG = \frac{\text{Total Moment}}{\text{Total Weight}}$$

   or:

   $$CG = \frac{79,674.2}{955} = 83.43 \text{ inches aft of datum}$$

3. Compare the calculated value to the allowed range for the position of the CG, 78.20 to 86.10. The calculated position is within the allowed range of both maximum weight and CG.

GLI
3862 [B] — (N21) — Soaring Flight Manual
Use the following steps:

1. Calculate the weight and moment of the equipment to be added using the formula:

   Weight x Arm = Moment

Item	Weight	Arm	Moment
Added equip.	35 lbs	43.8	1,533.0 lbs-in

2. Calculate the new total weight and moment.

Item	Weight	Moment
Old	945	78,000.2 lbs-in
Added	35	1,533.0 lbs-in
New Total	980	79,533.2 lbs-in

3. Calculate the old and new positions of the center of gravity using the formula:

   $$CG = \frac{\text{Total Moment}}{\text{Total Weight}}$$

   Original CG =

   $$\frac{78,000.2}{945} = 82.54 \text{ inches aft of datum}$$

   New CG = $\frac{79,533.2}{980}$ = 81.16 inches aft of datum

4. Compute change and direction of change of the CG.

Original CG	82.54
New CG	−81.16
	1.38 inches closer to datum (forward)

5. Compare the calculated values of weight and CG position to the allowed range shown in FAA Figure 54. The allowed CG range is 78.20 to 86.10 and the calculated value is within these limits.

GLI
3863 [B] — (N21) — Soaring Flight Manual
Use the following steps:

1. Calculate the total weight and moment using the information in the question and in FAA Figure 54, and the formula:

   Weight x Arm = Moment

Item	Weight	Arm	Moment
Empty weight	610	96.47	58,846.7 lbs-in
Pilot (fwd seat)	215	43.80	9,417.0 lbs-in
Passenger (aft seat)	215	74.70	16,060.5 lbs-in
Totals	1,040		84,324.2 lbs-in

2. Calculate the position of the CG using the formula:

   $$CG = \frac{\text{Total Moment}}{\text{Total Weight}}$$

   or:

   $$CG = \frac{84,324.2}{1,040} = 81.08 \text{ inches aft of datum}$$

3. Compare the calculated value to the allowed range for the position of the CG, 78.20 to 86.10. The calculated position is within the allowed range of both maximum weight and CG.

GLI
3864 [B] — (N21) — American Soaring Handbook, Chapter 6
Use the following steps:

1. Read the L/D ratio (which is numerically the same as the glide ratio) for a speed of 53 MPH from the graph (30.9:1).

2. Using the glide ratio of 30.9 feet forward for each foot of vertical sink, calculate the sink encountered in one statute mile (5,280 feet):

   $$\frac{\text{Distance}}{\text{L/D Ratio}} = \text{Vertical Sink}$$

   $$\frac{5,280}{30.9} = 171 \text{ feet vertical sink}$$

GLI
3865 [B] — (N21) — American Soaring Handbook, Chapter 6
Use the following steps:

1. Locate the sinking speed (V_S) curve and its associated scale (on the right side) of FAA Figure 55.

2. Read to the left from the 5 FPS position to the sinking speed curved scale.

3. Read downward from the point of intersection to the horizontal velocity (V) scale. Interpreting the horizontal scale gives a speed of 79 MPH forward.

GLI
3866 [C] — (N21) — American Soaring Handbook, Chapter 6
Use the following steps:

1. Locate the minimum sink speed (2.2 FPS at 44 MPH) on FAA Figure 55.
2. Determine the L/D (glide ratio) at 44 MPH by reading up from 44 MPH (on the V_S coordinate) to the intersection with the L/D curve. Read from that intersection to the left (L/D) coordinate. At 44 MPH the L/D ratio is 29.3:1.
3. Using the glide ratio of 29.3 feet forward for each foot of vertical sink, calculate the sink encountered in 5,280 feet (one statue mile):

$$\frac{\text{Distance}}{\text{L/D Ratio}} = \text{Vertical Sink}$$

$$\frac{5,280}{29.3} = 180 \text{ feet vertical sink}$$

GLI
3867 [B] — (N21) — American Soaring Handbook, Chapter 6
The L/D ratio is numerically the same as the glide ratio. Hence the best forward distance attained per foot of descent will be at the velocity which gives the maximum L/D.

GLI
3868 [C] — (N21) — American Soaring Handbook, Chapter 6
Use the following steps:

1. Locate 68 MPH on the V coordinate (at the bottom) on FAA Figure 55.
2. Read upward from the 68 MPH point to the intersection with the L/D curve.
3. Read to the left, from the point of intersection, to the L/D scale and read L/D, 28.5:1.

GLI
3869 [C] — (N30) — Soaring Flight Manual, Chapter 12
During all glider operations there should be a wing runner, if possible. Lowering the wing and raising the hands is the signal to hold position.

GLI
3870 [B] — (N30) — Soaring Flight Manual, Chapter 12
The wing runner moving his/her hand across the throat is the signal to release the towline.

GLI
3871 [C] — (N30) — Soaring Flight Manual, Chapter 12
Wing runners should use a paddle, flag or some signaling device that is easily visible to the tow pilot. Moving the signaling device and free hand back and forth over the head is the signal to stop operation.

GLI
3872 [A] — (N30) — Soaring Flight Manual, Chapter 12
To signal the towplane to turn, move the glider to the side opposite the direction of turn and gently pull the towplane's tail out.

GLI
3873 [B] — (N30) — Soaring Flight Manual, Chapter 12
If the glider cannot release, he/she should move to the right and rock the wings.

GLI
3874 [C] — (N30) — Soaring Flight Manual, Chapter 12
To signal the towplane or ground launch crew to reduce airspeed or ground launch speed, fishtail the glider.

GLI
3875 [C] — (N30) — Soaring Flight Manual, Chapter 12
After the glider has signaled that he/she cannot release, the towplane will attempt to release the glider. If the towplane cannot release, he/she should fishtail the towplane. A landing on tow will then be necessary.

GLI
3876 [B] — (N30) — Soaring Flight Manual, Chapter 12
Crab into the wind to maintain a position directly behind the towplane.

GLI
3877 [B] — (N30) — Soaring Flight Manual, Chapter 12
When a turn is begun too soon, the towplane's nose is pulled to the outside of the turn.

GLI
3878 [A] — (N30) — Soaring Flight Manual, Chapter 12
The glider should maneuver to the right of the towplane. The towplane should move over to the left. If there is a narrow runway, a full spoiler landing should be made as soon as possible.

GLI
3879 [C] — (N30) — Soaring Flight Manual, Chapter 12
At low altitude, the only alternative to landing straight ahead may be slight turns in order to reach a suitable landing area.

GLI
3880 [C] — (N32) — Soaring Flight Manual, Chapter 14
The correct recovery from a spiral dive is to relax back pressure on the stick and at the same time reduce the bank angle with coordinated aileron and rudder. When the bank is less than 45°, the stick may be moved back while continuing to decrease bank.

GLI
3881 [C] — (N32) — Soaring Flight Manual, Chapter 14
If a wing begins to drop during a turn, it is an indication of a stall. The nose of the sailplane should be lowered before applying coordinated opposite aileron and rudder to break the stall.

GLI
3882 [B] — (N32) — Soaring Flight Manual, Chapter 14
A spiral dive, as contrasted to a spin, can be recognized by rapidly increasing speed and G loading.

GLI
3883 [B] — (N32) — Soaring Flight Manual, Chapter 14
When using the forward slip to increase an angle of descent without acceleration, the dive brakes or spoilers are normally fully open.

GLI
3884 [C] — (N34) — Soaring Flight Manual, Chapter 16
It is always necessary to have a suitable landing site in mind. As altitude decreases, the plans have to get more specific. The area should be narrowed down at 2,000 feet and a specific field should be selected by 1,500 feet.

LTA
3885 [A] — (O02) — Taming the Gentle Giant, page 19
Since propane vapor is 1-1/2 times heavier than air, it can linger on the floor.

LTA
3886 [C] — (O02) — Taming the Gentle Giant
Precautions, such as wearing gloves, should be taken when filling the propane bottles.

LTA
3887 [B] — (O03) — Taming the Gentle Giant, page 22
Payload is the total weight of passengers, cargo, and fuel an aircraft can legally carry on a given flight, excluding weight of the aircraft and equipment.

LTA
3888 [C] — (O03) — Taming the Gentle Giant, Chapter 3
Use the following steps:
1. Locate the gross weight, 1,350 pounds, on the bottom of the graph in FAA Figure 57.
2. From that point, draw a line upward through the graph.
3. Locate the OAT +51°F on the left side of the graph.
4. From that point, draw a line to the right through the graph.
5. Note the point of intersection of the two lines, which in this case falls on the 10,000-foot curve.

LTA
3889 [C] — (O03) — Taming the Gentle Giant, Chapter 3
Use the following steps:
1. Locate the gross weight, 1,200 pounds, on the bottom of the graph in FAA Figure 57.
2. From that point, draw a line upward to the 5,000-foot pressure altitude line.
3. From there, draw a line to the left to the air temperature scale and read the maximum temperature, 100°F.

LTA
3890 [C] — (O03) — Taming the Gentle Giant, Chapter 3
Payload is the total weight of passengers, cargo and fuel an aircraft can legally carry on a given flight, excluding weight of the aircraft and equipment. Using FAA Figure 58, perform the following steps:
1. Enter the chart at an ambient temperature of 91°F. From that point, proceed upward to the 2,500-foot pressure altitude point (halfway between sea level and 5,000 feet).
2. From the point of intersection, proceed to the left to determine the gross weight for 2,500 feet (840 pounds).
3. Note that the empty weight is 335 pounds. Compute the payload using the formula:

   Payload = Gross Weight − Empty Weight
   Payload = 840 lbs − 335 lbs
   Payload = 505 lbs

LTA
3891 [B] — (O03) — Taming the Gentle Giant, Chapter 3
Use FAA Figure 58, and the following steps:
1. Enter the graph at the 1,100-pound gross weight point and proceed to the right to intercept the standard temperature curve.
2. Note that the intercept is between sea level and the 5,000-foot limit lines, and is much closer to the 5,000-foot line (4,000 feet).

LTA
3892 [C] — (O03) — Taming the Gentle Giant, Chapter 3
Use FAA Figure 58, and the following steps:
1. Enter the graph at the 1,000-pound gross weight point and proceed to the right to intercept the standard temperature curve.
2. Note that the intercept is just over 10,000 feet (11,000 feet).

LTA
3893 [B] — (O03) — Taming the Gentle Giant, Chapter 3
Use FAA Figure 58, and the following steps:
(The standard weight of propane is 4.23 pounds per gallon.)

1. Enter the chart at the 68°F ambient temperature value. Move upward to a point about 1/5 of the distance between the sea level and 5,000-foot pressure altitude curves.
2. From that point, draw a line to the left and read the gross weight as 1,040 pounds.
3. Calculate the weight of 20 gallons of propane:

    20 x 4.23 = 85 pounds

4. Compute the available lift:

Item	Weight
Gross weight	1,040 lbs
Empty weight	-335 lbs
Fuel weight	-85 lbs
Pilot and passengers	620 lbs

LTA
3894 [A] — (O03) — Taming the Gentle Giant, Chapter 3
Use FAA Figure 58, and the following steps:
(The standard weight of propane is 4.23 pounds per gallon.)

1. Enter the chart where 5,000 feet and the standard temperature line intersect.
2. From that point, draw a line to the left and read the gross weight as 1,090 pounds.
3. Calculate the weight of 20 gallons of propane:

    20 x 4.23 = 85 pounds

4. Compute the available lift:

Item	Weight
Gross weight	1,090 lbs
Empty weight	-335 lbs
Fuel weight	-85 lbs
Pilot and passengers	670 lbs

LTA
3895 [A] — (O05) — Taming the Gentle Giant
Burner output is dependent on fuel pressure. Proper valve operation is critical to safety and control.

LTA
3896 [C] — (O05) — Taming the Gentle Giant, page 104
A moderate-rate ascent is recommended initially to accurately determine the wind direction at various altitudes.

LTA
3897 [B] — (O05) — Taming the Gentle Giant, page 104
The positive pressure on the top of the envelope could force the deflation ports open.

LTA
3898 [A] — (O05) — Taming the Gentle Giant, page 104
The most efficient roundout is to reduce the frequency of blasts so that the envelope cools to a level flight temperature just as the balloon reaches the desired altitude.

LTA
3899 [C] — (O05) — Taming the Gentle Giant, page 104
The pilot should open another tank valve, open the regular, or blast valve and light off the main jet with reduced flow.

LTA
3900 [C] — (O05) — Taming the Gentle Giant, page 104
In a high-wind landing, the envelope should be ripped just prior to ground contact.

LTA
3901 [B] — (O05) — Taming the Gentle Giant, page 104
By facing forward with knees bent, the body is balanced and the legs act as springs, absorbing the landing shock.

LTA
3902 [C] — (O05) — Taming the Gentle Giant, page 104
By facing forward with knees bent, the body is balanced and the legs act as springs absorbing the landing shock. It is important that everyone remain in the basket until the envelope cannot lift the balloon back into the air.

LTA
3903 [B] — (O05) — Balloon Flight Manual, page 43
At one time or another a balloonist will be faced with the necessity of having to land in turbulent air. When this happens, the landing should be attempted in the middle of the largest field available.

LTA
3904 [C] — (O05) — Balloon Flight Manual, page 15
An envelope over-temperature can seriously degrade the strength of the envelope, so land as soon as is practical.

LTA
3905 [C] — (O10) — Taming the Gentle Giant
As a precaution against flameout, an ignitor must be carried to relight the burner. A second ignitor is necessary in case the first malfunctions or is lost overboard.

LTA
3906 [A] — (O22) — Taming the Gentle Giant, page 19
Propane is under pressure and has an artificial odor. If a leak exists, the fuel will 'hiss" out and can be smelled.

LTA
3907 [B] — (O26) — Taming the Gentle Giant, page 104
The desired envelope temperature for level flight is best maintained by short blasts at high frequency.

LTA
3908 [B] — (O30) — Taming the Gentle Giant, page 104
A free balloon will move about 100 feet per minute for every knot of wind. A pilot should allow 100 feet of travel for each knot of wind speed.

LTA
3909 [B] — (O30) — Taming the Gentle Giant, page 104
Turbulent airflow may extinguish the pilot light.

LTA
3910 [B] — (P03) — Balloon Flight Manual, page 14
A free balloon has no propulsion and so must take advantage of differing wind directions at various altitudes.

LTA
3911 [A] — (P03) — Balloon Flight Manual, page 42
Weather conditions during flight may take a sudden and unpredictable change. When this occurs and if powerful wind gusts, thermals, wind shears, or precipitation and lightning, are encountered, the appropriate action is to land as soon as possible.

LTA
3912 [C] — (P09) — Goodyear Operations Manual
A heavy airship should be trimmed tail heavy to provide dynamic lift during approach.

LTA
3913 [B] — (P09) — Goodyear Operations Manual
It is necessary to apply full power at the correct moment in an "upship" maneuver.

LTA
3914 [A] — (P09) — Goodyear Operations Manual
An airship is normally flown heavy, so a power reduction would cause a descent. Air should be taken into the forward ballonets.

LTA
3915 [C] — (P09) — Goodyear Operations Manual
An airship without power must be operated as a free balloon.

Cross-Reference A:
Answer, Subject Matter Knowledge Code & Category

The FAA does not publish a category list for any exam; therefore, the category assigned below is based on historical data and the best judgement of our researchers.

ALL .... All aircraft
AIR .... Airplane
GLI .... Glider
LTA .... Lighter-Than-Air (applies to hot air balloon, gas balloon and airship)
REC .... Recreational
RTC .... Rotorcraft (applies to both helicopter and gyroplane)

3001 .... [B] .... (A01) .... ALL	3037 .... [C] .... (A21) .... AIR, GLI
3002 .... [B] .... (A01) .... ALL	3038 .... [B] .... (A29) .... REC
3003 .... [A] .... (A01) .... ALL	3039 .... [B] .... (A29) .... REC
3004 .... [A] .... (A01) .... ALL	3040 .... [C] .... (A29) .... REC
3005 .... [C] .... (A01) .... ALL	3041 .... [A] .... (A29) .... REC
3006 .... [A] .... (A02) .... ALL	3042 .... [C] .... (A29) .... REC
3007 .... [A] .... (A02) .... AIR, GLI	3043 .... [A] .... (A29) .... REC
3008 .... [A] .... (A02) .... AIR, GLI	3044 .... [B] .... (A29) .... REC
3009 .... [C] .... (A02) .... AIR, GLI	3045 .... [B] .... (A29) .... REC
3010 .... [A] .... (A02) .... AIR, GLI	3046 .... [B] .... (A29) .... REC
3011 .... [C] .... (A02) .... AIR	3047 .... [C] .... (A29) .... REC
3012 .... [A] .... (A02) .... AIR	3048 .... [B] .... (A29) .... REC
3013 .... [C] .... (A15) .... ALL	3049 .... [C] .... (A29) .... REC
3014 .... [A] .... (A16) .... ALL	3050 .... [C] .... (A29) .... REC
3015 .... [B] .... (A16) .... ALL	3051 .... [B] .... (A29) .... REC
3016 .... [C] .... (A20) .... ALL	3052 .... [A] .... (A29) .... REC
3017 .... [C] .... (A20) .... ALL	3053 .... [C] .... (A29) .... REC
3018 .... [B] .... (A20) .... ALL	3054 .... [C] .... (A29) .... REC
3019 .... [C] .... (A20) .... ALL	3055 .... [A] .... (A29) .... REC
3020 .... [B] .... (A20) .... AIR, RTC, REC, LTA	3056 .... [B] .... (A29) .... REC
3021 .... [C] .... (A20) .... AIR, RTC, REC, LTA	3057 .... [B] .... (A29) .... REC
3022 .... [C] .... (A20) .... AIR, RTC, REC, LTA	3058 .... [C] .... (A29) .... REC
3023 .... [C] .... (A20) .... AIR, RTC, REC, LTA	3059 .... [C] .... (A29) .... REC
3024 .... [B] .... (A20) .... AIR, RTC	3060 .... [C] .... (A29) .... REC
3025 .... [B] .... (A20) .... AIR	3061 .... [C] .... (A29) .... REC
3026 .... [C] .... (A20) .... AIR	3062 .... [C] .... (A23) .... GLI
3027 .... [B] .... (A20) .... AIR	3063 .... [C] .... (A23) .... LTA
3028 .... [C] .... (A20) .... ALL	3064 .... [B] .... (A23) .... ALL
3029 .... [C] .... (A20) .... ALL	3065 .... [B] .... (A23) .... ALL
3030 .... [A] .... (A20) .... ALL	3066 .... [B] .... (A23) .... AIR, RTC
3031 .... [C] .... (A20) .... ALL	3067 .... [A] .... (A60) .... ALL
3032 .... [C] .... (A20) .... AIR	3068 .... [B] .... (A60) .... ALL
3033 .... [B] .... (A20) .... AIR, RTC	3069 .... [B] .... (A60) .... ALL
3034 .... [A] .... (A20) .... ALL	3070 .... [B] .... (B07) .... ALL
3035 .... [A] .... (A20) .... ALL	3071 .... [B] .... (B07) .... LTA
3036 .... [B] .... (A21) .... AIR, GLI	3072 .... [B] .... (B07) .... ALL

3073	[C]	(B07)	ALL	3120	[B]	(B08)	AIR, RTC
3074	[B]	(B07)	ALL	3121	[B]	(B08)	AIR, RTC
3075	[B]	(B07)	ALL	3122	[B]	(B08)	RTC
3076	[B]	(B07)	ALL	3123	[C]	(B08)	ALL
3077	[A]	(B07)	ALL	3124	[A]	(B08)	ALL
3078	[A]	(B07)	ALL	3125	[C]	(B08)	ALL
3079	[C]	(B07)	ALL	3126	[B]	(B08)	ALL
3080	[B]	(B07)	ALL	3127	[A]	(B08)	ALL
3081	[C]	(B07)	ALL	3128	[B]	(B08)	ALL
3082	[C]	(B07)	ALL	3129	[A]	(B08)	ALL
3083	[A]	(B07)	ALL	3130	[A]	(B08)	AIR, GLI
3084	[C]	(B07)	ALL	3131	[B]	(B09)	AIR, REC
3085	[B]	(B07)	AIR, GLI, RTC, REC	3132	[C]	(B09)	AIR
3086	[A]	(B07)	AIR, GLI, RTC, REC	3133	[A]	(B09)	RTC
3087	[B]	(B07)	AIR, GLI, RTC, REC	3134	[B]	(B09)	REC
3088	[C]	(B08)	ALL	3135	[B]	(B09)	REC
3089	[B]	(B08)	ALL	3136	[C]	(B09)	ALL
3090	[B]	(B08)	ALL	3137	[A]	(B09)	AIR, GLI, LTA
3091	[A]	(B08)	ALL	3138	[B]	(B09)	ALL
3092	[A]	(B08)	ALL	3139	[B]	(B09)	ALL
3093	[B]	(B08)	ALL	3140	[B]	(B09)	ALL
3094	[C]	(B08)	AIR, GLI, REC	3141	[A]	(B09)	ALL
3095	[C]	(B08)	ALL	3142	[B]	(B09)	AIR, GLI, RTC, LTA
3096	[B]	(B08)	AIR	3143	[A]	(B09)	AIR, GLI, LTA, REC
3097	[B]	(B08)	AIR, RTC	3144	[A]	(B09)	AIR, GLI, LTA
3098	[A]	(B08)	AIR, RTC	3145	[C]	(B09)	ALL
3099	[A]	(B08)	AIR, RTC	3146	[C]	(B09)	ALL
3100	[B]	(B08)	AIR, RTC	3147	[B]	(B09)	ALL
3101	[A]	(B08)	ALL	3148	[C]	(B09)	AIR, GLI, RTC, LTA
3102	[C]	(B08)	AIR, GLI, LTA, RTC	3149	[B]	(B09)	AIR, GLI, RTC, LTA
3103	[B]	(B08)	AIR, GLI, LTA, RTC	3150	[B]	(B09)	AIR
3104	[A]	(B08)	AIR, GLI, LTA, RTC	3151	[A]	(B09)	AIR
3105	[B]	(B08)	ALL	3152	[C]	(B09)	RTC
3106	[A]	(B08)	ALL	3153	[C]	(B09)	AIR
3107	[B]	(B08)	ALL	3154	[B]	(B09)	AIR
3108	[B]	(B08)	ALL	3155	[C]	(B09)	AIR, RTC
3109	[A]	(B08)	ALL	3156	[C]	(B09)	AIR, RTC
3110	[B]	(B08)	ALL	3157	[B]	(B09)	AIR, RTC
3111	[A]	(B08)	ALL	3158	[B]	(B09)	AIR, RTC
3112	[A]	(B08)	AIR, RTC	3159	[C]	(B11)	ALL
3113	[B]	(B08)	AIR, RTC	3160	[B]	(B11)	AIR
3114	[C]	(B08)	AIR, RTC	3161	[B]	(B11)	AIR
3115	[B]	(B08)	ALL	3162	[C]	(B11)	ALL
3116	[B]	(B08)	AIR, RTC	3163	[C]	(B11)	ALL
3117	[C]	(B08)	ALL	3164	[C]	(B11)	ALL
3118	[B]	(B08)	ALL	3165	[A]	(B11)	ALL
3119	[A]	(B08)	ALL	3166	[C]	(B11)	AIR, RTC

3167	[B]	(B12)	AIR, GLI, REC
3168	[A]	(B12)	AIR, GLI, REC
3169	[B]	(B12)	AIR, GLI, REC
3170	[A]	(B12)	AIR, GLI, REC
3171	[C]	(B12)	AIR, GLI, RTC, REC
3172	[A]	(B12)	AIR, GLI, RTC, REC
3173	[B]	(B12)	AIR, GLI, RTC, REC
3174	[A]	(B12)	GLI
3175	[B]	(B12)	GLI
3176	[C]	(B12)	GLI
3177	[B]	(B12)	GLI
3178	[B]	(B12)	AIR, GLI, RTC
3179	[B]	(B12)	ALL
3180	[B]	(B13)	ALL
3181	[A]	(B13)	ALL
3182	[B]	(B13)	ALL
3183	[B]	(B13)	ALL
3184	[B]	(B13)	ALL
3185	[C]	(B13)	ALL
3186	[C]	(B13)	ALL
3187	[C]	(B13)	ALL
3188	[A]	(B13)	ALL
3189	[B]	(B13)	AIR, RTC
3190	[B]	(B13)	AIR, RTC
3191	[C]	(B13)	ALL
3192	[C]	(B13)	ALL
3193	[A]	(B13)	ALL
3194	[A]	(G11)	ALL
3195	[C]	(G11)	ALL
3196	[B]	(G11)	ALL
3197	[A]	(G11)	ALL
3198	[B]	(G12)	ALL
3199	[C]	(G13)	ALL
3200	[C]	(G13)	ALL
3201	[A]	(H01)	ALL
3202	[A]	(H01)	AIR, GLI
3203	[B]	(H01)	ALL
3204	[A]	(H01)	ALL
3205	[A]	(H01)	AIR
3206	[A]	(H01)	AIR, GLI
3207	[A]	(H01)	AIR
3208	[B]	(H01)	AIR
3209	[B]	(H01)	AIR
3210	[B]	(H01)	AIR, GLI
3211	[A]	(H01)	AIR, GLI
3212	[B]	(H01)	AIR, GLI
3213	[A]	(H01)	AIR
3214	[C]	(H01)	AIR
3215	[C]	(H01)	AIR
3216	[B]	(H01)	AIR
3217	[B]	(H01)	AIR
3218	[B]	(H01)	AIR
3219	[C]	(H02)	AIR, GLI
3220	[A]	(H02)	AIR, GLI
3221	[B]	(H02)	AIR, RTC
3222	[C]	(H02)	AIR, RTC
3223	[A]	(H02)	AIR
3224	[A]	(H02)	AIR
3225	[B]	(H02)	AIR, RTC
3226	[B]	(H02)	AIR, RTC
3227	[A]	(H02)	AIR
3228	[A]	(H02)	AIR, RTC
3229	[C]	(H02)	AIR, RTC
3230	[A]	(H02)	AIR, RTC
3231	[C]	(H02)	AIR
3232	[B]	(H02)	AIR, RTC
3233	[B]	(H02)	AIR, RTC
3234	[A]	(H02)	AIR, RTC
3235	[C]	(H02)	AIR
3236	[A]	(H02)	AIR, RTC
3237	[C]	(H02)	AIR, RTC
3238	[C]	(H02)	AIR, RTC
3239	[B]	(H02)	AIR
3240	[B]	(H02)	AIR, RTC
3241	[A]	(H02)	AIR, RTC
3242	[A]	(H02)	AIR, RTC
3243	[C]	(H02)	AIR, RTC
3244	[C]	(H02)	AIR, RTC
3245	[A]	(H02)	AIR, RTC
3246	[B]	(H02)	AIR, LTA, RTC
3247	[B]	(H03)	AIR, GLI, RTC
3248	[C]	(H03)	ALL
3249	[C]	(H03)	ALL
3250	[C]	(H03)	ALL
3251	[C]	(H03)	ALL
3252	[A]	(H03)	ALL
3253	[B]	(H03)	ALL
3254	[C]	(H03)	ALL
3255	[A]	(H03)	ALL
3256	[A]	(H03)	ALL
3257	[B]	(H03)	ALL
3258	[B]	(H03)	ALL
3259	[B]	(H03)	ALL
3260	[B]	(H03)	ALL

3261	[C]	(H03)	ALL
3262	[C]	(H03)	AIR, GLI, RTC
3263	[C]	(H03)	AIR, GLI
3264	[C]	(H03)	ALL
3265	[A]	(H03)	AIR
3266	[C]	(H03)	AIR, GLI
3267	[C]	(H03)	AIR
3268	[C]	(H03)	ALL
3269	[C]	(H03)	ALL
3270	[B]	(H03)	AIR
3271	[C]	(H03)	AIR
3272	[C]	(H03)	AIR
3273	[B]	(H03)	AIR
3274	[C]	(H03)	AIR
3275	[A]	(H03)	AIR
3276	[C]	(H03)	AIR, RTC
3277	[C]	(H03)	AIR, RTC
3278	[C]	(H03)	ALL
3279	[C]	(H03)	ALL
3280	[B]	(H03)	AIR, GLI, RTC
3281	[C]	(H03)	AIR, GLI, RTC
3282	[C]	(H03)	ALL
3283	[C]	(H03)	ALL
3284	[B]	(H03)	ALL
3285	[B]	(H03)	GLI
3286	[A]	(H03)	AIR, GLI, RTC
3287	[B]	(H04)	AIR, GLI
3288	[A]	(H04)	AIR, GLI
3289	[C]	(H04)	ALL
3290	[C]	(H04)	AIR, RTC
3291	[B]	(H04)	AIR, RTC
3292	[C]	(H04)	AIR, RTC
3293	[C]	(H04)	AIR, RTC
3294	[C]	(H04)	ALL
3295	[A]	(H04)	ALL
3296	[C]	(H04)	AIR, RTC
3297	[A]	(H04)	AIR, RTC
3298	[A]	(H04)	ALL
3299	[B]	(H04)	ALL
3300	[B]	(H05)	AIR, RTC
3301	[A]	(H52)	AIR, GLI
3302	[C]	(H54)	AIR
3303	[A]	(H54)	AIR
3304	[A]	(H54)	AIR
3305	[A]	(H54)	AIR
3306	[A]	(H54)	AIR
3307	[C]	(H54)	AIR
3308	[B]	(H54)	AIR
3309	[C]	(H60)	AIR, GLI
3310	[A]	(H60)	AIR, GLI
3311	[C]	(H66)	AIR, GLI
3312	[A]	(H66)	AIR, GLI, RTC
3313	[A]	(H66)	AIR, GLI, RTC
3314	[B]	(H66)	AIR, GLI, RTC
3315	[B]	(H66)	ALL
3316	[A]	(H66)	AIR, GLI
3317	[A]	(H70)	RTC
3318	[A]	(H71)	RTC
3319	[B]	(H71)	RTC
3320	[C]	(H71)	RTC
3321	[A]	(H71)	RTC
3322	[B]	(H71)	RTC
3323	[C]	(H71)	RTC
3324	[C]	(H71)	RTC
3325	[B]	(H71)	RTC
3326	[C]	(H73)	RTC
3327	[B]	(H73)	RTC
3328	[A]	(H74)	RTC
3329	[B]	(H78)	RTC
3330	[A]	(H78)	RTC
3331	[C]	(H78)	RTC
3332	[B]	(H78)	RTC
3333	[C]	(H78)	RTC
3334	[A]	(H78)	RTC
3335	[C]	(H78)	RTC
3336	[B]	(H79)	RTC
3337	[C]	(H80)	RTC
3338	[B]	(H91)	RTC
3339	[B]	(H94)	RTC
3340	[C]	(N20)	GLI
3341	[B]	(N21)	GLI
3342	[B]	(N21)	GLI
3343	[B]	(N22)	GLI
3344	[C]	(N22)	GLI
3345	[B]	(N27)	GLI
3346	[A]	(N27)	GLI
3347	[B]	(N27)	GLI
3348	[C]	(N27)	GLI
3349	[B]	(N27)	GLI
3350	[A]	(N34)	GLI
3351	[C]	(O01)	LTA
3352	[C]	(O02)	LTA
3353	[B]	(O02)	LTA
3354	[A]	(O02)	LTA

3355	[A]	(O02)	LTA	3402	[C]	(I24)	ALL
3356	[C]	(O02)	LTA	3403	[B]	(I25)	ALL
3357	[A]	(O02)	LTA	3404	[A]	(I25)	ALL
3358	[B]	(O02)	LTA	3405	[A]	(I25)	ALL
3359	[A]	(O05)	LTA	3406	[A]	(I25)	ALL
3360	[A]	(O05)	LTA	3407	[C]	(I25)	ALL
3361	[C]	(O05)	LTA	3408	[A]	(I25)	ALL
3362	[C]	(O22)	LTA	3409	[C]	(I25)	ALL
3363	[B]	(O24)	LTA	3410	[B]	(I25)	ALL
3364	[A]	(O30)	LTA	3411	[C]	(I25)	LTA
3365	[C]	(O30)	LTA	3412	[A]	(I25)	ALL
3366	[C]	(O30)	LTA	3413	[A]	(I25)	ALL
3367	[C]	(O30)	LTA	3414	[C]	(I25)	ALL
3368	[C]	(P01)	LTA	3415	[B]	(I26)	ALL
3369	[B]	(P01)	LTA	3416	[B]	(I26)	ALL
3370	[C]	(P01)	LTA	3417	[C]	(I26)	ALL
3371	[C]	(P01)	LTA	3418	[B]	(I26)	ALL
3372	[A]	(P04)	LTA	3419	[B]	(I26)	ALL
3373	[A]	(P04)	LTA	3420	[C]	(I26)	ALL
3374	[A]	(P04)	LTA	3421	[C]	(I27)	ALL
3375	[A]	(P04)	LTA	3422	[A]	(I27)	ALL
3376	[C]	(P04)	LTA	3423	[A]	(I27)	ALL
3377	[C]	(P04)	LTA	3424	[C]	(I27)	ALL
3378	[C]	(P04)	LTA	3425	[A]	(I28)	ALL
3379	[B]	(P09)	LTA	3426	[C]	(I28)	ALL
3380	[C]	(P09)	LTA	3427	[B]	(I28)	ALL
3381	[C]	(I21)	ALL	3428	[C]	(I28)	ALL
3382	[A]	(I21)	ALL	3429	[C]	(I28)	AIR, GLI, RTC
3383	[C]	(I21)	ALL	3430	[C]	(I29)	AIR, GLI, RTC
3384	[A]	(I21)	ALL	3431	[C]	(I29)	AIR, GLI, RTC
3385	[A]	(I21)	ALL	3432	[A]	(I29)	AIR
3386	[A]	(I21)	ALL	3433	[B]	(I30)	ALL
3387	[C]	(I22)	AIR, GLI, RTC	3434	[B]	(I30)	ALL
3388	[B]	(I22)	ALL	3435	[B]	(I30)	ALL
3389	[C]	(I22)	ALL	3436	[A]	(I30)	ALL
3390	[C]	(I22)	ALL	3437	[B]	(I30)	ALL
3391	[B]	(I22)	ALL	3438	[A]	(I30)	ALL
3392	[A]	(I22)	ALL	3439	[A]	(I30)	ALL
3393	[C]	(I22)	ALL	3440	[B]	(I30)	ALL
3394	[B]	(I22)	ALL	3441	[B]	(I30)	ALL
3395	[B]	(I23)	ALL	3442	[C]	(I30)	ALL
3396	[A]	(I23)	LTA	3443	[A]	(I31)	ALL
3397	[C]	(I24)	ALL	3444	[C]	(I31)	ALL
3398	[B]	(I24)	ALL	3445	[B]	(I31)	ALL
3399	[A]	(I24)	ALL	3446	[C]	(I31)	ALL
3400	[A]	(I24)	ALL	3447	[C]	(I33)	ALL
3401	[B]	(I24)	ALL	3448	[C]	(I35)	GLI

3449	[C]	(I35)	GLI	3496	[A]	(I43)	ALL
3450	[C]	(I35)	ALL	3497	[C]	(I43)	ALL
3451	[C]	(I35)	GLI	3498	[B]	(I43)	ALL
3452	[A]	(I36)	ALL	3499	[A]	(I43)	ALL
3453	[A]	(I40)	ALL	3500	[B]	(I43)	ALL
3454	[B]	(I40)	ALL	3501	[A]	(I43)	ALL
3455	[A]	(I40)	ALL	3502	[B]	(I43)	ALL
3456	[C]	(I40)	ALL	3503	[A]	(I43)	ALL
3457	[C]	(I40)	ALL	3504	[C]	(I43)	ALL
3458	[C]	(I40)	ALL	3505	[C]	(I43)	ALL
3459	[A]	(I40)	ALL	3506	[B]	(I43)	ALL
3460	[A]	(I40)	ALL	3507	[A]	(I44)	ALL
3461	[A]	(I40)	ALL	3508	[B]	(I44)	ALL
3462	[C]	(I41)	ALL	3509	[A]	(I45)	ALL
3463	[B]	(I41)	ALL	3510	[C]	(I45)	ALL
3464	[A]	(I41)	ALL	3511	[B]	(I45)	ALL
3465	[B]	(I41)	ALL	3512	[C]	(I45)	ALL
3466	[B]	(I41)	ALL	3513	[B]	(I46)	ALL
3467	[A]	(I41)	ALL	3514	[A]	(I46)	ALL
3468	[A]	(I41)	LTA	3515	[B]	(I46)	ALL
3469	[C]	(I41)	LTA	3516	[C]	(I46)	ALL
3470	[C]	(I41)	GLI	3517	[B]	(I46)	ALL
3471	[B]	(I41)	GLI	3518	[C]	(I46)	ALL
3472	[C]	(I42)	ALL	3519	[B]	(I46)	ALL
3473	[C]	(I42)	ALL	3520	[B]	(I47)	ALL
3474	[A]	(I42)	ALL	3521	[A]	(I47)	ALL
3475	[B]	(I42)	ALL	3522	[A]	(I47)	ALL
3476	[B]	(I42)	ALL	3523	[A]	(I47)	ALL
3477	[C]	(I43)	LTA	3524	[B]	(I47)	ALL
3478	[C]	(I43)	ALL	3525	[A]	(I49)	GLI
3479	[C]	(I43)	ALL	3526	[A]	(H05)	ALL
3480	[C]	(I43)	ALL	3527	[B]	(H05)	ALL
3481	[C]	(I43)	ALL	3528	[C]	(H05)	ALL
3482	[A]	(I43)	ALL	3529	[C]	(H06)	ALL
3483	[B]	(I43)	ALL	3530	[A]	(H07)	ALL
3484	[B]	(I43)	ALL	3531	[C]	(H07)	ALL
3485	[B]	(I43)	ALL	3532	[B]	(H07)	ALL
3486	[A]	(I43)	ALL	3533	[C]	(H07)	ALL
3487	[A]	(I43)	ALL	3534	[B]	(H06)	AIR, RTC
3488	[C]	(I43)	ALL	3535	[B]	(H07)	ALL
3489	[C]	(I43)	ALL	3536	[C]	(H07)	ALL
3490	[A]	(I43)	ALL	3537	[B]	(H07)	LTA
3491	[C]	(I43)	ALL	3538	[C]	(H07)	AIR, RTC
3492	[A]	(I43)	ALL	3539	[A]	(H07)	AIR, RTC
3493	[B]	(I43)	ALL	3540	[C]	(H06)	AIR, RTC
3494	[A]	(I43)	ALL	3541	[C]	(H06)	AIR, RTC
3495	[C]	(I43)	ALL	3542	[B]	(H06)	AIR, RTC

3543	[B]	(H07)	ALL	3590	[A]	(H07)	ALL
3544	[A]	(H07)	LTA	3591	[B]	(H07)	ALL
3545	[B]	(H07)	AIR, RTC	3592	[B]	(H07)	ALL
3546	[A]	(H07)	AIR, RTC	3593	[A]	(H07)	ALL
3547	[A]	(H07)	AIR, RTC	3594	[B]	(H07)	ALL
3548	[B]	(H06)	AIR, RTC	3595	[C]	(H07)	ALL
3549	[B]	(H06)	AIR, RTC	3596	[B]	(H07)	ALL
3550	[C]	(H07)	AIR, RTC	3597	[C]	(H07)	ALL
3551	[A]	(H07)	AIR	3598	[C]	(J01)	ALL
3552	[A]	(H07)	ALL	3599	[C]	(J08)	ALL
3553	[B]	(H07)	ALL	3600	[B]	(J08)	ALL
3554	[C]	(H07)	AIR, RTC	3601	[A]	(J09)	ALL
3555	[B]	(H06)	LTA	3602	[B]	(J09)	ALL
3556	[A]	(H07)	ALL	3603	[A]	(J10)	ALL
3557	[B]	(H07)	LTA	3604	[A]	(J11)	ALL
3558	[A]	(H07)	LTA	3605	[B]	(J11)	ALL
3559	[B]	(H07)	LTA	3606	[A]	(J11)	ALL
3560	[A]	(H07)	ALL	3607	[A]	(J11)	ALL
3561	[C]	(H07)	ALL	3608	[C]	(J11)	ALL
3562	[A]	(H06)	AIR	3609	[A]	(J11)	ALL
3563	[A]	(H06)	AIR	3610	[A]	(J11)	ALL
3564	[B]	(H07)	GLI	3611	[B]	(J11)	ALL
3565	[A]	(H07)	AIR	3612	[B]	(J11)	ALL
3566	[A]	(H07)	ALL	3613	[A]	(J12)	ALL
3567	[A]	(H07)	ALL	3614	[A]	(J12)	ALL
3568	[C]	(H07)	ALL	3615	[C]	(J12)	ALL
3569	[B]	(H07)	LTA	3616	[C]	(J25)	ALL
3570	[C]	(H07)	ALL	3617	[A]	(J25)	ALL
3571	[C]	(H07)	ALL	3618	[A]	(J28)	ALL
3572	[B]	(H07)	ALL	3619	[B]	(J34)	ALL
3573	[C]	(H07)	ALL	3620	[A]	(J37)	ALL
3574	[B]	(H07)	ALL	3621	[B]	(J37)	ALL
3575	[C]	(H07)	ALL	3622	[A]	(J37)	ALL
3576	[A]	(H07)	ALL	3623	[C]	(J37)	ALL
3577	[C]	(H07)	ALL	3624	[A]	(J37)	ALL
3578	[B]	(H07)	ALL	3625	[C]	(J37)	ALL
3579	[A]	(H07)	ALL	3626	[B]	(J37)	ALL
3580	[C]	(H07)	ALL	3627	[B]	(J37)	ALL
3581	[C]	(H07)	ALL	3628	[B]	(J37)	ALL
3582	[C]	(H07)	ALL	3629	[C]	(J37)	ALL
3583	[B]	(H07)	ALL	3630	[A]	(J37)	ALL
3584	[C]	(H07)	ALL	3631	[C]	(J37)	ALL
3585	[A]	(H07)	ALL	3632	[C]	(J37)	ALL
3586	[C]	(H07)	ALL	3633	[A]	(J37)	ALL
3587	[B]	(H07)	ALL	3634	[B]	(J37)	ALL
3588	[C]	(H07)	ALL	3635	[A]	(J37)	ALL
3589	[C]	(H07)	ALL	3636	[C]	(J37)	ALL

3637	[B]	(J37)	ALL		3684	[C]	(H04)	AIR
3638	[B]	(J37)	ALL		3685	[C]	(H04)	AIR
3639	[B]	(J37)	ALL		3686	[C]	(H04)	AIR
3640	[C]	(J37)	ALL		3687	[B]	(H04)	AIR
3641	[B]	(J37)	ALL		3688	[A]	(H04)	ALL
3642	[C]	(J37)	AIR		3689	[B]	(H04)	AIR
3643	[B]	(J37)	ALL		3690	[A]	(H04)	AIR
3644	[C]	(J37)	LTA		3691	[C]	(H04)	AIR
3645	[B]	(J37)	LTA		3692	[C]	(H04)	AIR
3646	[C]	(J37)	LTA		3693	[B]	(H04)	AIR
3647	[B]	(N23)	GLI		3694	[B]	(H04)	AIR
3648	[C]	(N27)	GLI		3695	[B]	(H04)	AIR
3649	[B]	(N27)	GLI		3696	[C]	(H04)	AIR
3650	[C]	(N34)	GLI		3697	[A]	(H04)	AIR
3651	[A]	(H02)	AIR, RTC		3698	[B]	(H04)	ALL
3652	[A]	(H02)	AIR, RTC		3699	[B]	(H04)	RTC
3653	[A]	(H02)	AIR		3700	[A]	(H04)	RTC
3654	[B]	(H02)	AIR		3701	[C]	(H04)	RTC
3655	[B]	(H02)	AIR		3702	[C]	(H04)	RTC
3656	[A]	(H02)	AIR, RTC		3703	[C]	(H04)	RTC
3657	[B]	(H02)	AIR		3704	[A]	(H04)	RTC
3658	[B]	(H02)	ALL		3705	[B]	(H04)	AIR
3659	[A]	(H02)	ALL		3706	[B]	(H04)	AIR
3660	[C]	(H02)	ALL		3707	[A]	(H04)	AIR
3661	[A]	(H04)	AIR, RTC		3708	[A]	(H04)	AIR
3662	[C]	(H04)	AIR, RTC		3709	[B]	(H09)	ALL
3663	[C]	(H04)	AIR, RTC		3710	[B]	(H50)	ALL
3664	[B]	(H04)	AIR		3711	[A]	(H58)	AIR, RTC
3665	[B]	(H04)	AIR		3712	[B]	(H63)	AIR, RTC, LTA
3666	[A]	(H04)	AIR		3713	[A]	(H63)	AIR, RTC, LTA
3667	[B]	(H04)	AIR		3714	[C]	(H63)	AIR, RTC, LTA
3668	[C]	(H04)	AIR		3715	[A]	(H63)	AIR, RTC, LTA
3669	[A]	(H04)	AIR		3716	[A]	(H63)	AIR, RTC, LTA
3670	[B]	(H04)	AIR		3717	[C]	(H63)	AIR, RTC, LTA
3671	[C]	(H04)	AIR		3718	[B]	(H63)	AIR, RTC
3672	[B]	(H04)	AIR		3719	[C]	(H63)	AIR, RTC
3673	[B]	(H04)	AIR		3720	[C]	(H76)	RTC
3674	[A]	(H04)	AIR		3721	[A]	(H76)	RTC
3675	[B]	(H04)	AIR		3722	[B]	(H76)	RTC
3676	[A]	(H04)	AIR		3723	[B]	(H76)	RTC
3677	[B]	(H04)	AIR		3724	[A]	(H76)	RTC
3678	[C]	(H04)	AIR		3725	[B]	(H76)	RTC
3679	[B]	(H04)	AIR		3726	[B]	(H76)	RTC
3680	[B]	(H04)	AIR		3727	[C]	(H76)	RTC
3681	[B]	(H04)	AIR		3728	[B]	(H76)	RTC
3682	[C]	(H04)	AIR		3729	[A]	(H76)	RTC
3683	[B]	(H04)	AIR		3730	[A]	(H76)	RTC

3731	[B]	(H76)	RTC
3732	[C]	(H77)	RTC
3733	[B]	(H77)	RTC
3734	[B]	(H78)	RTC
3735	[C]	(H78)	RTC
3736	[C]	(H78)	RTC
3737	[A]	(H78)	RTC
3738	[B]	(H78)	RTC
3739	[C]	(H79)	RTC
3740	[A]	(H80)	RTC
3741	[C]	(H80)	RTC
3742	[B]	(H80)	RTC
3743	[C]	(H80)	RTC
3744	[C]	(H80)	RTC
3745	[B]	(H80)	RTC
3746	[B]	(H81)	RTC
3747	[A]	(H81)	RTC
3748	[C]	(H81)	RTC
3749	[A]	(H81)	RTC
3750	[B]	(I35)	GLI
3751	[A]	(I35)	GLI
3752	[C]	(I35)	GLI
3753	[C]	(I35)	GLI
3754	[A]	(I35)	GLI
3755	[B]	(I35)	GLI
3756	[B]	(I35)	GLI
3757	[B]	(I35)	GLI
3758	[A]	(I35)	GLI
3759	[A]	(J01)	ALL
3760	[B]	(J03)	AIR, RTC
3761	[A]	(J03)	AIR, RTC
3762	[C]	(J03)	AIR
3763	[B]	(J03)	AIR
3764	[C]	(J03)	AIR
3765	[B]	(J03)	AIR, RTC
3766	[B]	(J03)	AIR, RTC
3767	[B]	(J03)	AIR, RTC
3768	[C]	(J03)	AIR, RTC
3769	[B]	(J03)	ALL
3770	[A]	(J03)	AIR, RTC, LTA
3771	[B]	(J03)	AIR, RTC, LTA
3772	[B]	(J03)	AIR, RTC, LTA
3773	[B]	(J05)	AIR, RTC, LTA
3774	[B]	(J05)	AIR, GLI, RTC, REC
3775	[A]	(J05)	AIR, GLI, RTC, REC
3776	[C]	(J05)	AIR, GLI, RTC, REC
3777	[C]	(J05)	AIR, GLI, RTC, REC
3778	[C]	(J05)	ALL
3779	[C]	(J08)	ALL
3780	[C]	(J08)	ALL
3781	[C]	(J08)	ALL
3782	[C]	(J08)	ALL
3783	[B]	(J09)	ALL
3784	[A]	(J09)	LTA
3785	[C]	(J09)	AIR
3786	[B]	(J09)	ALL
3787	[C]	(J10)	ALL
3788	[C]	(J10)	ALL
3789	[C]	(J10)	ALL
3790	[C]	(J11)	ALL
3791	[C]	(J11)	ALL
3792	[B]	(J11)	ALL
3793	[A]	(J11)	ALL
3794	[C]	(J11)	AIR
3795	[C]	(J11)	AIR
3796	[A]	(J11)	AIR, RTC
3797	[C]	(J11)	AIR, RTC
3798	[C]	(J11)	ALL
3799	[A]	(J11)	ALL
3800	[C]	(J11)	AIR, RTC
3801	[A]	(J11)	ALL
3802	[A]	(J11)	REC
3803	[B]	(J11)	ALL
3804	[A]	(J12)	AIR, RTC
3805	[B]	(J13)	AIR, GLI, RTC, REC
3806	[A]	(J13)	AIR, GLI, RTC, REC
3807	[A]	(J13)	ALL
3808	[C]	(J13)	ALL
3809	[A]	(J13)	ALL
3810	[C]	(J13)	ALL
3811	[A]	(J13)	AIR, RTC
3812	[A]	(J13)	AIR, RTC
3813	[B]	(J14)	AIR
3814	[A]	(J14)	AIR, RTC
3815	[A]	(J15)	AIR, RTC
3816	[B]	(J15)	AIR, RTC
3817	[C]	(J15)	AIR, RTC
3818	[B]	(J15)	ALL
3819	[B]	(J22)	ALL
3820	[A]	(J22)	AIR
3821	[C]	(J22)	AIR
3822	[C]	(J22)	AIR
3823	[A]	(J25)	ALL
3824	[C]	(J27)	AIR, GLI, RTC

3825	[C]	(J27)	AIR, GLI, RTC	3871	[C]	(N30)	GLI
3826	[A]	(J27)	AIR, GLI, RTC	3872	[A]	(N30)	GLI
3827	[C]	(J27)	AIR	3873	[B]	(N30)	GLI
3828	[B]	(J27)	AIR, GLI, RTC	3874	[C]	(N30)	GLI
3829	[A]	(J27)	AIR, GLI, RTC	3875	[C]	(N30)	GLI
3830	[B]	(J27)	AIR, GLI, RTC	3876	[B]	(N30)	GLI
3831	[B]	(J28)	ALL	3877	[B]	(N30)	GLI
3832	[B]	(J31)	ALL	3878	[A]	(N30)	GLI
3833	[C]	(J31)	ALL	3879	[C]	(N30)	GLI
3834	[B]	(J31)	ALL	3880	[C]	(N32)	GLI
3835	[A]	(J31)	ALL	3881	[C]	(N32)	GLI
3836	[C]	(J31)	ALL	3882	[B]	(N32)	GLI
3837	[C]	(J33)	ALL	3883	[B]	(N32)	GLI
3838	[A]	(J34)	AIR, RTC	3884	[C]	(N34)	GLI
3839	[C]	(J34)	AIR, RTC	3885	[A]	(O02)	LTA
3840	[A]	(J34)	AIR, RTC, REC	3886	[C]	(O02)	LTA
3841	[B]	(J34)	ALL	3887	[B]	(O03)	LTA
3842	[B]	(J34)	ALL	3888	[C]	(O03)	LTA
3843	[B]	(J34)	ALL	3889	[C]	(O03)	LTA
3844	[A]	(J52)	ALL	3890	[C]	(O03)	LTA
3845	[A]	(J53)	ALL	3891	[B]	(O03)	LTA
3846	[A]	(J53)	ALL	3892	[C]	(O03)	LTA
3847	[B]	(J53)	ALL	3893	[B]	(O03)	LTA
3848	[A]	(J58)	ALL	3894	[A]	(O03)	LTA
3849	[C]	(J60)	ALL	3895	[A]	(O05)	LTA
3850	[B]	(J61)	ALL	3896	[C]	(O05)	LTA
3851	[A]	(J62)	ALL	3897	[B]	(O05)	LTA
3852	[B]	(J62)	ALL	3898	[A]	(O05)	LTA
3853	[A]	(J62)	ALL	3899	[C]	(O05)	LTA
3854	[A]	(M52)	ALL	3900	[C]	(O05)	LTA
3855	[B]	(M52)	ALL	3901	[B]	(O05)	LTA
3856	[C]	(M52)	ALL	3902	[C]	(O05)	LTA
3857	[A]	(N03)	GLI	3903	[B]	(O05)	LTA
3858	[C]	(N03)	GLI	3904	[C]	(O05)	LTA
3859	[C]	(N21)	GLI	3905	[C]	(O10)	LTA
3860	[B]	(N21)	GLI	3906	[A]	(O22)	LTA
3861	[C]	(N21)	GLI	3907	[B]	(O26)	LTA
3862	[B]	(N21)	GLI	3908	[B]	(O30)	LTA
3863	[B]	(N21)	GLI	3909	[B]	(O30)	LTA
3864	[B]	(N21)	GLI	3910	[B]	(P03)	LTA
3865	[B]	(N21)	GLI	3911	[A]	(P03)	LTA
3866	[C]	(N21)	GLI	3912	[C]	(P09)	LTA
3867	[B]	(N21)	GLI	3913	[B]	(P09)	LTA
3868	[C]	(N21)	GLI	3914	[A]	(P09)	LTA
3869	[C]	(N30)	GLI	3915	[C]	(P09)	LTA
3870	[B]	(N30)	GLI				

Cross-Reference B:
Subject Matter Knowledge Code & Question Number

The subject matter knowledge codes establish the specific reference for the knowledge standard. When reviewing results of your knowledge test, you should compare the subject matter knowledge code(s) on your test report to the ones found below. All the questions on the Recreational and Private tests have been broken down into their subject matter knowledge codes and listed under the appropriate reference. This will be helpful for both review and preparation for the practical test.

FAR 1: Definitions and Abbreviations

A01..... General Definitions
3001, 3002, 3003, 3004, 3005

A02..... Abbreviations and Symbols
3006, 3007, 3008, 3009, 3010, 3011, 3012

FAR 43: Maintenance, Preventive Maintenance Rebuilding, and Alteration

A15..... General
3013

A16..... Appendixes
3014, 3015

FAR 61: Certification: Pilots and Flight Instructors

A20..... General
3016, 3017, 3018, 3019, 3020, 3021, 3022, 3023, 3024, 3025, 3026, 3027, 3028, 3029, 3030, 3031, 3032, 3033, 3034, 3035

A21..... Aircraft Ratings and Special Certificates
3036, 3037

A22..... Student Pilots

A23..... Private Pilots
3062, 3063, 3064, 3065, 3066

A29..... (FAR 61)
3038, 3039, 3040, 3041, 3042, 3043, 3044, 3045, 3046, 3047, 3048, 3049, 3050, 3051, 3052, 3053, 3054, 3055, 3056, 3057, 3058, 3059, 3060, 3061

Cross-Reference B: SMK Code & Question Number

FAR 71: Designation of Class A, Class B, Class C, Class D, and Class E Airspace Areas; Airways, Routes; and Reporting Points

A60..... General: Class A Airspace
3067, 3068, 3069

FAR 91: General Operating and Flight Rules

B07..... General
3070, 3071, 3072, 3073, 3074, 3075, 3076, 3077, 3078, 3079, 3080, 3081, 3082, 3083, 3084, 3085, 3086, 3087

B08..... Flight Rules: General
3088, 3089, 3090, 3091, 3092, 3093, 3094, 3095, 3096, 3097, 3098, 3099, 3100, 3101, 3102, 3103, 3104, 3105, 3106, 3107, 3108, 3109, 3110, 3111, 3112, 3113, 3114, 3115, 3116, 3117, 3118, 3119, 3120, 3121, 3122, 3123, 3124, 3125, 3126, 3127, 3128, 3129, 3130

B09..... Visual Flight Rules
3131, 3132, 3133, 3134, 3135, 3136, 3137, 3138, 3139, 3140, 3141, 3142, 3143, 3144, 3145, 3146, 3147, 3148, 3149, 3150, 3151, 3152, 3153, 3154, 3155, 3156, 3157, 3158

B11..... Equipment, Instrument, and Certification Requirements
3159, 3160, 3161, 3162, 3163, 3164, 3165, 3166

B12..... Special Flight Operations
3167, 3168, 3169, 3170, 3171, 3172, 3173, 3174, 3175, 3176, 3177, 3178, 3179

B13..... Maintenance, Preventive Maintenance, and Alterations
3180, 3181, 3182, 3183, 3184, 3185, 3186, 3187, 3188, 3189, 3190, 3191, 3192, 3193

NTSB 830: Rules Pertaining to the Notification and Reporting of Aircraft Accidents or Incidents and Overdue Aircraft, and Preservation of Aircraft Wreckage, Mail, Cargo, and Records

G10 .... General

G11 .... Initial Notification of Aircraft Accidents, Incidents, and Overdue Aircraft
3194, 3195, 3196, 3197

G12 .... Preservation of Aircraft Wreckage, Mail, Cargo, and Records
3198

G13 .... Reporting of Aircraft Accidents, Incidents, and Overdue Aircraft
3199, 3200

AC 61-23: Pilot's Handbook Of Aeronautical Knowledge

H01..... Principles of Flight
3201, 3202, 3203, 3204, 3205, 3206, 3207, 3208, 3209, 3210, 3211, 3212, 3213, 3214, 3215, 3216, 3217, 3218

H02..... Airplanes and Engines
3219, 3220, 3221, 3222, 3223, 3224, 3225, 3226, 3227, 3228, 3229, 3230, 3231, 3232, 3233, 3234, 3235, 3236, 3237, 3238, 3239, 3240, 3241, 3242, 3243, 3244, 3245, 3246, 3651, 3652, 3653, 3654, 3655, 3656, 3657, 3658, 3659, 3660

H03..... Flight Instruments
3247, 3248, 3249, 3250, 3251, 3252, 3253, 3254, 3255, 3256, 3257, 3258, 3259, 3260, 3261, 3262, 3263, 3264, 3265, 3266, 3267, 3268, 3269, 3270, 3271, 3272, 3273, 3274, 3275, 3276, 3277, 3278, 3279, 3280, 3281, 3282, 3283, 3284, 3285, 3286

H04..... Airplane Performance
3287, 3288, 3289, 3290, 3291, 3292, 3293, 3294, 3295, 3296, 3297, 3298, 3299, 3661, 3662, 3663, 3664, 3665, 3666, 3667, 3668, 3669, 3670, 3671, 3672, 3673, 3674, 3675, 3676, 3677, 3678, 3679, 3680, 3681, 3682, 3683, 3684, 3685, 3686, 3687, 3688, 3689, 3690, 3691, 3692, 3693, 3694, 3695, 3696, 3697, 3698, 3699, 3700, 3701, 3702, 3703, 3704, 3705, 3706, 3707, 3708

H05..... Weather
3300, 3526, 3527, 3528

H06..... Basic Calculations Using Navigational Computers or Electronic Calculators
3529, 3534, 3540, 3541, 3542, 3548, 3549, 3555, 3562, 3563

H07..... Navigation
3530, 3531, 3532, 3533, 3535, 3536, 3537, 3538, 3539, 3543, 3544, 3545, 3546, 3547, 3550, 3551, 3552, 3553, 3554, 3556, 3557, 3558, 3559, 3560, 3561, 3564, 3565, 3566, 3567, 3568, 3569, 3570, 3571, 3572, 3573, 3574, 3575, 3576, 3577, 3578, 3579, 3580, 3581, 3582, 3583, 3584, 3585, 3586, 3587, 3588, 3589, 3590, 3591, 3592, 3593, 3594, 3595, 3596, 3597

H09..... Appendix 1: Obtaining FAA Publications
3709

AC 61-21: Flight Training Handbook

H50..... Introduction to Flight Training
3710

H52..... Introduction to the Basics of Flight
3301

H54..... Ground Operations
3302, 3303, 3304, 3305, 3306, 3307, 3308

H58..... Landing Approaches and Landings
3711

Cross-Reference B: SMK Code & Question Number

H60..... Proficiency Flight Maneuvers
3309, 3310

H63..... Night Flying
3712, 3713, 3714, 3715, 3716, 3717, 3718, 3719

H66..... Principles of Flight and Performance Characteristics
3311, 3312, 3313, 3314, 3315, 3316

AC 61-13: Basic Helicopter Handbook

H70..... General Aerodynamics
3317

H71..... Aerodynamics of Flight
3318, 3319, 3320, 3321, 3322, 3323, 3324, 3325

H73..... Function of the Controls
3326, 3327

H74..... Other Helicopter Components and Their Functions
3328

H76..... Weight and Balance
3720, 3721, 3722, 3723, 3724, 3725, 3726, 3727, 3728, 3729, 3730, 3731

H77..... (AC 61-13)
3732, 3733

H78..... Some Hazards of Helicopter Flight
3329, 3330, 3331, 3332, 3333, 3334, 3335, 3734, 3735, 3736, 3737, 3738

H79..... Precautionary Measures and Critical Conditions
3336, 3739

H80..... Helicopter Flight Maneuvers
3337, 3740, 3741, 3742, 3743, 3744, 3745

H81..... Confined Area, Pinnacle, and Ridgeline Operations
3746, 3747, 3748, 3749

Gyroplane Flight Training Manual—McCulloch

H91..... Gyroplane Terms
3338

H94..... Basic Flight Maneuvers (Gyroplane)
3339

AC 00-6: Aviation Weather

I21 ...... Temperature
   3381, 3382, 3383, 3384, 3385, 3386

I22 ...... Atmospheric Pressure and Altimetry
   3387, 3388, 3389, 3390, 3391, 3392, 3393, 3394

I23 ...... Wind
   3395, 3396

I24 ...... Moisture, Cloud Formation, and Precipitation
   3397, 3398, 3399, 3400, 3401, 3402

I25 ...... Stable and Unstable Air
   3403, 3404, 3405, 3406, 3407, 3408, 3409, 3410, 3411, 3412, 3413, 3414

I26 ...... Clouds
   3415, 3416, 3417, 3418, 3419, 3420

I27 ...... Air Masses and Fronts
   3421, 3422, 3423, 3424

I28 ...... Turbulence
   3425, 3426, 3427, 3428, 3429

I29 ...... Icing
   3430, 3431, 3432

I30 ...... Thunderstorms
   3433, 3434, 3435, 3436, 3437, 3438, 3439, 3440, 3441, 3442

I31 ...... Common IFR Producers
   3443, 3444, 3445, 3446

I33 ...... Arctic Weather
   3447

I35 ...... Soaring Weather
   3448, 3449, 3450, 3451, 3750, 3751, 3752, 3753, 3754, 3755, 3756, 3757, 3758

I36 ...... Glossary of Weather Terms
   3452

AC 00-45: Aviation Weather Services

I40 ...... The Aviation Weather Service Program
   3453, 3454, 3455, 3456, 3457, 3458, 3459, 3460, 3461

I41 ...... Surface Aviation Weather Reports
   3462, 3463, 3464, 3465, 3466, 3467, 3468, 3469, 3470, 3471

Cross-Reference B: SMK Code & Question Number

I42 ...... Pilot and Radar Reports and Satellite Pictures
  3472, 3473, 3474, 3475, 3476

I43 ...... Aviation Weather Forecasts
  3477, 3478, 3479, 3480, 3481, 3482, 3483, 3484, 3485, 3486, 3487, 3488, 3489, 3490, 3491, 3492, 3493, 3494, 3495, 3496, 3497, 3498, 3499, 3500, 3501, 3502, 3503, 3504, 3505, 3506

I44 ...... Surface Analysis Chart
  3507, 3508

I45 ...... Weather Depiction Chart
  3509, 3510, 3511, 3512

I46 ...... Radar Summary Chart
  3513, 3514, 3515, 3516, 3517, 3518, 3519

I47 ...... Significant Weather Prognostics
  3520, 3521, 3522, 3523, 3524

I49 ...... (AC 00-45)
  3525

AIM: Aeronautical Information Manual

J01 ..... Air Navigation Radio Aids
  3598, 3759

J03 ..... Airport Lighting Aids
  3760, 3761, 3762, 3763, 3764, 3765, 3766, 3767, 3768, 3769, 3770, 3771, 3772

J05 ..... Airport Marking Aids and Signs
  3773, 3774, 3775, 3776, 3777, 3778

J08 ..... Controlled Airspace
  3599, 3600, 3779, 3780, 3781, 3782

J09 ..... Special Use Airspace
  3601, 3602, 3783, 3784, 3785, 3786

J10 ..... Other Airspace Areas
  3603, 3787, 3788, 3789

J11 ..... Service Available to Pilots
  3604, 3605, 3606, 3607, 3608, 3609, 3610, 3611, 3612, 3790, 3791, 3792, 3793, 3794, 3795, 3796, 3797, 3798, 3799, 3800, 3801, 3802, 3803

J12 ..... Radio Communications Phraseology and Techniques
  3613, 3614, 3615, 3804

J13 ..... Airport Operations
  3805, 3806, 3807, 3808, 3809, 3810, 3811, 3812

J14 ..... ATC Clearance/Separations
3813, 3814

J15 ..... Preflight
3815, 3816, 3817, 3818

J22 ..... Emergency Procedures Available to Pilots
3819, 3820, 3821, 3822

J25 ..... Meteorology
3616, 3617, 3823

J27 ..... Wake Turbulence
3824, 3825, 3826, 3827, 3828, 3829, 3830

J28 ..... (AIM)
3618, 3831

J31 ..... Fitness for Flight
3832, 3833, 3834, 3835, 3836

J33 ..... Pilot Controller Glossary
3837

J34 ..... Airport/Facility Directory
3619, 3838, 3839, 3840, 3841, 3842, 3843

J37 ..... Sectional Chart
3620, 3621, 3622, 3623, 3624, 3625, 3626, 3627, 3628, 3629, 3630, 3631, 3632, 3633, 3634, 3635, 3636, 3637, 3638, 3639, 3640, 3641, 3642, 3643, 3644, 3645, 3646

AC 67-2: Medical Handbook For Pilots

J52 ..... Hypoxia
3844

J53 ..... Hyperventilation
3845, 3846, 3847

J58 ..... Carbon Monoxide
3848

J60 ..... Night Flying
3849

J61 ..... Cockpit Lighting
3850

J62 ..... Disorientation (Vertigo)
3851, 3852, 3853

Cross-Reference B: SMK Code & Question Number

Additional Advisory Circulars

M52 .... AC 00-2, Advisory Circular Checklist
3854, 3855, 3856

American Soaring Handbook—Soaring Society of America

N03 ..... Ground Launch
3857, 3858

Soaring Flight Manual—Jeppesen-Sanderson, Inc.

N20 ..... Sailplane Aerodynamics
3340

N21 ..... Performance Considerations
3341, 3342, 3859, 3860, 3861, 3862, 3863, 3864, 3865, 3866, 3867, 3868

N22 ..... Flight Instruments
3343, 3344

N23 ..... Weather for Soaring
3647

N27 ..... Computations for Soaring
3345, 3346, 3347, 3348, 3349, 3648, 3649

N30 ..... Aerotow Launch Procedures
3869, 3870, 3871, 3872, 3873, 3874, 3875, 3876, 3877, 3878, 3879

N32 ..... Basic Flight Maneuvers and Traffic
3880, 3881, 3882, 3883

N34 ..... Cross-Country Soaring
3350, 3650, 3884

Taming the Gentle Giant—Taylor Publishing

O01 .... Design and Construction of Balloons
3351

O02 .... Fuel Source and Supply
3352, 3353, 3354, 3355, 3356, 3357, 3358, 3885, 3886

O03 .... Weight and Temperature
3887, 3888, 3889, 3890, 3891, 3892, 3893, 3894

O05 .... Balloon Flight Tips
3359, 3360, 3361, 3895, 3896, 3897, 3898, 3899, 3900, 3901, 3902, 3903, 3904

Flight Instructor Manual—Balloon Federation of America

O10 .... Flight Instruction Aids
   3905

O22 .... (Flight Instructor Manual)
   3362, 3906

Propane Systems—Balloon Federation of America, 1991

O24 .... Repair and Maintenance
   3363

O26 .... (Propane Systems)
   3907

Powerline Excerpts—Balloon Federation of America

O30 .... Excerpts
   3364, 3365, 3366, 3367, 3908, 3909

Goodyear Airship Operations Manual

P01 ..... Buoyancy
   3368, 3369, 3370, 3371

P03 ..... Free Ballooning
   3910, 3911

P04 ..... Aerostatics
   3372, 3373, 3374, 3375, 3376, 3377, 3378

P09 ..... (Goodyear Airship Operations Manual)
   3379, 3380, 3912, 3913, 3914, 3915

FAA Accident Prevention Program Bulletins

V01 ..... FAA-P-8740-2, Density Altitude

V02 ..... FAA-P-8740-5, Weight and Balance

V03 ..... FAA-P-8740-12, Thunderstorms

V04 ..... FAA-P-8740-19, Flying Light Twins Safely

V05 ..... FAA-P-8740-23, Planning Your Takeoff

V06 ..... FAA-P-8740-24, Tips on Winter Flying

Cross-Reference B: SMK Code & Question Number

V07 ..... FAA-P-8740-25, Always Leave Yourself an Out

V08 ..... FAA-P-8740-30, How to Obtain a Good Weather Briefing

V09 ..... FAA-P-8740-40, Wind Shear

V10 ..... FAA-P-8740-41, Medical Facts for Pilots

V11 ..... FAA-P-8740-44, Impossible Turns

V12 ..... FAA-P-8740-48, On Landings, Part I

V13 ..... FAA-P-8740-49, On Landings, Part II

V14 ..... FAA-P-8740-50, On Landings, Part III

V15 ..... FAA-P-8740-51, How to Avoid a Midair Collision

V16 ..... FAA-P-8740-52, The Silent Emergency

Note: AC 00-2, Advisory Circular Checklist, transmits the status of all FAA advisory circulars (ACs), as well as FAA internal publications and miscellaneous flight information such as Aeronautical Information Manual (AIM), Airport/Facility Directory, practical test standards, knowledge test guides, and other material directly related to airman certificates and ratings. To obtain a free copy of AC 00-2, send your request to:

U.S. Department of Transportation
General Services Section, M-45.3
Washington, DC 20590

More Private Pilot Products from ASA

ASA has many other books and supplies for the Private Pilot. They are listed below and available from an aviation retailer in your area. Need help locating a retailer? Call ASA at 1-800-ASA-2-FLY. We can also send you our latest ASA Catalog which includes our *complete* line of publications and pilot supplies… for all types of pilots and aviation technicians.

Private Pilot Books

	Product Code	Suggested Price
Flight Training by Trevor Thom	ASA-PM-1	29.95
Private & Commercial by Trevor Thom	ASA-PM-2	29.95
Private Pilot Syllabus	ASA-PM-S-P	10.95
The Complete Private Pilot by Bob Gardner	ASA-PPT	18.95
The Complete Private Pilot Syllabus	ASA-PPT-S	8.95
The Complete Private Pilot Workbook	ASA-PPT-W	8.95
The Complete Manuevers Manual	ASA-PPT-MM1	10.95
Private Oral Exam Guide	ASA-OEG-P	9.95
Private Pilot Airplane Practical Test Standards	ASA-8081-14S	4.95
Private Pilot Test Prep	ASA-TP-P	14.95
Private Pilot Test Guide	ASA-P010G	14.95
Aeronautical Chart User's Guide	ASA-CUG	13.95
Dictionary of Aeronautical Terms	ASA-DAT-2	16.95
Flight Training Handbook	ASA-AC61-21A	12.00
Aviation Weather Combo Pak	ASA-AC00-6A-45D	22.95
Pilot's Handbook of Aeronautical Knowledge	ASA-AC61-23B	14.95
FAR/AIM	ASA-FR-AM-BK	12.95

Private Pilot Supplies

Pilot Logbook	ASA-SP-30	$6.95
Flightlight™	ASA-FL-1	14.95
Flight Planner Sheets	ASA-FP-2	4.95
Long Tri-Fold Kneeboard	ASA-KB-3L	34.95
E6-B Flight Computer	ASA-E6B	22.95

All prices based on U.S. currency.
Prices subject to change without notice.

Call **1-800-ASA-2-FLY** for the retailer nearest you.

New Products from ASA

Improved, expanded and updated: ASA's product line continues to evolve. The products listed here are brand new. For a copy of our latest ASA Catalog, which includes many other products, call 1-800-ASA-2-FLY.

New Pilot Supplies...

Lexan® Plotters
Durable Lexan® resin won't melt, warp or break in extreme temperatures—guaranteed! Each plotter features 8 scales to meet the needs of all VFR aeronautical charts—nautical on one side, statute on the flip. Nautical and Statute conversion scale also included.

Ultimate Fixed Plotter. 13¼" long.
#ASA-CP-1LX $7.95

Ultimate Rotating Plotter. 13¼" long.
Features rotating azimuth which eases flight planning with direct readout of course.
#ASA-CP-RLX $9.95

Ultimate Micro Plotter. 8" long, convenient for flightbag, shirt-pocket, or airplane storage.
#ASA-CP-MLX $4.95

Lexan is a registered trademark of the General Electric Company.

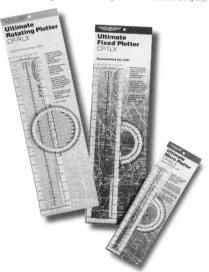

New Practical Test Standards
These are fundamentals to a successful checkride and include the skills and knowledge required for each license or rating. Instructors, students, and examiners use these books to prepare, review, take, or issue the checkride.

Private, Single-Engine, Land .... #ASA-8081-14S $4.95
Baker's Dozen .... #ASA-8081-14S-13 .... $59.40
Private, Multi-Engine, Land .... #ASA-8081-14M $4.95
Baker's Dozen .... #ASA-8081-14M-13 .... $59.40
Private & Commercial, Single-Engine, Sea .... #ASA-8081-SEA $4.95
Baker's Dozen .... #ASA-8081-SEA-13 .... $59.40

Flight Maneuvers Handbook and Manual
ASA now provides the standard in maneuvers manuals, previously published by Haldon Books, Inc. Both books provide excellent learning and teaching aids for instructors and students, and cover all maneuvers necessary for FAA certification. Each maneuver is described in step-by-step detail with many supporting graphics, and all are described according to the type of aircraft (high or low wing) the lesson will take place in. Through the use of these handbooks, the student will have a more thorough understanding of the maneuvers, creating a safer and more competent pilot—thereby shortening each flight instruction period.

Pilot Examiner's Handbook
Reprint of the official FAA Order 8710.3B of September 1994. Required for Designated Pilot Examiners, and an excellent reference book for flight instructors.
#ASA-8710.3B $14.95

New Books...

Say Again, Please
Guide to Radio Communications
by Bob Gardner

Mr. Gardner's manual provides a clear, conversational approach to aviation communications. The text features examples of typical radio transmissions that explain how the air traffic control system works, and presents a simulated flight to demonstrate the correct procedures for communicating in each class of airspace. This hands-on book covers: the ABCs of communicating, understanding radio equipment, communication etiquette and rules, VFR, IFR and emergency communication procedures, air traffic control facilities and their functions, and a review of airspace definitions.
#ASA-SAP $14.95

Visualized Flight Maneuvers Handbook
Based on high-wing aircraft. Known as the "Blue Maneuvers Book."
#ASA-FM-HI $19.95

Flight Maneuvers Manual
Based on low-wing aircraft. Known as the "Red Maneuvers Book."
#ASA-FM-LO $19.95

More New Books...

A Pilot's Guide Series
by Jeremy Pratt

Each Pilot's Guide is a comprehensive book on the fundamentals of flying the airplane. Subjects covered in detail include an overall description of the aircraft, limitations, handling characteristics, and loading/performance data. All the information is gleaned from flying experiences by experts in the industry, and is presented in an easy-to-read format. Pilots will find each guide in the series an invaluable companion to the aircraft's Flight Manual and an excellent sourcebook for the aircraft's principal characteristics.

Cessna 172: A Pilot's Guide	#ASA-PG-C-172	$14.95
Cessna 152: A Pilot's Guide	#ASA-PG-C-152	$14.95
Cessna 150: A Pilot's Guide	#ASA-PG-C-150	$14.95
Piper Warrior: A Pilot's Guide	#ASA-PG-PA-28W	$14.95
Piper Cherokee: A Pilot's Guide	#ASA-PG-PA-28C	$14.95
Piper Tomahawk: A Pilot's Guide	#ASA-PG-PA-38	$14.95

Aviation Weather Services Workbook
by John Holley

Designed to be used in conjunction with *Aviation Weather Services*. Contains text and exercises to increase reader's knowledge of weather and weather services. Previously published by IAP, Inc.

#ASA-WX-WK $7.95

Aviation Weather Services
Reprint of the newly updated FAA AC 00-45D we've all been waiting for! Includes information in all areas of weather reports, forecasts and analysis with all new charts.

#ASA-AC00-45D $14.00

Flying Ultralights
by Doug Chipman

Ultralights are becoming one of the fastest growing sectors in the general aviation market. These aircraft provide the experience of flying in a manner which is much less expensive, and much less regulated, than traditional airplanes. *Flying Ultralights* provides a framework for learning in a safe, efficient, and inexpensive environment. The book includes a series of lessons and exercises, making it an excellent syllabus for students and instructors alike.

#ASA-ULF $14.95

For FAA testing centers and flight schools:

Private Pilot Test Prep Course
Organized into a 2-day exam review seminar, this course can be used as final preparation for the FAA Knowledge Test. The Instructor's guide follows ASA's *Private Pilot Test Prep* chapters in subject order for classroom presentation, and offers airplane-only questions for faster review. Students are expected to follow along using the ASA *Private Pilot Test Prep*. Additional memory aids, hints, and many overhead transparencies are included.

#ASA-TPC-P $100.00

Global Navigation for Pilots
by Dale DeRemer and Donald McLean

Presents background needed by pilots to learn international and oceanic operations. Glossary and index included. Previously published by IAP, Inc. 421 pages.

#ASA-GNP $28.95

Air Traffic Control Test Prep Study Guide
by Patrick Mattson

Prepares reader for the Air Traffic Control test, and includes questions, answers, application procedures, employment and training information, and test-taking strategies.

#ASA-ATC $19.95

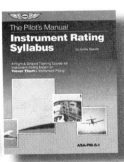
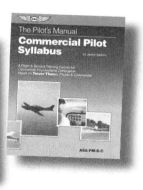

Where Am I?
Previously published by Haldon Books, Inc., this is an instructional manual on the use of today's standard instruments in navigation. The book explains, with practical applications, the use and understanding of ADF and OMNI (VOR). The text is supported by many graphics throughout.

#ASA-WHERMI $15.95

The Pilot's Manual Series Syllabi
by Jackie Spanitz

These syllabi meet all Part 141 requirements and supplement Trevor Thom's textbooks: *Flight Training*, *Private & Commercial*, and *Instrument Flying*. The syllabi have been reviewed by the FAA, present a fresh approach, and offer the most integrated, comprehensive, and simple flight and ground training programs available. Flight lessons are presented side-by-side with their coordinating ground lessons. Each syllabus comes with appropriate Stage Exams.

Private Pilot Syllabus	#ASA-PM-S-P	$10.95
Instrument Rating Syllabus	#ASA-PM-S-I	$10.95
Commercial Pilot Syllabus	#ASA-PM-S-C	$10.95

All prices based on U.S. currency.
Prices subject to change without notice.

Call 1-800-ASA-2-FLY for the retailer nearest you.

ASA's CX-1a Pathfinder™: State-of-the-Art in Flight Computers.

Pilots choose the CX-1a Pathfinder™ from ASA's AirClassics™ collection because it is easy to use and it has many outstanding features:

- Large LCD screen shows entire problem as it is being worked, including:
  a six-line display, prompts, units reference and menu
- Prompts guide you through each problem
- 18 formulas provide an incredible 31 aviation calculations, quickly and easily
- 14 conversion functions at your fingertips
- Calculator can be used alone or in any aviation mode
- Chain calculation results are easily stored and instantly recalled
- Easy battery access
- Authorized for use on FAA tests

The CX-1a Pathfinder™ is a favorite of pilots at all levels—from student pilots to 777 captains. This computer's time-proven success speaks for itself.

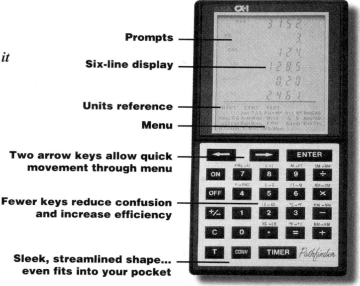

Prompts
Six-line display
Units reference
Menu
Two arrow keys allow quick movement through menu
Fewer keys reduce confusion and increase efficiency
Sleek, streamlined shape... even fits into your pocket

AirClassics and CX-1a Pathfinder are trademarks of Aviation Supplies & Academics, Inc.

#ASA-CX-1a $69.95

ASA's AirClassics™ HS-1 Headset

The most advanced technology, high-quality components, sleek look, reasonable price, maximum comfort, and a lifetime warranty—your wish list is complete!

Features

- *Earcups of high-density acoustic foam provide best passive noise attenuation*
- *High fidelity speakers for clear, natural sound*
- *Electret, noise-canceling microphone reduces background noise and allows clearest voice transmission*
- *Gold-plated microphone and headphone plugs ensure best connection and resist corrosion*
- *High-grade multi-strand wire improves cable life*
- *Stereo/mono capability*
- *Large, dual controls for quick, easy volume adjustment for each ear*

- *Microphone muff*
- *Adjustable headband with easy thumb screws for maximum comfort, eliminates "hot spots," and accommodates eyeglasses and any head size*
- *Quality foam ear seals and light weight add to overall comfort*
- *Sleek, all-black design with ASA wings attractively silk-screened on each earcup*
- *Sturdy, high-quality and reliable— yet reasonably priced for maximum value*

LIFETIME WARRANTY

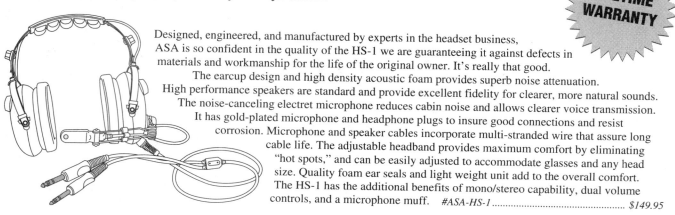

Designed, engineered, and manufactured by experts in the headset business, ASA is so confident in the quality of the HS-1 we are guaranteeing it against defects in materials and workmanship for the life of the original owner. It's really that good.
The earcup design and high density acoustic foam provides superb noise attenuation. High performance speakers are standard and provide excellent fidelity for clearer, more natural sounds. The noise-canceling electret microphone reduces cabin noise and allows clearer voice transmission. It has gold-plated microphone and headphone plugs to insure good connections and resist corrosion. Microphone and speaker cables incorporate multi-stranded wire that assure long cable life. The adjustable headband provides maximum comfort by eliminating "hot spots," and can be easily adjusted to accommodate glasses and any head size. Quality foam ear seals and light weight unit add to the overall comfort. The HS-1 has the additional benefits of mono/stereo capability, dual volume controls, and a microphone muff. #ASA-HS-1 .... $149.95

Call **1-800-ASA-2-FLY** for the retailer nearest you.